Village Work

NEW AFRICAN HISTORIES

SERIES EDITORS: JEAN ALLMAN, ALLEN ISAACMAN, AND DEREK R. PETERSON

Village Work

Development and Rural Statecraft in Twentieth-Century Ghana

༔

Alice Wiemers

OHIO UNIVERSITY PRESS ༔ ATHENS, OHIO

Ohio University Press, Athens, Ohio 45701
ohioswallow.com
© 2021 by Ohio University Press
All rights reserved

Printed in the United States of America
Ohio University Press books are printed on acid-free paper ∞ ™

31 30 29 28 27 26 25 24 23 22 21 5 4 3 2 1

Library of Congress Cataloging-in-Publication Data
Names: Wiemers, Alice, 1982– author.
Title: Village work : development and rural statecraft in twentieth-century Ghana /
Alice Wiemers.
Description: Athens : Ohio University Press, 2021. | Series: New African histories
series | Includes bibliographical references and index.
Identifiers: LCCN 2020048199 (print) | LCCN 2020048200 (ebook) | ISBN
9780821424452 (hardcover) | ISBN 9780821447376 (pdf)
Subjects: LCSH: Local government—Ghana. | Central-local government relations—
Ghana. | Economic development—Ghana. | Ghana—Politics and government—20th
century.
Classification: LCC JS7655.3.A3 W54 2021 (print) | LCC JS7655.3.A3 (ebook) | DDC
320.809667—dc23
LC record available at https://lccn.loc.gov/2020048199
LC ebook record available at https://lccn.loc.gov/2020048200

For my family

Contents

Illustrations

Acknowledgments

Writing is usually thought to be a lonely process. I feel very lucky that the many years in which I have been researching and writing this book have been surprisingly social, collaborative, and fun. Nearly everything in this book was developed and refined through extensive conversation, both formal and informal, in Ghana and in the United States. I am deeply grateful for these conversations and the relationships that have developed around them. I want to thank a number of people, groups, and institutions in particular.

Research for the book began as a dissertation project at Johns Hopkins University. Sara Berry and the late Pier Larson were a generous and dynamic pair of advisers and wonderful mentors. Sara's mentorship inspired and shaped this work in countless ways, and she continues to shape my identity as a scholar and as a person. She encouraged me to take the research where it led and to think deeply and creatively about what I was seeing and what I had to say. Pier shared his boundless intellect and kindness, challenging me to make my writing clear and focused and helping me take a broad view of the themes that emerge in the work. I will continue to miss him. In Randall Packard, I was fortunate to find a critical and constructive third reader who gave generously of his time and expertise, and Lori Leonard and Bill Rowe served as careful readers and critics during my dissertation defense. The weekly interdisciplinary Africa Seminar was my intellectual home at Hopkins, and I am indebted to the faculty members, graduate students, and visiting scholars who read and commented on drafts of nearly every chapter in this book, both during my time at Hopkins and after. I want to thank, especially, Jeffrey Ahlman, Matt Bender, Claire Breedlove, Kirsten Chalke, Thomas Cousins, Julia Cummiskey, Kelly Duke Bryant, Jane Guyer, Siba Grovogui, Anatoli Ignatov, Isaac Kamola, Lori Leonard, Lindsay Reynolds, Elizabeth Schmidt, and Elizabeth Thornberry.

In Ghana, my greatest continuing debt is owed to interviewees who were generous with their time, memories, and knowledge. I am also grateful to a number of people in Kpasenkpe, Walewale, Tamale, and Accra who helped to shape this work. In Kpasenkpe, Nelson Ndimah, Agnes Sebiyam, and their family members generously opened their home and shared their food, conversation, and kindness. Solomon Dawuni Sebiyam, who spent long hours facilitating and interpreting interviews in Kpasenkpe, shared his amazing good humor and his wide-reaching network of friends in town. Seiya Namyoaya Enoch helped enormously by facilitating and interpreting additional interviews in 2013, and in 2019 Emmanuel Sebiyam graciously helped me return to those I had interviewed to confirm their contributions before the book would be published. In Kpasenkpe and Accra, Professor J. S. Nabila was a gracious host, particularly because of his commitment, as an academic colleague and as a chief, to giving full reign to my scholarly inquiry. I am grateful for the early support of several scholars who helped get my research in Ghana off the ground, including Kofi Baku, Susan Herlin, Wyatt MacGaffey, Laura McGough, and Dzodzi Tsikata. I am also indebted to the staff of the West Mamprusi District Assembly and of World Vision International for welcoming me during my first months in Walewale, particularly Mr. Andani, Abigail Sulemana, Fati Alhassan, and Andrew Kuyipwa. Robert Kwame Boateng introduced me to a variety of former civil servants and teachers, for which I am grateful. The staff of the East Mamprusi District Assembly, the Northern Region Ministry of Food and Agriculture, the Savanna Agricultural Research Institute, the Tamale Institute of Cross-Cultural Studies, and the West Mamprusi District Assembly generously opened their libraries and archives to me. I am deeply thankful for the staff of the Public Records and Archives Administration Department (PRAAD) in Tamale and Accra, in particular Mr. Mahama in Tamale, whose commitment to assisting research went far beyond what was required.

My research in Ghana was made possible by funding from a Dissertation Proposal Development Fellowship from the Social Science Research Council, the Boren Fellowship from the National Security Education Program, as well as generous institutional support from the Institute for Global Studies and the Center for Africana Studies at Johns Hopkins and faculty research funding from Otterbein University and Davidson College. In Walewale and Tamale I have been lucky to find a community of colleagues and neighbors to whom I am indebted in innumerable ways and whose friendships I continue to cherish. Among these, in particular, are Nineveh Ndimah, Georgina Niber-Ang, and their daughter Irene for years of fellowship and laughter; Victoria Chirapanga for untold hours of companionship; and Edward Salifu Mahama, Mary Mahama, and their daughters Evelyn, Louisa, and Titi, for over a decade of conversation and ongoing collaboration.

At Otterbein University I found a welcoming department for my first academic appointment. I would like to thank Deborah Solomon, in particular, for her friendship and support. During a 2013–14 fellowship at the Kellogg Institute for International Studies at Notre Dame, I found a dynamic intellectual environment that helped me reconceive significant parts of the manuscript. I want to thank especially Adam Auerbach, Paul Ocobock, Derek Peterson, and Meredith Whitnah for formal and informal conversations that pushed the work forward. At Davidson College, my academic home since 2014, I have benefited immensely from the personal and institutional support of the History Department and the Africana Studies Department. My colleagues in both departments have mentored me and helped me grow as a scholar, teacher, and community member. It is a joy to work alongside them. I am also grateful to current and former Davidson students Jessie Cohen, Yunah Han, and Brian Wood for invaluable research assistance.

This book would not have been possible without the support of a wider community of scholars who have provided valuable feedback and advice at every stage of the manuscript. First there are the participants in my book workshop, made possible by Davidson, at which Emily Lynn Osborn, Laurian Bowles, and Jessie Cohen generously provided detailed comments and advice that strengthened the manuscript immensely. Jeffrey Ahlman, Julia Cummiskey, and Lacy Ferrell gave me the gift of our writing group. I owe thanks to a number of people for commenting on the manuscript in formal and informal settings and for convening panels and conferences that became valuable spaces to work through my ideas, including John Aerni-Flessner, Nana Akua Anyidoho, Kofi Baku, Thomas Bierschenk, Clifton Crais, Leslie Hadfield, Jennifer Hart, Takiyah Harper-Shipman, Jacqueline Ignatova, Jack Lord, Stephan Miescher, Kara Moskowitz, Bianca Murillo, Paul Nugent, Jean-Pierre Olivier de Sardan, Benedetta Rossi, Pamela Scully, Sebastiaan Soeters, Paul Stacey, Rhiannon Stephens, and Benjamin Talton. I am grateful to Kristy Johnson for editing the prose at several points in the process and to Nick Cuba for designing the maps. The manuscript was helped immensely by feedback from participants at conferences and workshops organized by the Ghana

Studies Association; the Africana Studies Department at Davidson; Emory University's Institute of African Studies; the Institute of African Studies at Columbia University; and the History Department at the University of Ghana, Legon. I am indebted to my undergraduate mentors, Marcia Wright and Greg Mann. I am also grateful to the numerous friends and colleagues who have been writing companions over the years, especially Ian Beamish, Anelise Shrout, Laura Sockol, Caroline Weist, and members of the faculty writing collective at Davidson.

I consider myself extremely lucky to have been able to work with the staff and editors at Ohio University Press. Jean Allman, Allen Isaacman, Derek Peterson, Stephanie Williams, Gillian Berchowitz, and Rick Huard have believed in the book's potential and offered invaluable guidance throughout. Special thanks to Jean Allman for her keen insights into the source material and for widening my vision of the book's audience. I am deeply grateful for the comments of two anonymous readers whose critiques and suggestions helped me solve old dilemmas and see new possibilities in the work. Sally Welch, Andrea Gapsch, Tyler Balli, Lee Motteler, Beth Pratt, and Zoë Bossiere provided invaluable assistance with the production and copyediting of the book. Cambridge University Press and Elsevier gave me permission to use adapted and revised versions of material that previously appeared in *International Labor and Working-Class History*, the *Journal of African History*, and *World Development*.

Friends and family have talked through the ideas of this book and have provided encouragement and escape during the process of getting it written. I am lucky to have dear friends in Davidson and also those who make the trek here regularly from far-flung and ever-changing locales. I am grateful for strong networks in Atlanta, Baltimore, and New York that are a joy to return to. Special thanks to E. R. Anderson, Ian Beamish, Alison Bory, Laurian Bowles, Will Brown, Julia Cummiskey, Natalie Elder, Martha Herbers-Sanger, Takiyah Harper-Shipman, Katie Hindmarch-Watson, Andy King, Sara Luce Look, Sarah Reidy, Jackie Reitzes, Anelise Shrout, Laura Sockol, Trish Tilburg, Sarah Waheed, and Caroline Weist. My oldest friends Christine Suwendy, Michaela O'Neill, and Tim Whittemore have reminded me, always, of who I am. Angie has been her troublesome and sweet self throughout. Most of all, I want to thank my family, to whom this work is dedicated. My parents, Nancy Jennings and Gene Wiemers, and my sister Emily Wiemers have given me unconditional support and encouragement as well as examples of how academic work can be part of a life that is thoughtful, responsible, caring, and fun. They have read and discussed nearly every aspect of the manuscript, and I am especially grateful to my father for years of kind and careful editing. My extended family of aunts, uncles, parents- and siblings-in-law, nieces, and nephews have shared their joy and love. Finally, I am deeply grateful to my husband, Gabe Klehr, and more recently to our son, Solomon. They have enriched my life and work in ways I could never have imagined and have made for years full of goofiness, meaning, and possibility.

Introduction

Villages and States in Twentieth-Century Ghana

IN THE early twenty-first century, when residents or visitors rode market trucks, motorbikes, or 4x4s on the bumpy forty-five-minute ride from the district capital of Walewale to the small settlement of Kpasenkpe, they were surrounded by evidence of village development projects. Entering Kpasenkpe, they would pass the Kpasenkpe Health Center, built in the 1970s and more recently restocked and staffed by the Ghanaian government and Columbia University's Millennium Villages Project that ran from 2012 to 2016. Continuing into town, they would pass boreholes and hand-dug wells constructed with funds from Oxfam and the international Christian nongovernmental organization World Vision in the 1980s, 1990s, and 2000s. At the market site in the center of town, they would see a baobab tree surrounded by market stalls that were first built in the 1950s as part of the first wave of community development initiatives in the region. Past two churches and a mosque, they might take a path that leads to the primary and middle schools, which were first established by the colonial and nationalist governments of the 1940s and 1960s, then revamped with school gardens in the 1970s, and rebuilt by World Vision as part of a community development project in the 1980s. Following the main road out of town, they would reach the White Volta River, spanned, since 2007, by a bridge funded by the French and British governments and built on contract by a Chinese engineering firm. Glancing to their right from the new bridge, they might notice the pillars of a bridge that was half-built in the

1950s and 1960s, called locally "Nkrumah's bridge," and be reminded that new ideas are rarely, well, new. Regardless of the decade, the government in power, and the source of funding, almost all these structures were built, without pay, by Kpasenkpe residents themselves. The road itself holds the longest such history, having been cut initially in the 1920s by Kpasenkpe residents who did the back-breaking work of clearing trees under a colonial regime of forced labor.

For residents and others who know the place, Kpasenkpe's public infrastructure tells a story of governments come and gone, of personal and professional relationships, and of both the hard work and contestations inherent in pairing outside funding with demands for local self-help. Elders' brutal stories of colonial forced labor still hang over current residents, as do fond memories of working with neighbors on a shared project, and the bitter disappointments about hoped-for transformations that never came. For visitors from state or nongovernmental agencies that sponsor such projects, however, the emphasis can be quite different. Regardless of how familiar these visitors might be with Kpasenkpe or how well they might know the details of its history, when contemplating the area's future there is little room for these memories. Like generations of developers before

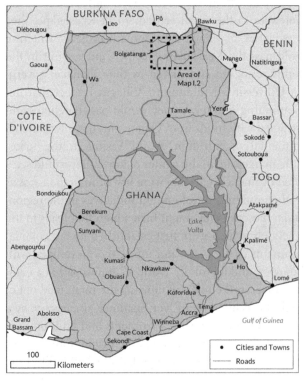

MAP I.1. Ghana. Map by Nicholas Cuba.

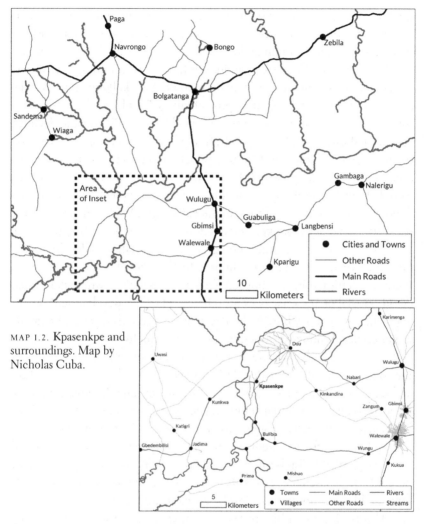

MAP I.2. Kpasenkpe and surroundings. Map by Nicholas Cuba.

them, they come to classify Kpasenkpe as just a northern village, like many others, where another new project has the potential to take shape.

In many ways, Kpasenkpe is indeed like other northern Ghanaian settlements. Here, as in other villages in hinterland regions of the global South, the stuttering, project-based system of village development is a large part of what "the state" looks like.[1] With an economy built on small-scale agriculture and a history of relatively stable local politics, states have rarely spent time or money on instruments of violence, redistribution, or export production here. Instead, despite the end of colonial rule and dramatic swings in postcolonial political and economic life, many of the central mechanisms and foci of statecraft remained the same. Through colonial, civilian, and military rule, and under nominally capitalist and nominally socialist regimes, Kpasenkpe residents saw wave after wave of governments ask for their labor as a means or an end for something they called "development."

In other ways, Kpasenkpe stands out from its surroundings because of the concentration and longevity of development work. It arguably qualifies as what Ben Jones has called a "project village," a place where "development agencies ha[ve] focused their efforts."[2] Repeatedly over the decades, agents of thinly staffed and poorly funded government and nongovernmental agencies fanned out from regional and district capitals to identify a handful of villages in which they could set up small-scale projects that would stand for development in the region as a whole. Kpasenkpe was often one such place. Beginning in the early 1940s, Wulugunaba Sebiyam, the young chief of Kpasenkpe and a self-styled "progressive," began to court new colonial interest in, and funding for, northern Ghana's development.[3] Over the five decades of his chieftaincy, the Wulugunaba and, increasingly, members of his family, established Kpasenkpe as a place where developers could raise labor and enact various schemes of village development, swiftly and with minimal trouble. By the late twentieth century, agents of state, international, and nongovernmental agencies would likely have worked with colleagues who had family ties to Kpasenkpe and surroundings, most likely the sons and daughters of the Wulugunaba, all of whom went to school and many of whom pursued careers in civil service and development work. Over the years, the national actors and goals of development changed from colonial and nationalist proponents of community development to agricultural extension officers intent on creating a Ghanaian "green revolution" and then to World Vision International's project of "transformational development." In Kpasenkpe, residents and leaders made space for both continuity and local innovation as developers came and went.

This book is not a history of a particular village. Instead, I situate this story in Kpasenkpe to illustrate how multiple actors, institutions, and performances have reinforced the centrality of village development in the practice and rhetoric of rural statecraft. The book argues that the dynamic between particularity and generalizability—between the story of how Kpasenkpe residents and leaders fought for its projects and the fact that projects were always conceived for a generic number of villages—is what makes this detailed local history so revealing of the central and enduring dynamics of twentieth-century government in rural hinterlands. Small settlements like Kpasenkpe are frequently referred to colloquially as villages (*tinkpaŋŋa* in Mampruli) in Ghana, and Ghanaians use references to an ancestral village or hometown to tell complex and layered stories about belonging, identity, and history.[4] A variety of actors in this book, however, decided to minimize this complexity by invoking an alternate image of undifferentiated rural space occupied by interchangeable villages. They did so because it was a convenient way to allocate or attract limited resources, to highlight or downplay struggles over power, and to forge national and international networks. The treatment of the region as a sea of villages was always combined with the scarcity of funding and attention characteristic of government in a rural hinterland. This dynamic resulted, paradoxically, in the creation of an uneven landscape in which certain rural spaces and people became particularly tied to regional, national, and international institutions of development. Meanwhile, developers' consistent demands for community self-help allowed systems of labor extraction to remain the backbone of rural development.

Local actors were not passive recipients of developmentalist visions, and as this book endeavors to show, it was largely through daily practices at the district and village level that the conditions for both continuity and change were forged. District and regional officials, working under conditions of scarcity, leaned on fictions of village homogeneity and interchangeability in order to make decisions. Local leaders and constituents, for their part, learned and tested what claims they could make on the government and what they would need to demonstrate in return. As the stakes of development increased over the twentieth century, the urgency of this work grew, even as residents of Ghana's North found it more and more difficult to contest the underlying marginality of their concerns to successive governments.

Focusing on a variety of village-level projects in a hinterland region over several decades offers a number of contributions to the historiographies of development and statecraft in Africa and the global South. First, the book uses long-term, historically grounded, rural research to tell a story that de-emphasizes the sweeping plans and pronouncements of governments and focuses instead on the piecemeal, contingent, and largely improvised ways in which both development and states are enacted and experienced. Long-term studies of development as a twentieth-century project in Africa tend to focus on big projects and national plans, while small-scale studies are prone to center on specific projects and cover relatively limited time frames. In contrast, this book uncovers long-term patterns of interaction around local labor and leadership that are all but invisible in the context of individual projects or eras. This scope reveals how the daily work of rural people and local officials helped create the conditions and shape the terms on which development continued as a state practice.

Second, my choice of scope and method offers readers new entry points into longstanding discussions about power and discourse in development.

Since the 1990s, an important strain of scholarly focus has been to reveal the discursive apparatuses created by development initiatives. Scholars have shown how development projects naturalize and depoliticize structures of power by constructing their own objects and categories of analysis. With few exceptions, however, these studies have taken snapshots of discursive regimes in particular projects and eras. In contrast, *Village Work* follows the example of a handful of works that trace how categories of development have been created and contested over time. I use this historical perspective to answer Paulla Ebron's call to bridge gaps between analysis of performance and representation, a method that allows us to see how "high players as well as low" become "enrolled in the rhetorics, the stances, and the subject positions" that development entails.[5]

Third, this book positions rural development at the heart of rural statecraft in the twentieth century. While there is frequent recognition that rural areas represent a key arena of development and poverty reduction, debates about twentieth-century African statecraft and its relationship to development have been almost exclusively waged on the level of central government policy, large projects, or aggregate indicators. This book, in contrast, argues that development in Africa has not become statecraft exclusively when states have had a grand plan. Instead, most people made sense of developmentalist government as they experienced it over time, from projects that were accompanied by little to no external fanfare or critique. The stories in this book show people figuring out how to interact with government institutions for which they were only sporadically a concern, and from which they often wanted to attract the right kind of attention and avoid the wrong kinds of demands. I argue that this experience is not the absence of something called "the state" but instead reflects a particular mode of governing, which I term "hinterland statecraft," that allowed for village development to emerge and endure as a central piece of government. Over time, bureaucrats, leaders, and residents invested in and improvised with the categories of village development and self-help. Along the way, they shaped twentieth-century government in ways that unsettle common ideas about how and by whom states are made.

Fourth, by centering its history of twentieth-century statecraft on village development projects, the book draws attention to the continued role of unremunerated labor in mediating relationships between governments and the governed. This theme has received comparatively little attention in studies of both development and statecraft, particularly in the postcolonial period. State officials, chiefs, and development practitioners used labor to implement and legitimize development work, while rural people repeatedly tested the political possibilities of labor by complying, resisting, and leveraging their work to make demands.[6]

Finally, this is a book about how certain people were able to use "local" development projects to cultivate translocal, national, and international networks of state engagement. While studies of small-scale development projects have offered excellent explorations of development projects' effects on local differentiation by class, gender, and education, they have tended to pay less attention to the differential ways that rural people accumulated ties to structures of development over time and across projects. The book's attention to the institution of chieftaincy as well as to the family network of Wulugunaba Sebiyam shows how developmentalist states have both driven and been driven by disparities along lines of lineage, gender, and schooling. At the same time, the book's attention to one family network over a long period of time helps show how rural people built varied and enduring networks that could both exacerbate and unsettle growing inequities in state engagement and attention.

The book delineates four broad eras in which particular logics of development and labor extraction configured relationships among residents of Ghana's North, local leaders, and agents of government. In the interwar period, the colonial state pursued the simultaneous (and often incompatible) goals of forced labor, fiscal stringency, and political quiescence. It was out of the quintessentially colonial tensions among these objectives, along with residents' obvious and widespread resistance to forced labor, that colonial officials developed a cheap, flexible, and resilient model of governing that downplayed the particularities of rural places and required unpaid labor as a condition of spending. Second, the book considers the period that began in the early 1950s and continued through independence in 1957 until the coup against Ghana's first president, Kwame Nkrumah, in 1966, a period termed locally "Nkrumah's time" that corresponds roughly to what Frederick Cooper calls "the development era" for the continent as a whole.[7] In these years, as development became both a popular demand and a legitimating ideology of states, both colonial and nationalist governments embraced a globally popular framework of village development and self-help labor. Village development backed by unremunerated labor became an adaptable mode of statecraft that could operate in the face of ongoing tensions between the demands of developmentalism and the continued treatment of certain regions as economic and bureaucratic hinterlands.

The third period spans the late 1960s and 1970s, a time of struggle and contradiction across the continent in which, as Greg Mann argues for the Sahel, "no single over-arching narrative can embrace all of the processes at work."[8] In northern Ghana, two simultaneous global trends shifted the ground on which development struggles were waged. The global economic crises of the 1970s tightened already strained development budgets and intensified political upheaval. Meanwhile, the North became one of the hinterland regions across the continent on which governments and international lenders pinned hopes for an African "green revolution" that would follow perceived agricultural successes in Asia and Latin America. As citizens and local officials navigated crisis and opportunity, they improvised on existing models of development, leadership, and self-help, transforming them into malleable templates for engaging ever-changing configurations of government. The book ends with the period of the 1980s and early 1990s, when World Bank– and IMF–mandated structural adjustment programs dismantled state development agendas across the globe and when, in their wake, a growing army of international nongovernmental organizations (NGOs) found themselves with ample opportunities to take up village development. While scholars have often studied the neoliberal era in isolation, I use the illustrative example of World Vision International's work in Kpasenkpe to show how citizens, officials, and NGO staff drew on what were by then familiar models of exchanging labor for scarce resources—work that grew ever more urgent as village projects became the dominant form of government in the region. By 1992, on the eve of Ghana's return to party politics and as mainstream development institutions embraced a depoliticized vision of participation, residents of Ghana's northern regions were deeply engaged with the state, but they also faced powerful institutional mechanisms that discouraged dissent and demanded specific performances of village leadership and community support.

DEVELOPMENT AT SCALE AND IN PRACTICE

Scholars have long identified the "marvelous ambiguity of the word development" to alternately denote a naturalized process, an idealized model of change, a goal of state policy, and a justification for state intervention to achieve it.[9] Those who wish to study development as a social and political process are thus faced with myriad options about how to define their scope, materials, and methods of analysis. On the macroscale of empire and nation, scholars have examined the long intellectual and political history of the concept of development. This literature reveals remarkable continuities in the long-term relationships among racial and political hierarchies, resource extraction, and knowledge production in development, at the same time that it emphasizes the development concept's capacity to allow multiple people and institutions to pursue parallel as well as competing political, social, and intellectual projects.[10]

Drawing on these insights, my work takes a deliberately open approach to defining what development entails. The book focuses on the small-scale projects that have been labeled "development" in Ghana's rural North—schools, clinics, roads, water projects, market structures, and interventions in community development and small-scale agriculture—not because they stemmed from a coherent theory or stable plan for development, but because they have been the focus of a tremendous amount of government involvement in rural hinterlands across the global South. At different times, the bundle has taken on different labels for governments— "amenities," "basic needs," "small-scale public goods," or "village-level interventions," to name a few. For Kpasenkpe residents, these projects have also been associated with terms and ideas of improvement (*maaligu*), enlightenment (*ninneesim*) and help (*suŋŋi*). What emerges from this view is not so much a tightly bound "apparatus" of village development as it is a field of interaction where multiple actors pursued multiple agendas over long periods of time.

By departing from historians' tendency to focus on the large-scale or high-profile projects that preoccupied central governments and commanded the attention of admirers and critics, the book demonstrates the value of what Leslie Hadfield and John Aerni-Flessner term "localizing the history of development."[11] In recent years, a number of excellent studies of large-scale development projects that spanned colonial and postcolonial eras have brought attention to their exploitation of people and environments as well as the mixed opportunities they created for Africans to engage with states.[12] Other scholars have drawn attention to how the paradigms that underpinned such initiatives went far beyond them, pointing out how, for example, idioms of modernization were shared between and among colonial and postcolonial states and their broader publics.[13] Villages often enter conversations about development only in the cases where states became particularly preoccupied with them, most notably when Tanzania embarked on its high-profile project of *ujamaa* villagization. While the rich scholarship on *ujamaa* contains robust and important debates about the relationship between theory and practice and about the nature and extent of state control, it remains bounded by the temporal and geographic scope set by the architects of the project.[14]

As Hadfield and Aerni-Flessner argue, examining less high profile local projects helps to decenter national governments and international agencies, "forc[ing] us to consider, with equal importance, the role played by 'lay people' in . . . contestations over development."[15] This insight, long known by anthropologists and critical development studies scholars who have produced a wide array of insightful studies on the local politics of development, has recently been taken up by historians of Africa's twentieth century.[16] With few exceptions, both clusters of works are closely bounded in time, with anthropologists largely focusing on the neoliberal era and with historians focused on the middle part of the century.[17]

Following a range of village development projects over a long period of time led me to questions about the discursive and conceptual categories that underpin development work, principally the category of "village" as a unit of development. Decades of poststructuralist analyses have shown that the creation and re-creation of development fictions in official documents is not misunderstanding but instead serves as what James Ferguson termed an "anti-politics machine," in which universal categories help developers naturalize the existing structures of state power and present systems of inequality as "simple, technical problems."[18] More recently, Sabelo Ndlovu-Gatsheni has drawn on postcolonial and decolonial theory to think of development discourse as part of ongoing "global imperial designs" that combine regimes of knowledge production and material exploitation.[19] As Tania Murray Li argues in her sweeping study of "the will to improve" in Indonesia, however, discursive regimes are never really separate from the worlds they create. Instead, we need to examine what she terms the "witches brew of processes, practices, and struggles" that emerged, over time, when discursive and institutional attempts to depoliticize meet the "practice of politics."[20]

Village Work also builds on scholarship that historicizes the global intellectual and diplomatic roots of the idea of village development. In the years following the end of the Second World War, as the model of "tribal" governance invoked by indirect rule became increasingly untenable as a basis for administration, colonial administrators found a powerful new way to draw older ideas of rural community into emerging discourses of development. As Nicole Sackley and Daniel Immerwahr both argue, the midcentury idea of community development gave governments across the globe a new "universal category."[21] The idea of the village accommodated social scientific interest in rural modernization at the same time that it assured administrators that plans for rural change would contain the forces of development in stable social units, knowable by experts, and applicable across geographies of empire, nation, and the Cold War theaters of the Third World.[22] In Ghana, as elsewhere, the category proved portable enough to be taken up by anticolonial nationalists and the independent government they created. In this long-term view, "village development" became what Cornwall terms a "fuzzword," referring to the way that buzz-words become "concepts that can float free of concrete referents, to be filled with meaning by their users" and that are thus able to "shelter multiple agendas, providing room for maneuver and space for contestation."[23]

The village concept that emerged in the interwar era, hardened in the midcentury, and continues through the present has relied on two central imaginaries. First was an idea of each village as a homogenous, bounded, and often unchanging or isolated community. This imaginary has, rightly, received a good deal of scholarly criticism, some (but only some) of which has filtered into recent development discourse.[24] In order for the idea of village development to be put into practice, however, a second imaginary had to be at work: the idea that villages are the same. For developers to extrapolate lessons from individual rural development projects, the places in which they took place needed to be imagined as representative of a more generalized set of social, political, and economic structures.

As this book shows, state agents' role in shaping a village imaginary has gone beyond the pages of official documents. Practitioners, confronted with the urgency of enacting policies in real circumstances, worked to create useable fictions, not simply tidy ones. In this view, common ideas and practices emerged over time, shared by colonial and nationalist officials, agricultural extension workers in the 1970s and 1980s, and the nongovernmental organization employees that have in recent decades come to dominate the development scene on the continent. *Village Work* focuses less on the plans that these actors produced and more on the relationships that underpinned their day-to-day practice. The book follows Nana Akua Anyidoho's suggestion that development projects be understood in terms of "sense-making," in which both policy makers and ordinary people make decisions about how to interact based on accumulated ideas and experiences.[25] As illustrated throughout these chapters, development fictions became useable because a wide range of people decided to use them.

Governments in twentieth-century Ghana rarely sought to explicitly define or structure village space.[26] Instead of pinning down what "village" meant, officials found it useful to build in several ambiguities: about the criteria by which communities would be identified, about the demands that could be placed on villagers, and about what success or failure in one village would mean for the region as a whole. Throughout the twentieth century, it was rarely seriously imagined that governments could reach all settlements in northern Ghana with the roads, schools, clinics, and wells that constituents increasingly demanded. Instead, planners looked for certain villages where projects could be undertaken easily and then hoped, imagined, or pretended that further spending or spontaneous community action would follow in surrounding areas. Planners searched for "project villages" precisely because they recognized that they were different from other spaces. In doing so, development practitioners both acknowledged and suppressed the realities of rural difference. The situation in which any village (but not all villages) could be a site for development encouraged competition and inequality. In the region overall, critiques and challenges to the model of village development were inhibited by the scarcity and transience of projects that were, themselves, often in high demand. Within villages, scarcity and competition also had the effect of suppressing critique, thus encouraging rural people to reaffirm development tropes of homogenous, consensual communities.

DEVELOPMENT, LABOR, AND HINTERLAND STATECRAFT

This book shows village development schemes to be a forum for statecraft, by which I mean the formation of systems that organize how people interact with governments. On a broad scale, the centrality of development to African statecraft has been clear. As Kwesi Prah argues, development has been an "obsessive object" of African governments and elites, remaining an "espoused *raison d'être*" despite wide variation in political and developmental ideology across the continent and over time.[27] For much of the period discussed in this book, from the midcentury to the early 1990s, debates about development and African states followed the focus of both national governments and international institutions on central governments, large projects, and macroeconomic processes and indicators. Then, over the course of the 1990s and early 2000s, as the World Bank and other development institutions looked to counter growing criticism and explain failures of structural adjustment, they located responsibility in the internal workings of African states.[28] As Thandika Mkandawire shows, the focus on "good governance" that emerged from this era selectively drew on scholarship that cast the institutions and practices of African governments as the root of development failures and interpreted scholarship in such a way that it would not challenge fundamental tenets of the neoliberal agenda.[29] In the end, this vilification of African states reinforced the austerity agenda of structural adjustment while intensifying reliance on development mechanisms that would bypass central governments, either via decentralization policies or by funding development through bilateral, nongovernmental, and civil society organizations.

Despite this "local turn" in development thinking, recent development efforts have reflected scant attention to how government has been practiced over time, particularly at regional and local scales.[30] A range of critical examinations shows that new projects often ignore or exacerbate relations of power at the local level, though in the scholarship, as well, the focus is rarely on long-term dynamics.[31] *Village Work* extends the time frame through which we examine the local life of development in order to show how small-scale projects were woven into the twentieth-century practice of rural government over decades. In this view, developmentalist statecraft was neither created merely by governments nor simply imposed on the governed. Rather, it was jointly constructed over time through the interactions between them.

I use the phrase "hinterland statecraft" to characterize patterns of government that extend from the colonial period on into the present. The marginality of hinterland regions has made them the frequent targets of development projects, but states have rarely imposed a strict vision of developmentalism. With few exceptions, central governments allocated few resources and exercised little close oversight of small-scale projects. If government agents could keep relative peace, maintain the basic economic and political hierarchies, and report something that they could call success, they were given wide latitude to define how and where projects took place. *Village Work* tells stories of people making do, working with the tools they have and improvising on the margins. A key insight of the book is that improvisation is just as necessary for district officials and project leaders as it is for the so-called targets of development. Strapped for resources and hoping to show progress, these actors cultivated productive ambiguities over the terms of progress and relied on usable fictions like the idea that villages were, for the purposes of government, interchangeable.

Most of all, developers required villagers to work. Throughout the twentieth century, governments and local leaders relied on residents to provide unremunerated labor for development, molding cement blocks, carrying water and stones, and plastering walls. Reinvented in the late colonial period to replace labor taxes, this labor has gone by different names, first as "communal labor," and then "self-help," and in more recent development projects simply "participation." Developers imagined that rural residents would contribute labor as a kind of political engagement: as a tribute to chiefs, as a service to the nation, or because of "community spirit."

Scholars have demonstrated that at some key historical moments, states have cast village development labor as evidence of support for unpopular policies and have mobilized the idea of participation to suppress critique and preserve existing structures. A cluster of recent works on the relationship between forced labor and developmentalism under colonial rule across the continent demonstrates that the idea of communal labor emerged in the 1920s and 1930s as a rhetorical and legal strategy of colonial governments that faced mounting critiques of forced labor. Benedetta Rossi, Opolot Okia, and others provide clear evidence that force and compulsion, often enacted by chiefs, could maintain a range of activities under the guise of development.[32] Decades later, in the 1990s and 2000s, the World Bank and other international development institutions coopted radical ideas of participation to rebrand their policies in the face of discontent over structural adjustment programs and to justify continued liberalization of markets and reductions in state funding.[33] Other scholars have noted that, at different historical moments, unremunerated self-help labor appeared as part of more sustained efforts to reshape mechanisms of popular participation. Scholars of the early postcolonial period, for example, have uncovered a range of strategies adopted by self-help laborers as they attempted to cope with the ambiguous links between labor and citizenship in developmentalist nation-building projects.[34]

Despite these insights into specific eras, scholars have struggled to understand why states continued to rely on unremunerated rural labor across decades. *Village Work* traces the pathways of coercion that bridged the colonial and developmentalist orders and allowed for continued appropriation of labor over the course of the twentieth century.[35] Looking at the practice of self-help over several decades shows how and why local people and officials repeatedly invested in constructs of development, even as they came to see their limitations as a form of politics. As a historian, the most intriguing and challenging aspect of studying collective unpaid labor is interpreting people's labor contributions in terms that neither replicate the assumptions of developers (who read labor as support) nor assume a priori that all labor was the result of state control. Historians are drawn to conflict for various reasons. At a basic level, conflict tends to produce documents and, at a broader level, it reveals the fault lines of social interaction. In contrast, successful calls for labor leave no such traces.

Why did men and women in Kpasenkpe and surrounding areas respond to collective calls to dig wells, mold blocks, and plaster walls? Residents may have shown up because of the threat of punishment by chiefs, the government, or both. A series of laws consistently reproduced a 1930s-era exception for "minor communal services" in the definition of "forced labor," allowing states and local leaders to enforce collective labor exactions. Records of this enforcement are few and far between, of course, but it is difficult to imagine that the threat of repercussions for refusal was not widely experienced and known, particularly in the colonial period. Alternately, residents may have shown up to engage with chiefs or government officials. Responses to labor requests could serve as a relatively low-cost way to demonstrate support (or opposition) for certain leaders or regimes and, conversely, to make demands on these leaders for reciprocity. Last, residents may have shown up because they simply supported the projects on which they were asked to labor—needing a school or a well, they responded to demands that they build it. This book is full of examples of each of these dynamics. In their recollections of performing unremunerated labor, Kpasenkpe residents offered accounts that included multiple motivations, often at the same time, revealing how individuals navigated development demands in ways that defy singular explanations and simple dichotomies between coercion and choice.

If we step back from the stew of individuals' motivation for contributing or refusing labor, however, we can instead ask what labor allowed people, as individuals and collectivities, to do and to demand. In other words, we can begin to see the possibilities and limitations that self-help labor presented as a form of twentieth-century political action. Like other forms of state appropriation, governments treated constituent contributions of labor as both budgetary necessities and as demonstrations of belonging and support—for chiefs, for the state, or for a project itself, and often for all three combined. Unlike most forms of taxation, however, labor demands were always both envisioned and enforced as collective exactions on an undifferentiated set of villagers. Developers showed remarkably little interest in determining which people came out to perform labor or in how this labor was raised. Collective, project-based demands had the effect of building in individual flexibility and variation. They also circumscribed the options for rural people to link their contributions and refusals of labor to larger political goals. As long as local leaders could muster a group of laborers for an allotted time, developers would read these performances as representing the support of the whole community, no matter how many people stayed home out of protest or lack of interest. Furthermore, when citizens performed or refused labor to oppose leaders or assert support for alternate orders, their efforts were easily read as narrow support or rejection of a certain project, rather than part of a larger agenda.

Even if we limit our vision to the politics of development funding, we can see how collective, village-level labor extraction had a depoliticizing effect. Over time, rural people came to know that developers expected performances of community support, and that without it there were limited options for attracting a school, a well, or a road. In this context, it is easy to see how thinking of coercion and threat of punishment on an individual level limits historians' perspective and how structures of funding and consistencies in official ideology could constrain people's options in ways that are not easily reflected in documents on specific projects or articulated by individual participants. Reasonably, people in various places tended to channel their energy into competing for projects, rather than calling attention to the overall scarcity of development resources. Meanwhile, officials and politicians could use examples of labor from disparate village projects, regardless of their scope, as evidence that they were developing the region as a whole and with popular support.

CHIEFS, FAMILIES, AND STATES

While development schemes often imagined and treated rural villagers as undifferentiated and "local" populations, for some Kpasenkpe residents village projects became a way to cultivate careers and reputations that connected them to regional and national centers. The book spends a lot of time on the topic of chieftaincy and with Kpasenkpe's long-serving chief, Wulugunaba Sebiyam, as well as the men and women associated with his compound as wives, siblings, and children. Institutions of chieftaincy offer important windows into the ambiguities of colonial and postcolonial statecraft. In part because of ongoing discussions about the relationship between statecraft and the concept of tradition, scholars of chieftaincy have had to think flexibly about the ideologies, discourses, and practices of local politics. In the Ghanaian context, several scholars have worked to uncover mechanisms by which chiefs retained or captured political and economic relevance over the course of the twentieth century, focusing especially on claims to land and belonging.[36] In a variety of contexts elsewhere on the continent, historians have shown the ways that chieftaincy became imbricated in the politics of development projects as chiefs alternately courted and criticized the work of developers.[37]

Less attention has been given to the practical ways in which chiefs became involved in the daily bureaucracy of development projects and to how performances of technical competence and local mediation became key elements of chiefly authority in the decades after the end of indirect rule and as chiefs navigated the postcolonial period. As a result, scholars have tended to see a recent resurgence of chiefly influence as a consequence of neoliberal statecraft, showing how donor-enforced reforms across Africa in the 1980s, 1990s, and 2000s (policies under the labels of structural adjustment, good governance, and decentralization) allowed chiefs to cultivate outside recognition and participate in an invigorated "politics of custom."[38] *Village Work* shows how the long history of chiefly engagement with development forged patterns that have been ripe for intensification in the twenty-first century.

Kpasenkpe is located in the heart of the old kingdom of Mamprugu, where Mamprusi kings centralized their authority from the late seventeenth to mid-nineteenth centuries by incorporating groups of traders and spiritual specialists, regulating the slave trade, and managing tributary relations with the expanding Asante state to the south.[39] Under colonial rule, the Mamprusi chiefly hierarchy held on to claims to local authority by nimbly engaging with colonial administrative structures and performing administrative functions.[40] By the 1930s, colonial officials came to rely on chiefs who demonstrated an ability to command "followers" and undertake projects on "their own initiative." When these roles crystalized into the concept of "progressive chieftaincy," they allowed chiefs to remain both indispensable and palatable to post–World War II planners, nationalist politicians, and successive postcolonial states that looked to implement (but often not pay much for) development projects in the North.

These aspects of chieftaincy can be understood as a repertoire of roles and scripts that chiefs accumulated over decades and that they could use to engage with multiple audiences. In the text, I sometimes use the language of performance—particularly the idea of scripts and improvisation—to describe the interactions among chiefs, constituents, and developers. Over the course of the twentieth century, chiefs sometimes took on roles as clients of powerful outsiders. Casting themselves as both agents of change and custodians of community stability, chiefs found ways to remain relevant to the daily work of developmentalist statecraft even as its representatives and demands transformed by the decade. At other moments, chiefs took on a role as hosts, paving the way for newcomers' work and expecting that developers conform to locally recognized roles and responsibilities.[41] Paying attention to these performances of leadership, *Village Work* offers a framework for understanding the longevity of chiefly authority that relies on the work that chiefs have done, rather than their perceived relationship to concepts like tradition or modernity. In addition, the book shows how chiefs' ability to perform these roles has implicated wider networks of people and cemented personal and professional connections between chiefs and state and nongovernmental organizations.

Wulugunaba Sebiyam was chief of the Kpasenkpe division for fifty years, from 1942 to 1992. He appears frequently in the pages of this book, as do members of his wider family network. Their careers often anchor my discussion of wider connections among development, statecraft, and chieftaincy as well as the role of family, schooling, and gender in shaping rural people's engagement with village development. Moving to the more granular narrative of one chief and one family network allows me to explore how the institution of chieftaincy and the practice of family evolved over decades of engagement with development projects, often in ways that both resulted from and reproduced differential opportunities and life courses based on people's lineage, gender, and schooling.

In the first decades of his chieftaincy, Sebiyam's embrace of progressive chieftaincy relied on a network of people whose life paths brought them into little formal contact with developmentalist states. The labor of men and women who came to the chief's compound as his wives and brothers supported the expansion of farming and schooling that became central to Sebiyam's engagement with successive colonial and postcolonial states. In later decades, Kpasenkpe continued to be an attractive site for village projects because of the work of family members other than the chief. As increasing numbers of Sebiyam's siblings and, eventually, all several dozen of his sons and daughters attended school and many took up jobs in the civil service and nongovernmental organizations, they accumulated expertise in development work and strengthened Kpasenkpe's connections to national development networks.

Stories of the Sebiyam family network disrupt imagined divisions between "local" elites and "outside" developers. Locally, Sebiyam's brothers served as local council president and local tax collector, and his sister worked on Nkrumah-era community development projects. His children, at some point, became headmasters of every successive school in Kpasenkpe, served as local representatives of major political parties and every government that has emerged in postcolonial Ghana, and family members became the local organizers for the locally influential international NGO World Vision and a variety of successive "village" projects by other organizations. Sebiyam's siblings and children who started their careers locally became district and regional directors of education and social welfare. His eldest son became a minister of state and a university professor. Large networks of daughters and sons forged careers in medicine and education. As family members made careers in civil service, politics, and international development, they forged connections among siblings and with aunts and uncles that allowed them to weather the political and economic volatility of late twentieth-century Ghana. In turn, connections that crisscrossed the country raised family members' abilities to act as "local" hosts for successive governmental and nongovernmental village development projects.[42]

What should scholars take from the evidence of the close involvement of so many Sebiyam family members with village development? A rich range of literature explores how efforts at "grassroots" or "decentralized" development often entrench, rather than disrupt, local hierarchies and inequality.[43] Indeed, tracing Kpasenkpe's chiefly family illustrates one way that village development reproduced inequality by lineage and schooling. Developers' search for leaders who were at once "local" and "progressive" often allowed educated family members to take an outsized role in development practice in Kpasenkpe, both because of their individual experience and training and because of the connections they forged with one another. In doing so, they increased distinctions between themselves and other Kpasenkpe residents (including many in their own family network). Scholarship on development and rural differentiation forms an important counternarrative to the imaginaries of village development projects, which too often relied on assumptions of homogeneity within villages. However, models that would decry the story of Kpasenkpe's chiefly family as "nepotism" or "capture" have the effect of treating familial connections as a deviation from some imagined norm, rather than seeing them as a key way in which rural constituents have navigated developmentalist states.[44]

Anthropologists and historians have long appreciated that family networks are deeply important in the ways that people, in Africa and elsewhere, have navigated the century more broadly, and there is extensive literature on contemporary family networks, particularly with regard to transnational migration.[45] As historians such as Emily Lynn Osborn have aptly shown, the idea that state and family are "separate spheres" is a colonial construct, and one that has left a long legacy in policy making as well as scholarship.[46] By following the accumulated engagement of one family network, this book brings forward the claim that, at least in northern Ghana, the separation of family and state was never a practical reality, especially for chiefs. Moreover, developers' inability to recognize the centrality of family networks often had the perverse effect of both heightening and obscuring mechanisms of differentiation within and among rural settlements. This book suggests that scholars and practitioners of rural development should take family networks, like village projects, to be a key site where statecraft happens.

Within and beyond the Sebiyam family, differentiation by lineage and schooling intersected with the gendered enterprise of twentieth-century statecraft. Developers' ideas about villagers and village life shaped how men and women across the region encountered the state. Colonial gender ideologies made men and boys the primary targets for forced labor requisitions as well as agricultural interventions and government schooling. While postcolonial regimes often paid lip service to addressing the resulting inequalities in schooling and access to agricultural inputs, they often reinforced them in practice. For example, "green revolution" interventions in the 1970s and 1980s continued to imagine "key farmers" as men, despite widespread recognition of the importance of women as cultivators.[47] Similarly, both governmental and familial ideas about gender continued to limit girls' access to schooling. When postcolonial village development programs self-consciously aimed to reach women and girls, they often did so in ways that reinforced colonial gender binaries, as is evident in the antinudity campaigns of the Nkrumah era (chapter 3). Throughout the period, developers identified men as their primary interlocutors, with the exception of initiatives that specifically sought to reach women.

Interviews showed the range of ways that men and women in Kpasenkpe navigated and reflected upon the gendered aspects of village development. Men in Kpasenkpe could make use of developers' ideas to reinforce local hierarchies. For example, when Sebiyam created a new (male) titled elder position for "chief farmer" in the 1940s, he drew resources to the area while bolstering colonial ideas that both leadership and farming were men's work. Interviews also helped draw attention to the gaps between the ways that developers imagined gender hierarchies and the realities of village life. For example, evidence from several successful women farmers in Kpasenkpe reveals that, while agricultural extension activities in the town were focused on men, women were adept at using familial and commercial networks to access government-subsidized inputs. Additionally, Kpasenkpe residents' ideas about gender and labor shaped their interaction with village development projects. For example, when women organized Amasachina self-help initiatives in the 1970s, they did so by drawing on common mechanisms for organizing women's labor on farms and in compounds.

Gender mattered in the chiefly family as well. Wulugunaba Sebiyam made the unusual decision to send both his sons and daughters to school. While this decision makes his family something of an anomaly among Kpasenkpe residents and among chiefly families across the region, it also means that tracing his children's careers helps to illuminate the different paths available to educated men and women in successive eras of the postcolonial civil service.[48] Sebiyam's prosperity as a farmer was also somewhat unusual in Kpasenkpe (though less so than his emphasis on girls' education). In contrast to families that relied more heavily on women's farm labor, Sebiyam's wives successfully used normative ideas that women did not farm as a way to protect their labor and invest resources in individual trading enterprises. Like in other compounds across Ghana, however, this power declined over the course of the late twentieth century, as wives invested increasing amounts of labor and resources to support their children's feeding and schooling. Studying family networks can help illuminate how people navigated the twentieth century not only as women and men but also, as Christine Okali puts it, as "spouses, siblings, offspring, and parents."[49]

SOURCES AND METHODS

At present, the proliferation of development agencies in northern Ghana is obvious even from casual observation. On my daily walk to the archives in the regional capital of Tamale, when I began this research in 2008, I passed a corner where a large sign for a local NGO Youth Alive was surrounded by a cluster of international, bilateral, and other local agencies: the Government of Ghana's Northern Region Poverty Reduction Programme, the Canadian International Development Agency (CIDA), and the international NGOs Basic Needs and Action Aid (see fig. I.1).

For someone familiar with the literature in development studies, the North's development scene evidenced what Charles Piot, looking at a similar cluster of signs in northern Togo, terms "NGO fervor," flourishing in West

FIGURE I.1. Street corner in Tamale, northern Ghana, 2008. Author's photo.

Africa's poorest regions in the wake of structural adjustment programs in the 1980s and 1990s.[50] As my work went on—over fifteen months of research between 2008 and 2011 and shorter visits in 2013, 2015, and 2019—I became increasingly aware of the continuities between present practices and the waves of development interventions Ghanaians had navigated in the preceding decades. As these successive waves are within the living memory of many people in northern Ghana, I became interested in meeting people who had this depth of experience. I decided early on to spend several weeks moving between archival work in Tamale and a stay in Walewale, the current capital of one of the districts that kept surfacing in my archival research. Splitting my time in Walewale between the West Mamprusi District Assembly and the offices of the prominent NGO World Vision, I spoke with staff about their careers and observed the kinds of questions and struggles that came up in current work as agencies sought to optimize slim budgets and show success in small-scale projects.

It was through this initial research that I first began to think about villages, like Kpasenkpe, that emerged in both streams of research—places where activist local leaders and a long-standing web of connections to state agents seemed to make development work endure. As I turned from work in the district capital to research in Kpasenkpe itself, I followed the networks (both official and personal) that had connected the town to national and international institutions of development practice. Interviews and daily conversations in Kpasenkpe—with about one hundred different residents over five years of visits—focused on personal and occupational histories, and I learned a great deal about both the shared and divergent ambitions and struggles that shaped individuals' lives. I always began by explaining my interests, and conversations often tended toward discussions of the specific past projects about which individuals either knew the most or, often, about which they had the strongest opinions. A surprising strength of this method was that I realized a lot of people had much to say about previous development projects, both in praise and critique. Like development planners, people in Kpasenkpe were interested in evaluating past projects, and, like development planners who have worked for more than a few years in the business, they were often simultaneously jaded about the litany of past failure and hopeful for future success. As it became clear that I had no hand in bringing developers to town, I turned out to be an adequate sounding board for the kinds of reflections that developers themselves rarely hear.[51] I appreciated the candor with which a variety of town residents told stories about how development had shaped—or not—the town as well as their own lives.

When I embarked on this project, I realized that I could not imagine tracing local-state relationships without grounding my understanding in a particular place and set of people. However, there are real risks of using this scope while trying to challenge an idea that villages are all the same. I frequently found myself asking (and being asked) if Kpasenkpe was "representative" of other villages in northern Ghana, Africa, or around the world, even as I realized that I needed to question and historicize that desire to generalize. Instead of making Kpasenkpe representative of the region's villages, I aim to illustrate the links that connected village development in Kpasenkpe to regional, national, and international processes of statecraft. These specific links are, of course, particular to Kpasenkpe, but the mechanisms of connection are not. So, between trips to Kpasenkpe, I returned to Walewale, Tamale, and Accra to find oral historical and documentary sources that illuminated Kpasenkpe's connections to district, regional, and national capitals. As I tried to understand how Kpasenkpe had become a site for a series of development initiatives over time, I worked extensively with documentary material housed in official archives, individual ministries, and the frequently uncatalogued files of the West and East Mamprusi District Assemblies. So as to position Kpasenkpe's politics of development in conversation with other northern settlements, the book also draws on a database I created of over two hundred petitions sent to district and regional officials across Ghana's North from 1957 to 1992. This material also led to fifteen interviews with former and current staff of local government bodies, the Ministry of Agriculture, and World Vision. Throughout my research, I used documentary evidence to shape the questions that I asked of the people I spoke to, and vice versa. In interviews, my familiarity with the archives and secondary literature allowed me to offer time lines and interpretations that either prompted specific memories or allowed people to dispute my interpretation of the written record and comment on the arguments of other historians.

It was here, as I traced Kpasenkpe's history of development, that I began to realize the depth of influence exercised by the family of the former chief of Kpasenkpe, a network that articulated in complex ways with official channels of development practice. At the same time, and on a more personal level, I found myself engaging with members of the Sebiyam family, often before I knew of their family connections. As I learned more about family history, I began to understand the variety of ways I had encountered family members in my initial research—in archival records and among Ghanaian academics and civil servants. I realized that I was the latest in a long string of outsiders interested in development for whom Kpasenkpe had become a site and the Sebiyam family had acted as hosts. From this realization, I found it necessary to make these connections the subject of my research by turning my attention to historical dynamics that made such associations long lasting.

My interest in speaking with people who had been most involved with village development initiatives meant that my selection of people to speak within Kpasenkpe often reflected the biases of lineage, gender, and schooling that characterized village development in the region overall. Of the 106 Kpasenkpe residents with whom I spoke, 32 were in the chiefly family, including Sebiyam's wives and brothers' wives (14), siblings (10), and children (8). In the rest of my seventy-plus interviews in Kpasenkpe, I attempted to interview a large percentage of residents who had lived in the village between 1942 and 1992, a period in which Kpasenkpe's population ranged from seven hundred to thirteen hundred residents.[52] I paid particular attention to people who were remembered as being notably involved in development initiatives, either as leaders or participants. I sought out women who had been involved in development initiatives, either as leaders or participants, but even then, my interviews reflected the gender biases of development, with women making up about 30 percent of the Kpasenkpe residents with whom I spoke. Twenty interviews were with men who, by the time of my interviews, had become titled elders, chiefs, or regents. As scholars of Mamprugu point out, in the historically multiethnic Mamprusi political system, distinctions among elders (*kpaamba*), commoners (*tarima*), and recent immigrants (*saama*) are often fluid and change over time. In addition, disputes over who can claim descent from ruling lineages are common.[53] Since my interviews were not focused on matters of descent or ethnic identification, I have decided not to adopt Mamprusi terminology with reference to particular people. However, I do include traditional titles when referring to individual people if they specified that this was how they would like to be named in the book.

In my interviews with members of the Sebiyam family network, I focused most heavily on interviews in Kpasenkpe itself, where I met and interviewed extended patrilineage members, including Sebiyam's brothers, sons, daughters, and select others. I also spoke to Sebiyam's wives and brothers' wives who were still alive and residing in Kpasenkpe at the time of my research. Beyond Kpasenkpe, I was more selective and (somewhat artificially) focused on the network of Sebiyam's direct children, of whom I spoke to sixteen outside of Kpasenkpe, as well as one nephew. I traced networks to regional and national centers most closely, speaking to his children currently residing in Walewale, Tamale, and Accra. Where possible, I supplemented interviews with documentary evidence from district and regional government and NGO documentation.

The book's strength in following networks of engagement with development, particularly through the chiefly family, also limited my interviews in important ways. Kpasenkpe is quite a small place, and I was clearly networked through members of the chiefly family which, as the book points out, included people active in multiple aspects of traditional, governmental, and nongovernmental authority. As a result, though I interviewed a large number of people, I was unlikely to hear about certain subjects, such as disputes over chieftaincy. While I heard more than a few critiques of Sebiyam and his family members, it is also possible that some interviewees muted their appraisals.

Ebron reminds us that interviews often enact the performances that scholars wish their interlocutors to discuss.[54] Certainly, as a stranger who had come to talk about development, I fit into a familiar script. Like other strangers, I relied on local hosts, working primarily with two research assistants and interpreters whose positions and reputations also shaped the course of the research.[55] Solomon Dawuni Sebiyam, with whom I worked over several years, is one of Wulugunaba Sebiyam's sons, but he is also someone whose biography and personal struggles led him to develop local networks and relationships that often placed him outside the dominant arenas of familial influence. As I moved to interview a wider set of Kpasenkpe's elders, I worked with Seiya Namyoaya Enoch, a young part-time teacher who has cultivated an interest in elders' stories. We were sometimes perceived as a surprising combination of listeners: an outsider interested in complaints about past development projects rather than setting up present ones, a family member whose path through town and the late twentieth century had kept him from the centers of local leadership, and a young person who cared about history. Our conversations were shaped by the combination of the predictability of our roles—an interested outsider, a local host—and the oddity of our task. While some avenues of inquiry were closed off, this dynamic allowed for often vibrant and multifaceted conversations about the local structures and dynamics of development and the familial, professional, and personal relationships that had connected local people to larger networks.

ORGANIZATION

Village Work is organized chronologically, but it also makes connections across scale, weaving stories of Kpasenkpe and its chiefly family with stories of local and regional government and of national and international trends. Along the way, the book traces a genealogy of village development and hinterland statecraft that begins with colonial strategies for labor extraction and administrative austerity, continues through experiments in self-help and labor extraction in the late colonial, nationalist, and postnationalist eras, and ends with the hardening of village development and self-help labor as the primary focus of rural statecraft in the neoliberal era.

Beginning the book with a regional view, chapter 1 charts the emergence of hinterland statecraft in northern Ghana in the interwar period, showing how systems of labor extraction for development and models of progressive chieftaincy emerged out of the dynamics of colonial forced labor. Colonial officials combined force and flexibility as they endeavored to commandeer northern labor for roads in the face of limited budgets and widespread resistance. By the 1920s, officials used an imaginary of undifferentiated villages to direct resources and attention to chiefs who could appropriate labor "on their own initiative," a practice that also provided cover as international critiques mounted against forced labor. Over time, chiefs learned to work with and around the contours of the hinterland state. The last section of the chapter shows how certain northern chiefs forged new models of rule, laying down scripts of progressive chieftaincy that linked labor extraction to new ideologies of development and incorporated them into performances of modernization, largesse, and power.

Chapters 2 and 3 bring the focus to Kpasenkpe as a wide range of residents as well as a young chief and his family navigated the confluence of development, decolonization, and nation building in the 1950s and 1960s, a period that is commonly referred to as "Nkrumah's time," for Ghana's first president. Chapter 2 shows that the colonial government and the Nkrumah state used a framework of village development—combining models of progressive chieftaincy, demands for self-help labor, and a fiction of undifferentiated rural space—to serve a variety of ideological, political, and practical needs. Residents used arguments about village development and small-scale funding to affirm, contest, or alter the shape of government in the emerging independent state. In Kpasenkpe, Wulugunaba Sebiyam and residents worked to attract development funds, imbuing labor and leadership with ideas of modernization and help while remaining attuned to the demands of a shifting political landscape. Nkrumah's time was marked by local improvisation and innovation, but struggles over the terms of village development and self-help labor also worked to reinforce their centrality, setting the boundaries of what residents of Ghana's northern regions could demand of the new Ghanaian nation.

Shifting the lens to the chief's family, chapter 3 shows how village development work became enmeshed in the careers and family dynamics of those who became agents of state-led development. As Sebiyam's educated siblings and children began to build regional and national careers, they also came back to Kpasenkpe as the face of the state, shoring up a connection between chieftaincy and development amidst the uncertainties of decolonization and nationalist politics. In the family, like the town, engagement with development relied on labor. Men and women who entered Sebiyam's compound as wives and brothers rarely interacted directly with development projects, but it was their work on family farms and in the compound, as well as their ingenuity in maintaining family stability, that made development a family enterprise.

Chapters 4 and 5 continue to trace the story of village development through regional trends as well as granular histories of Kpasenkpe and its chiefly family. Chapter 4 turns to the years of national political and economic upheaval that followed Nkrumah's ouster in 1966. In these years, increasingly desperate governments looked on the northern hinterland as a place of untapped agricultural potential, partnering with international and donor agencies to subsidize and distribute "green revolution" technologies. It was a paradoxical time in the rural North, and the chapter traces how agricultural spending reached into the daily lives of farmers even as residents faced governments that could not build the roads, schools, or clinics they might have hoped would accompany increased state attention. Using district-level budgets, ministry records, petitions, and oral histories, this chapter maps out a surprisingly vibrant period of rural engagement with developers and governments. In Kpasenkpe and the region more broadly, village projects became unmoored from well-defined, state-centered networks, and officials, leaders, and constituents used performances of self-help and village leadership in a variety of political and economic projects, to demonstrate support or opposition to chiefs and elders, influence disputes over administrative and traditional boundaries, or attract funds from officials and international sources. The multiplicity of strategies people employed in the period is nowhere more evident than in the chief's own family network, where wives, brothers, and children used family connections to navigate both uncertainty and opportunity.

Chapter 5 shows how experiences from the previous decades allowed officials, leaders, and constituents to cope with the fundamental contradictions of the early neoliberal era, when the self-styled revolutionary PNDC government of J. J. Rawlings implemented World Bank–supported structural adjustment programs. In the rural North, neoliberal reforms slowly dismantled agricultural programs and the government turned to a flood of nongovernmental actors to undertake village development work in the face of state austerity. In Kpasenkpe, this dynamic was dramatized by its 1986 selection for a community development project by the international Christian NGO World Vision. Reanimating older models of community responsibility and local initiative, PNDC and World Vision officials used demands for self-help to depoliticize the scarcity and competition that undergirded programs of "people's power" and "participatory development." In turn, local PNDC cadres, church officials, and constituents used performances of leadership and labor to navigate this complex terrain, solidifying Kpasenkpe's reputation as an attractive site for developers and reprising the Wulugunaba's role as host to development projects. A focus on this work, alongside a section on the growing network of educated members of the chiefly family, allows for an inversion of an image of village residents as simply local clients of outside developers, showing instead how village labor and leadership became enmeshed in regional, national, and international networks of expertise and employment.

The book concludes by bringing its detailed long-term analysis of village development to bear on recent debates about the impact of neoliberal restructuring on the politics of development in rural Africa. Rather than a sharp break with the past, I suggest that recent decades have forced rural people to rely even more heavily on existing repertoires of performance and strategies for engaging governments and nongovernmental organizations. As the book overall shows, these strategies have drawn rural people and leaders into wide-ranging local, regional, and national networks even as they have reinforced the centrality of models of community cohesion and local initiative. Together, these dynamics suggest a new perspective on Ghana's much-heralded stability in the 1990s and 2000s.

1 ↜ Labor, Chieftaincy, and Colonial Statecraft

> His Excellency presumes that no village would agree of its own
> initiative to maintain, still less construct, its section of a road un-
> less the work were regarded by the village as being for the direct
> benefit of its own community.[1]

IN MARCH of 1936, Chief Commissioner W. J. A. Jones recommended
that one of the first British colonial development grants in the hinterland regions of colonial Ghana's Northern Territories Protectorate be
allocated to build a dispensary in the out-of-the-way town of Sandema.
Despite having little revenue, he argued, the Builsa "people under the
active leadership of the head chief have shown highly commendable
initiative in the development of their country" by building a school,
constructing latrines, undertaking sanitary measures approved by the
medical officer, and building roads that despite being "maintained without payment, are among the best in the Protectorate."[2] Jones had good
reason to present this as a simple story of a rural community voluntarily
mobilizing in its own "interests."[3] By the early 1930s, the British government faced increasing criticisms from African anticolonial activists and
international organizations about the forced labor that they extracted
from colonial hinterlands. Officials in British colonial Africa began to
cast about for new rationales and practices of labor extraction. In colonial Kenya, officials began aggressively expanding their reliance on
chiefs for communal labor to pursue increasingly unpopular antierosion
schemes.[4] On Zanzibar's clove plantations, officials cast about for a new
rationale for compelling cultivation until finding it in a "Grow More
Food" campaign during the Second World War.[5] In the Gold Coast's
Northern Territories, reports like Jones's allowed the state to make much
of their meager outlays for local projects, reframing labor extraction as

"local initiative" and providing examples that they could use to paint a picture of consensual, contained, and gradual progress in the North.

For Builsa's newly installed Sandemnaab Azantilow, the young chief to whom Jones referred, the matter was not simple at all. Over the preceding decades, Azantilow had come of age as the effects of colonial rule took shape around him. He had seen his predecessors, like other chiefs in the region, strive to satisfy the insatiable British demand for labor. They conscripted local men into journeys to the South, where they would serve in the colonial military, take up the most undesirable positions in gold mines, and build the roads and railways that facilitated colonial extraction.[6] More locally, chiefs had appropriated labor from local men and women to build the roads and rest houses that served as the administrative infrastructure of British colonial rule. Forced labor was deeply resented, and colonial clerks' desks were covered with reports from chiefs on constituents' refusals to follow their demands for local road building. Resistance to forced labor had stymied colonial officials, while officials' responses had underscored for residents that colonial rule was to be sporadic, unpredictable, and underwritten by violence. Throughout, struggles over labor defined the practice, experience, and limits of colonial authority in the region.

Using records from the broader region in which Kpasenkpe is located (called, from 1921 to 1946, the Northern Province), this chapter traces how, over this period, systems of labor extraction for development emerged from colonial forced labor regimes. Over the interwar period, I show how the colonial state's treatment of the region as an economic and bureaucratic hinterland incentivized officials to embrace both force and flexibility in statecraft. By the mid-1920s, colonial officials began to experiment with a pragmatic framework of backing chiefs who could raise road labor. An approach that treated villages as indistinct and substitutable proved useful, allowing officials to demand labor while cultivating ambiguity over where, how, and by whom it could be demanded. In these years, administrators simply identified chiefs who were able to build roads and rest houses "on their own initiative" and then downplayed or ignored the ongoing coercion and exploitation that made such efforts possible. Over time, chiefs learned and tested the possibilities of rule, incorporating labor extraction into their struggles to attract followers and manage the burdens of an extractive state.[7] By the 1930s, chiefs like Azantilow did not simply extend a system of colonial labor extraction. Instead, they reinvented it for a new era.[8] In their interactions with colonial officials, Azantilow and others laid down a script of what became known as "progressive" chieftaincy, raising labor for small-scale development projects and garnering visibility and state funding in return. To constituents, progressive chiefs crafted performances that linked modernization, largesse, and power, and which buried the coercion of labor extraction under a new rhetoric of indirect rule and development. It was out of the ambiguities, limitations, and opportunities of hinterland statecraft that chiefs and officials forged models and imaginaries of statecraft that would become the backbone of rural development in the decades to follow. In the village of Kpasenkpe, some thirty miles east of Sandema, the future chief, Sebiyam Barijesira, watched and learned.

LABOR AND RULE IN A COLONIAL HINTERLAND

By the time that British forces arrived in what would become the Northern Territories Protectorate, generations of residents of the historically mobile, multiethnic, and politically diverse savanna region had already experienced life on the margins of empires. In the seventeenth and eighteenth centuries, an expanding Asante empire to the south treated the region as a source of tribute, often levied in enslaved people. Nineteenth-century incursions from the new Sahelian armies of Babatu and Samori intensified or reintroduced instabilities of enslavement in many areas.[9] Over these centuries, enterprising community builders in the region crafted a diverse array of political and social structures that allowed people to participate in, cope with, or avoid the predations of empires. Kingdoms, including Mamprugu, emerged with centralized political structures that institutionalized hierarchies and organized exploitation, while other areas developed decentralized and overlapping systems of authority over land, people, and ritual.[10] Meanwhile, ideas of some or all northern people as "primitive" and "savage" flourished in coastal and forest regions and in the Atlantic world overall, shaping the ideological terrain on which colonial policy would unfold in the twentieth century.[11]

When British officials sought to expand colonial occupation inland from the Gold Coast Colony in the late nineteenth century, they were thus primed to think of the northern savanna as marginal to their interests. Extending into the region only as a matter of speculation and military strategy, they reinscribed the region as the "Gold Coast hinterland" or the "Asante hinterland" and began to cast about for a way to make colonial administration both economically and fiscally feasible.[12] Labor soon emerged as the center of colonial thinking about the region's potential on both fronts, with plans for industrial and commercial growth in the export-producing South reliant on continued flows of cheap or coerced northern labor and resulting in what scholars have characterized as the "underdevelopment" or "non-development" of the region.[13] People from the Northern Territories were forcibly recruited for underground work in the gold mines, as colonial soldiers, and as laborers on the large-scale road, railway, and port infrastructure in the South.[14] Southern economic expansion also created the conditions under which migrants searched for labor opportunities on their own, particularly during the rise of cocoa production in the early decades of the twentieth century.[15]

While colonial officials raised concerns about the effects of migrants' mobility and access to new sources of wealth and knowledge, they imagined that colonial policies could contain the influence of returning migrants.[16] In this view, colonial administrators could cast the North's hinterland status as a virtue, particularly in contrast to what they saw as the "uncontrolled" or "premature" development of the southern economy and politics. This framework allowed officials to square their treatment of the region as a labor reserve with ideas of colonial trusteeship, using, as Jeff Grischow argues, "invo[cations] of community . . . to maintain state power while exploiting [local] resources."[17] The history of enslavement in the region provided official rationale for colonial labor demands, which were cast as an extension of tributary relationships that, officials argued, had been disrupted by slave raiding and imperial conquest by Asante, Babatu, and then the British. Imagining that residents had long been subjected to coercive labor regimes, colonial officials argued that the colonial state and its agents were the legitimate beneficiaries.[18]

British colonial constructions of the region as an economic hinterland made it into an administrative backwater as well. If, as Sara Berry argues, colonialism in West Africa as a whole aimed for "hegemony on a shoestring," the Northern Territories was an area where the concerns about shoestring budgets predominated over ambitions for strict control of people and resources.[19] When district commissioners (DCs), the British civilian staff who replaced military officials in 1907, arrived at postings in the Northern Territories, they found themselves with tremendous autonomy and very few resources. Between 1908 and 1930, the total number of DCs and clerks in the region was between twenty and twenty-seven, creating a ratio of one official to nearly thirty-five thousand residents and an area of nearly two thousand square miles.[20] Direct taxation quickly proved impractical, and in 1907 the colonial government eliminated tolls on the caravan trade, the only revenue stream that made significant contributions to the Northern Territories budget.[21] Colonial agents faced the colonial government's strict unwillingness to expend resources on the region—a sentiment notably captured by Governor Thornburn's 1912 statement that "the Northern Territories must be content to wait their turn" in favor of government investment in the South.[22]

In lieu of taxation, the Northern Territories administration again turned to labor, placing demands directly on the bodies of colonial subjects.[23] Officials required labor to satisfy DCs' constant preoccupation with "trekking" through large districts.[24] Residents were ordered to clear and clean the roads that ran between district capitals, served as boundaries between districts, and gave officials access to towns and villages they wished to visit. They built rest houses for officials and, before the widespread use of official motorcars in the 1920s, DCs on tour had an almost inexhaustible demand for "carriers" (head porters). Road labor quotas were officially set at six days per quarter for adult men, though demands varied in practice over time and space, and women as well as men were targeted. Demands for carriers and rest house building were officially sanctioned, but there was no set quota, or limit, on these impositions.[25] At the discretion of individual DCs, demands for labor were arbitrary, sporadic, and highly localized.[26] As administrators shuffled among districts, labor regimes could change dramatically and unpredictably. Latitude for official violence was profound, but the practical extent of enforcement was consistently limited.

The state's desire to extract labor from the region without allocating funds or personnel encouraged officials to find useable fictions and simplified strategies of administration. As scholars of northern Ghana have amply demonstrated, colonial officials layered a homogenous institutional framework over the diversity of political formations in the region, recognizing the authority of a variety of earth priests, chiefs, and local strongmen.[27] Officials were more than willing to unseat chiefs who failed to meet administrative demands and, conversely, to support appointed "sergeant major chiefs" who often appeared to be nothing more than hired guns.[28] Names and lists of villages became a technology for defining and ordering the colonial state in the Northern Territories. At a practical level, officials often cared about jurisdiction only insofar as chiefs could translate their authority over particular settlements into forced labor. By identifying the villages that were "under" a certain leader's jurisdiction, colonial officials found simple ways to map imagined political hierarchies without pinning down the details of boundaries. Similarly, colonial officials used the label of "village" to describe a variety of rural settlements, some with clustered settlement patterns and others that consisted of more dispersed networks of households and farms. Instead of being concerned with territory itself, these designations helped officials create colonial administrative units and identify seats of "head" chiefs who could serve as the counterparts of DCs.

"A COMPLAINT OF MUCH ELASTICITY OF MEANING": ADMINISTRATION AND FORCED LABOR TO 1920

Residents of the Northern Territories contested labor extraction from the very beginning, a fact that is evident even from the official diaries kept by British officials as they attempted to enforce colonial demands in the region. Diaries from 1919 and 1920 reveal that people faced uneven and changing regimes of official violence and that they worked creatively to contest the demands placed upon them. From January to November of 1919, the district commissioner of the Navrongo-Zuarungu District was A. W. Cardinall.[29] Cardinall was a scholarly-minded official who was not particularly enthusiastic about labor requisition and who came to the district while he was working on his book, *The Natives of the Northern Territories of the Gold Coast*, and his daily records reveal his growing recognition of how administrative demands burdened colonial chiefs.[30] The most common notes in his records concern constant complaints from chiefs that locals would not "follow" them. He wrote that this was "a complaint of much elasticity of meaning" and, later, that the term "'follow' is a word I have never understood."[31] From his published writings about the area, it is clear that Cardinall was not confounded by the region's diverse systems of authority in general but was rather pointing out that chiefs' complaints about "following" did not correspond to what he knew about these systems. Cardinall's diaries chronicle his dawning understanding that chiefs used the complaint not as a commentary on the general state of their authority but instead to explain and excuse inability (or refusal) to raise forced labor. Cardinall alternated between critiquing Britain for undercutting its own rhetoric of "democracy" and writing longingly of the ways a "benevolent despot" would be able to realize what he saw as the agricultural and trade potential of the region.[32] He often concluded such scholarly and ideological musings with more practical recognition that the handful of administrators who enacted policy in the region did not need to concern themselves with the workings of authority as much as they simply needed newly colonized subjects to meet colonial requirements. "From an administrative point of view," he wrote in July 1919, "it matters little whom they 'follow' as long as law and order is observed."[33]

In November of that year, just prior to the yearly demand for dry season labor (from December to March), Cardinall was replaced by W. E. Gilbert, a thirty-four-year-old recruit who came directly from his military service in the First World War.[34] Over the eight months that Gilbert worked in Navrongo-Zuarungu, he saw with fresh eyes the extent of local resistance to forced labor, and his responses reveal the violence with which officials often responded. While on "trek," Gilbert's usual practice was to stop in a town and note the condition of the roads and rest house under a chief's jurisdiction. He then spoke (through an interpreter) to the chief. Nearly everywhere he stopped, Gilbert fielded complaints that certain sections or towns had refused to "follow" chiefs with respect to forced labor. Consulting his lists of villages, Gilbert determined whether the chief had jurisdiction over the area mentioned and, if so, arrested the headmen he found responsible and imposed collective or individual fines.

Speaking to elderly people in the area in the 1990s, Jean Allman and John Parker found that memories of violence, punishment, and its threat pervaded narrations of forced labor in the first decades of colonial administration, when government-recognized chiefs found their work crystalizing around the role of labor recruiter.[35] Detention and flogging of chiefs were frequent responses, and when chiefs identified specific people who "refused to follow" them, those individuals were given similar punishments. Some hints of more generally applied violence and its threat appear even in the self-reported diaries of officials such as Gilbert, who noted the "Maxim Gun for this Station" when it was returned from Tamale, and, when he turned the post over to his successor in July of 1920, he described the process as "handing over the books and ammunition."[36] While Gilbert was imposing fines and other punishments to enforce labor demands in Navrongo-Zuarungu, the DC of Gambaga District instead meted out gunpowder to chiefs, refusing to distribute it until roads and towns were cleared and rest house repairs and construction complete.[37]

In Lawra-Tumu District, forced labor demands for local roads were particularly onerous. Between June and August of 1920, C. B. Shields was posted to the sparsely populated western side of the district to make residents build and maintain the hundreds of miles of roads that connected the area to the more densely populated regions to the east and north. Shields spent three months trying to force constituents to comply with the "road scheme," which, he argued, called for "every available man" to be put to work.[38] His frustration with constituent resistance was evident. On the first day of a tour, he remarked that inspecting roads made him "furiously angry. . . . The only way to get anything proper is to stand all day and watch every inch of it." In one of the roads near Tumu, Shields found that a constable had "taken it into his head that there should be a . . . bulk across the road. . . . It will take 20 men all day tomorrow to unmake it." In Pina, "nothing has been done on . . . the road that I wanted, but some that I did not want has been done." In Dolbizan, where a "Constable could only raise 19 men" of the hundred that Shields had demanded, he found that they had "done a little work, where it was already very good and left all bad places." In Jeffisi, he found that constituents had spent "20 days messing up the road where it was already good."[39] For a brief period, direct supervision and threat of force allowed DCs like Shields to meet administrative demands for road labor. Returning along these roads late in the month, Shields paused to count the hundreds of workers on each section, and "stopped" to "speed things up" where necessary.[40] By August, when Shields was nearing the end of his term, he had concluded that "in the future unless I can be there personally I shall not start any work."[41]

Fines, imprisonment, and the threat of violence were the constant tools of colonial administration, but it is important to remember that the extent of official intervention was often limited.[42] The sheer regularity with which colonial officials reported labor refusals suggests that for many chiefs much of the time, complaints regarding "not being followed" could explain months in which colonial rule had been more or less ignored and allowed officials to cast vague, collective blame that resulted in the punishment of a few. In some cases, colonial officials hesitated before punishing local chiefs who seemed to be able to maintain colonial authority more generally. Between 1919 and 1920, successive DCs in both Navrongo-Zuarungu and Gambaga noted repeated refusals of labor and loyalty by followers of Anam, the chief of Yoragu, just outside the town of Bolga-tanga. Despite being fined and imprisoned, Anam persisted, and officials were loath to unseat a chief who had the power to organize constituents, even though they concluded he was "doubtless at the bottom of all the trouble in this part of the District."[43]

In other cases, officials observed that they had little understanding of or control over the local practice or politics of labor. In October, when a young official named A. C. Duncan-Johnstone took over as DC of Lawra-Tumu, he observed the aftermath of Shields's work. It was an uneven landscape. The residents of Golu, taken with their chief to work on the road to the east of town, had left "a very bad piece of road." At Pullima the road was "as good as anything in the LORHA district," and in Bellu, a site of frustration for Shields, Duncan-Johnstone remarked that "Not only have [constituents] turned out in large numbers, but they have done very excellent work, and from what I saw of the crowds on the road today, seem to be most cheerful, the work being performed to much singing and dancing." The same day, he mentioned that he could "not say the same for the DASIMA division. . . . They have done very little work and very few people have turned out."[44] In August, after reporting on long-standing recruitment issues in the town of Ulu, Duncan-Johnstone reflected on his limits by ruefully quoting a 1911 poem by an administrator in Nigeria called "The Passive Resister." The chosen passage read, "Of course it's all right if he means to fight / You can easily burst his bubble. / But if he sits tight, then it's hell's delight / He can give a whole world of trouble."[45]

Monthly diaries suggest that at times officials, like chiefs, were drawn into the complex process of coercing labor. In Southern Mamprusi, the DC began to recruit labor for railway work, implementing the "new labour scheme" that gave chiefs a quota for laborers but insisted that it be recruited "voluntarily."[46] After informing chiefs of their respective quotas, he argued that Northern Territories residents would then "see its benefits when the line is extended North" and that "if they want to stop our continual calls for head transport they must send boys down."[47] By March of 1920, the DC noted he was "not very successful" in getting "purely voluntary labor" for the railroads and elaborated that in Navrongo-Zuarungu Gilbert had said young men were willing to leave but not to "report to him for subsistence, papers, etc.," because "they prefer not to tie themselves up in that way."[48] By July, administrators were under pressure to deliver on recruits. While there were occasional spikes in recruitment, desertion was frequent and workers who returned often listed complaints about the road, the difficulty of getting work and pay, and the nature of the work itself.[49] Despite DCs' attempts to "make an example of" particular chiefs and imposing fines for "obstructing recruiting," they ended up simply paying extra travel money for laborers to return south.[50]

More generally, because colonial policy and economic change continued to encourage people from the Northern Territories to be mobile, colonial officials found themselves enmeshed in larger processes whereby chiefs and communities struggled to attract residents and secure their labor and loyalty. The ability of even small groups of people to cross district boundaries to avoid labor demands presented new challenges to state coercion, forcing colonial officials to treat labor not just as something that could be extracted from bodies but also as a political act involving subjects, chiefs, and officials.[51] In these cases, DCs became the leaders that constituents refused to "follow."

In January of 1919, Michael Dasent, then DC of Tumu, visited Sante-jan, a chiefly jurisdiction on the district's far eastern border. Stopping in the town of Gwosi, he reported that residents had refused to do road and rest house work and, it was suggested, had burned down the commission-er's stables in protest. When the Santejan chief said that "he could never get labour and that they took no notice when he told them to clean the road," Dasent moved through his arsenal for enforcing labor demands. After the Santejan chief fined the town ten sheep, Dasent "addressed" them "on the subject of their evil ways," replaced the Gwosi chief and stationed a constable to the town. These reports occasioned no comment from Dasent's superiors. The Santejan chief made similar complaints about the people of Kalarsi and Nbenya, but then he added an allegation that became a major source of administrative anxiety. He reported that the residents of Nbenya had not only refused to work but, in addition, were "migrating to the Navarro District."[52] The following month, Dasent's replacement E. O. Rake sent an inquiry to Northwestern Provincial Com-missioner H. M. Berkeley about the Santejan case. Reporting that "the people of a village called NAMANEA [Nbenya] . . . have crossed over into the NAVARO district, their complaint being that there was too much work in this District," Rake pointed out that while he was "of the opinion that a native is allowed full liberty in choosing his place of residence," he knew that policies might differ at his new post and asked "what steps," might be necessary "to get these men back."[53]

Over the next ten months, Rake's inquiry sparked debate over the relationships among labor, authority, and development that expose com-petitions among administrators to keep potential laborers within their jurisdiction. In 1919, the boundary between Lawra-Tumu and Navrongo-Zuarungu Districts also separated the Northeastern and Northwestern Provinces. Berkeley wrote to his counterpart in the Northeastern Province with the seemingly straightforward request that he "instruct" the DC of Navrongo-Zuarungu to "send these people back." "They ran away to avoid work when called upon by their Chief," he argued, and "if this is allowed . . . the people [would] desert from one side or the other according to the way they are called upon to supply labour."[54] Berkeley and Rake's counterparts in the Northeastern Province, however, saw things differently. Provincial Commissioner S. D. Nash and DC Cardinall, who both displayed an early interest in northern small-scale agriculture, began to craft an argument against "interfering with free migration," if "the natives . . . have changed their residence merely to get better farming land."[55] Cardinall moved from the specific to the general, arguing that "it seems to me to involve grave issues," involving the principle of "freedom of choice" and the risk of colonial chieftaincy becoming "tyrannical."[56] Nash sent a curt note back to Berkeley stating that he would take no action against the migrants.[57] When Berkeley turned the case over to Chief Commissioner H. W. Leigh, he contrasted Nash and Cardinall's defense of "freedom" with fundamental concerns for authority and respect, calling the migration "a deliberate attempt to scorn the headchief and so the District Commissioner."[58]

The letters between Nash and Berkeley reveal the administrative pressures and competitions that motivated their high-minded debates between "freedom" and "authority." Tumu, where DC Shields was about to undertake his major push for road construction, was sparsely populated. Recognizing the reality of widespread discontent, Berkeley sought to use district boundaries to set a limit on residents' options for avoidance of labor in the district. In contrast, Nash and Cardinall, seeing migration as a benefit to agricultural production and labor supply on their side of the boundary, had every reason to defend freedom of movement.[59] Over the subsequent years, debates between Lawra-Tumu and Navrongo-Zuarungu became more entrenched, even as the Northern Territories administration shuffled officials among districts.[60] Like the chiefs to whom they delegated the task of raising labor, DCs found that competition for followers could be fierce.

VIOLENCE, DENIABILITY, AND DEVELOPMENT IN THE 1920S

Concerns about labor continued to shape colonial practice as the first, limited plans for colonial development began to take shape in the region. At the same time, Northern Territories residents became more familiar with both the demands of administrators and the inconsistencies of colonial administration, finding new ways to navigate colonial rule. In 1919, Gold Coast governor Frederick Gordon Guggisberg released a ten-year development plan for the colony, the first of its kind in British colonial Africa.[61] Guggisberg focused primarily on the South, but the plan also articulated a vision for longer-term growth in northern agriculture, education, social welfare, and infrastructure. Transport was both the literal and figurative instrument for this transformation, and planners envisioned an extension of the railway (and later, the road network) as the "Highway of Progress" for the North.[62] Throughout the decade, however, officials continued apace in their labor demands. The Highway of Progress for colonial

Ghana's hinterlands, it seemed, would be an unpaved road, requiring annual maintenance by local labor.[63]

Administrators adapted old methods to the new tools and demands of developmentalist administration.[64] At the height of the rains, DCs in motorcars monitored the effects of water on roads and bridges, noting the improvements that would need to be made. Then, as the rains began to ebb, the real work began. In October of 1926, for example, Provincial Commissioner P. F. Whittall recounted his varied practices for controlling labor. On the second, he sent a contractor, Abudulai, to oversee labor on the main Tamale-Navrongo road. On the seventh, Whittall asked the Builsa chief to initiate and supervise construction of a "dry-weather motortrack" connecting his jurisdiction to the main road, reporting the chief's assurance that "the work can be done without any trouble at all." On the twelfth, Whittall went to visit the DC of Southern Mamprusi as he supervised construction of a low-cost bridge over the White Volta River, checking up on Abudulai's work on the way home. Back in his headquarters, Whittall arranged for a special road to be made simply so that the governor could visit a government cattle kraal by motorcar, reporting on the success of his brick-making scheme and its promise for future roadwork.[65] Meanwhile, resistance to labor demands continued. In Wa District, for example, DC Sumner complained consistently from 1926 to 1928 about "refusals." In response, he turned to the toolkit of punishments, fines, and oversight forged by his colleagues in the early 1920s — "rais[ing] a big row" (August 1926), issuing fines and assigning extra work as punishment (June 1926, September 1928, October 1928), arresting compound heads (October 1928), and using orderlies and constables to "put the fear of the D.C." into recalcitrant workers (October 1928).[66]

As people in the Northern Territories became more familiar with colonial administration, they continued to elaborate strategies for avoiding colonial labor demands. One of the most successful strategies continued to be mobility, which exploited tensions among officials' concurrent hopes for gradual development and their desires to appropriate labor and keep administrative order. On the border between Navrongo-Zuarungu and Southern Mamprusi Districts, frustrations with constituents' mobility came into conflict with nascent concerns about agricultural stability. In March of 1926, facing complaints that several compounds on the Navrongo-Zuarungu District border would not "follow" the Builsa chief, Provincial Commissioner Whittall responded by instructing them to move across the boundary to Southern Mamprusi, where, he hoped, migration would also encourage an expansion of small-scale farming.[67] In October, however, when Whittall became aware that several compounds in the settlement of Wiasi wanted to make a similar move, officials raised concerns that it was because of a "desire to avoid work . . . by crossing over to Southern Mamprusi which has a reputation for being rather more somnolent," and DC Freeman prevented the move.[68] In November, Whittall expressed his happiness at reports that there was "a good deal of migration into Southern Mamprusi District" from Navrongo-Zuarungu, even as Freeman lamented that "neither Commissioner or chiefs could have any hold over people who slip across the border and settle without any reference to anyone."[69] By 1928, the issue of mobility caused Whittall to abandon his hopes for migration, consider the whole area a problem, and conclude that "there is something wrong in that corner."[70]

Some chiefs, meanwhile, capitalized on officials' desperation for road work and crafted their own systems of labor exploitation. In the last months of 1920, Duncan-Johnstone began to report the surprising fact that some chiefs in Lawra-Tumu District had taken up road widening and local road construction "by themselves" or on their "own initiative."[71] The administration was pleased, even if Duncan-Johnstone knew little about how or why chiefs had suddenly found road building to serve their economic, personal, or administrative purposes. As chiefs in the district gained greater experience with labor recruitment over the course of the 1920s, DCs began to report more cases. In December of 1926, DC Eyre-Smith reported that a series of chiefs had made roads "on their own initiative." On the third of December, he wrote that he "was amazed to find the Chief of NANDOM had bridged the KAMBA on his own, getting nails made in his division" (yielding a comment of "Splendid. Very satisfactory" from Whittall).[72] On the fourteenth, he added that chief Kayani of Tumu and the chief of Nandom had both built "excellent" roads and bridges "without help or supervision," praised Kayani's bridge as "show[ing] up any other work on roads in the district," and remarked that "the Public Works Department could take a lesson from the job of work."[73]

Official diaries show the contrast between the concern over local politics that administrators showed when residents resisted labor demands and their comfort with ignorance when receiving reports that chiefs were raising road labor on their own. A good example of this contrast took place in the town of Tizza, which in the mid-1920s was engaged in what Carola Lentz characterizes as a "bitter power struggle" with the site of the recently designated head chieftaincy in Jirapa.[74] When residents refused to perform labor, Eyre-Smith did not hesitate to send constables to conscript residents into additional labor as punishment.[75] Eyre-Smith described his efforts to investigate local politics, assuming that local disputes, not the labor itself, were the root of the problem.[76] In the midst of these accounts, however, he also noted, with no apparent concern, that labor requisitions were going on without his knowledge, stating, "To my surprise I find the chief of DURI has built a motorable road with a very good surface 18ft. wide to TIZZA and TIZZA people have carried it on, this has been done on their own initiative entirely and taps a very thickly populated and good shea butter area."[77]

Officials' dependence on chiefs who could take on colonial road building was so acute that it could overshadow growing administrative concerns that chiefs were using colonial backing to accumulate power and wealth. I return to the case of Kayani of Tugu.[78] In 1920, at the time that Duncan-Johnstone reported that Kayani could make "roads without assistance," DCs supported the chief by punishing "malcontents" who refused to follow him.[79] Six years later, Kayani was among those chiefs who earned Eyre-Smith's praise for continuing to meet new demands for motorable roads.[80] Just eight months after Eyre-Smith's glowing reports of Kayani's roads, however, a broader investigation into chiefly affairs in the area raised official concern about his ability to exploit constituent labor for his own farms, and the DC attested that Kayani was "using the people in his villages as his slaves."[81] He went on to argue that colonial labor demands had provided Kayani with excuses to punish his opponents throughout the 1920s.[82] In response, Kayani was removed from his chieftaincy in October of 1927. His compound was demolished, his farms were seized, and he was sentenced to six months in prison in Tamale.[83] By April of 1930, however, the next DC of Lawra-Tumu complained that Kayani's replacement was failing, as constituents refused to work and "ran 'for bush'" when the DC summoned them. Arguing that the administration needed "a man with a heavy hand [to be] installed as chief," he advocated that the administration again turn to Kayani and, in June of 1930, Northern Province commissioner Whittall approved his reinstatement as chief of Tugu.[84]

INDIRECT RULE, "COMMUNITY INTEREST," AND PROGRESSIVE CHIEFTAINCY

In addition to widespread local refusals, Northern Territories officials faced regional and global resistance to forced labor practices. Across colonial Africa, forced labor practices were central to the extractive ambitions and practices of rule.[85] By the 1930s, however, activism by colonial subjects against forced labor, along with the passage of the 1930 Forced Labor Convention by the International Labor Organization (ILO), put pressure on colonial governments to reframe, if not reform, the extractive practices of rule.[86] Since the British government was a signatory to the ILO convention, the colonial administration in the Gold Coast scrambled to bring the colony's laws in alignment.[87] As Sarah Kunkel persuasively argues, concerns about labor and the ILO convention dominated official discussions during the imposition of indirect rule in the Northern Territories in the 1930s.[88] Codified and popularized by Frederick Lugard's 1922 publication of the *Dual Mandate in Tropical Africa*, the theory of indirect rule asked that chiefly administration of colonial demands be bureaucratized through the creation of "Native Authorities" that would have their own courts and clerks and (in theory) would finance themselves through local taxation.[89] The imposition of indirect rule sought to formalize the positions of chiefs through the Native Authority system and, at the same time, to respond to forced labor bans by creating a layer of deniability about the structures of colonial coercion.[90] Here, officials' refusals to investigate chiefly coercion came in handy. Colonial officials sought creative ways to continue forced road labor into the 1930s and to enshrine demands in the emerging policy of indirect rule. Where loopholes could not be found, officials simply failed to inquire, report, or change their practices.[91]

The ILO's definitions of coercion also had the effect of enshrining chiefs' latitude for commandeering labor under the mantle of "community."[92] The convention outlined two classes of rationale by which colonial officials could continue to demand unpaid labor. Article 2 specified one of the few exceptions to the ban to be "minor communal services performed by members of a community and in the direct interest of the community," and article 10 elaborated additional cases where forced labor "exacted as a tax . . . for the execution of public works by chiefs who exercise administrative functions" would be acceptable, at least for the short term, as long as it was, among other things, of "direct interest for the community called."[93] While administrators recognized that most roads did not fit into either exception, they affirmed that labor for more "local" infrastructure and services like dams and wells fell firmly in the category of "minor communal services." In these cases, Chief Commissioner Jones recommended that officials defer to "native customs" but then recommended that limits be set at the same level as the previous road work quotas, "restricting to twenty-four the number of days on which a person may be required to work during a year." (He went on to note that even this would be only a fiction, because "for several years to come, it will be impossible to enforce such a Regulation, as there will be no clerks to keep records."[94])

It was a loophole through which the northern administration could attempt to slide all manner of development demands in the coming years, and officials did so with free rein. Just a year later, in May of 1936, the Colonial Secretary's Office even briefly attempted to put northern roads back into this category, pointing out that there was "nothing in [the Labour Ordinance No. 33 of 1935] to prevent a chief and his people maintaining and clearing any road by mutual consent in accordance with native custom, provided that only voluntary labor is employed."[95] After administrators officially devolved labor responsibilities to chiefs under indirect rule, both the extent and mechanisms of coercion become even harder to garner from the archival record. But given the contentious history of forced labor, it is clear that chiefs could not simply depend on voluntary contributions, nor could they easily impose a regime of force on a highly mobile population who had years of experience defying colonial demands. By paying attention to how both chiefs and officials instrumentalized colonial imaginaries of "community," it is possible to trace how new models of appropriation emerged.

As in previous years, colonial officials looked for modes of administration that fit the financial and personnel constraints of hinterland statecraft. In the 1930s, when colonial officials attempted to establish Native Authorities, they spent countless hours hearing and investigating the disputes over political hierarchy and jurisdiction that were baked into the infrastructure of indirect rule across colonial Africa.[96] Scholars of northern Ghana in recent decades have shown that Northern Territories residents were active in shaping and contesting the categories and structures of indirect rule, often in ways that enshrined disputes over land and belonging.[97] They have paid less attention to the ways that officials, facing the labyrinthine negotiations over the codification of chiefly hierarchy, often threw up their hands and, wherever possible, adopted practices to avoid, downplay, or ignore the complexities of local politics. One powerful mechanism was an increased reliance on chiefs who officials considered "progressive"—each of whom could be, as Lentz puts it, "a capable and at the same time obedient administrator, who allowed himself to be incorporated into the bureaucratic hierarchy."[98]

Progressive chiefs began to take a particularly prominent role in colonial gestures toward supporting "development" through indirect rule. In 1935, aware of the "meagre" resources raised by many Native Authorities, the governor proposed to divert some revenue collected under the Land and Native Rights Ordinance and the Mineral Rights Ordinance to fund "works of local benefit" in the Northern Territories, at least in "those native administrations whose poverty, need, and eagerness to progress would make them deserving cases." The "sums allocated could not be large" (approximately £1,000 annually for the entire region) but would "encourage progressive local authorities."[99] The introduction of this development funding promised to confront officials with the question of how government grants could support progressive chiefs without creating new claims on the colonial state or (of even greater concern to officials) providing opportunities for Native Authorities to enrich themselves. In order to smooth over the tensions of local governance, administrators turned to the familiar strategy of requiring chiefs to raise labor. Officials hoped that labor would reduce costs, limit opportunities for personal accumulation, and serve as an affirmation of local support. When deciding where to demand labor and where to commit colonial funding for infrastructure, officials often paired the idea of progressive chieftaincy with an imaginary of the North as a sea of undifferentiated village communities, attempting to divorce their support of particular chiefs from messy questions of hierarchy and power. Rhetorically, officials could present any Native Authority project as proof that indirect rule was a success while, practically, officials could work with chiefs who, for their own reasons, found such projects to be beneficial to their rule. Chiefs, for their part, crafted new models of chieftaincy that emerged alongside indirect rule but would, in the end, far outlast it.

Azantilow was born shortly before British occupation of Builsa began in 1902. Like many areas of northern Ghana, political organization in what became Builsa District frustrated colonial officials who sought clear hierarchies and defined boundaries. While there are debates about the extent of British influence on Builsa chieftaincy, it is clear that there was no Builsa "paramount," or "head" chief before 1911, when the British designated the office of Sandemnaab (chief of Sandema) as the seat of the paramountcy.[100] As the brother of two of the first three paramount chiefs in Sandema, Azantilow witnessed their position crystalize around recruitment of forced labor.[101] In the 1920s, he also saw the consequences of colonial labor demands. His predecessors received medals and commendations from the colonial state for their labor recruitment at the same time that they faced constituent refusals to "follow" them and, in at least one case, constituents who defected to other chiefs in response to labor demands.[102] When Azantilow became Sandemnaab in 1932, on the eve of the imposition of indirect rule and the creation of the Builsa Native Authority, he worked out possibilities for change and continuity in chieftaincy amidst the ongoing contradictions of colonial rule.

In the early years of indirect rule, Azantilow took up the project of education by raising labor to construct a primary school without government funds. In recollections gathered for his funeral, authors stated that "he refused an offer of a loan from the British colonialists and rather offered £10 of £15 that was needed to complete the school project."[103] When colonial officials began to contemplate where to spend new funds, they were thus able to frame grants to Builsa as responding to contributions already raised by the chief. In March of 1936, when Chief Commissioner Jones recommended allocating one of the first grants to Sandema, he argued that funding would serve a political as well as economic purpose, by offering the administration "great assistance in proving the value of local government" despite a lack of local tax revenue.[104] Over the subsequent years, Azantilow interacted frequently with colonial officials who sought to identify sites where constituents would supply labor for village schools, dams, and the like.

Colonial officials, as in the past, showed little interest in ascertaining how the Sandemnaab and other chiefs raised labor for local public works. Unless demands for unpaid labor generated formal complaints or contributed to chieftaincy disputes, officials were content to interpret labor as a sign of popular support. However, because they could simply choose alternate sites if confronted with resistance, there is also very little evidence that officials explicitly authorized force. This is in contrast to other northern development initiatives, such as tsetse eradication, for which colonial officials were more than willing to authorize chiefly coercion and punishment with respect to unpaid labor.[105] Across the White Volta from Builsa, for example, the Kpasenkpe area continued to be seen as mired in jurisdictional disputes and, as a result, worthy of being ignored.[106] By raising labor without colonial involvement, chiefs like the Sandemnaab effectively demonstrated their ability to manage the popular and political implications of colonial funding.

Azantilow's "active leadership" continued to impress colonial officials. In 1939, Jones recommended additional funding to build wells and maintain the Sandema school, noting the efficiency with which Builsa chiefs collected taxes, if not the amounts raised.[107] Officials praised Azantilow's growing knowledge of English and the comparative ease of practicing indirect rule in the area.[108] The Sandemnaab replicated his predecessor's drive for military recruitment, leading Jones to argue that further grants should be made "in recognition of the splendid work of the Headchief and his council not only in the administration of their country but in the raising of recruits, of whom some 350 were forthcoming in a few days."[109] Azantilow's reputation was buoyed by his embrace of colonial "mixed farming" and his willingness to engage in antimeningitis campaigns by "call[ing] in on" or "deal[ing] with" patients and chiefs.[110]

It is difficult to access the Sandemnaab's early motivations for engaging with colonial developmentalism, but the effects of these activities on his relationships with administrators are clear.[111] Several episodes in 1940 demonstrate that Azantilow found new leverage to contest colonial plans. While narratives were written by district officials, the Sandemnaab's negotiations are evident. In February of 1940, after expressing his "amazement" with the Sandemnaab's "knowledge of the works that are being undertaken and of their cost," the DC of Navrongo reported the chief's insistent requests for a new Native Authority lorry. Monthly diaries highlight Azantilow's willingness to show local projects to visiting technical officials, but they also demonstrate his disdain for recommendations that poor districts rely on inexpensive technologies. After an April 1940 collapse in the temporary "bush-stick bridge" that had been constructed according to government requirements, Azantilow arranged for the Builsa Native Authority to begin construction of a permanent bridge. The DC averred: "It will cost a lot of money, but the Builsas are going to attempt it," because "the Sandemnab hates bush-stick bridges."[112]

The Sandemnaab's performance of progressive chieftaincy was also clearly geared to audiences beyond the colonial administration. In a region where modernity, development, and knowledge of the world were increasingly associated with southern Ghana and with young migrants, the Sandemnaab was likely interested in showing constituents that he was mobile and able to harness the newest improvements.[113] Azantilow's use of the Native Authority lorry, for which he lobbied DCs furiously, helps illuminate his efforts.[114] In preparation for a government-sponsored trip to Salaga, Azantilow insisted that the lorry drive from the town lorry park "some 100 yards" to collect him at his house, while other chiefs walked.[115] The connection between technology, status, and power was likely not lost on the audience of visiting chiefs and town residents. Similarly, the Sandemnaab was careful to plan a lorry trip that took all his subchiefs on a visit to his "enormous" bullock-plowed farm. One of the chiefs, obviously thinking of perennial efforts to raise farm labor from constituents, noted that he would "need nearly 100 hoes to do the same work."[116] Family members and local residents recall, more broadly, that the 1940s and 1950s were a time when Azantilow involved constituents in a variety of interlinked initiatives in farming, education, and health—including the institution of a cattle kraal, promulgation of a compulsory call for universal education in 1949, and calls for unpaid labor to build primary schools in surrounding towns.[117] In 1953, the Sandemnaab reinforced this reputation by accepting an invitation to England to attend the coronation of Queen Elizabeth II.[118]

By the 1940s, progressive chieftaincy, unpaid labor, and government grants had become key elements of indirect rule, so much so that officials and chiefs actively avoided the substitution of direct taxation for unpaid labor during and after the Second World War, even as access to wage labor increased.[119] Hopes for taxation reflected a growing ambivalence about the role of chiefs in colonial administration, including fears that mixed farming had become a mechanism of accumulation.[120] Soon, though, taxation emerged as yet another source of official anxiety. District files are replete with Native Authority plans to capture greater fees and taxes from constituents, with chiefs remarking that the "people were now full of money" and that there was "more money about than ever before." While district officials had applauded the efficient (if modest) collection of taxes in previous years, the prospect of increased taxation raised fears that chieftaincy would become a "money making business like [it is in] some other parts of the Colony."[121]

The continued role of chiefs in the provision of wells, schools, and dispensaries allowed Azantilow and others to avoid a resurgence of colonial concern about chiefly accumulation after World War II. In the 1920s officials were willing to support chiefs like Kayani of Tugu, despite their obvious ability to use colonial demands to their personal advantage. Chiefs like Azantilow, in contrast, presented their ability to raise labor as a bulwark against chiefly accumulation. In April of 1943, Builsa's DC Davies remarked with alarm the "determined effort on the part of the [Builsa] chiefs to raise their salaries" and related with appreciation that the Sandemnaab "did more than I to dissuade them."[122] More practically, the work that the Sandemnaab and other progressive chiefs did to recruit labor allowed officials to make decisions about where to allocate grants, favoring places where projects could happen with "a little N.A. money and a lot of local co-operation."[123] Monthly diaries of district officials in the 1940s continued to emphasize the multiple roles of the Sandemnaab as a mixed farmer, a supporter of local development, and a source for local labor. Nearly all small-scale projects were undergirded by unpaid labor, and Azantilow raised labor to build, among other things, a bridge, a teacher's compound, and a number of local dams and wells.[124] In January of 1944, ten years after the first development grants had been disbursed in the Northern Territories, Davies showed the chief commissioner of the Northern Territories some of the new projects that the colonial government had begun to fund in Builsa district—latrines, schools and teacher housing, dispensaries, rural roads and bridges, and dams and wells. To Davies and the chief commissioner, the projects could be deemed successful because the Sandemnaab had supplied the government with labor: "Nearly all the labourers, I find, whom Your Honour saw working on the new Sandema dam, are voluntary workers—there are only seven names on the time sheet, which is encouraging."[125]

↩

The early twentieth century saw the development of hinterland statecraft in colonial Ghana's Northern Territories Protectorate. Names and lists of villages were a basic technology of rule, as officials traveled through districts demanding that chiefs supply labor from "their" villages and then noting and punishing chiefs whose constituents refused to "follow" colonial demands. In the face of widespread resistance and avoidance, officials began to abandon efforts to extract labor evenly, instead relying on chiefs who were able to raise labor "on their own initiative." As the case of Kayani of Tugu illustrates, officials were more than willing to support the violence of colonial rule when enacted by such chiefs, repackaging labor appropriation as in the "interest of the community." Chiefs and residents were not simply bystanders in the construction of the state. In addition to continued efforts to avoid forced labor, some chiefs and their constituents also began to forge new connections between labor and government, particularly when the state began to disburse nascent funding for small-scale projects. As the case of the Builsa Sandemnaab Azantilow suggests, a script of progressive chieftaincy could simultaneously enlist colonial officials in projects to bolster chiefly power and capitalize on ideologies of modernity and development circulating in the region.

Across the White Volta River from Builsa, in the village of Kpasenkpe, a chief twenty years Azantilow's junior took office in 1942, just as the colonial government began to put an unprecedented amount of state funding into small-scale public projects in the region. Over the next decade, British officials who had hoped that development would relegitimize empire soon found themselves ceding power to nationalist politicians for whom development was a powerful tool for imagining and building a postcolonial order. As development became the subject of intense political struggles, a variety of actors found new uses for models of progressive chieftaincy and demands for communal or self-help labor. Thus, as the next chapter will show, after two decades of widespread daily resistance and legal bans on forced labor, and in the face of rising political mobilization against colonial exploitation, labor extraction by chiefs became a normal part of what residents of Ghana's North could expect from development.

2 ∽ Statecraft and Village Development in "Nkrumah's Time"

> Every village . . . should provide itself with water. The villagers
> should be made to understand that they would be provided with
> money and cement and that they should do the sinking of wells
> or dams themselves. The Commissioner was sure that by the next
> session, the water problem should have been solved.[1]

In 1942, when he was appointed Kpasenkpe's chief after his father's
death, Wulugunaba Sebiyam was young, ambitious, and vulnerable. By
the 1940s, colonial officials in northern Ghana relied on chiefs to manage the tensions between the extractive, developmental, and conservative
ambitions of indirect rule. Only some had figured out how to do so. The
clearest path for Sebiyam to garner influence was, it seemed, to follow
the model forged by chiefs like Azantilow in the 1930s, in which demonstrations of so-called progressive chieftaincy and an ability to raise unpaid
labor allowed for a measure of chiefly autonomy while linking chieftaincy
to new state initiatives. Like many Ghanaians in the midcentury, however,
Sebiyam forged his path in the midst of deep uncertainty, figuring out
his place in the rapidly changing politics of decolonization and independence and testing what government could mean for leaders like himself
and their constituents.[2]

Four years into Sebiyam's chieftaincy, in the last months of the Second World War, the visiting governor of the Gold Coast called a meeting
of Northern Territories chiefs. After announcing constitutional changes
that would take place in 1946, he gave a promise that after the "difficulties"
of the war, "no time will be lost in the carrying out of the plans which have
already been made" to include the Northern Territories in a colony-wide
"programme of post-war development."[3] In the years that followed, the
Gold Coast government, backed by new sources of metropolitan funding,

put millions of pounds into development projects. For districts in the Northern Territories, funding doubled, and then doubled again.

As was true across postwar Africa, the colonial government used funding for and arguments about development to both relegitimize rule and intensify the empire's extractive ambitions.[4] Meanwhile, as Frederick Cooper argues, the framework of development was malleable enough to be embraced both by late colonial powers, who hoped to quell popular dissent, and by anticolonial activists, who found it to be a powerful new framework for claim making.[5] In a pattern that would be repeated across the continent, colonial subjects' mass mobilization against key structures of economic and political control in colonial Ghana forced the British government to consider fundamental changes in—and ultimately the end of—rule itself. After begrudgingly allowing popular elections in 1951, the British faced a sweeping electoral victory by the nationalist Convention People's Party (CPP) and found themselves releasing its leader Kwame Nkrumah from prison to take his place as "leader of government business" and then, in 1952, as prime minister. By the mid-1950s, increasing certainty about the coming of independence accelerated, rather than diminished, an outpouring of debate over the shape of postcolonial modernization and development.[6] In the Northern Territories, struggles over who would plan and who would control government infrastructure—about who would do the work and who would benefit—were simultaneously the subject of debate and a forum through which residents and their leaders imagined the future. The choice often seemed stark: the political economy of northern regions would either continue to be marked by labor extraction, in which residents were seen as simply "hewers of wood and drawers of water," or it would be transformed by development.[7]

After it became the first sub-Saharan African colony to gain independence in 1957, Nkrumah's Ghana served, for many in the country and around the world, as the lodestar of African nation building and development. The CPP pursued an ambitious program for industrial development, symbolized by the massive hydroelectric Akosombo Dam and the planned city of Tema, embedded in a wider project of pan-African modernization that entailed an array of educational, infrastructural, and cultural programs aiming for personal and institutional as well as economic transformation.[8] In the northern hinterlands, sweeping changes coexisted with powerful mechanisms of continuity. The CPP embraced ideas of regional equity, but the overwhelmingly rural and food-crop-producing northern Ghanaian economy was often secondary in state modernization plans.[9] Even so, the rapid expansion of schooling and smaller-scale development resources markedly increased government's role in everyday life.[10] Residents across the North worked to shape the meanings of nationalist and pan-African mobilization, often in ways that challenged local as well as national structures of power and exclusion.[11] Meanwhile, the CPP government often reinvigorated colonial strategies of differential governance in the North and South. This was done, for example, by sidestepping its antichieftaincy stance in the North and by, at times, reaffirming long-standing notions of northern difference.[12]

Kpasenkpe was far from the centers of both colonial developmentalism and nationalist mobilization in Ghana, but, as this chapter argues, administrative and economic hinterlands like northern Ghana have much to show us about the mechanisms of change and continuity in the midcentury. Here, officials from both the late colonial and Nkrumah governments took up models of village development, unremunerated labor, and chiefly authority. Village development became a flexible mode of statecraft that could operate in the face of ongoing contradictions between demands for development and the reality of limited funding and between state rhetoric about local cohesion and ample evidence of contestation.

The overlapping chronologies of developmentalism, decolonization, and nation building in Africa have challenged historians to describe change and continuity in ways that capture what Cooper terms the "possibility and constraint" of the era.[13] Scholars have shown that marking time with categories such as "the development era" or "the age of modernization," which span the postwar and early independence years, can help illuminate the shared conceptual ground on which retreating colonial powers and nascent nationalist governments imagined and negotiated the terms of a postcolonial future.[14] A number of recent works highlight how, in the years of decolonization and nation building, citizens and state agents across the continent reshaped the meaning of independence by imagining, demanding, and navigating new configurations of development, citizenship, pan-Africanism, and self-reliance.[15] This chapter tackles the challenge of narrating the midcentury by paying attention to the ways that rural people delineated and characterized change and continuity. Kpasenkpe residents, like many Ghanaians, have a deceptively simple shorthand that does just this. "Nkrumah's time," the periodization commonly used to refer to both the 1950s and 1960s, spans formal independence in 1957 and downplays state-centered narratives of the nationalist government's rise, its increasingly repressive rule, and its ultimate downfall.[16] Used frequently in Ghana, the term "Nkrumah's time" elegantly frames the period by its internal continuities as well as by what set it apart. Kpasenkpe residents' use of the term associates decolonization with a wide set of changes in local life, minimizes the differences between late colonial and nationalist development projects, yet imbues the whole period with the vitality, ambition, and uncertainty of Nkrumah's time in power.[17] Kpasenkpe residents talked only rarely of the dramatic constitutional and institutional changes in local government and development planning. Instead, in "Nkrumah's time," local actors improvised, invented, and muddled through the massive project of redefining government.

The rest of the chapter is organized in four sections. The first section details Sebiyam's early efforts to craft his role as a progressive chief as postwar colonial development initiatives took hold in the region. The next two sections consider the politics of development in the 1950s in Kpasenkpe and the North as a whole, first through the lens of the local politics of unpaid labor and next through examining the entanglement of development and nationalist politics. The chapter concludes by considering the Nkrumah government's unsuccessful efforts to institutionalize self-help in the 1960s, showing how residents in Kpasenkpe and elsewhere observed and responded to the increasing importance of political connections in the distribution of development resources.

POSTWAR DEVELOPMENT AND THE POSSIBILITIES OF PROGRESSIVE CHIEFTAINCY

Kpasenkpe is located in the central part of the old kingdom of Mamprugu, one of the three major precolonial kingdoms in northern Ghana, where the colonial conception of hierarchical political space fit more neatly than in Azantilow's seat of Sandema. Mamprusi settlements, whether smaller villages (*tinkpaŋŋa*) or larger towns (*tiŋŋa*), are located in political space by historical and genealogical narratives that recognize overlapping layers of subchieftaincies.[18] Even though Kpasenkpe was a small settlement, it claimed an important place in the chiefly hierarchy as a seat of a divisional chieftaincy, responsible for enskinning subchiefs in the surrounding area.[19] Thus, in the interwar period, Kpasenkpe was easily identified as among the handful of settlements that the Gambaga DC visited regularly. Nonetheless, in the first decade of his chieftaincy, Kpasenkpe's Wulugunaba Sebiyam followed the model of progressive chieftaincy that Azantilow and others had forged in the 1940s, engaging in a number of activities that secured Kpasenkpe's place in a newly developmentalist colonialism.

As funding for agricultural extension activities came into South Mamprusi, Sebiyam recruited several of his brothers to train in bullock farming at an extension plot in the nearby town of Gbimsi. By the late 1940s, the agricultural extension services had approved the establishment of a demonstration farm in Kpasenkpe itself, known locally as *nigi puu* (or "cow farm").[20] During the same period, Sebiyam also participated in a colonial finance committee designed to "provide an opportunity for the younger and more progressive members of the community to associate themselves more closely with the Native Administration," and officials found his work "excellent."[21]

Over the subsequent decade, the pace and volume of demands on progressive chiefs grew along with funding for village development. District records reveal dramatic increases in the "Ordinary Grants-in-Aid" allocated to northern districts, from just over £51,000 in 1946–47 to over £220,000 in 1955–56. Additional funding for "Development Grants-in-Aid" climbed from an initial £70,000 in 1948–49 to over £132,000 in 1957–58, with similar amounts available for "Regional Development" by the mid-1950s, under the purview of Kwame Nkrumah as prime minister.[22] Ministries such as the Department of Social Welfare and Community Development supplied additional funding for development projects, particularly through the Mass Education Programme. Officials imagined the Northern Territories as significantly less politically advanced than the South, and development plans were intended to "preserve community" and provide a bulwark against mass political action—what Jeff Grischow calls "economic development without social transformation."[23] As the model of "tribal" governance invoked by indirect rule became increasingly untenable as a basis for administration, colonial administrators found, in the idea of village development, a powerful new way to reframe interwar ideas of community into a vision of modern government and development.[24] As Carola Lentz articulates, with respect to the Mass Education program, officials began to imagine "that the village, 'a genuine closely knit community' (Sautoy 1958: 13), not the clan, the tribe or the native state, was the traditional social unit of greatest significance."[25]

Colonial plans for community development, in northern Ghana as elsewhere, clearly drew on practices of forced and so-called communal labor from the interwar period.[26] By the 1950s, however, colonial governments in Africa could also place themselves in conversation with initiatives for village development and rural self-reliance that were rooted in diverse political and ideological projects across the globe, from postcolonial nation building to social scientific knowledge production to US Cold War military strategy.[27] Community development was, for example, the communitarian counterpoint of large-scale modernization plans in newly independent India.[28] Building on an idiosyncratic experiment in the villages of Etawah District and bolstered by subsequent American funding, community development became a central plank of Indian national development policy and, eventually, served as a model for US anti-Communist initiatives across the world as well as national community development plans across Asia, the Middle East, and North Africa.[29] Meanwhile, in Kenya, community development became a central tool of British social engineering during the Mau Mau emergency.[30] Colonial community development initiatives in the postwar era were thus part of the larger push to renew the terms of colonial rule in a Cold War world, an effort that Low and Lonsdale termed a "second colonial occupation" for the variety of new intrusions brought into the daily lives of colonial subjects.[31] As Joseph Hodge observes, this form of occupation ignited new and lasting forms of governance, a "triumph of the expert" that gave primacy to specialist knowledge and technical expertise.[32]

Much like in the interwar period, however, administration in northern Ghana was piecemeal, sparsely funded, and largely improvised by officials and residents alike. Regular grants-in-aid flowed into districts with even less programmatic guidance than Mass Education (which was, itself, rife with shortages of funding and personnel).[33] In October of 1948, chief commissioner of the Northern Territories, W. H. Ingrams, presented DCs with a plan for regional development.[34] Exhorting DCs to devise strategies for simultaneous investments in "economic . . . civic, political, and social services development," he encouraged them to delegate paperwork to African staff, to work on "getting people to realise their duties and leaving them to perform them," and to "regard yourself more as the man with the oilcan not, more than you can help, as part of the machinery." At the same time, Ingrams suggested that "a pioneering spirit" should inspire them to propose their own plans and take charge of implementation as they saw fit, warning, "if we are too cautious and try to co-ordinate too much we will just go on in the same old way."[35] A response to Ingrams's letter circulated by the DC of Bawku summed up an underlying administrative principle: "The most efficient committee is composed of two members of which one is permanently away ill."[36]

In theory, after 1951, community development was to be implemented through the new system of District and Local Councils that were established

to replace indirect rule. Over the course of the 1950s, however, the government continued to leave budget allocations in the hands of British DCs.
The Ministry of Local Government allocated funds among northern districts but paid very little attention to how projects were allocated within
districts.[37] DCs continued to rely on head chiefs, like Sebiyam, whom they
perceived as progressive, to implement projects and cultivate local support, and the ability of chiefs to raise "communal" or "self-help" labor soon
emerged as a key measurement of the feasibility and efficiency of potential
projects. The earliest discussions of development grants set the pattern for
subsequent years. One district official worried that labor demands would
seem "like a reversion to the forced labour days" and that residents would
be reluctant to participate.[38] As a defense against this impression, colonial
officials introduced a principle of matching "local initiatives" with government funding. "Much can be achieved with comparatively slender funds,
and the extent of such an achievement will be the measure of the people's genuine desire for advancement to improved standards of living," a
central government memo argued, "self-help will beget, and will deserve,
help from external sources." Officials envisioned that "local development
committees" would be set up in each area to "foster local enthusiasm and
initiative," arguing, "the surest way of stimulating enthusiasm is to give the
community reason to believe that the ideas and plans put forward are their
own."[39] District officials, however, had little direction as to how to set up
such a committee, and they hesitated to put new funding into local government bodies that were supposed to raise their own funds. Instead, they
simply made ad hoc choices to fund particular projects.[40]

The dynamics of hinterland statecraft in northern Ghana left ample
room for local officials and colonial subjects to set the agenda for and
attempt to shape the meaning of development. In the late 1940s and the
1950s, chiefs like Sebiyam encountered a cohort of DCs who had been
trained in postwar ideals of planning, local government, and development.[41] Neil Dobbs, the official with whom the Wulugunaba worked most
closely, fit the mold. Raised in Kenya as the son of an Irish colonial administrator, Dobbs entered the colonial service in 1941 at twenty-four years old,
after graduating (with first-class honors) from Trinity College Dublin, and
was sent to Mamprusi District for his first post.[42] In 1949, Dobbs was briefly
transferred to Gonja to set up the Gonja Development Scheme, the sole
colonial experiment in large-scale mechanized agriculture in the region.
He returned to Mamprusi District in early 1951 hoping to use what he had
learned. Monthly diaries reveal that in the early 1950s, like other Northern

Territories DCs, he found himself managing an unprecedented level of funding for local projects. Even though he supported local government reform, he was chronically disappointed with local councils and tended to rely instead on chiefs whose visions of progress aligned with his own.[43] For Dobbs, who was given wide latitude to choose where to spend new colonial resources, Sebiyam's performance of progressive chieftaincy promised to smooth the way for colonial development.

Concentrating solely on Sebiyam's relationship to colonial officials causes us to miss other audiences and other actors who influenced Sebiyam's performance of progressive chieftaincy and to see how the larger political and economic context contributed to the sense of change and possibility in postwar Kpasenkpe. Recognition from constituents and an ability to harness their knowledge and connections had long been central to chiefly power in Kpasenkpe. Scholars of the Mamprusi heartland emphasize the element of Mamprusi politics known as *naam*—an essence of political and spiritual authority that is assigned to chiefs hierarchically by the Mamprusi king, the Nayiri, but is ultimately reinforced by proper recognition from constituents and has been an important binding element in the multiethnic Mamprusi polity.[44] Authorized to allocate land to strangers but not to collect significant rents from it, Mamprusi chiefs from the seventeenth century onward have focused on regulating local access to broader networks of trade and labor and to states and other centers of outside power.[45] In the early twentieth century, colonial political and economic changes heightened demands that rural chiefs manage connections to wider networks. In Kpasenkpe, as elsewhere in northern Ghana, short- and long-term labor migration to southern Ghana had become a stable part of the trajectory from youth to adulthood.[46] In light of the growing opportunity and instability in southern labor markets during and following the Second World War, Sebiyam became a local booster, seeking to attract migrants (and their earnings) back to town. Kpasenkpe's older residents recall their stints working in the South, often on cocoa farms but also for government agencies and small- and large-scale enterprises.[47] Sakparana Sandow Batisima recalled going to Kumasi for one farming season to work on a cocoa farm and "just to see the city." "As a young man," he explained, "you had to roam."[48]

Returning migrants remember coming back from the South with new skills, technologies, and resources that were valued both by their families and by the chief. Balihira Seiya was the daughter of Sebiyam's uncle, Seiya Hammi.[49] In the postwar era, after marrying and having her first two children, Balihira Seiya traveled south with her husband to work on cocoa farms. While there, she carried firewood for an Asante woman who brewed *akpeteshie* (locally produced gin), through which she learned the trade and its potential.[50] When she returned to Kpasenkpe in the 1950s, she began her own *akpeteshie* business, investing the profits in a grinding mill and becoming one of the few women in town to establish her own farms.[51]

Sebiyam drew a sense of change and opportunity to Kpasenkpe by crafting his early chieftaincy around what Mampruli speakers call *nin-neesim*. Often translated as "enlightenment," *ninneesim* (like *anibue* in Twi and *olaju* in Yoruba) refers to an idea of broadening one's knowledge of the world.[52] When attributed to Sebiyam, *ninneesim* referred to his knowledge of and ability to connect Kpasenkpe to new and outside influences. Kpasenkpe residents remember Sebiyam's enthusiasm for recognizing the contributions of outsiders who brought new skills and knowledge to town. Bugurana Ibrahim Manmara remembered that, in the early 1940s, Sebiyam invited teachers from Bawku to stay and teach lessons in town.[53] Pastor Daniel Barijesira Azundow, the chief's brother, who became Kpasenkpe's first Assemblies of God pastor, spoke of missionaries from Walewale who came to teach the Mampruli gospel, leading to the formation of the first Christian congregation in town in 1951.[54] Alhassan Pusu, one of the early Muslim converts in town, associates *ninneesim* with Hausa migrants who came in the postwar era to fish near Kpasenkpe and "got him to know God" through Qu'ranic schooling. Soon after, the Muslim community in Kpasenkpe and the neighboring settlement of Nabari chose an Imam who Sebiyam formally recognized.[55]

Starting in the late 1940s, government projects began to fit into this larger framework. Kpasenkpe was chosen in 1947 as a site for one of the first expansions in government primary schools in the region.[56] The teacher posted to the new Kpasenkpe Primary School was Mumuni Bawumia, the young son of a Mamprusi chief who had just completed his training at the newly established Tamale Teacher Training College.[57] Sebiyam was an enthusiastic supporter of the new school, but schooling was by no means a popular demand in the late 1940s. After decades of restrictions in northern education and limited avenues for school leavers to advance beyond the lower rungs of the colonial bureaucracy, parents across the region were understandably skeptical, and in the Kpasenkpe division Sebiyam drummed up students by requiring each household in Kpasenkpe and each chiefly family in his wider jurisdiction to send one boy or girl.[58] Meanwhile, adult literacy classes through Mass Education started in 1951, attracting a variety of participants who had not gone to government schools.[59] Alhassan Sulemana remembered that, when the Kpasenkpe Primary School opened, his parents sent one of his sisters so that he could tend sheep and help with farming. By the 1950s, he sought out Mass Education so that he, too, could learn to read and write.[60]

Farming was as integral to Sebiyam's reputation as an agent of change in Kpasenkpe as it was to his interactions with colonial officials. Men who became involved in early colonial agricultural initiatives remember experimenting with rice and cotton at a riverside farming area that had been previously uncultivated. After the chief's demonstration farm, *nigi puu*, had been established in Kpasenkpe, agricultural officers sought out households who had cattle and asked them to send members to train in bullock traction, then offered them loans to purchase plows.[61] As Sebiyam worked to further entrench the connections between colonially supported farming initiatives and traditional male office in Kpasenkpe, he established a new titled elder position of *kakpanaba*, or chief farmer, and awarded it to a local lineage head who was heavily involved with colonial agricultural extension initiatives.[62] Even those who were less directly involved with particular initiatives felt their effects, including the diversification of the crops and markets with which they engaged and periodic access to mechanized and industrial inputs. Wurugurunaba Nsoanyanni Sandow remembers that after people in town started using bullock plows, farmers began to sell excess food crops for the first time, buying sheep and cattle that they could then sell "if they had a problem."[63] Adam Abdullai Seiya remembers that children learned to use bullock plows on their fathers' farms after senior family members had completed formal training.[64] Adisa Tampulima, one of the few women who cultivated her own plots in this era, recalls that while she did not engage directly with agricultural extension agents, she was always able to hire bullock and tractor services from neighbors or government agents.[65] On an informal but no less important level, residents remember Sebiyam as a zealous advocate for local farming. Bugurana Ibrahim Manmara offered the common image of the young chief, in knee-high rubber boots, riding his bicycle to his farm and scolding any young men he saw sitting down to come and pick up a hoe.[66]

LABOR AND DEVELOPMENT IN "NKRUMAH'S TIME"

Soon, Sebiyam's relationships with colonial officials began to reshape the physical landscape of the Kpasenkpe area. DCs allocated development grants for the construction of the Kpasenkpe Primary School, wells in each section of town, and extensive road clearing and repair. In the early months of 1955, Sebiyam was able to persuade DC Dobbs and Mass Education organizers to relocate the Kpasenkpe market away from the existing site—which was in an area associated with an opposing candidate for the chieftaincy—toward a site directly behind his own palace.[67] Most ambitiously, Dobbs and the Wulugunaba found a common desire to transform Kpasenkpe into a gateway to the agricultural lands on the western side of the White Volta River. After the Wulugunaba had organized his constituents to clear and repair the Kpasenkpe road "without spending much money," Dobbs arranged for a grant to support a larger project to bridge the river. Between December of 1954 and May of 1955, Dobbs visited the Wulugunaba and the Kpasenkpe bridge project several times a month.[68] For Dobbs, the bridge project was a way of demonstrating his ambition and vision. DCs had long spoken of "opening up" western Mamprugu, and Dobbs was the first to make a concrete attempt. For Sebiyam, the bridge was a demonstration of his zeal for change and of his prominence among the head chiefs of western Mamprugu (the Kpasenkpe site having eclipsed plans by the neighboring chief of Wungu to build a bridge farther downstream). Dobbs pointed out that the Wulugunaba compared the bridge to the work of the Italian engineering firm Stirling-Astaldi on the northern trunk road. At one point, the pair visited the Stirling-Astaldi contractors to "see if [they] were in need of any advice."[69]

While the chief and colonial officials emphasized the novelty of these projects, they continued to rely on the local labor force that had been reframed in the 1930s as in the "interest of the community." Colonial development grants provided cement for buildings, and officials brought machinery to blast the foundation for the bridge, but they requisitioned local stones and mud for the rest of the construction. Most strikingly, they required that Kpasenkpe residents (and, for the bridge, residents of Kunkwa) provide all of the unskilled labor for construction.[70] As demonstrated in chapter 1, after the northern administration implemented bans on forced labor in the 1930s, officials were happy to cultivate a studied ignorance of how chiefs mobilized labor. Little changed about this dynamic in the 1950s. The injection of new funding, however, changed the practical possibilities for chiefs as they sought to meet government demands.

In Kpasenkpe, Sebiyam managed to build on multiple scripts and sources of influence to mobilize labor.[71] Structurally, his calls for labor for the market, road, bridge, and well projects of the 1950s built on an existing form of chiefly labor mobilization, called *nayiri kpaariba*, that allowed the

FIGURE 2.1. Ministry of Information publicity for self-help in the North. Clockwise from top left: "Bo-Naba, the Chief of Bongo, welcoming Mr. D.F. Buafor, the regional education officer to Bongo where the inhabitants are helping themselves to improve the town through communal labour"; "The inhabitants of Bongo going to do communal labor"; "Women in Bongo carry water to the men in communal work"; "The District Commissioner for Savelugu, Mr. Majied, and the Chief of Daire [sic] and his subchiefs clearing the site." Photos by Opong Gyima and Iddi Braimah, courtesy of the Ministry of Information, Ghana, Information Services Photographic Library, Ref. no.s R/9788/1-3, R/R/2770/10.

chief to request that each farm under his jurisdiction send one worker for a one-day to one-week shift on his farms, in acknowledgement of which workers were fed and housed.[72] For development work, the Wulugunaba called on subsets of his constituents in shifts, asking them to mold blocks, carry stones, and fetch water, for which the chief's wives prepared them a daytime meal from the household's food store. In turn, the Wulugunaba used the presence of government funding for development and the attendant recognition of his authority to strengthen his demands for constituent labor on his farms.[73] Echoing the complaints levied against chiefs by constituents across the north in the interwar period, Bugurana Ibrahim Manmara recalled the simultaneous increase in labor demands by arguing that residents did not have much choice: "Whether or not you liked it, you would go."[74]

Despite this critique, there was also a sense in which Sebiyam's use of the *nayiri kpaariba* system sought to distance new demands from recent memories of forced labor. Older residents also made these distinctions in their recollections. According to Pastor Daniel Barijesira Azundow, development work was fundamentally different from the "forced work" (*mugsigu tuma*) required for the Tamale-Bolgatanga trunk road. The fundamental illegitimacy of that work, he argued, was encapsulated in a work song he had learned in his youth that highlighted how colonial planners made demands without any knowledge of or concern for the human or ritual landscape: "We are forced to be here, so the spirits too will have to step aside, for he too knows the power of the white man."[75] In what has become a common story about the intrusive demands of colonial administrators, Sakparana Sandow Batisima used vivid imagery from his childhood of being asked to carry heavy loads—even colonial administrators themselves—across the river.[76] "There were no vehicles to transport the white men to Kpasenkpe. We therefore had to carry them from village to village. The people of the various villages carried them in turns. Wulugu people carried them to Nabari, Nabari people carried them to Duu, Duu people carried them to Kpasenkpe, Kpasenkpe people carried them to Kunkwa." The contrast with Nkrumah's time was clear: "It was only during the regime of Kwame Nkrumah," he argued, "that we had lorries [so that government officials carried themselves]."[77] Similarly, Bugurana Ibrahim Manmara argued that, in contrast to the earlier labor demanded through chiefs by colonial officials, development work in the 1950s represented the change to "Nkrumah's time." In the 1950s, labor requisitions were matched by "help" (*suŋŋi*) in the form of government funding of materials and skilled planners. Furthermore, while Sebiyam could announce that labor was required and could attempt to impose fines or alternate work for those who refused, his requests were no longer backed up by the threat of violence from the colonial state. Whereas colonial officials might imprison or fine those who refused forced labor in the 1930s and 1940s, by the 1950s residents would only have to reckon with the chief himself, who would, for example, assign special additional tasks to those who had failed to arrive when called.[78]

Other elderly Kpasenkpe residents recounted their own histories of contributing labor in ways that revealed new motivations for and flexibility in labor recruitment. Wudana Daboo Saka and Kambonaba Ziblim Takora explained that they had contributed labor because of their own interest in *maaligu*, meaning improvement, a term whose equivalent was explicitly adopted by Mass Education in neighboring Dagbani-speaking areas.[79] Memumbla Boonba recalled carrying stones to build the first school and other projects, even when she was pregnant, because she, like the chief, wanted *maaligu* for the town. "By that time," she argued, people "wanted development" so much that anytime the government asked them for labor, they would "come out, very fast."[80] Pastor Azundow recalled that the Wulugunaba promoted concepts of *suŋŋi* (help) and *maaligu* to encourage development labor, urging Kpasenkpe residents to "help" those who had "come to develop the place."[81] This connection suggests the efficacy of campaigns by Mass Education and Sebiyam himself to reframe the purpose of labor, but it also suggests that Sebiyam was able to make connections between labor and development meaningful to a range of people, at least in retrospect. It is also clear that not everyone had to comply. When recalling the rash of development projects in the 1950s, a number of elderly residents explicitly rejected the idea that Sebiyam had called for their labor to build them, leaving the strong impression that development labor was more sporadic and easily avoided than in previous decades.[82] The variation in whether and why Kpasenkpe residents performed labor, however, mattered very little to colonial officials. The evidence that villagers were working for their chief and laboring for development reaffirmed officials' impression that Kpasenkpe was a village to come back to and an example of, as Dobbs wrote, "what can be done" when locals "take an interest in what is going on."[83]

VILLAGE DEVELOPMENT AS POLITICS AND GOVERNMENT

As Sebiyam mobilized labor and crafted his reputation in Kpasenkpe, other residents of the Northern Territories used development to negotiate the broader question of how decolonization would configure relationships among citizens, chiefs, and the state.[84] While colonial officials saw northern development as a source of political stability, the region's politicians envisioned development as a way to radically change the North's place in the colonial economy. Politicians agreed on the need to increase state spending to spur northern development, but bitter disputes emerged about how it would be accomplished. In 1949, a number of prominent activists from the North joined the CPP because they wanted just such a transformation.[85] Over the course of the early 1950s, apprehension grew over the effects of the CPP's demands and platform of "self-government now," and some Legislative Assembly members from the Northern Territories became concerned over the place a less-developed Northern Region would end up taking in the independent nationalist state. In response, the Northern People's Party (NPP) was launched in 1954 on an explicit platform of northern development and regional autonomy.[86] While activists from the region did not dominate national politics, party political debates were no less vibrant in the North. In parliamentary elections in 1954 and 1956, residents mobilized around Nkrumah's CPP as well as the opposition NPP, both of which shared broad rhetorical and practical commitment to northern development but offered contrasting arguments about the pace and terms of independence that would facilitate it. In the elections, voters often made decisions based not only on these party platforms but also on politicians' positions in ongoing local disputes over how and by whom development resources would be allocated.[87]

The linchpin of Kpasenkpe's connection to national politics was Mamprusi politician Mumuni Bawumia, who had started his career as a teacher in the Kpasenkpe school and maintained strong connections to Kpasenkpe and to the Wulugunaba. As personal secretary to the Nayiri and as the clerk of the Mamprusi District Council, Bawumia was elected to the Gold Coast Legislative Assembly in April of 1952 and was a founding member of the NPP. As he campaigned for the NPP, Bawumia continued as the clerk to the Mamprusi District Council and became a member of the Northern Territories Council, serving on committees on education and development.[88] Emerging as what Paul Ladouceur terms "the most important of the politician-patrons" in the North, Bawumia secured the political support of the Nayiri in the elections of 1954 and 1956. In transcripts of legislative debates excerpted in his memoirs, Bawumia can be seen advocating not only for development in the North as a whole but also for specific development projects in Mamprugu.[89] Rather than make Kpasenkpe a safe stronghold for the NPP, Bawumia's close involvement in the area simply highlighted the value of party political organization in the reconfiguration of local authority. Residents in the Kpasenkpe area joined both the CPP and NPP for a variety of reasons, and the NPP won by only slim margins in Kpasenkpe.[90]

Electoral politics is never simply about official platforms, and it was in daily negotiations over votes and projects that people came to work out the meaning and weight of party political disputes. The language of village development and the underlying questions of how state spending would be distributed in the North were woven through disputes across the region. A collection of thirty-three petitions from 1957 and 1958 that were filed at the regional commissioner's office in Tamale in the months following independence show the diversity of strategies that chiefs, local government officials, and others used to engage the new government. Drawing on existing practices used to petition colonial officials as well as new networks of party organization, writers attempted to influence chiefly and local government jurisdiction, advocate for local needs, and draw official recognition for local disputes, often in overlapping ways. Some petitions were addressed to the regional commissioner's office itself, while other petitions ended up in the commissioner's hands through the extensive and creative use of the petition's "copies to" line, in which petitioners multiplied the potential audiences for their arguments.[91] Unsurprisingly, many petitions cluster in some of the places in the North where conflicts, often entwined with party politics, were particularly virulent in the late 1950s.[92]

Several petitions came in the form of welcome addresses to newly appointed regional commissioners. Here, prominent chiefs advocated for projects directly, reminding the government of the developmentalist promises of independence and suggesting their own role in delivering on them. In Eastern Gonja, for example, the Kpembewura apologized in advance for expressing their grievances about the unfulfilled promises of postwar development, arguing for the piped water and town planning that "the Government has promised to carry out since from 1952 [sic]."[93] In Navrongo, the Navropio thanked "the Prime Minister, Dr. Kwame Nkrumah, his Cabinet, yourself, and the government as a whole . . . [for] . . . all that has been done to develop this district." He then went on to list a wide array of additional projects in water, education, agriculture, town planning, and health "for which they stand in dire need" but that would also serve the new government by making the area "impressive and modern enough befitting independent Ghana."[94] In Yendi, the Ya Na thanked "the present Government" for projects they had undertaken "since they came into power in 1951 . . . including new trunk roads and the construction of big bridges . . . feeder roads, improved water supplies, Hospitals and Dispensaries, Secondary Middle and Primary Schools, Agriculture and Veterinary services, introduction of the system of Local Government, Health services Septic tank latrines, new Markets and many others too numerous to mention." He went on to advocate for "further more excellent schemes for the development of the Country, and particularly the Dagomba State" and reminded government representatives of their commitments by way of thanking them for "re-arrang[ing] the pattern of life so that both young and old may enjoy greater welfare in our new Ghana."[95]

Other petitioners used development to argue for new relationships among chiefs, government, and constituents. W. H. Wahab, the CPP propaganda secretary in Yendi, outlined how parties had mobilized hopes and critiques of taxation. As a party organizer, Wahab said, he felt it was his duty to advocate for local taxation schemes by telling residents that "the money was going to be collected and used for their benefit," even as opposition activists were "telling people that the Government is aiming at making the country poor." He noted, however, that it was fortunate that the government had alleviated the need for dispute by responding to the £8,000 raised in Yendi with £19,000 worth of development grants for market and latrine projects.[96] In Eastern Gonja, national negotiations about northern development became mobilizing tools for local electoral disputes. The government agent at Salaga forwarded a fictitious document he said was being circulated by opposition activists that purported to detail a secret CPP meeting in Accra where party officials discussed the need to "reconsider" the Northern Territories Development Plan because people in the region "have a very strong physic and for that matter are best used in our unskilled labour camps; to bring them to our level means to reduce our unskilled labour force."[97] In the Lawra Confederacy, petitioners used arguments about development in myriad ways, reflecting the salience and malleability of the concept: to express chiefs' support for the CPP ("We . . . are after developments in this area and the country as a whole; so we support the party and the government"); to advocate for local recognition by organs of the state ("Nandom is the only state within the District where the policies of [the United Ghana Farmers Council] could easily be carried out; members of the C.P.P. are citizens and who are really farmers"); and to criticize Catholic activists for provoking "lawlessness" by opposing chiefs and disrupting taxation ("There is no negligence however to recognize the value of Catholicism and the development it has been bringing to Nandom but diligently request Catholics of Nandom to refrain from the present caustic ways").[98]

In the Kpasenkpe area, too, local politics became intimately connected to developmentalist decolonization. In the local government elections of 1958, the Wulugunaba's appointee in Kunkwa, Anabila, ran for a Local Council seat on a CPP platform, challenging a pro-NPP candidate supported by Bawumia.[99] In Kunkwa and Duu, CPP and NPP supporters made rival claims to chieftaincy, and over the next several years petitions continued to stream in, not only about chieftaincy but also about the drawing of local government boundaries.[100] Disputants in Kunkwa and Duu turned to the Nkrumah government to renegotiate their place in the new order. In a petition to Kwame Nkrumah, the CPP-supporting claimant to the Duu chieftaincy argued that Bawumia and others were preventing his people from enjoying the "fruits of Freedom and Independence" and asked that the president intervene.[101]

In the end, village development worked better as a tool for consolidating party networks than as a basis for new claims on the government. When the NPP leadership recalibrated political strategy after massive losses in 1958 local government elections, they recognized that CPP party networks were crucial to meeting their own needs and those of their supporters.[102] After "crossing the carpet" to join the CPP, Bawumia, for example, was rewarded with political appointments as ministerial secretary of Works and Housing in November 1960 and as regional commissioner for the Northern Region in 1962, where he presided over development budgets for village projects throughout the region.[103] When Kunkwa's Anabila found his ambitions for Kunkwa stymied by the ascension of the old NPP leadership, he wrote to Nkrumah advocating for a separate subdistrict in order to "preserve peace and order and to prevent oppression and tension."[104] Like a previous attempt he had made to move Kunkwa to the Builsa District, Anabila's claims were rejected by the Gambaga DC, who invoked the history of village development. The Kunkwa area was in its rightful place, argued the DC, because it had benefited "in the administration of local services" since the late colonial period. Moreover, as long as these services were provided, he held that places like Kunkwa should not have direct networks to the president, because Kunkwa was "a village among the countless villages which make up the Mamprusi state" and that "it is not the policy of the Government to recognize villages as states."[105]

In Kpasenkpe as elsewhere, however, constituents had options for political action that went beyond formalized appeals. From the evidence of petitions and district correspondence, it would be easy to conclude that challenges to the Wulugunaba's jurisdiction in surrounding towns had come only from party activists. Oral historical research on labor organization, however, revealed that these disputes also had profound impact on the Wulugunaba's ability to mobilize *nayiri kpaariba* labor for his farms. A wide range of interviews with Kpasenkpe residents and Sebiyam family members date a dramatic reduction in the scope of *nayiri kpaariba* to the period of nationalist political dispute. After the mid-1960s, the Wulugunaba ceased to rely on constituents outside of Kpasenkpe for farm labor. Though Pastor Azundow argued that those villagers who had "respect for tradition" continued to contribute *nayiri kpaariba*, he admitted that their numbers suffered a drastic decline from which they never recovered.[106] By the 1960s, refusals to perform farm labor for the chief became a well-established form of protest by CPP supporters in the surrounding area.

"SELF-HELP" AND THE BUREAUCRACY OF NKRUMAHISM IN THE NORTH

When Kwame Nkrumah and his senior ministers stood on the podium at midnight on March 6, 1957, during the independence ceremonies that marked Ghana as Africa's first nation to emerge from colonial rule, they were strikingly clad in woven smocks from the North. Nkrumah no doubt meant the choice to signal the symbolic incorporation of the Northern Territories into the new nation of Ghana and the wider project of pan-African liberation and modernization, but audiences from the North were reminded of the region's uncertain future in an independent Ghana, wherein resources and opportunities for schooling were concentrated in the South.[107]

To Nkrumah, decolonization was not simply the transferal of bureaucratic control, it was the creation of new men and women, involved and invested in making Ghana the center of a modern pan-African state.[108] New mechanisms for popular participation in state development, including the Young Pioneers, the Builder's/Workers Brigade, and the State Farms Corporation, aimed to create what Ahlman calls a "new type of citizen" in which a "pan-African and socialist citizenry [was] constructed around an ethics of discipline, order, and civic activism."[109]

By the 1960s, ideas of self-help and community development became central to the development philosophies and programs of newly independent states across the African continent. In each of the often-contrasted regimes of Tanzania under Julius Nyerere and Kenya under Jomo Kenyatta, national programs of self-help were grounded in transnational discourses of self-reliance as well as utopian models of precolonial community solidarity. In both places, as recent books by Priya Lal and Kara Moskowitz demonstrate, citizens navigated the spaces among the rhetorical, practical, and political possibilities of self-help.[110] In Lesotho, self-help became a way for the ruling party, the opposition, and a wide variety of youth and community groups to debate and articulate contrasting visions of independence.[111] Meanwhile, African governments could draw funding and support for rural and village projects from sources as diverse as the United States government, the People's Republic of China, and the World Bank.[112] Thus, when Kwame Nkrumah incorporated self-help into a larger vision of pan-African citizenship, he participated in a widespread and multifaceted global reworking of the possibilities of rural development.

Despite the centrality of ideas of self-help to Nkrumah's philosophy of development, however, rural residents of Ghana's northern hinterland occupied an ambiguous place in the CPP's plans. Unlike theories of pan-African modernization focused on village life (most notably, Julius Nyerere's project of *ujamaa* in Tanzania), Nkrumah's vision of development was decidedly industrial and export oriented. Thus, despite the CPP's professed commitment to rural self-help, plans for northern villages were a mere remainder of nationalist projects focused elsewhere. The Young Pioneers, Builder's Brigade, and other horizontally organized organs of the Nkrumahist state did little to address what the CPP, like the colonial government before it, imagined to be the elusive political power of village community. As Kate Skinner points out, Nkrumah lamented that even with new systems of local government, "the internal life of particular villages, therefore, remains substantially unadministered."[113] In practice, the CPP reproduced the late colonial state's ambivalence about a wholesale restructuring of rural life in northern Ghana, combining rhetorical attacks on chieftaincy with the pragmatic recognition that it lacked the commitment, power, and popular support to fundamentally reshape rural government.[114] Most practically, ongoing local activism in the region, such as that which Benjamin Talton highlights in Konkomba areas, had clearly reinforced to the Nkrumah administration that both village development and unpaid labor would not easily be separated from thorny political questions.[115]

By the early 1960s, struggles to mobilize village community proceeded against the backdrop of the government's efforts to prune back the welfare promises of the state. As Skinner argues, "the CPP's programme indicated that while in the 1950s Ghanaians had become accustomed to reaping the benefits of the party's struggle for independence in the form of ever-expanding governmental provision, such expectations must now be curbed: political education, discipline and sacrifice were the order of the day." This turn blended ideological and practical concerns. Ghana's 1961 budget and 1962 Programme for Work and Happiness aimed to focus increasingly limited state resources on what they considered "productive" projects for infrastructure and industry. In the face of falling cocoa prices that threatened the national budget, Nkrumah's government hoped that rural development could replace funding with a national spirit of "self-help."[116] Reductions in development grants reversed the rise in local development funding that had characterized the previous decade for northern Ghana.[117] The model of "self-help" that had developed in the postwar period was particularly poorly suited to reductions in expenditure. In the 1950s, modest local efforts at taxation and communal labor in places like Kpasenkpe had attracted the attention from DCs who had grants they needed to distribute. The CPP's vision, instead, sought to bring state control over a series of efforts that it was no longer able to fund.[118]

A June 1962 meeting between the regional commissioner's office and district officials, held in the weeks following Nkrumah's May 5 announcement of the "Programme of Work and Happiness," demonstrates the ways that messages of fiscal stringency and self-help were intertwined.[119] In his opening address to DCs, Regional Commissioner Bawumia presented the sacrifices that would be made for national development, announcing that a "great deal of money was required by the Government to complete such projects as the Volta River Project and to establish a lot of essential industries which would ensure the economic stability of the Country." Echoing the formulations that postcolonial officials like Ingram had made fourteen years previously, he "advised the District Commissioners to possess creative abilities in order that they might bring developments to their areas without much expense." The CPP's plan for rural development called for formation of town and village development committees, unofficial bodies that would, as Bawumia noted, nonetheless "be responsible for the development of every village in their districts" and would bring the "village chief" together with party representatives and other "influential people."[120] Despite subsequent exhortations that "it was the wish of Osagyefo [Nkrumah] that the villagers themselves should develop their own villages" and attempts to make chiefs even more central to the effort, it is apparent that development committees reported little success and were never formed in nearly half of the districts.[121]

Thus, despite the Nkrumah government's rhetorical emphasis on self-help, the state was surprisingly bad at rewarding it. Instead of trading self-help for government funds, by the 1960s the surest way for a rural settlement to gain governmental attention was to become a district capital. In 1957, the Nkrumah government adopted the recommendations of the Greenwood Commission for Local Authorities, which drastically reduced the number of local government bodies.[122] Almost immediately, however, Ghanaians began to lobby for new districts, applying strategies that they had previously used in struggles over chieftaincy and Native Authority jurisdiction. It was clear why. When a settlement was designated as a district capital, the government funded district offices and bungalows, and it quickly became a higher priority for road improvements, schools, and other small-scale projects.[123] Staff and civil service positions played a dual role, offering employment to educated and well-networked locals and also providing services, like paid road work and agricultural extension, that promised to fulfill the visions of development for which northern politicians had so vociferously advocated.

In 1961, when the Nkrumah government authorized a more than doubling of the number of local government capitals, Kpasenkpe became one of them.[124] Sebiyam's history of attracting projects and his connections to Mumuni Bawumia, now regional commissioner, allowed it to be designated as the capital of one of three new districts, carved out of the South Mamprusi District, that lasted from 1962 until they were dissolved after the 1966 coup.[125] The DC posted to Kpasenkpe was Damma Wuni, a longtime NPP supporter who had clerked under Bawumia for the South Mamprusi Local Council.[126] A medical field unit and agricultural, veterinary, and social welfare officers were posted to the town.[127] Tindana Issa Tongo recalls that his brothers pooled their money to purchase a bullock plow for their food plot from agricultural extension officers at the same time that he signed up to cultivate an acre of cotton in a large farm that was plowed by government tractors.[128] Development grants, now extremely reduced from the 1950s, were consistently distributed to newly appointed DCs with little follow-up about how they were spent, apart from weak admonitions that all local government members should be "vigilant," and should "check inefficiency and waste or extravagance."[129] Damma proved able at lobbying for Kpasenkpe in this situation.[130] In May of 1963, Damma successfully argued for the allocation of a £1,000 road grant for the spur road to Kpasenkpe out of a drastically reduced 1963 allocation of £19,400 in regional development funds for the entire region.[131] Assorted development reports from the 1962–66 period demonstrate continuous funding for this road, frequently to the exclusion of other proposed projects.[132] While no additional primary schools were opened in the district during the 1962–66 period, a new middle school was constructed in Kpasenkpe town, drawing students from throughout the region.[133]

Kpasenkpe residents, for their part, were keenly attuned to the changing performances that would support a new political economy of development that was centered on party networks and demonstrations of national unity rather than on shows of local solidarity. People who remembered the preceding decade as a time of village development projects instead recalled the Kpasenkpe district as a time of central government recognition and engagement. Duundana Yakubu Kolugu and Sakparana Sandowbila recalled fierce competition to secure positions on a road crew that was paid by the government.[134] Jacob Pitigi Tampulima got a job maintaining the DC's bungalow that paid 8 1/2 shillings a month.[135] Older men remembered joining groups of *toosiwaa* dancers that Damma organized to travel, present at CPP agricultural shows, and welcome visits of the regional commissioner.[136]

By the 1960s, the nationalist government had forged powerful new networks that allocated resources along lines of party influence. Rather than downplaying the postwar model of unpaid labor for village development, however, the Nkrumah state persisted in reinforcing it. State officials hoped and pretended that if DCs could not simply harness the local spirit of self-help, they could instead manufacture it. Announcing the "Provide Yourself With Water" campaign in October of 1962, for example, Regional Commissioner Bawumia announced that "every village . . . should provide itself with water. The villagers should be made to understand that they would be provided with money and cement and that they should do the sinking of wells or dams themselves." Self-help would allow for DCs to "ensure that a majority of the people benefitted from the Government," and it was therefore their job to "put the spirit of communal labor into the people." He added, absurdly, that he "was sure that by the next session, the water problem should have been solved."[137]

↜

From the end of the Second World War to Nkrumah's ouster in 1966, residents of Ghana's North improvised the local politics of development, decolonization, and nationalist statecraft in the northern hinterland. With the first development grants that trickled into the North in the 1930s (chapter 1), officials began to strategically reward chiefs who had figured out how to manage the local politics of ongoing colonial demands for unpaid labor. Over the course of the 1940s, 1950s, and 1960s, however, as development came to dominate both late colonial and nationalist mobilization in the region, new funding for small-scale projects opened new opportunities for local negotiation. Development as a discourse and projects as practice became the subject of debate and strategy, not just for politicians but for Ghanaians seeking to test the possibilities of the era.

A new global postwar imaginary of village development appealed to a broad range of actors by seeming to reconcile modernization with community and state funding with unpaid self-help labor. By pairing the ambitious, politically infectious framework of development with a globally relevant imaginary of villages, officials could leave rural settlements to compete for development funds by asking them to demonstrate self-help. For colonial administrators, a simplified framework of undifferentiated villages and the continued reliance on communal labor and chiefs they considered "progressive" allowed them to make decisions about where to allocate funds while sidestepping the complex political dynamics of decolonization and local government reform. For the Nkrumah government, the idea of village development by self-help allowed for a convenient slippage between the rhetoric of socialist transformation and the realities of limited budgets for rural development and continued reliance on chiefs in the North. By the 1960s, as the independent state faced even larger cuts to local funding for rural development, the designation of district capitals allowed for village projects to be apportioned along new networks of party influence. Residents of the region continued to be, if not exactly hewers of wood and drawers of water, at least clearers of roads and molders of blocks.

If colonial and nationalist development imaginaries set the contours of midcentury government, they nonetheless continued to exercise little control over the meanings that people in the North would make of a new era of government intervention. Petitioners across the region used demands for local projects to reaffirm, contest, or alter the relationships among politicians, bureaucrats, chiefs, and their constituents. Chiefs like Kpasenkpe's Wulugunaba Sebiyam could tie colonial and nationalist development projects into widely circulating ideas about knowledge and improvement, opening space to reinvent both the scope of labor demands and the ways constituents viewed them. At the same time, constituents used contributions and refusals of labor to support and contest the chief's entanglement with the developmentalist state. As this chapter shows, the new politics of labor and leadership was not automatic or permanent. In the 1950s, constituents imbued unpaid labor with multiple meanings and began to use it as an instrument of protest. By the early 1960s, while rhetoric of self-help abounded, residents largely abandoned unpaid labor in favor of maintaining connections to the Nkrumahist state through more focused political networks and performances of support. Nevertheless, the Nkrumah state's persistence in affirming the imaginary of undifferentiated rural villages limited residents' ability to use these networks to transform the essential mechanisms of government in the region. Despite the diversity of meanings with which people imbued their actions, the end results were powerful continuities in the means that citizens used to engage the state, affirming the centrality of unpaid labor and progressive chieftaincy. As the next two chapters show, these performances both relied on wider familial, professional, and personal networks and produced an enduring repertoire of practices that citizens used to navigate the tumultuous decades to come.

3 ↬ Labor and Statecraft in a Chiefly Family

WHEN WULUGUNABA Sebiyam and the newly posted teacher Mumuni Bawumia mobilized local labor to build the Kpasenkpe primary school in 1947, more than a dozen hesitant girls and boys had already been pledged by their families to attend.[1] While their neighbors stacked stones and carried water, the "pioneer" class of children met in Sebiyam's compound or in the DCs' rest house and investigated this novelty: a village school. Among them were Sebiyam's young sister, Pawura Paulina Barijesira, and his first son, John Sebiyam Nabila. Like other schoolchildren, Nabila and Pawura likely saw the purpose of their training largely in terms of fulfilling obligations to their families. Bawumia could relate, as the son of a chief who had, just thirteen years earlier, also been sent to satisfy his family's obligation to the colonial state.[2] For Bawumia and other aspiring politicians from the North, however, the purpose of schooling was beginning to be much broader. Over the course of the 1950s, as Kwame Nkrumah ascended to power and Kpasenkpe's first graduates began middle school, northern Ghana's political elite successfully linked the demand for northern education to a vision of regional development. They held that, if students like those in Kpasenkpe could not take over the civil service from a retreating colonial state, there was little hope that the new nationalist state would ever serve the North.[3] Thus, as Nabila and Pawura passed through the Kpasenkpe school and took up civil service jobs, they were, as much as any village project, part of the emergence of a developmentalist state in the 1950s and 1960s.

Sebiyam's educated children did not simply leave to join a distant state apparatus. Instead, like earlier generations who passed through the limited colonial school system in the Northern Territories, they became the face of government across the region. At certain points, schooling and careers would take them to regional and national capitals, allowing them access to centers of government power. At other points, they would travel to districts and villages across the region, implementing programs aimed at educating, healing, and developing the rural North. Frequently, the work would also bring them back to Kpasenkpe and its surroundings, as grown and established agents of state-led development. In careers that emphasized their expertise as much as their lineage, the chief's educated siblings and children took up and extended the Wulugunaba's engagement with government agents and projects. They forged new models of how and by whom development could be done and diversified the ways Kpasenkpe was connected to networks of state power, both regionally and beyond. Meanwhile, in the chief's compound, as elsewhere, relatives of school-goers and newly minted civil servants navigated the expansion of the developmentalist state as a matter of labor, investment, and opportunity that took place in their own families. Over the first quarter century of his chieftaincy, Sebiyam married over a dozen women and girls.[4] During the same period, a series of men came to the compound to take up roles as Sebiyam's brothers, tasked with working on the chief's expanding network of family farms. As Sebiyam worked to craft his reputation as a progressive by expanding his farms and by sending his children to school, lineage, gender, and education differentiated how members of Kpasenkpe's chiefly family engaged with the emerging developmentalist state.[5]

The developmentalism that emerged in mid-twentieth-century Africa was built on well-established colonial models of government that treated families as an object of state intervention but rarely paid attention to how Africans negotiated government as members of actual families. As Emily Lynn Osborn argues with respect to French colonial rule, "The effort by French colonial officials to disaggregate the household from the state—both their own households and those of their African colonial subjects—was, in fact, a distinctive feature of colonialism."[6] At the same time, despite colonial officials' refusal to recognize them, family networks were central to how both African subjects and European officials navigated state making across colonial Africa.[7] In northern Ghana, the dynamics of hinterland statecraft meant that chiefly families became a key site of engagement with colonial development. This chapter initiates the examination of one such family network, returning to "Nkrumah's time" to follow Kpasenkpe's chiefly family as its role as an engine of developmentalist statecraft began to take shape. It traces the careers of the first cohort of Sebiyam's siblings and children who went to school and became both beneficiaries and agents of state-led development, as well as the wives and brothers who formed the backbone of his compound.

In doing so, the book shifts scope and register rather significantly, illuminating how developmentalism was forged by labor and relationships in compounds and farms, in schools, and for frontline civil service workers. By extending an analysis of family networks beyond a historiography centered on the colonial period, this chapter shows that the entanglements of family and state both continued and transformed during the era of decolonization and development. Just as Kpasenkpe emerged as a model site for generically conceived village development projects, the chief's educated siblings and children became models of rural success and village leadership in the eyes of a state that ignored or downplayed their family connections. As a result, chieftaincy as an institution was reinforced by its growing links with other networks of state-led development, particularly the civil service. At the same time, like other aspects of village development in Kpasenkpe, the expansion of schooling and government employment relied on the labor and commitment of people who were not its public face. While children went to school and took up state employment, Sebiyam's wives and brothers crafted a household that could accommodate the children's mobility and maintain stability in the years when the new Ghanaian state became, in many ways, a family matter.

CHIEFLY FAMILIES AND THE COLONIAL STATE IN NORTHERN GHANA

Men in chiefly lineages were central to the vision and practice of colonial rule in the North long before Sebiyam became chief. As in most aspects of colonial policy in the region, administrative attitudes toward chiefly families reflected a dual desire to save money and to keep both chiefs and school-leavers from gaining the political and economic power of their counterparts in the South. In educational policy, colonial officials turned to chiefly families to supply students with the aim of creating a class of young men who could link chiefs to the "world on paper," but who, they hoped, would present little challenge to the colonial project itself.[8]

The career trajectories of Sebiyam and his next eldest brothers reflect the elaboration of this policy. Sebiyam's father, the Wulugunaba Barijesira, became the chief of Kpasenkpe in the interwar period.[9] In the 1930s, Barijesira's two eldest sons, Sebiyam and his older brother, were in charge of household matters, while their younger brothers, E. B. Mansu and B. B. Wahaga, were recruited to attend the government primary school over forty miles away at Gambaga.[10] After schooling, while their older brothers took up roles as chiefs, Mansu and Wahaga began careers as African staff of the Northern Territories Protectorate, Mansu as a revenue collector and Wahaga as a teacher. The state's attention to chiefly lineages was also strengthened by officials' reliance on schools and chiefs' farms in efforts to spur agricultural change. For example, the young agricultural officer who spearheaded demonstration farming in the region, Charles Lynn, wrote in his letters home about his hopes that both the Native Administration schools and the sons of chiefs would serve as entry points for state-sponsored farming initiatives to take root in the region.[11] In the early years of his chieftaincy, Sebiyam responded to such calls by sending two brothers to train in bullock farming.

Chiefly families could also, however, become the focus of colonial anxieties. Mamprusi chiefs, like local leaders across the region, accumulated authority and demonstrated wealth by acquiring dependents. In Mamprusi terminology, they took on the role of "landlord" (*yiddaana*) both in their own households and in their jurisdictions, a position that implied both responsibilities as a host and access to the labor and other resources brought by those they termed guests.[12] As Allman and Parker superbly illustrate in their study of the ritual networks of the Talensi god Tongnaab, leaders could accumulate political, economic, and spiritual power in ways that colonial officials neither controlled nor understood.[13] Watching for signs that chiefs were pursuing "individualism," officials paid attention to the size of chiefs' farms, their compounds, and especially to the number of wives they married.[14] In this context, development projects were often conceived as an antidote to chiefly accumulation and an engine for collective progress.[15] When the progressive chiefs who championed local projects began then to show their success by growing their farms and compounds, colonial officials may have raised an occasional eyebrow, but they largely decided to read this accumulation as an advertisement for development rather than an impediment to it.[16]

In the early years of Sebiyam's chieftaincy, his reputation as a progressive allowed him to thread this needle, highlighting his family's engagement with early colonial efforts in farming and education and packaging it as evidence that development was taking place, rather than as a sign of personal gain. Sebiyam began to engage with state agricultural programs, he became a successful farmer, and he built a reputation as a progressive that reinforced his engagement with the state for decades to come.[17] Other family members also began to engage with the state investment in education that began to trickle into Kpasenkpe in the 1940s. Sebiyam's younger brother, Daniel Barijesira Azundow, began to work with Christian missionaries who introduced him to the colonial Mass Education scheme. Azundow learned to read and write in English and Mampruli, becoming the first pastor of the Assemblies of God Church in Kpasenkpe and strengthening the popular associations among chieftaincy, development, and *ninneesim*, or "enlightenment."[18] Then, beginning with Nabila and Pawura, Sebiyam sent all of his children to school. In the 1950s and 1960s, as Nkrumah's time took shape, at least twenty Sebiyam children attended school in Kpasenkpe. Over the period, Sebiyam's educated siblings and children burnished his reputation as a progressive chief and strengthened his engagement with the nationalist state. Sebiyam's embrace of his children's mobility through schooling and civil service work, however, can easily obscure the zealousness with which the chief pursued a more common model of success. As women and girls came to the compound as wives and male family members came to the compound as brothers, they built a household that became central to the family's engagement with a changing state.[19]

MAINTAINING A PROGRESSIVE FAMILY IN NKRUMAH'S TIME

Sebiyam's growing reputation as a progressive farmer, as well as the schooling of his children and siblings, depended on the labor of a number of family members whose direct engagement with state development initiatives was quite minimal. Schoolchildren needed to be fed and clothed on a daily basis, yet their ability to contribute to and participate in household and farming tasks was diminished. Moreover, the implications for the future were hazy, as family members likely sensed that Sebiyam's sons were not preparing to enter work on his farm, nor were they expected to bring wives home to the compound. For the dozens of men and women who came to the chief's compound in these years, the first decades of Sebiyam's chieftaincy are known not only for the chief's embrace of state initiatives in farming and education but also by the labor that supported these efforts.

Like other residents, surviving members of the first cohort of wives and brothers characterize Kpasenkpe's history during Nkrumah's time as a period of rapid change that brought along new opportunities and challenges. However, when they reflected on the same period with respect to life in Sebiyam's compound, they spoke of a time when family members upheld "old" norms of familial responsibility and reciprocity even as the household swelled with new members.[20] In particular, descriptions of family labor patterns relied on two normative models of familial responsibility and reciprocity: in "those days," wives and brothers recalled, "brothers farmed together" and "we all ate from one pot." Family members often used normative descriptions in response to many of my specific questions about what made new agricultural practices and children's schooling possible. How did one family farm grow so big? ("Brothers farmed together"); How did they feed both farm workers and all the schoolchildren? ("We ate from one pot").

As scholars have amply demonstrated, historians do well to understand that people often use the seemingly timeless language of normative kinship and farming arrangements to tell stories about change and personal initiative.[21] When brothers and wives recounted the longer sweep of their careers as farmers and traders, parents, and members of diverse family networks beyond the chief's palace, they often emphasized individual entrepreneurship, luck, and change. In contrast, description of their collective responsibilities in Nkrumah's time emphasized regularity and equity, downplaying the possibility of conflict. Normative ideals allowed newcomers to the compound to create a set of relationships through which they could manage new responsibilities and strengthen principles of continuity and household reproduction while accommodating the family's investment in children's schooling. The timelessness of these descriptions, in other words, often functioned to mark them very specifically in time, part of the story of how family members encountered the forces of farming and schooling.

The reality of differentiation by schooling was the backdrop against which wives' and brothers' stories were told. Among men in the lineage, schooling created sharp differences, as brothers who worked on Sebiyam's farms rarely experienced the career opportunities of those who went to school and began to become enmeshed in village development work. Among women in the compound, lineage became a clear differentiator, as Sebiyam's daughters and sisters went to school and his wives did not. By declining to dwell on these or other tensions in the household, Sebiyam's wives and brothers clearly avoided mentioning potentially damaging or personal stories of familial discord. Instead, they chose to emphasize unity and common enterprise, marking out how their labor not only made the household prosperous but how the consistency of their efforts forged unity in a time when tensions could easily have boiled over. Moreover, they made it possible for family members who would otherwise disappear from the story of village development to center their own role in creatively knitting together continuity and stability in a period of change.

A handful of Sebiyam's brothers engaged directly with agricultural extension by training in bullock farming, but a much wider circle of family members supported Sebiyam's efforts to expand and use new agricultural techniques on the family farm.[22] In the 1940s, Sebiyam opened a new and expansive farm, called Barangaŋi, located several miles away from Kpasenkpe in the relatively more fertile lands around the town of Kinkandina.[23] Apart from a few very small-scale rice plots nearer to Kpasenkpe, all the family's growing food needs were met by the new farm at Barangaŋi. Family members emphasized the unusual size of the farm by the standards of the time, for example by explaining it was so big that "if you were on one end of the farm weeping, no one would know you were there."[24] Bullock farming and access to inputs from the Ministry of Agriculture facilitated the expansive farming at Barangaŋi and the riverside, but it by no means resulted in a reduction of labor demands.[25] As Barangaŋi expanded over the course of the 1940s and 1950s and Sebiyam opened new farms to take advantage of state agricultural programs, his demands for regular farm labor also increased.[26] He also welcomed a series of men to the compound, each of whom took up responsibility for family farming.

As it was for many other Mamprusi families in the mid-twentieth century, farming in the Wulugunaba's family was conceived of as a joint project among male lineage members, led by a father or senior brother who was designated as the household head or "landlord" (*yiddaana* or *yiridaana*). "At that time," older people in Kpasenkpe invariably recall, brothers often took over their fathers' plots and farmed together.[27] In their descriptions of farm work, Sebiyam's family members invoke what Barbara Cooper terms a "normative farming arrangement."[28] In this idealized account, after a father's death the senior brother would serve as "head" of the farm, but both labor and produce would be shared among the brothers in the family. This period of cooperation would be followed by processes of fission, in which senior brothers married and established their own farms.[29] A look at the composition of the workforce on Barangaŋi from 1942 to 1966 reveals the extent to which the concept of "brothers work together" hides a more complex set of choices and relationships on Sebiyam's farms. By the 1950s, half of Sebiyam's direct brothers (Barijesira's sons) were pursuing careers away from the family farm. Instead, it is clear to see that while some of Barijesira's sons worked with Sebiyam, it might be more accurate to say that work on the farm determined the extent to which a male relative came to be considered a brother.

In some cases, the term "brother" applies, as it often does in Kpasenkpe, when describing men of the same generation who belong to the same patrilineage.[30] A small number of farm workers were in this model of classificatory brother. But it is also clear that some relatives became brothers through the process of working on the farm. In addition, many other relatives came to work on the farm whose ties were familial but who could also easily be thought of as dependents or migrants. One brother recalled coming to Kpasenkpe with his mother as a young child, being taken in by Sebiyam as one of his "children," and working full time on the farm until he took on a job in the Kpasenkpe District in 1962. Another handful of brothers was described by others as having a health status that made them unable to establish their own farms. Many of these stories emphasize newcomers' own decisions, but the chief was also clearly interested in directing this expansion of dependents. For example, after several years working on Sebiyam's farms in the 1940s and early 1950s, one brother traveled south and secured a position as a watchman at the Aburi Gardens north of Accra. While he remembers the pride of having this position, recalling that Sebiyam traveled south "especially to see him!" he also pointed out that it was upon this visit that Sebiyam informed him that he had to end his employment and return to the family farms in Kpasenkpe, "to help."

The farming responsibilities of Sebiyam's wives were also shaped by normative ideas that constructed women as nonfarmers while requiring them to play important roles at the stages of sowing, harvesting, and post-cultivation processing. As Agnes Atia Apusigah highlights, this designation both limited women's farming burden and constrained their ability to make claims on land, produce, and a role in decision making.[31] In interviews, wives insisted that their labor on Sebiyam's farm conformed to this ideal, meaning that concentrated labor demands were limited to planting and harvest.[32] As the size and number of crops under cultivation on Sebiyam's farms increased over time, however, labor demands on the wives as a group certainly expanded. The distance of Barangaŋi figured prominently in memories—when sowing or harvesting at Barangaŋi, wives would have to leave early in the morning and come back late at night.

Farming grew apace with the expanding palace compound, and when brothers and wives came to Sebiyam's palace they made room for themselves, both metaphorically and literally. As Susan Drucker-Brown suggests, midcentury Mamprusi compounds like Sebiyam's were organized to emphasize seniority and gender divisions.[33] Like other household heads at the time, Sebiyam occupied a large structure, or "room," at the front of the compound, facing the room of his senior wife (*paanni*) Adisa, while unmarried brothers slept in a young men's section of the compound. When children were born and after they were weaned, regardless of who their mother was, they would sleep in Adisa's room. As they grew, boys would then move to a young men's section of the compound, while daughters would stay in the main yard. Until circumstances allowed her to build her own room, a new wife would join the children in Adisa's room. Over time, junior wives built rooms, arranging themselves in a semicircle further back in the compound. As they married, brothers and brothers' wives built rooms in a similar pattern in a far wing of the compound.[34]

The majority of Sebiyam's wives who were alive at the time of my interviews had married Sebiyam in the period from 1942 to 1966.[35] Their explanations for marriage reveal the range of avenues by which individual women would come to the compound.[36] One woman recalls a simple story of Sebiyam "seeing her" on a visit to the neighboring village of Duu

FIGURE 3.1. Sebiyam's compound in 2019. Author's photo.

and then initiating marriage proceedings after she agreed. But others re-count more complicated stories. One woman recalls her parents objecting to her choice of a husband, bringing a case against him that was resolved when Sebiyam agreed to marry her. In contrast, another woman remembers that, while another man wished to marry her, she married Sebiyam "so not to suffer," because he was "strong." Remaining wives came to the compound as young girls, promised in marriage to Sebiyam but taking up roles as his "daughters" until they came of age. In their recollections, their young marriages were the result of individual circumstances, many of which reflected marginal positions in their families. For Sebiyam's compound, however, they were also a new class of junior dependents, who, although growing up beside his daughters in the patrilineage, were not sent to school but rather took up the daily work of the household.

The large open space in the center of the palace compound, marked by the common granary and hearth, was dominated by the increasingly large enterprise of processing, preparing, and allocating food for brothers, wives, children, and farm laborers. Between 1942 and 1966, it was common that upwards of thirty adults and twenty children would need to be fed daily. In addition, during periods of peak labor demand, they were joined by weekly crews of ten or more farm laborers from among the Wulugu-naba's constituents in surrounding towns. All the family members I spoke with insisted on the importance of the normative Mamprusi system at the time, by which the whole household was fed from "one pot." Each day, one wife would be in charge of food preparation for the entire group—a lunch of rice or millet porridge, bean cakes, and so on; then millet, rice, or maize in the evening, with soup. The only women exempted from this rotation were the two senior wives, who cooked a separate pot for the chief to eat alone.[37]

The "one pot" system served as the point at which farm produce was shared among family members and farm workers.[38] The senior wife would set aside the grain at the start of the week to those wives whose turn it was to cook for the family, and each wife would then be in charge of apportion-ing the evening meal, preparing and sending grain to feed farm workers and preparing lunch for wives and children. The common silo and hearth also meant that the considerable work of processing grain (shucking, win-nowing, grinding, etc.), along with harvesting and preparing relish ingre-dients was idealized as a common task, and there was plenty of such work to go around. As many of Sebiyam's children noted, more daily differences could easily emerge, as responsibilities could often fall more heavily on junior family members and become sources of tension in the compound. When I asked wives about exceptions to the rigid descriptions of group labor, they similarly acknowledged that "of course" women often stayed behind when they were sick, tending to young children, or otherwise engaged. Likewise, while the overwhelming sense of this period was of a time when the "silo was always full," wives would sometimes discuss occasions on which they used their own income to feed children in times of need. The compound was, of course, also busy with work other than household feeding. Nearly every wife, like most Mamprusi women, pursued individual small-scale trading, often of prepared food to sell in local markets, though wives recall that the task of household management was so big that their success in this early era paled in comparison to later periods.[39] In emphasizing regularity and shared responsibility, however, wives recalled the ways they accommodated individual needs while maintaining a sense of equity and stability in a period when inequalities by schooling and lineage were beginning to be quite pronounced.

SCHOOLING AND THE STATE

While their uncles and mothers worked on the farm and compound, Sebiyam's children went to school. In doing so, they also benefited from the work of a previous generation of committed activists who saw education as the key to the ability of the regions' residents to participate equally in a postcolonial state. These activists were also, largely, the educated members of chiefly families. When Nabila, Sebiyam's eldest son, and Pawura, his younger sister, finished middle school in the mid-1950s, however, these plans for northern advancement were still just plans, and it was by no means clear how, exactly, their schooling would serve themselves, their families, or the emerging Ghanaian nation. Nabila's early career demonstrates how engagement with programs for northern education could launch some on paths of individual and familial accumulation that, at least initially, seemed to distance them from village development work. Nabila attributes his education to his father, who, he argues, was motivated by a lifelong wish to have attended school himself. After completing primary school in Kpasenkpe, Nabila, like his uncles and much of the early generation of colonially educated men in the region, began to pursue a career in teaching.[40] In the 1950s, teachers were in high demand in the region, thanks to the expansions in northern primary education that continued throughout the decade. At the same time, expanding access to teacher training meant that middle school graduates like Nabila were encouraged to continue their schooling to meet this demand.[41] Shortly after completing middle school in 1956, he enrolled in Pusiga Teacher Training college and then took positions in Nalerigu and Kpasenkpe before gaining admission to Tamale Training College to complete his Certificate A in teaching.[42]

Nabila continued to pursue his personal goal of attending university, a rare path for Northern Territories residents at the time. He heard from a former teacher about correspondence courses that he could order from London, and he completed his O-level course work through Mayflower Correspondence College. At the same time, he sat for an exam and interview that qualified him for the "Special Scholarship Scheme," a program established upon Ghana's independence that provided students from the North with training and scholarships to attend universities in the South.[43] After qualifying as one of the ten yearly recipients, Nabila was able to accelerate his studies, sit for A-level exams, and gain admission to the University of Ghana. It was during this time when he traveled south to pursue a degree, which very few from the North had ever completed, that Nabila noted "everything changed."[44] His new salary, provided by the government as he pursued his studies, along with the connections he began to make in Accra, promised to facilitate his siblings' schooling and to widen the network of the family as a whole. It was unclear where these new networks would lead. For the time being, they led Nabila far away from Kpasenkpe.

If the outcome of Nabila's schooling was uncertain, it was even more so for his aunt and his classmate Pawura. As elsewhere, the colonial state in the Northern Territories had been a masculinist enterprise. Women were largely excluded from both schooling and civil service work until the 1940s, and even then the expansions were contested and their outcomes unknown.[45] However, by the 1950s educated women from the region had fought for greater opportunities, and by the early 1960s the Nkrumah government took up at least a rhetorical commitment to revolutionary gender equality.[46] Women were primarily encouraged to take up positions in teaching and nursing, fields that had been dominated by men but were increasingly feminized over the late colonial and early nationalist period.[47] The newly established Department of Social Welfare and Community Development also sought women as agents, particularly for what it called "women's work."[48] As a result, women like Pawura were able to imagine that, after "pioneering" the schools they attended, civil service employment might follow.

Pawura started her postprimary education at Bagabaga (Girls) Middle School in Tamale, and after completing in 1956 she returned to the Kpasenkpe area to serve as a "pupil teacher" (i.e., with no further training) in Wungu, Walewale, and Kpasenkpe. There, she met and married her husband, a young teacher from the far western side of the district, and gave birth to a daughter. In 1963, during a short-lived dispute between her husband and her family that made her eager to get away, she heard from a friend about a training course in community development that the government was offering in Accra. When Pawura went to see the director of the Social Welfare office in Tamale, it was not her schooling but her experience, language skills, and familiarity with the rural North that impressed them: "You are the people that we are after," she recalled him saying, because "you will really do the work!" In a story whose humor and drama had been sharpened by frequent retellings, Pawura used the story of her first airplane ride to highlight the contrast between her village upbringing and the world that professional government work opened up to her. She recollected, with a laugh, that when the director asked, "Have you ever flown?" she replied, "Have I got wings?" After recounting a series of hijinks as she learned about tickets, seat belts, and takeoffs, she ended the story with a reflection on the new order the plane ride represented. In the rainy season, when lorry travel south was difficult, she pointed out that the airplane flew her, a village woman, over the heads of men who "could not go." As she went on, she paused to savor the memory of receiving her first month's salary in Accra ("I said YEAHHH") before narrating how she arranged to be posted back to the Mamprusi District, where her language skills and personal connections would be most valuable.

Unlike Nabila, Pawura found that her education and training would quickly bring her back to Kpasenkpe as an agent of the state. In this era, she, more than Nabila, would demonstrate the new face of village work in the North. Work as a Mass Education assistant allowed Pawura to draw on both her professional training and her connections to the region.[49] When engaged in what the department called "women's work," she described "educating the women to take care of the children" by giving department-approved lessons in breastfeeding, bathing, and seeking medical care. When she worked in Mass Education campaigns, she taught women to read and write, sometimes linking the work to small-scale enterprise training in soap making. As was standard practice, she worked with each village's chief and *mangasiziiya* (women's leader) to call group gatherings of women and then proceeded with house-to-house and small group visits. Recalling the Mampruli phrases she would use to introduce her work, Pawura highlighted the terminology of help and development that Kpasenkpe residents associated with small-scale development projects spearheaded by Sebiyam and government officials in the preceding years.[50] As Skinner notes, when referring to social work as a whole, agents like Pawura were asked to "navigate precise configurations of power in highly localised settings, using personal relationships and resources to build alliances between chiefs, party branches, government departments and local councils."[51]

Pawura's most memorable work of the era by far was working on the Nkrumah government's so-called antinudity campaigns, which sought to "modernize" women's dress by enforcing their use of cloth in areas where women wore waistbands with leaves or bark, rather than the manufactured cloth that the government considered respectable. Pawura's stories about her work on the antinudity campaigns reflect the complex mix of advocacy, professional pride, and state violence that scholars have charted in a program that aimed to bring women, by force if necessary, in line with imposed definitions of "Ghanaian culture."[52] As Jean Allman argues, antinudity campaigns affirmed long-standing notions of northern "savagery" and otherness, but they also showed how, over time, such notions shifted from the whole colony to the North, then from men to women, and finally from all women in the region to just members of "target" groups and districts.[53] Pawura's recollections clearly reflected such displacement as well, as she pointed out that it was not "the Kpasenkpe people" who had been targeted by the campaign but rather Builsa people from "across the river" who came to Kpasenkpe on market days. When recounting her work, Pawura also emphasized, however, that as an educated woman from the North, she was motivated to work not only toward what she thought of as the advancement of the region's people but also to improve its reputation in national and international discourse. "They said we should get up, and go and fight for our people!" she recalled, because "We shouldn't let them be abusing us like that. We are not animals!"[54]

At the same time, like other antinudity campaigners from the North, she sometimes thought of the campaigns as occurring within her home and her family. Pawura affirmed that her family connections to the area mattered. While her patrilineage was clearly associated with Mamprusi chieftaincy, her "grandmother's side" was comprised of Builsas from Kunkwa, people with whom she had spent considerable time in her youth. She highlighted that her ability to speak Buli as well as Mampruli and her familial connections to the area gave an intimacy to her work, while also providing her with specialized knowledge that she could use.[55] She recounted, for example, incorporating antinudity work, such as tie-and-dye demonstrations and the sale of subsidized cloth, into her usual program of "women's work" that included a broader platform of women's advocacy.[56] In these ways, her reminisces of early efforts were similar to those of Builsa campaigners, including the Sandemnaab's daughter Margaret Azantilow, who was an early antinudity activist.[57]

Ultimately, it was not her identity by region, gender, ethnicity, or lineage that most shaped Pawura's own commitment to the campaigns but rather her position as a representative of the developmentalist state. As the Nkrumah government became more explicit in its authorization of force for antinudity work, antinudity workers were encouraged to impose the bans explicitly, particularly in markets. Pawura worked with her brother Sebiyam to design a scheme that would allow them to enforce the bans by confining women on a market day until they complied. At first, the plan was simply to trap offenders in a room, but when a group of women began easily brushing past a man posted to keep them confined, Pawura recalls thinking quickly: "You are my grandmothers," she said, "but I will do something to you." Using her scissors, presumably handy because of the sewing demonstrations that accompanied her work, she snipped the belts of women as they tried to escape confinement and then waited with them as relatives went to fetch them cloth to cover themselves. In recounting the episode, Pawura downplayed the violence and humiliation of her tactics. Instead, she emphasized the logic of developmentalism in which she, as an agent of the state, had both the expertise and the responsibility of ensuring the success of a government program. When she recalled the campaigns, her ideas about clothing and respectability were clearly overshadowed by the importance of development work itself. "Government has got some money, given to us [the Department] . . . for you people to become Ghanaians! Why," she recalled thinking of the women she targeted, "why are you trying to fail us?"[58]

Meanwhile, in less explicit and dramatic ways, Pawura's nieces and nephews also learned to navigate their emerging roles as agents of Ghanaian statecraft. Family members who were just a few years junior to the "pioneers" began to benefit from the combined effects of a growing network of relatives who had jobs and lodgings across the North.[59] For example, when a son abruptly shifted from training for agricultural extension work in Walewale to pursue teacher training in Bolgatanga, he was able to lodge with one uncle and seek the support of an uncle in the Department of Education who could look out for his career interests. Some children pursued new kinds of specialties and took appointments in new locations. After schooling in Bolgatanga and Tamale in the 1960s, one daughter decided to pursue nursing. Hearing about openings at the mission hospital in

Bawku, she started a career that lasted decades and established Bawku as a base for junior siblings who also went into nursing. Others, like Pawura before them, began to return to Kpasenkpe and its surroundings for civil service postings, navigating their dual roles as agents of the state and members of the chiefly family.[60]

~

When Kwame Nkrumah was overthrown by a coalition of military officers in February of 1966, it was seen by supporters and critics alike as a watershed moment for the country—and, indeed, the continent.[61] Sebiyam appears to have taken the national upheaval to heart, advising his children strongly to avoid party politics in favor of the relative stability of civil service work.[62] Family members' stories of Nkrumah's time, however, have few such sharp dividing lines. Wives and brothers recall their own careers as farmers and traders, punctuated by births and deaths and by new farms and changes in family fortune. Nabila and Pawura, for their parts, recounted a decade marked more by the rhythms of schooling and employment than by political transition. Since the National Liberation Council maintained the Special Scholarship Scheme, Nabila continued his schooling at the University of Ghana. Pawura stayed with the Department of Social Welfare and Community Development, which transferred her to Walewale and then for several years to Eastern Region in southern Ghana.

These stories highlight the mundane and daily work of both household and government, but they also belie the enormity of the changes they effected and made possible. Colonial and nationalist officials recognized Sebiyam's family farm and his commitment to education as part of his reputation as a progressive, allowing him to remain relevant to a rapidly changing political environment. Meanwhile, divisions of gender, lineage, and schooling shaped individuals' relationships with the emerging postcolonial order, as educated family members' ability to join the state apparatus relied on the ongoing labor and relationship work of wives and brothers who rarely engaged formally with development. Over time, these efforts led some members of the Sebiyam family to take up positions in the growing apparatus of state-led development in the North. At times, the work brought them back to Kpasenkpe, further cementing the connection between chieftaincy, development, and statecraft. Moreover, as they forged connections that spanned the country and crossed civil service agencies, they created a durable network that would far outlast the Nkrumah government itself.

4 ⤳ Improvising Government in the Granary of Ghana, 1966–81

It is hoped that with your help our sweat and toil will not be fruitless.[1]

I N 1 9 7 5, after his government proudly announced that Ghana had become self-sufficient in rice production, General I. K. Acheampong visited the country's Northern and Upper Regions on a congratulatory tour.[2] Acheampong, who represented the third of seven administrations that would rule Ghana in the tumultuous fifteen years after the coup against Kwame Nkrumah, proclaimed to an audience of chiefs and officials that they could "now be accorded the honorary title of Granary of Ghana."[3] While Acheampong credited the growth in northern production to his government's "Operation Feed Yourself" platform, this policy was only the latest in a string of national and international efforts to transform Ghana's northern hinterlands into a breadbasket for a hungry nation. As subsidies for fertilizer and seeds started to filter into farming life, residents cautiously speculated about the dawn of a new era of development in which the North would take center stage. They might well have recognized, of course, that successive governments' focus on the region reflected the increasing desperation of the economic situation in the country as a whole. Amidst constant government upheavals and the effects of a growing global recession, successive regimes struggled to maintain support in the face of mounting external debts, volatile international prices for Ghana's key imports and exports, and declining productivity in mining and cocoa. Government coffers emptied, and successive states struggled to maintain the most basic infrastructure of rule.

The years after Kwame Nkrumah's ouster marked a paradoxical time in northern Ghana. For governments that sought new sources of political and economic stability, the historic poverty and neglect of Ghana's northern hinterland suddenly made it an attractive focus for development, and their hopes were bolstered by a new international push to bring recent methods and techniques from Asia and Latin America to create an African "green revolution." International agencies supported government plans to promote high-yielding varieties of staple crops, chemical fertilizer, and pesticides through state-funded distribution networks, access to credit, and guaranteed markets.[4] As a result, northern Ghana became one of several areas of sub-Saharan Africa, including Zambia's Northern Province, Zimbabwe's white-owned estates, and parts of Nigeria and Ethiopia, in which governments and international donors invested heavily in subsidies and extension services to encourage farmers to adopt new technologies and crops.[5] While the long-term agricultural outcomes of these interventions were ambiguous at best, the era gave people a glimpse of what a different political economy of development could look like. Living in a center of national development planning, residents could find multiple channels for accessing state programs and making claims on government resources.

These openings, however, were rife with paradoxes of their own. Citizens who were surrounded by agricultural activity faced states that were persistently less willing and able to expend resources on the roads, wells, and clinics that they hoped might accompany agricultural programs. Across the region, chiefs, local youth associations, literates' groups, and self-help societies organized work crews and wrote petitions appealing for materials and expertise. In Kpasenkpe and its surroundings, residents who hoped to maintain road access to market their crops tried at least twice to build a new road. Sending requests to successive governments for machinery and supplies, they organized themselves to do the work by hand.[6] Their efforts signal a newfound optimism for engaging with governments that paid so much lip service to their development, but they also demonstrate the stark reality that they would have to build most of it themselves.

Africa's 1970s have often been overlooked in studies of development, appearing as a blank space between the ambitious era of postwar and nationalist planning and the retrenchments of the neoliberal era.[7] In broader discussions about African political economy in the twentieth century, a focus on development in the early postcolonial period gives way to stories of political upheaval and economic decline, detailing how a wave of coups in the 1960s and early 1970s that toppled pioneering nationalist leaders across the continent were followed over the course of the 1970s by the economic fallout of global oil shocks and, in West Africa, of successive large-scale droughts.[8] Social scientists who wrote about Ghana in the period's immediate aftermath likewise emphasized the bleak continuities—terming it the time of "political recession," "the era of decline," or simply the "black years."[9] Historians' subsequent neglect of Ghana's 1970s has much to do with the scarcity and difficulty of accessing documents from the period due to the state of archival data collection and preservation that resulted from political upheaval and economic decline—a situation that reaffirmed, in circular fashion, the impression that because the records are absent, so was the government's influence during the decade.[10] Without more detailed histories, these characterizations can give the impression that both governments and citizens stopped debating the terms of state intervention and the goals of development.[11] Recent works by Jennifer Hart and Bianca Murillo, in contrast, confirm that in crucial arenas of life, including automobility and consumer politics, the 1970s was a period in which citizens actively engaged with governments over the terms of what Hart calls "economic morality" and what Murillo describes as the "intimate effects of scarcity and economic uncertainty."[12] In this chapter, I suggest that histories of hinterlands like Ghana's northern regions can also help reframe scholars' ideas of how states work in times of tumult and hardship.

Because it is a period in which documentary evidence is fragmented, oral historical work on this period becomes extremely important, not just for filling in gaps but for continuing to offer alternate chronologies and interpretations of government practice than is suggested by the archival record.[13] Like scholars, Kpasenkpe residents often elide the differences among the regimes of the period (referring to all of it as simply "Busia's time" or "Acheampong's time"). However, instead of bleak national trends, Kpasenkpe residents emphasize the innovations and survival strategies that they patched together at the local level. This chapter shows how, in the face of changing national priorities and unpredictable national politics, local actors improvised new and lasting modes of government interaction by working with existing scripts. With respect to agriculture, officials at "Agric" (as the Ministry of Agriculture was colloquially called) picked up on some of the practices of previous decades, rewarding performances of progressive farming through identifying groups of "key" or "lead" farmers. Both the Wulugunaba and a selection of men in Kpasenkpe used established models of progressive farming to engage directly with extension agents who were flush with funding from international and bilateral donors. Conversely, a wider array of men and women encountered new state initiatives without having to rely on local leaders at all, quietly altering their farming practices by accessing newly subsidized inputs in networks of relatives and neighbors. The multiplicity of strategies people employed in the period is nowhere more evident than in the chief's own family network, where wives, brothers, and children used family connections to navigate both uncertainty and opportunity.

As regional emphasis shifted to agriculture and fiscal problems mounted throughout the decade, local government officials and constituents alike looked for ways to continue to build the schools, roads, hospitals, and wells that central governments often saw as consumption that they could ill afford. While their rationales and rhetoric of intervention varied, successive waves of officials took up and adapted well-worn models of village development from the late colonial and nationalist periods. Local government officials who were increasingly divorced from centralized channels of state influence and who had few options for enforcing labor demands simply decided to direct scarce resources to places where local people were willing to extract labor for the state by organizing themselves. Local efforts drew on colonial and nationalist scripts of self-help and community interest, but they were taken up by a new variety of organizers who challenged Nkrumah-era networks of chiefs and politicians and attempted to reshape the terms of government in the region. Organizers across the region showed that demands for village development could be incorporated into diverse political projects.

A "TIME OF AGRIC"

Following a crash in the price of cocoa in the mid-1960s and rising food prices in urban areas, successive post-Nkrumah regimes put new hopes in northern development. To a number of English speakers, particularly those who had worked with or for the Ministry of Agriculture, the period between the 1966 coup and the early 1980s is referred to simply as the "time of Agric," or "the time when Agric was strong," phrases that are illustrative of how state agricultural programs, more than national political changes or broader economic trends, dominated memories. The early centerpiece of these efforts was the promotion of large-scale mechanized rice cultivation, using high-yielding varieties promoted by the government, in previously uncultivated *fadama* (seasonally flooded) lands in Ghana's Volta River Basin.[14] One such area of rice production was in the Fumbisi Valley, just across the White Volta River from Kpasenkpe. Given the prominence of estate farming in scholars' accounts of the period, I was surprised to find that few of the changes in farming practice in Kpasenkpe related directly to rice cultivation or the proximity of the rice estates.[15] Instead, residents recalled the availability of subsidized fertilizer and the popularization of new varieties of maize, reflecting the more widespread impact of agricultural policy as, over the course of the 1970s, small-scale farmers became an increasingly explicit focus of government and bilateral initiatives.[16] Subsidies, especially for fertilizer, became the backbone of these policies—with fertilizer prices reflecting between 50 and 80 percent subsidies in all the years between 1970 and 1985.[17]

A crucial element of policy continuity was the growing influence of international and bilateral donors. The government of Ghana drafted policies designed to attract support from different constellations of funders.[18] In 1967–68, USAID drafted and supported an initiative called the "Focus and Concentrate Programme," which aimed to direct agricultural interventions toward "progressive" or "innovative" farmers, working to develop detailed farming plans and, ultimately, relying on the idea that they would set examples for their neighbors. Two years later, in 1970, the vision of northern Ghana's agricultural transformation was taken up by the West German government, which established the Ghana-German Fertilizer Project (GGFP) in 1970 and the Ghana-German Agricultural Development Project (GGADP) in 1974. Former Ministry of Agriculture staff remember the Ghana-German project (which lasted, in one form or another, until 1987), as a time when national and international support brought unprecedented influence to staff and vastly increased the scope and reach of their work in rural areas.[19] A 1980 report from the German development agency GTZ reported that over the first ten years of the GGADP program, 43 million deutsche marks had been put into the project ($78 million in 1980 US dollars), about one-quarter in the form of no-cost imports of over thirty thousand tons of fertilizer.[20]

Compared to the Nkrumah government's halting experiments in northern agriculture and industry, new support for green revolution interventions was sustained and comprehensive. By setting up zonal offices to coordinate input distribution and extension at the subdistrict level, GGADP staff attempted to reach "every farmer" who wanted information and access to fertilizer, seeds, and new technologies. Staff remember the responsiveness of the programs to changing needs—after starting with simple distribution of fertilizer, the GGADP expanded to include extension services, mobile information units, research and seed multiplication, and dam construction.[21] Eventually, the GGADP built a farming implement factory to better supply the region with plows and other equipment.

The combination of ambition and funding is summed up in an anecdote by a former Ministry of Agriculture information officer, recounting his pattern of work with German colleagues: "We were evaluating the 'compact farmer approach' which was an extension approach they were using. We had to put motos [motorbikes], and put bicycles [in the back of the pickup]. We would get to some place, and we'd have to ride motos. You'd [then] get to some place and have to say 'Oh, as for now . . . the way is too much for moto, we have to use the bicycles.' Then we would leave it and take bicycles. To get to the farmers, to get to the farmers' level."[22]

Despite this dramatic change in the scope and available resources for state intervention, new agricultural initiatives continued a long-standing government focus on men who were deemed progressive. Agricultural extension programs relied on the assumption that the farmers to reach were those who made decisions about inputs, rather than everyone who farmed.[23] Thus, in the construction of policy, a "farmer" was almost always the senior man in a household or, in some cases, widows or junior men who pursued farming on supplemental plots.[24] Agents, furthermore, hoped to glean which of these men would most easily adopt and spread information about fertilizer, bullock and tractor plowing, high-yielding seed varieties, and agrochemicals. The fundamental organizing principle of agricultural extension was each village's list of farmers group participants. Ministry of Agriculture efforts aimed to "focus and concentrate" extension and inputs on these farmers and to use farmers groups to lead innovations.[25] Extension agents identified farmers by asking for lists, generated locally, naming members of each village's group. Groups continued to be recognized by successive governments and agricultural projects. In Kpasenkpe, when I asked Suurana Yakubu Pusu, a former leader, if the group membership changed with each new government, he said of course not, and instead highlighted the importance of local intermediation and bureaucratic inertia. "Every government wanted to form groups," he said, and "when they came in and opened the books, our names were already there."[26]

The Wulugunaba found that agricultural officials' demands for local leadership allowed him to draw on well-established models of progressive chieftaincy. In addition to demonstrating personal interest in new agricultural technologies, the Wulugunaba continued to show his ability to mobilize and manage local interactions with government. One of the most concrete ways that the Wulugunaba shaped agricultural opportunities for Kpasenkpe's residents was by his role in the farmers group. Though the group's chairman lived across town, the tractor for the group was kept at the Wulugunaba's palace, so that he could exercise his judicial powers, "in case there were any problems."[27] Later, the Wulugunaba bought out the group's tractor loan and used the tractor on his own farms. Most crucially, the Wulugunaba worked with the Ministry of Agriculture officer in identifying farmers to participate in the group. Farmers who had been asked to join the group attributed their selection to the Wulugunaba's impression of the "seriousness" of their farming habits, regardless of their previous use of agricultural inputs. As Suurana Yakubu Pusu put it, "He [the Wulugunaba] would look at you and if you were seriously working then he would tell them to pick you."[28]

Participating in a farmers group became a new way for individual farmers to gain recognition from government agents and negotiate access to state development initiatives. In Kpasenkpe, the farmers group expanded the small riverside tobacco and cotton group farms from the Nkrumah era to include staple crops—millet, rice, and increasing amounts of maize. Instead of farming collectively, men in the farmers group were allocated ten- to twenty-acre plots and given access to tractor services and government buyers.[29] The farmers group brought members new access to agricultural inputs. Members collected seed and fertilizer on loan, and parcels of land designated for the groups were tractor plowed, first by government tractors sent from the district capital and later by the group's own tractor, secured by an African Development Bank loan in the early 1970s.[30]

The current *kakpanaba* (chief farmer), Somka Nluki, is the son of Kpasenkpe's first *kakpanaba*, who was installed in the early postwar era. Somka Nluki started farming on his own in the late colonial period, likely around the time of his father's appointment. He recalls that in the late 1960s and 1970s a role as a lead farmer could bring numerous benefits, often well beyond the activities on the farmers group. Like other early enthusiasts of state-sponsored farming activities, he was well placed to take advantage of intensified government interest in agriculture. When he served as chairman of the farmers group in the late 1960s and 1970s, he opened a bank account and collected seeds and fertilizer on loan from the Ministry of Agriculture, paying extension agents back with produce at harvest time. The group soon took out a loan for a tractor. Members of the group received free tractor services, and the group also hired out the tractor to area farmers, earning money to invest in inputs. Members of the farmers group cultivated rice in a group plot—of which they were each designated several acres—and then sold the produce to government buyers. But, for him, this was less significant than the expansion of his own farms of millet, maize, and groundnuts that was made possible by access to fertilizer and tractor services. Like other farmers in Kpasenkpe, he experimented with new high-yielding varieties of maize. He fed his family, sold produce both locally and to traders from surrounding towns, and continued to expand his fields. Fertilizer became standard on his fields, and like many farmers he added his own plots along the riverside to take advantage of seasonal flooding for irrigation of high-yielding varieties.[31] These benefits were not reserved for group leadership. Naaichi Maka arrived in Kpasenkpe from Nigeria shortly after Acheampong came into power in 1972, coming initially to join other Hausa speakers who concentrated on fishing.[32] When government agents encouraged the formation of a fishing group, Naaichi and others organized themselves to collect dues, make bank deposits, and secure loans for investment in boats and materials. At the same time, Naaichi enthusiastically sought to join the farmers' group, farming rice and also rapidly expanding his own millet and maize farming with the help of fertilizer access through the group.[33]

Farmers groups often reinforced existing hierarchies and patterns of government engagement, and depending on who was narrating the story, perspectives on the farmers group could vary quite a bit. Sandola Tampuri, a small-scale farmer who had achieved longevity but not significant accumulation as a farmer in Kpasenkpe, told a story that drew knowing laughs from the group of men who were sitting with us. At first, he said, he took a plot at the riverside rice farm organized by the group. Soon, however, he realized that not everyone was having the same experience with government agents. While he and many other farmers used their produce to repay Ministry of Agriculture loans of seeds and fertilizer, others who had ties to the government would simply "take and they would not pay back."[34] Consequently, he and others also refused to pay, ultimately ending their involvement with the group and, he implied, curtailing the government's hopes for the rice scheme as a whole.[35]

The Wulugunaba's ability to engage with government interventions was further strengthened by Kpasenkpe's proximity to the rice estates of the Fumbisi Valley where, as in other areas of the North, a small group of people used connections to the state and access to capital to take up large-scale mechanized estate farming.[36] In these areas, chiefs were often well-positioned to gain from their relationships with newcomers.[37] In Kpasenkpe, residents remember the arrival of "Bolga farmers," estate owners from the towns of Bolgatanga or Tumu, some of whom stayed in

Kpasenkpe for months at a time while they supervised their hundred-plus-acre rice farms on the other side of the river.[38] Evidence regarding large-scale rice cultivation largely confirms the argument of Konings and others, that the gains from estate agriculture accrued primarily to estate owners, to the limited number of urban workers employed in permanent positions on their farms, and to a small set of local elites. The Wulugunaba appears to have been the only Kpasenkpe resident to start a large-scale rice farm across the river in the Fumbisi Valley.

However, transformations wrought by government agricultural interventions were not limited to large-scale farming, or even members of the farmers group and the Wulugunaba, who were heavily involved with particular government initiatives. Like residents of Ghana's North as a whole, Kpasenkpe residents felt the effects of the broader influx of subsidized agricultural inputs.[39] Agricultural initiatives for fertilizer, seeds, plows, and tractors brought government services onto the farms and into the households of a wide range of Kpasenkpe residents. Though strongly associated with government, they were not networked through recognizable channels that directed government intervention in the past. Kofi Nabila began farming his own farm in the late 1960s, enthusiastic to take up both established and new farming technologies. He first saved to buy a bullock and then a plough, accessing a loan scheme through the Ministry of Agriculture. It was here that he spoke of engaging directly with government agents, who knew he was "serious on farming" after inspecting his farm.[40] When chemical fertilizer became available in the 1970s, he purchased it from Walewale, using it widely on his farms. While he continued to farm millet, as well as yellow corn, yams, and dry season crops, he also remembers intercropping millet with new varieties of white maize. "Damongo" maize arrived in the 1970s when Sebiyam brought seeds back from Damongo. After seeing it grow tall on Sebiyam's farm, Kpasenkpe residents took it up. "Agric" maize, in contrast, was distributed by extension agents but also quickly took hold in local networks.[41]

Chiefs, local government officials, and party networks are mostly absent in these accounts—replaced by interactions with traders, neighbors, and family members. It is likely that some farmers used commercially produced fertilizer before the 1960s, but in the immediate post-Nkrumah years farmers recall the sudden and overwhelming abundance of fertilizer.[42] They recount that in sharp contrast to the present, low-priced fertilizer became available to nearly everyone: whether you got it from government or traders, recalled Sandow Kundunkurigu, "it was cheap."[43] Hajia Musah

Ladi pointed out that "at that time if you had some small money you could buy," a sentiment echoed by Adam Abdullai Seiya's more stark claim that farmers "could buy fertilizer at that time even if [they] were poor."[44] Fertilizer made possible experiments with new varieties of white maize that were popularized both by the chief and by extension agents, and mentions of "Agric" maize and "Damongo" maize brought out a flood of memories from a wide range of men and women in Kpasenkpe.[45] Meanwhile, residents' use of bullock plows and tractors expanded rapidly.[46]

The handful of women in Kpasenkpe who cultivated their own farms in this era, while not involved in Kpasenkpe's farmers groups or trained by extension agents, nonetheless found ways to make use of new technologies as and when they found them to be useful.[47] Balihira Seiya, who returned north from the Asante region in the 1950s and began selling akpeteshie in Kpasenkpe, invested her profits first in a grinding mill and then in her own farms.[48] She recalled bartering grain for a bullock from herders across the river in the early 1970s, and so joined the growing number of farmers who started using animal traction during that time, two decades after people like Somka Nluki had begun doing so. Since she owned the bullock and made money from akpeteshie sales, she was able to hire labor and expand her farms.[49] Around the same time, she became interested in experimenting in new crop varieties after she heard about them in town. She never grew rice, and while she sold maize, she does not recall interacting with government buyers. Sometime in the 1970s, she began to use fertilizer on her new maize and groundnut crops, which she was able to purchase freely because, at that time, she noted, "it was not costly." Like Somka Nluki, fertilizer allowed her to open new farms at the riverside.

Kpasenkpe residents who did not directly purchase plows and fertilizer encountered government initiatives through labor markets, cash exchanges, and relationships among neighbors and family members. This group consisted of a wide range of people, including those who made input decisions as well as a variety of women and junior men who did not. Residents recounted a general expansion in both the volume and variety of daily waged labor opportunities (called "b-day") facing small-scale farmers and the expansion of small-scale farmers' own use of wage labor.[50] Men farmers nearly all recall that by-day labor figured into some part of their farming career, usually when they were still young. Similarly, almost every farmer, men and women, listed by-day laborers as a source of labor on their own farms at least since the late 1960s. Farm heads met peak labor demands with a diverse combination of family, by-day, *kpaariba*, and small reciprocal labor-sharing groups referred to as *nangbanyinni* (meaning "one mouth," or, more loosely, "unity").[51] From the perspective of plow owners and users, cash exchanges were mixed with claims of obligation and reciprocity. Several plow owners remember exchanging bullock services for labor—particularly by requesting that recipients organize *kpaariba* labor during peak weeding periods.[52] But by far the most common description of plowing arrangements concerned "not being able to refuse" a family member who begged for "help." In this way, plow owners became conduits through which greater numbers of people accessed government subsidies. In a metaphorically loaded description, Alhassan Pusu illustrated the reciprocity implicit in his provision of bullock services: "You know the bullocks, they can get lost, and if you haven't helped your family, who will come search for it with you?"[53]

Not all farmers in Kpasenkpe, to be sure, experienced dramatic and coherent changes in their farming practices in the 1970s. Zamma Voonaba recalled buying a bullock plow, which he then used every year to raise labor, but he also recalled being unable to afford fertilizer on a yearly basis.[54] Others recalled using fertilizer sporadically.[55] Many residents simply recollected years of good eating.[56] Most notably, farmers remember struggling with the risks and sensitivity of new varieties and new inputs. Fati Zebagane recalled that Damongo maize, prized for its height and ability to withstand early floods, would break in high winds.[57] Adisa Tampulima and Nelson Danladi pointed out that, because Agric maize did best with fertilizer, it became important that farmers have timely access to it.[58] Naaichi Maka spoke of the need to repurchase seeds every three years.[59] Many farmers recall ceasing to grow rice when both the rains and the timing of government purchasing became unpredictable. As a number of scholars have demonstrated with respect to more recent decades, input-intensive agriculture has intensified labor demands and increased vulnerability to climate and market shocks, particularly after broad-based agricultural supports were discontinued in the mid-1980s.[60] In fact, Kpasenkpe residents often told stories of the late 1960s and 1970s as a way of highlighting contrasts to more recent times, when farmers have been left to bear these risks without the cushion of government support. As Balihira Seiya described evocatively, agricultural supports allowed farmers to weather growing risks. "Even if the river water came and washed away your fertilizer," she recalled, it was so inexpensive that farmers did not suffer.[61]

Successive governments placed their hopes for northern Ghana's economic transformation on the Ministry of Agriculture and the GGADP, reserving little attention or resources for social and economic infrastructure more broadly. Local government officials, chiefs, and their constituents were left to figure out how to pursue, on the margins, the roads, schools, wells, and other small-scale projects that they might have hoped would accompany agricultural investment. One surprising resource local governments had at their disposal was stability. Despite national political upheaval, local government personnel often remained at their posts. Even though, in the immediate aftermath of Kwame Nkrumah's overthrow, district commissioners like Damma Wuni were jailed and Mumuni Bawumia left for London to pursue a law degree, by the late 1960s many CPP staff had again found positions in the North.[62] In part, this was because it was an unpopular posting. In October of 1967, for example, District Administrative Officer E. Ansah-Aboagye suggested building an "Officers Club" in Gambaga so that "Senior Officers . . . feel happy about their being in the district and [would be able] to disregard the impression that they were sent here as punishment."[63] By 1970, Damma Wuni appeared on the staff of the Walewale/Kpasenkpe Local Council as a clerical officer, and by 1971 and 1972 he became treasurer and clerk of council in Yendi and Bole Districts.[64] Subsequent coups and civilian transitions often had even less impact on local administrative positions. For example, C. K. Amanfu, who began as the district administrative officer (DAO) of Gambaga under the National Liberation Council (NLC) government in early 1969, continued in Gambaga through the transition to Busia's civilian regime later that year. After Acheampong's coup against Busia in 1972, Amanfu continued as Gambaga DAO, eventually serving in Damongo and Salaga Districts throughout the mid-1970s.[65]

In the post-Nkrumah years, career government workers accumulated strategies for coping with tumultuous politics and uncertain budgets. Like their predecessors in the late colonial and early nationalist eras, officials made repeated attempts to use self-help or communal labor to make projects cheaper and to identify areas where they could demonstrate development success. In February and March of 1969, the clerk of the Walewale/ Kpasenkpe Local Council asked DAO Amanfu to fund the maintenance of roads that had fallen into disrepair since the coup. In response, Amanfu declined to fund the projects outright but argued that if the council would "encourage communal labor," the district might "put in our bit to make the work complete."[66] In August of 1970, Amanfu asked the chief of Bunkpurugu to organize communal labor to "supplement the efforts made by Government" in road repair after severe flooding, stating in a letter that "it is expected of every Chief to organise his people to supplement the efforts made by Government."[67]

Governmental failure to fully institutionalize communal labor is evident in the repeated attempts to "revive" town and village development committees. After finding the North's CPP development committees "inactive" in 1966, NLC officials soon attempted to use the same model in their own development practice.[68] When the Gambaga Town Development Committee was reestablished in 1968, with DAO E. Ansah-Aboagye as its chairman, he told members that "God helps those who help themselves. It is the same with Government." He "explained that the main task facing committee members is not the technical aid but rather how to convince the people to do Communal Labour on their own," and he "expressed the hope that perhaps members would do better in their persuasion [than he had] since they speak the same language and know their own people better."[69]

When A. B. Naah came in as the Gambaga District administrative officer under Busia's civilian Progress Party in 1969, however, he again found that "Town and Village Development Committees" in the district "existed only on paper." Undaunted, he toured the district to revive the concept in what he deemed to be all of the "large and accessible village[s]" in his jurisdiction. In a generic speech he gave at each location (fittingly titled in his notes, "The Need for a Village/Town Development Committee in Your Village/Town"), Naah argued that because the Busia government had "inherited a difficult financial situation . . . an active and efficient Village/Town Development Committee will help you provide yourselves with those amenities which Government is unable to give you, by planning, organising, and supervising communal labour."[70] Nonetheless, by 1974 the Department of Social Welfare and Community Development in Gambaga found, yet again, that development committees in South Mamprusi were "either not in existence or inactive." In a memo circulated to Mamprusi divisional chiefs that instructed "all chiefs to revive and reactivate" committees in their area, Senior Assistant Community Development Officer M. D. Bonirima gave a surprisingly candid assessment of why demonstrations of grassroots effort felt so urgent. "Please note," he concluded, "that the success of every government worker depends on these development committees."[71]

Absent a strong institutional structure to demand self-help, local officials adopted a piecemeal approach of focusing efforts on places where they thought they could show success. Chiefs emerged as nimble cultivators of multiple personae as they attempted to attract and manage state support. In the newly created Northern Region House of Chiefs, chiefs portrayed themselves to the central government as agricultural entrepreneurs, seeking to tap into new avenues of state support. In other forums, however, these same actors sought small-scale public grants through well-established claims to community leadership and village solidarity. For example, at the same time that Sebiyam used his role as a progressive farmer to "focus and concentrate" agricultural efforts on a circle of men in town, he also worked to renew his reputation as a chief who could mobilize a broad swath of constituents for development. In May of 1970, the Northern Territories Planning Committee commissioned an "on the spot survey" of far western Mamprugu, to "look into the problems of the area," and to give "a pep talk . . . on the importance of communal labor."[72] At a stop in Kpasenkpe, they interviewed the Wulugunaba about the possibilities of "self-help labor" in the area. The survey team recorded that the chief acknowledged the erosion of his ability to mobilize labor during the time of the Kpasenkpe District. He "talked at length on the history of community development in his Division . . . [and] . . . said that some of the factors that encouraged them to give full support are no longer there." However, when the delegation informed him that they "expected renewed vigour in the way [Mamprusis] approached Self-Help Projects," the Wulugunaba "pledged his full support."[73]

Monthly reports of DAOs for Northern Region from 1972 to 1974 show administrators routinely visiting villages in their districts to "organise" or "meet [the] local chief" about communal labor on particular projects, as well as visiting projects that had been successfully organized.[74] While officials occasionally raised the specter of state punishment—as when the chairman of the Walewale/Kpasenkpe Local Council "emphasized that the Clerk of Council should inform police whenever there is any difficulty about communal labour"—in practice a lack of community action simply meant projects did not move forward.[75] Instead, officials looked for particular places as potential sites to demonstrate success. In certain cases, the search for "village" sites was so focused on success that definitions proved malleable, as in a 1970 "aided self-help scheme" that identified the large, historically important towns of Gambaga and Salaga as sites that they "agreed [could] be regarded as villages under this pilot scheme."[76]

SELF-HELP AND CLAIMS ON THE STATE

As government agents struggled to figure out a reliable way to extract labor for small-scale development, people in the North set about doing it themselves, using contributions and refusals of labor and demonstrations of leadership to serve a variety of political and developmental efforts. In the process, while broad attempts to institutionalize self-help failed, practices and arguments around local initiative both spread and took root. Rural people weathered political instability by using existing scripts of village community and governmental obligation to test and shape the possibilities of government.

In a collection of sixty-five petitions about local development projects that ended up in Gambaga District and Northern Region files for the years from 1968 and 1979, twenty-five invoke communal labor and local financial contributions in their arguments.[77] Some of these petitions, an intriguing handful, suggest that communal labor worked its way into a range of disputes across the region. A 1968 petition from a "communal labor group" in Bunkpurugu announced that several lorry owners would be blocked from using locally constructed bridges because they had refused to lend their vehicles to the construction effort.[78] A group of "school leavers" (likely middle school graduates) in Gambaga argued that they should not be overlooked for employment because they had "worked during the communal labor hours" to build a community center.[79] In a revived dispute over the chieftaincy in Kunkwa, some residents protested the chief's moving of the market and the school by citing the communal labor involved in both projects.[80] Communal labor surfaced in the long-running dispute over efforts by dissident minority groups to gain political recognition in East Gonja, when a group of Gonja chiefs argued, to the electoral commissioner in 1971, that the use of communal labor for a water project in Kpandai validated the effectiveness of the East Gonja District.[81]

Most striking are fourteen petitions from across the Northern Region in which a variety of local groups use communal labor and "voluntary contributions" to make the case that they, not government-organized groups, would lead the way. Petitioners included chiefs, youth associations, clerks of council, literates' groups, some town development committees, and others. In February of 1968, for example, just one day before he unsuccessfully attempted to reconstitute the Gambaga Town Development Committee, Gambaga DAO Ansah-Aboagye wrote to the Ministry of Agriculture asking for tractors to help with the Walewale-Wungu-Yama road. "The people of Wungu, Yama, Bubillia [sic] and Kpasenkpe have expressed their wish to work on the above road through Communal Labor," he wrote, and therefore, "The Walewale Local Council and the Regional Organisation Gambaga have also agreed to play their part in this noble task." While he pushed for "Town/Village Development Committees" that would bring such projects under government direction, Ansah-Aboagye seemed more than willing to let this proposed project proceed "under the supervision of Reverend Arthur E. Hockett of the Assemblies of God Mission Walewale," who had "kindly agreed to advise on and supervise the entire project" and had "already won the confidence of the people."[82] Three and a half years later, a different configuration of roadside residents petitioned to construct a section of the same road, arguing that they, the "Executive Members of the Yaama, Bulibia, and Zua villages," could claim to have directed citizens' efforts and therefore deserved government support. "It is hoped," they argued, "that with your help our sweat and toil would not be fruitless."[83]

Given the variety of actors involved in these projects and the distance among them, they reveal a striking consistency in their form of argumentation. Petitioners first argued for the necessity of a project—a road that was too bad in the rainy season for sick people to reach the hospital or was necessary for farmers to get produce to markets; dams that would save lives in the dry season. Petitioners then listed the contributions that had been made: reconstructing a Tolon area road "through self-help;" constituents in the Kpasenkpe area "express[ing] their wish to work on . . . the road through Communal Labor"; 600 cedis for a dam from the "chief and people" in Jukuru; "token voluntary contributions" to the Bole Local Council for a drinking water project; and a levy for a dam on house and cattle owners by a newly formed Takoro-Belega Development Committee.[84] Petitioners further asserted that government assistance would be met with additional community support, with people "prepared to do communal labor," "ready to provide labor," and "ready to contribute our quota."[85] Ultimately, petitioners argued that the government should match voluntary efforts with funds, materials, and skilled labor. The Chief of Lungbun asked that "the social welfare would come into help us with this crusade."[86] Petitioners in Yapei pointed out that the government "gives aid to people in rural areas to improve their standing," but only after they demonstrated "self-reliance and not always to be waiting or looking for the Government to do every possible thing."[87] Petitioners called attention to the limits of what they could do themselves, requesting cement, machines, and technical advice in building local works.

In their repetition of a basic formula, these petitions reveal the extent to which a wide range of actors understood the weight that government officials had placed on evidence of local support in previous decades. These were no generic gestures toward the importance of self-help, but rather explicit and concrete arguments that local initiative could continue to be the basis for government spending. However, petitioners also sought to ground claims in new arguments about the basis of community and its connection to development. Some petitions continued to make claims that the "chiefs and the people" would form the basis of community action, but they were not the only claimants. For a brief period after their revival in January of 1974, organizers of new Town Development Committees used the committees as a platform from which to argue for government funds. The Zabzugu Youth Association cited the "spirit of the revolution" as animating their efforts toward a community center, suggesting that they sought to tie local demands to national political ideologies.[88] Meanwhile, "literates" in Yapei invoked generation and class as a basis for leadership, contrasting their efforts at self-help with the lackluster performance of town elders, who "hate educated children" and neglected development of the town.[89] In their varied appeals, different sets of petitioners sought to be recognized as local leaders and to make claims to government resources. At the same time, they acknowledged a situation in which such claims were confined to established scripts of village labor and progressive leadership, in which they would have to compete for scarce funds.

KPASENKPE:
DEVELOPING THE VILLAGE IN A TIME OF FERTILIZER

If Kpasenkpe's farming seasons in the 1970s were marked by new structures of agricultural support, the dry season was, as in previous decades, a time for building. After being identified in 1968 as a site for one of fifty-four rural health posts to be constructed around the country, Kpasenkpe attracted modest funding from successive states to purchase cement and hire lorries, while constituents supplied labor.[90] The result was the largest public building project Kpasenkpe had seen: the Kpasenkpe Health Post, known locally as the hospital. Work began on the hospital just two months after Wulugunaba Sebiyam's conversation with the Northern Territories Planning Commission's survey team, in which he "pledged his full support" to raising communal labor for state projects.[91] To raise labor, the Wulugunaba turned again to the structures of *nayiri kpaariba* with which he had acquired labor for a variety of projects in the 1950s. Constituents came for one-day shifts from each section or quarter (*fɔŋŋu*) of Kpasenkpe as well as each of the surrounding towns under the Wulugunaba's jurisdiction (including those towns that had been involved in Nkrumah-era political disputes).[92] However, as with projects mentioned in petitions across the region, the hospital project drew not just on the chief but also on a variety of organizational energies in town. After the Kpasenkpe District was dismantled in 1966, and as Kpasenkpe residents navigated new relationships with the Ministry of Agriculture, they improvised widely on scripts of labor and leadership that had been cemented in the prior decades.

For many Kpasenkpe residents who were born in the 1950s and 1960s, the hospital was their first and only experience with communal labor until the mid-1980s, and they attributed their contributions of carrying water, molding blocks, and plastering walls to a variety of motivations. Like their elders who had come of age in the late 1950s, memories of labor were tied to arguments about collective responsibility, couched in terms of their interest in town development (*maaligu*), or simply unity (*nangbanyinni*, for which they employed the word that described the shared farming arrangements flourishing at the time). They also remembered it as a source of personal opportunity, often framed in terms of the food they were fed by the chief and occasional cash payments they received from the project's contractor.[93] Many of these memories involved Wulugunaba Sebiyam's efforts to call and to compensate labor. Some remember that residents came, in the words of one hospital employee, Jacob Pitigi Tampulima, "because of the food and because it would help them."[94] More simply, recalled Wurugurunaba Nsoanyanni Sandow, "They fed us WELL."[95] Unlike Nkrumah-era projects, calls for development labor in the 1970s were not paired with calls to perform labor on Sebiyam's own farms. In light of this, it seems likely that labor for the hospital—called in the dry season—also became a relatively painless way for constituents to recognize *naam* without going through the more onerous duties of *nayiri kpaariba*, or the political trouble of refusing the chief when he called.

One group that exhibits the vitality of local organizing in the era and became particularly active during the hospital's construction was the local branch of the Amasachina organization. Started by university students from the North in the 1960s, Amasachina groups spread to locations across the region through organizing efforts of its founders and others.[96] In Kpasenkpe, this initiative was from W. W. Zakari, a young Amasachina organizer from Tamale teaching in Kpasenkpe, who started the local branch of the group in the early 1970s. A variety of residents remember

Zakari, but beyond that their memories of Amasachina diverge. The variety of activities attributed to Amasachina was significant: fishing, building projects, road repair, groundnut farming, soap making, and purchasing gifts for visiting officials. Several people recalled that men and women joined a fishing group, while others insisted that Amasachina was centered only on women.[97] Adisa Tampulima, who was one of the group's leaders, recalls the work as a mixture of government assistance, obligation to the chief, and commitment of members to each other. Women contributed money to a group farming enterprise, but the government supplied them materials for soap and pomade making. Sometimes the chief would give them guinea fowls and rice, and they would dance and convince women to go in for group farming. Other times they would contribute money to buy guinea fowls themselves, to honor visitors to the town. They would carry sand and fill potholes on the road, and "if there was any building" they would help by carrying water and stones.[98] Here, work on the hospital appeared as one of many local improvements that residents organized themselves to build.

Despite the variety of agendas that constituents brought to the hospital project, however, their performances of unpaid labor primarily succeeded in cementing the reputation of Kpasenkpe as a place where the chief could get things done. Sebiyam used the project to call for reciprocity from government officials. After the building was initially completed in February of 1975, the regional commissioner visited the site to congratulate the community. In his remarks during the commissioner's visit, Sebiyam took the opportunity to make requests for additional projects that would build on its success. He asked that the government fund additional works that would allow residents to better take advantage of it, including pipe-borne water and reconstruction of the road and completion of the bridge to Kunkwa. In his plea, he pledged that residents would give communal labor to lay the pipes and, for good measure, he threw in an additional request for a dam so that residents could also have water for farm animals.[99] Officials, in turn, used projects like the Kpasenkpe Health Post to demonstrate their own success and to call for communal labor in other northern villages. When the regional commissioner inaugurated the Northern Region House of Chiefs on May 23, 1975, he listed the Kpasenkpe project among those that had been "initiated or completed" since he took office, arguing that chiefs should see these as an example of what could be possible if chiefs decided to "think of how best to assist this Government in developing your Region."[100]

The ambiguities of the era were reflected in patterns of accumulation and differentiation within the chiefly family as well. In some ways, it was a time in which Sebiyam loomed large. The Wulugunaba was by far the best-positioned farmer in Kpasenkpe to take advantage of state subsidies and loans for chemical inputs and mechanized farm equipment. The sudden availability of fertilizer and other industrial inputs, as well as tractor services, ushered in a period of rapid expansion and diversification of Sebiyam's farming activities. As in Kpasenkpe as a whole, however, opportunities and upheavals often worked to decenter Sebiyam and allow new networks to grow. Wives and brothers who had created stable systems that valued unity and equity in the Nkrumah era were able to protect their labor and pursue individual accumulation, again by hewing to normative ideas of familial relationships and gendered farming responsibilities. Meanwhile, a new cohort of Sebiyam's children who finished their schooling and entered government work amidst budgetary and political upheaval relied increasingly on the assistance and advice of an expanding network of educated siblings, aunts, and uncles. In the Sebiyam family, new agricultural technologies and rapid changes in civil service prospects did not correspond to a larger collapse in relations of obligation and reciprocity with Sebiyam's family network, but they did radically alter the terms and content of those relations. For children, taking up a position as an agent of the state now relied not just on access to schooling but on navigating uncertain times through family support. For wives and brothers, state investment in agriculture and the chief's involvement with it became only the backdrop to stories of personal drive and accomplishment that were dependent on their own initiative.

Over the course of the late 1960s, 1970s, and into the 1980s, Sebiyam purchased several tractors, opened a series of new farms on which he grew cotton, tobacco, and new varieties of maize, and made widespread use of fertilizer and other chemical inputs. Instead of concentrating on production at one large plot at Baraŋaŋi, which had expanded throughout the 1950s and early 1960s, Sebiyam opened a number of new more specialized farms in the Kpasenkpe area. In addition to expanding output and shifting production toward cash crops, these changes altered both the geography and labor demands of Sebiyam's farms. The first and largest of the new farms was a plot in the uplands immediately adjoining Kpasenkpe town, at an area called Kpawaŋa.[101] Smaller than Baraŋaŋi and much closer to the palace, it was at Kpawaŋa that Sebiyam began to rely heavily on fertilizer and tractor farming. Around the same time, Sebiyam opened number of riverside farms, cultivated new maize varieties, and intensified his cultivation of rice, first in a series of tractor-plowed rice plots around Kpasenkpe and then at a commercial rice farm across the river. The expansion of the group cotton and tobacco farms along the riverbank was another source of cash income. The yield in food and money made possible by new crops and by government subsidies allowed Sebiyam to hire increasing numbers of by-day laborers and to take on new seasonal dependents in the form of migrants from Burkina Faso or drought-stricken areas of Ghana.[102]

While family members' accounts of Nkrumah's time emphasize normative arrangements of brothers farming together and eating from one pot, they speak of the next period, in which Sebiyam's commercial farming took off, as a time of change and opportunity when "the brothers separated."[103] The idea of separation itself was consistent with an idealized model of family farming in which a period of joint farming by male lineage members would be followed by a period in which junior men married and began their own family farms. As in previous decades, however, family members invoked timeless norms to describe how they navigated specific periods of change. As Sebiyam's farming enterprise began to rely more heavily on industrial inputs, labor exchanges with constituents, and hired by-day labor, it made possible fundamental changes in the organization of labor and patterns of accumulation within Sebiyam's family. Of the over a dozen brothers who worked full-time at Baranaŋgi in the 1940s and 1950s, two-thirds stopped working on Sebiyam's farms in the late 1960s and 1970s.[104] After this period, the permanent family workforce on Sebiyam's farm consisted of four brothers and one son that Sebiyam incorporated in the 1960s.[105]

Separation created opportunities for junior brothers to make independent farming decisions while they fashioned new forms of reciprocity with Sebiyam. In addition to paying the marriage greetings for the brothers who separated, Sebiyam continued to support their careers in multiple ways, often capitalizing on access to state recognition and resources. Sebiyam was instrumental in brothers' limited forays into off-farm careers — most notably through enskinning one brother as chief of the nearby town of Jadema, but also by securing a brother's position with the district administration and by providing regular work to a brother who had trained as a tailor in Bolgatanga (before Sebiyam "called him back" to Kpasenkpe, among other things to sew school uniforms for Sebiyam's children). On the farms of brothers who separated, Sebiyam's role was also prominent. Two brothers recall Sebiyam providing them with free fertilizer and bullock or tractor services throughout the 1970s and 1980s. While other farmers in Kpasenkpe would trade labor for tractor services and fertilizer, Sebiyam would provide them to brothers, "because they were brothers." Another brother remembers a variety of additional ways that Sebiyam's involvement with state agricultural projects benefited family members, including Sebiyam's ability to "cut" portions of group farm land for brothers' use or to secure access to loans through group farming schemes.[106] New inputs and labor arrangements had effects even for brothers who continued to work on Sebiyam's farms, as there were possibilities for personal advancement within the family farming network during the expansions of the 1960s and 1970s. One brother gained some status in the family farm when, in the late 1960s, Sebiyam sent him to manage a millet farm he had established in the neighboring town of Duu. Others recount cultivating small additional plots of their own, using fertilizer and tractor services they obtained from Sebiyam. Some brothers who did not separate, however, reflect on the period with more ambivalence, regretting lost opportunities in schooling, off-farm employment, or commercial farming.[107]

Though rarely mentioned explicitly, "separation" also signaled a period in which Sebiyam's wives gained greater control over their own time and labor and were able to pursue individual enterprise.[108] In previous years, Sebiyam's frequent marriages had been instrumental in his success as a farmer and his investment in his children's schooling. Wives' work on the farm and, more crucially, in household feeding had supported the labor-intensive expansion of Sebiyam's farms in the 1950s and 1960s. Meanwhile, the young girls that Sebiyam had married in the Nkrumah era began to reach maturity, have children, and establish themselves in the compound and in their own enterprises.[109] The increased number of adult women in the compound expanded the number of wives participating in the cooking rotation for household feeding, even as "separation" and the end of *nayiri kpaariba* reduced the number of adults living in the compound. By the late 1960s, each wife would be called to cook only once every three weeks, and the rest of the time, in the words of one wife, "you would just be chopping." Added to reduced labor demands were the material benefits of Sebiyam's growing involvement with commercial production. Wives remember being rewarded for their work sowing and harvesting rice, cotton, and tobacco: "As a wife, when he [Sebiyam] sells [cotton or tobacco], by all means [one] would get something out of it!" Sebiyam's prosperity as a farmer also provided ancillary benefits for domestic labor and budgeting. For example, when Sebiyam bought a grinding mill, wives did not have to "walk somewhere and pay someone" to grind grain.

Sebiyam's wives spent newly gained time and resources on a variety of trading ventures, many of which began to take off. One younger wife who married Sebiyam in the early 1970s recalls beginning to fry and sell doughnuts to Hausa fishermen at the riverside, eventually beginning to sell *kenkey* in Kpasenkpe (which she continues to do).[110] Other wives, both those who married Sebiyam in the 1970s or who came as young girls in the 1960s and came of age in this era, remember the market for *kenkey* in Kpasenkpe being so saturated by Sebiyam's wives that several junior wives went to find a market across the river in Kunkwa. Senior wives expanded and diversified their trading enterprises. One senior wife had long been selling *pito* (millet beer) out of the compound, but sometime in the 1960s and 1970s another began selling *akpeteshie*, an endeavor also taken up by some of the more junior wives. Women remember reinvesting their trading profits in their own ventures. Even those wives who had to travel to Kunkwa to sell *kenkey* recall a time of accumulation. One would buy millet and maize from farmers in Kunkwa with the money she collected, bringing it back to market in Kpasenkpe and to prepare her *kenkey* for the next day. Another participated in a *susu* rotational savings group, briefly setting up a similar arrangement among several of the younger wives. Recollecting her time selling *akpeteshie*, one wife laughed along with one of Sebiyam's children as they recalled the compound buzzing with activity from all of the "drunks" that would come to the house—so many, that Sebiyam eventually banned his wives from selling.[111] While selling *akpeteshie*, she said, she accrued significant profit, not just the small gains she acquired from selling food. She recounted accumulating decorative bowls so that, when people came to her room, they would know she had done well. At that time, she argued, trading was so good that displays of personal accumulation were expected: "If you didn't have them, people would insult you!"

Meanwhile, for Sebiyam's children, the promise of personal success became more tenuous even as more of them followed the path from school to state employment. In the late 1960s and 1970s, another two dozen of Sebiyam's children attended the Kpasenkpe primary school and then the Kpasenkpe middle school, which was opened in 1964. This cohort, unlike their senior siblings, entered the civil service during the political and economic volatility of the decades following the coup against Nkrumah. Nevertheless, networks among educated family members now mitigated the uncertainties of employment. Pawura and her husband had established a household in Walewale by the 1970s. Other siblings and uncles had households in Bolgatanga, Tamale, Damongo, and Bawku. Meanwhile, Nabila won a government scholarship to pursue a PhD in the United States, at Michigan State University, after which he returned to Ghana in 1974 to take a position as a lecturer at the University of Ghana, later becoming an MP for Walewale. Siblings, nieces, and nephews came to Accra to stay with him as well. In the elections following Rawlings's first coup in June of 1979, Dr. Nabila became minister for presidential affairs, a senior cabinet position in the government of Hilla Limann.[112] In addition to bringing Sebiyam's children to district and regional capitals, civil service jobs continued to bring some back to the Kpasenkpe area as agents of the state. For example, in 1978, when the Acheampong government began instituting continuation middle schools that would adapt educational curricula to what it perceived as the needs of rural areas, one senior son returned to Kpasenkpe as the headmaster, and another was posted to Kpasenkpe as a postal agent in 1977.[113] Another senior son argued that family members' visible ability to pursue careers in and out of Kpasenkpe served as an advertisement for schooling, but it also drove home the fact that it was the network of educated family members, not just the school itself, that allowed them to accumulate access to state employment at a time when it was in short supply.[114] Perhaps most strikingly, Sebiyam himself fades from these stories, appearing to advise or to support but rarely to direct the way that his children navigated the vicissitudes of the postnationalist era.

↬

Writing about the long 1970s, scholars of Ghana have argued that, in the absence of strong centralized government, citizens relied on local institutions of chieftaincy and civil society.[115] This chapter confirms that practices of government in the 1970s reduced the importance of particular, state-centered networks in accessing government services. Instead of seeing people fall back on stable or unchanging local institutions, however, it demonstrates that state agents, local leaders, and citizens were all engaged in the ever-messy, yet surprisingly vigorous process of determining what government could be and do. Through a widespread network of agricultural interventions, people made government policy part of some of their most crucial daily livelihood decisions. They formed new associations, organized self-help labor, and initiated claims on government resources, even as chiefs and officials continued to downplay or ignore the political nature of this work. The chief's family experimented with new modes of organization and connection that built on state-led development but also wove them into personal strategies for survival and accumulation. In the process, these actors breathed new life into colonial and nationalist models of leadership, development, and self-help, making them flexible frameworks for engaging the ever-changing and ever-multiplying set of institutions of government. As chapter 5 shows, these daily innovations established practices through which citizens could interpret and cope with the transformations of the neoliberal era.

5 ⤳ Project Village
Government by Village Work, 1982–92

> The need for continuous offer[s] of self-help and self-sacrifice
> toward the national good cannot be over-emphasized. You must
> work with other Non-Governmental and International Agen-
> cies to uplift your own social image . . . and free [your]selves of
> mental slavery and the erroneous thinking that there is somebody
> somewhere known as Government . . . [which] comes out to dish
> out gifts to the people.[1]

AFTER YEARS of gazing at television and newspaper images from
"famine-stricken Africa," a donor in the US or the UK in the mid-1980s
might have reached for the phone to sponsor a child through World Vision
International.[2] The generic image of a starving African child in the sponsor's head might likely have been from the widely photographed famine
camps in Ethiopia, but by 1986 or 1987 the child's picture, when it arrived,
might be from northern Ghana—might, indeed, be from Kpasenkpe.[3]
The note attached might further inform the sponsor that their funds were
designated not just for that child but instead for community development
initiatives in their village as a whole. The sponsor might not notice either
of these substitutions. Staff at World Vision International fundraising offices, in turn, looked at the donations streaming in from such sponsors and
saw something different: an opportunity to leverage Christian compassion
into "transformational" development in communities across what they
called the "Two-Thirds World."[4] Recently reorganized to integrate child
sponsorship and relief work with a professionalized development agenda,
World Vision International was, like a number of other nongovernmental
organizations (NGOs) with projects in Africa, poised to take advantage of
the concurrent outpouring of popular interest in famine relief and the imposition of an international development agenda that slashed government
budgets and funneled resources into NGOs. Meanwhile, in northern

Ghana, educated professionals who considered their job prospects in light of their personal convictions and ambitions (not to mention a shrinking pool of civil service jobs) might have seen working for World Vision as an opportunity to marry their work with their faith, to find an alternative to the civil service, or to be closer to their families. They might obtain a copy of World Vision's magazine *Together*, read debates about the nature and purpose of development alongside critiques of global and local inequality, and see themselves as part of a community of motivated Christian activists who would help Ghana's villages.[5] An individual sponsor, a World Vision policy maker, and a local World Vision staff member may have differed profoundly in their vision of development, but they agreed on a couple of things. They hoped that what they were doing would, indeed, transform development. And they truly believed that it was new.

Looking out from northern Ghana's villages, as residents greeted visitors from World Vision (and Oxfam, and CIDA, and others), the view could be quite different. Some of what this new crop of developers brought did seem new. But, for the most part, despite differences in funder, ideology, and focus, village projects looked quite similar, not only to one another but also to past initiatives. In this frame, it was not Africa's children or the villages of the global South that seemed interchangeable but rather the funders themselves. This chapter opens with an image of World Vision not because it was unique but because it happened to be the organization that, in the 1980s, identified Kpasenkpe as a site for a multiyear and multipronged community development initiative. Like countless other NGOs and donors that began to flood into northern Ghana and like decades of government officials that preceded them, agents from World Vision framed their work as village development. They decided which local groups and individuals to work with, building relationships that were increasingly cast as "partnership." They, yet again, asked for local labor, now increasingly framed as "participation." What was truly new about these projects would only emerge with time and repetition, as residents of Kpasenkpe and across the region came to see that piecemeal, project-based development would be the primary basis of rural statecraft in the emerging neoliberal order.

As in previous decades, Ghana in the 1980s was a "pacesetter" for political economic trends across Africa. In 1983, it became one of the first states to accept the World Bank and IMF-enforced policy reversals known as "structural adjustment," which made it a condition of lending that governments across the global South follow a neoliberal agenda of market liberalization, reductions in public sector spending, and civil service retrenchment.[6] The resulting influx of organizations like World Vision put Ghana as a whole, and northern Ghana in particular, on the leading edge of another hallmark of the era: the rapid rise of NGO involvement in African development. This two-pronged reversal in previous patterns of state-led development, in which governments were thrust out of interventionist roles at the same time that new extragovernmental institutions took them up, has generated a wide variety of studies on the practice of small-scale rural development in the 1980s and 1990s. In northern Togo, Charles Piot shows how rural citizens navigated both the material and affective implications of rapidly multiplying and often ephemeral NGO initiatives.[7] In the Gambia, Richard Schroeder shows how rural livelihoods could be upended by abrupt shifts in NGO focus, as when in the mid-1980s the popularity of agroforestry as a means to "sustainable development" swiftly undercut what had been an NGO-supported boom in women's gardening.[8] In northern Tanzania, in contrast, Dorothy Hodgson shows how NGO initiatives encouraged Maasai leaders to rearticulate long-standing gendered images of timeless Maasai pastoral livelihoods.[9] With the prominent exception of Hodgson's work on Tanzania, scholars of development in Africa have tended to study the neoliberal era on its own, rarely tracing processes of change and continuity that link the period to the twentieth century as a whole.[10] This chapter, in contrast, shows how residents and officials shaped, navigated, and made sense of neoliberal development by improvising on patterns of state engagement from previous decades.

As food agriculture receded from the national spotlight and as structural adjustment policies further entrenched northern Ghana's status as a hinterland of development planning, local officials turned to NGOs and donor programs to fund small-scale development projects. The "rollback of the state" in northern Ghana could thus require quite a bit of energy on the part of government agents who worked to coordinate and facilitate external funding and deal with its contradictions. Local officials and NGO staff scouted sites and identified target villages for funders who treated villages as interchangeable sites for projects, creating a political economy of scarcity and competition. Meanwhile, a variety of actors in Kpasenkpe reinvigorated its role as a "project village," a place that developers repeatedly saw as an attractive site for projects. Local organizers from the Assemblies of God church acted as World Vision's "hosts" and "landlords," a role forged by Wulugunaba Sebiyam in the 1950s and 1960s and, before that, by the first wave of progressive chiefs like Sandemnaab Azantilow. Kpasenkpe residents responded to calls for unremunerated labor and helped to down-play local political wrangling over projects, cognizant of the threat that projects would disappear if labor extraction could not be packaged as local support. As in previous decades, local actors struggled to define the possibilities and limitations of self-help, but as projects came and went, and as it became increasingly clear that they would be the only game in town, the possibility of using local labor to make larger claims on the state receded farther into the distance. Meanwhile, for some Kpasenkpe residents, including members of the chief's family, village development projects that were conceived by funders as isolated and local were deeply bound up in regional and national networks, playing key roles in careers that spanned decades and crossed regional and institutional boundaries.

REVOLUTION ON A SHOESTRING

As Paul Nugent points out, Ghana in the early 1980s was an "unlikely candidate" to become Africa's emblem of structural adjustment reform.[11] A final round of coups, both by Jerry John Rawlings in 1979 and 1981, brought Rawlings' self-styled revolutionary Provisional National Defense Council (PNDC) into power. In addition to the ongoing economic and fiscal problems from the 1970s, the PNDC was soon facing additional crises, including large-scale droughts in 1982–83 and a massive resettlement of over a million Ghanaian migrants who were expelled from Nigeria in January 1983.[12] In dire need of foreign exchange and emergency funding, the Rawlings regime acceded to demands of international lenders by devaluing the Ghanaian currency and adopting of series of reforms in its 1983 and 1987 Economic Recovery Programmes (ERPs) that aimed to "stabilize, rehabilitate, and liberalize" the Ghanaian economy.[13] The ERPs slashed government payrolls and services, instituted user fees for health and education, and defunded agricultural programs, particularly those aimed at food production.[14]

A central tension of the PNDC government, then, was its attempt to maintain its popular appeal and revolutionary image while implementing structural adjustment reforms. In both the self-proclaimed "house-cleaning" coup of June 4, 1979, and the "revolution" of December 31, 1981, Rawlings had promised not only to address the economic and fiscal crises of the 1970s but to do so by reshaping the terms and mechanisms of political participation in Ghana. Eschewing electoral politics as "sham democracy," the PNDC set up alternate structures of local governance—starting with the establishment of "People's Defense Committees" and "Workers

Defense Committees" and later turning to the more ominous sounding "Mobisquads," "Committees for the Defense of the Revolution" (CDRs), and "People's Militia"—which were called collectively the "revolutionary organs" and their members the "cadres."[15] The Rawlings revolution sought to build national government on a coalition of "small boys" who had, for the most part, been excluded from formal politics since the early Nkrumah era, and who had suffered most from the economic crises of the 1970s: urban workers, students, and lower-ranking military officials.[16] After the adoption of structural adjustment plans, the regime's populist rhetoric was continually challenged by the social and economic effects of neoliberal reforms, which threatened the economic prospects of many of those who the regime had initially galvanized.[17] The political necessity of mobilizing new constituencies competed with a perennial shortage of fiscal resources to meet their needs and demands.

Rural northern Ghana was positioned to feel particularly acute effects of structural adjustment policies.[18] While the effects of 1970s agricultural subsidies on small-scale farmers in northern Ghana were far from uniformly positive, the abolition of subsidies and collapse of extension services in the mid-1980s made these inputs more difficult for smallholders to obtain and use.[19] More broadly, a national reorientation away from promoting food agriculture once again placed Ghana's northern regions on the periphery of national development planning. To many people in the North, and particularly to civil servants who worked with farmers, the important dividing line for the Rawlings era was not the 1981 coup nor the adoption of structural adjustment in 1983 but rather the gradual elimination of agricultural funding over the course of the 1980s, culminating in what several former Ministry of Agriculture staff refer to as the "collapse of Agric" in the late 1980s.[20]

Even in small settlements like Kpasenkpe, the revolutionary ambitions of the Rawlings government came into direct conflict with its fiscal policies. Rawlings's coups could not be said to have had revolutionary implications in Kpasenkpe (they did not, as Nugent terms it, "ignite" any "combustible social material"), but, at least at first, the PNDC's program of "people's power" deemphasized the chief's role and elevated leaders in Kpasenkpe whose support the Rawlings regime would have welcomed— "small boys," or people often referred to as "youth."[21] However, the disintegration of state funding structures for agriculture, public works, and services meant that the PNDC cadres in Kpasenkpe soon found themselves unable to play a meaningful role in the delivery of state services.[22]

Both critics and supporters of Rawlings in Kpasenkpe emphasize that the PNDC was not "interested" in development. While the Rawlings regime made occasional gestures toward mobilizing communal labor, the cadres, like their counterparts in the district and regional civil service, were unable to command any significant national funding. The farming and fishing groups organized in the 1970s continued to exist on paper, but in practice residents either remember that "nothing" was happening with them or that cadre leaders took what little funding they supplied.[23] One resident told me bluntly that, while during the 1970s the government was helping farmers, by the 1980s they were simply "doing their own farming."[24]

THE NGO-IFICATION OF STATECRAFT
IN THE NEOLIBERAL NORTH

Over the course of the 1980s, as government officials felt the brunt of reductions in public sector funding, they began to rely on NGOs and international donors to undertake small-scale development projects. Paul Nugent summarizes the multiple forces that resulted in the proliferation and growing influence of Northern NGOs in Africa in the 1980s and 1990s, including increased international interest in (and funding for) humanitarian relief, donors' increasing interest in channeling funding through nonstate actors, and governments' own needs to replace services cut under neoliberal austerity measures.[25] All of these factors were at play in Ghana, and analysts have charted the rapid rise of NGOs in late twentieth-century Ghana—from 10 registered in 1960 to 350 in 1991 (and ballooning to nearly 4,500 by 2009).[26] The relative poverty of northern Ghana made it a particular focus for donors and NGOs. Lynne Brydon and Karen Legge point out that the regional capital of Tamale was the "obvious choice for the converging of international aid agencies" as well as a variety of nongovernmental organizations, local and international.[27]

Meanwhile, by the mid-1980s, the World Bank and IMF were themselves under pressure to address some of the most obvious detrimental livelihood effects of structural adjustment. Ghana became the first African country to implement a program under the new World Bank policy to address the "Social Dimensions of Adjustment" and put forward "adjustment with a human face." In 1987 the government launched the donor-supported "Program of Actions to Mitigate the Social Costs of Adjustment" (PAMSCAD).[28] PAMSCAD aimed to "enhance the sustainability and acceptability of the Economic Recovery Programme" by starting programs to assist those (like farmers, the unemployed, the North, and the poor) that were said to have been most hurt by the ERPs.[29] While PAMSCAD was administered by the Ghanaian government, it operated by channeling donor funds into a series of project-based initiatives and donor-funded initiatives and looked, for all intents and purposes, like other donor or NGO projects.[30]

Because of its focus on reducing the public sector, the neoliberal turn in African development policy often lends itself to descriptions of state withdrawal or absence. Scholars have been quick to point out, however, that neoliberalism has required quite a bit of statecraft.[31] By the mid-1980s in Mamprusi District, the PNDC government had come to rely programmatically on NGOs and international donors to fund a variety of small-scale public works projects. District administrative documents reveal this shift most dramatically in their accounts of the funding and implementation of village projects in the period. A list of "self-help projects completed and ongoing 1986–1989," for example, includes forty-two projects (twenty-four classrooms and day care, eight boreholes, three clinics, four assorted building projects, two small-scale agricultural projects, and one project for road repair). Of these, twenty received funding from NGOs (including eight from World Vision and six from a Canadian-funded initiative called NORRIP), nine were funded locally by village development committees, and only six are listed as being organized by the Department of Community Development or the newly created District Council.[32]

Former district staff members remembered the pervasive dependence on outside funding. A former staff member of the National Mobilization Programme (NMP), which grew out of the relief efforts of 1981–83 and then became the de facto development ministry of the PNDC, described the organization's antideforestation work in West Mamprusi almost exclusively in reference to the donor agencies and NGOs with whom he had worked. They wanted community members to contribute labor for tree planting, he explained, but it was difficult to get them to come out, "because we had nothing to give them." As a result, he applied to a variety of NGOs and donors, eventually securing support from a food-for-work grant from the Adventist Relief Agency (ADRA), an organization of the Seventh-Day Adventist Church.[33] District records confirm that by the late 1980s, donor funding requests constituted a significant portion of NMP activity.[34] For example, in 1985 the NMP plan for district development listed World Vision, NORRIP, and "local contributions" as the primary sources of funding for projects.[35] To get a broader sense of where this NGO interaction fit in the daily work of a district official, I inquired about the budget from the national government. "Ha!" the former NMP official laughed. "There was no budget!" There was only "community work through NGOs and voluntary labor." As a result, much of his daily work centered on interactions with NGOs, including ADRA, World Vision, and UNICEF. That is why, when describing his work, he said that he was "always doing project proposals."[36]

As government officials scrambled to piece together funding for local projects, they found themselves contending directly with the tensions and contradictions of village development work as it was practiced by NGOs and international donors in the early neoliberal era. With the exception of the World Bank's nod toward the "social dimensions of adjustment," discussions of village projects and self-help were nearly absent from the mainstream structural adjustment project in the 1980s.[37] However, in the realm of project-based rural development, the 1980s saw the ascendance of "participation" as a tenet of mainstream development discourse and project design.[38] Discourses of participation drew from diverse global intellectual strains, including those, like models of participatory action research emerging from the global South, that sought to use participatory processes to challenge structures of oppression and redefine the terms of political participation.[39] However, particularly when it was taken up by donors and northern NGOs, participation quickly and frequently lost its political valence, rendering it a "technical method of project work rather than [a] political methodology."[40]

Writing on the Northern Regional Rural Integrated Programme (NORRIP), one of the flagship development projects of the 1980s, Karl Botchway argues that projects in northern Ghana took up the rhetoric of "participation" and "empowerment" that pervaded international discourses and used them to fit multiple and often conflicting goals, many of which had little to do with the interests or ideas of rural constituents.[41] Planners focused on asking local people to contribute time, labor, and money to projects whose vision and parameters were largely predetermined and then used these structures to save money and to avoid fundamental questions about local hierarchies and the structural position of northern communities in regional and national economies. Ultimately, he argues, the structures of community participation rendered "villagers . . . simply a resource for development."[42]

District documents reveal the contradictions officials navigated under these circumstances. On March 16, 1989, the Ministry of Local Government in Accra sent a telegraph message to all regional secretaries about a World Bank/PAMSCAD program to fund eight "Community Initiative Projects," or "CIPs," in each district in the country. In its telegraph, the Ministry of Local Government specified that these projects should be "feasible simple projects nearing completion" that would receive between 100,000 and 1 million cedis to be completed in three to six months. Projects could include a range of activities under the village development rubric: "primary school or JSS blocks, health posts, KVIPs, latrines, hand dug wells, desilting of dams, planting of woodlots, and repair of access roads."[43] Along with the telegraph, the ministry sent a form that district officials could fill out, which had lines for each "amount spent by community" and a "remarks" section for discussions of labor and levies.

Two weeks later, PNDC district secretaries across the Northern Region received the PAMSCAD Secretariat's "Guidelines and Criteria for Selection of PAMSCAD CIPs." The criteria from the PAMSCAD Secretariat set out a minefield of conflicting goals and demands. At the outset, the PAMSCAD Secretariat indicated its intention to fund "self-help projects initiated by communities themselves" that were in the late stages of completion. At the same time, reflecting PAMSCAD's mandate to narrowly target those most effected by structural adjustment (even in regions where the effects of austerity and privatization were widespread), the secretariat indicated that projects should focus on the "most vulnerable communities." The secretariat foisted the problem of their uncomfortably matched goals onto local officials, who were tasked with simultaneously focusing on the neediest communities and finding places where local residents could spare time and money for projects. "Priority must be given to the poorest communities," they wrote, "especially those that are prepared to make the greatest contribution to voluntary labor and/or cash to a particular project." Similarly, the PAMSCAD Secretariat specified that communities should "select and initiate" their own projects, but it listed only seven types of projects that would be considered for funding. With apparently no sense of irony, the memo asserted that the project was designed to "help . . . in the most flexible and nonbureaucratic way possible."[44]

While both the sophistication and absurdity of the bureaucratic slight-of-hand in this document are notable, the process that they outline would have been legible, and even familiar, to those involved in village development in the district. Sometimes lost in debates about the recent mainstreaming of "participation," are the ways that, in places like northern Ghana, much of what new projects required fit into longer-standing patterns of hinterland statecraft that had, for decades, relied on

FIGURE 5.1. A childcare center under construction, 1991. Photo by Clement Zori, courtesy of the Ministry of Information, Ghana, Information Services Photographic Library, Ref. no PD/410/31.

unremunerated labor and treated villages as interchangeable. District officials and local organizers navigated donor and NGO requirements by drawing on existing practices and, yet again, tested the possibilities of a new development order.

Because the version of participation that NGOs and international donors put forward was familiar, district officials could readily assimilate demands for labor into their existing work. PAMSCAD wanted to fund only eight CIPs per district, so the task for district officials was to figure out which existing initiatives could be packaged to fit the criteria. PAMSCAD's criteria fit into patterns officials had already established to cope with declining government coffers and a proliferation of NGOs. In the months after the CIP memo was circulated, Mamprusi District files show how readily district officials identified projects and, conversely, how little effort the PAMSCAD Secretariat put into ensuring that these projects met the complex web of criteria it had put forward. On April 18 of that same year, PNDC District Secretary and District Administrative Officer A. K. Obeng forwarded to the regional administrative officer a succinct plan of action written by District Community Development Officer Ali Mintabah that outlined four priority areas of action (adult education, self-help construction, hand-dug wells, and home science activities) and identified eleven projects—six school-building projects, one day care, one teachers' quarters, two clinics, and one hand-dug wells project—that he felt met criteria for PAMSCAD funding. In each case, the projects were undertaken with "community involvement" in the form of labor and small contributions, as well as "technical assistance" from the Department of Community Development or others. From marginal notes on Mintabah's list, it seems that the regional administrative officer simply selected eight of the eleven projects for inclusion in the district's application for PAMSCAD funds.[45] Nor was PAMSCAD funding the only game in town, for in fact the CIP project coincided with an unrelated project funded by the Canadian government, in which the "Canadian Fund for Local Initiative" similarly asked districts to identify projects that would match donor funding for materials with local offers of communal labor.[46]

For the variety of local actors who had begun to petition government for local projects in the 1970s, the influx of donors brought new audiences for old strategies of turning participation into demands on the state. Some petitioners continued to appeal to government agents directly, as when the Wungu Town Development Committee wrote to the Ghana Highways Authority in August of 1985 to inform them that "the people ha[d] been mobilized" to repair the Wungu-Walewale road and to ask for materials, or when the Diani Town Development Committee asked the Department of Community Development to provide roofing materials for a school project, promising that the sixty-five hundred potential beneficiaries were "also in the front line to provide communal labor."[47] Other petitioners, however, recognized the increasing dependence of local government officials on outside funding. For example, in February of 1988, town development committees paired with CDR officials in Shelinova and Wungu to appeal to World Vision directly for boreholes, arguing in each case that "it is therefore our hope that World Vision International" would "come to our aid to save our lives."[48] By 1989, town development committee leaders in Walewale and Wungu simply filled out and attached the form for PAMSCAD assistance that had been sent to district officials from the PAMSCAD Secretariat, suggesting that the processes of requesting projects and offering community contributions had been routinized on the local level as well as by district officials.[49] Government agents and local leaders alike required local labor as a way to satisfy outside funders' needs for "participation" and to allow continued "partnership" between PNDC agents and new outside funders. For rural residents, it was likely increasingly clear that labor was the currency with which villages would attract projects.

PROJECT VILLAGE: LANDLORDS AND LABOR
IN A WORLD VISION COMMUNITY DEVELOPMENT INITIATIVE

By the mid-1980s, a few of the numerous NGOs active in the Mamprusi District initiated projects in and around Kpasenkpe. A NORRIP borehole in Kpasenkpe is listed on the 1985 National Mobilisation Programme for the district, and several boreholes now present in Kpasenkpe were, according to residents, constructed by Oxfam in the early 1980s. World Vision International, meanwhile, had begun work on schools in the nearby village of Wulugu.[50] In Kpasenkpe, there were plenty of experienced organizers and participants for NGOs to work with, as the Amasachina group continued and, even without government support, farming and fishing groups remained organized, if not particularly active.[51] The Kpasenkpe Town Development Committee, never particularly prominent in town, began initiating school construction and the construction of a Farm Services Center.[52] Then, between 1986 and 1994, World Vision International began a comprehensive village development project in Kpasenkpe, working primarily with members of the local Assemblies of God church. The project funded the construction of a kindergarten and primary school, a middle school, teacher's quarters, a guesthouse, several boreholes and began work on a community center. It also distributed occasional food aid and sponsored local children they identified as "the poorest of the poor." Not since the late colonial period had there been so much construction of small-scale public works in town.[53] As in the district as a whole, residents of Kpasenkpe engaged with World Vision by improvising on existing patterns of state engagement.

World Vision was founded in the 1950s as an American evangelical organization that funded missionary orphanages in Asia, but by the late 1970s it had grown to include donor offices in Canada, Australia, New Zealand, and South Africa and had "field" offices in countries around the globe. The heart of World Vision's funding model was child sponsorship, in which individual donations were earmarked, directly or indirectly, for the care of a particular child about whom sponsors would get updates and with whom they might correspond.[54] The organization's rapid growth in the 1970s was spurred by successful television campaigns that circulated images of starving Africans and encouraged sponsors to personalize their relationship to poverty and Christian humanitarianism. The messages sponsors received were at once specific, in that they focused sponsorship on one child in a particular place, and also generalized, in that they promoted a depoliticized and homogenized image of the global South.[55]

World Vision's growth relied on selling funders a simplified vision of global poverty, but, as it grew, the organization went through a variety of changes that reflected its growing ideological, theological, and geographic diversity. In the 1960s and 1970s, the organization's leadership sought to professionalize its ranks and gain legitimacy as a development organization that would be authorized to receive grants from the US government and international agencies. In 1978, the organization reorganized its board to form World Vision International, a move that gave immediate representation to all of the donor countries and provided a pathway for future representation from "field" offices in the global South. Decentralized decision making allowed both donor and field offices to exercise some autonomy over programming.[56] As a result, when World Vision began work in Ghana in the late 1970s, it relied heavily on Ghanaian staff to both plan and implement development projects under the umbrella of World Vision's agenda.

To reconcile its commitments to child sponsorship and evangelism with its growing interest in development work in the early 1980s, World Vision instituted a policy of pairing child sponsorship with Christian-led community development efforts by pooling resources from sponsors in each recipient community and using some of the funds to support small-scale projects.[57] Small-scale projects and community involvement became the focus of the organization's emerging model of "transformational" development, which embraced increasingly popular models of participatory development from secular development theorists like Robert Chambers alongside its foundational ideas of Christian community and evangelism.[58] In this idealized process, World Vision imagined that community members' contributions of time and labor in meetings and workshops would not only produce a plan but would engender a new affective relationship to development itself, summed up in the idea of "ownership."[59] As community members began to create and "own" the plan, they were then expected to offer local labor as a solution to practical problems, seeing community contributions of labor as readily available "resources" that could substitute for more expensive or politically difficult solutions. World Vision agents were thus encouraged to see unpaid labor as both a tool for development and as evidence that it was working, a costless "win-win" that conveniently avoided questions of how, why, and by whom such labor would be done.

World Vision's work in northern Ghana began in earnest in response to the 1982–83 drought, when World Vision Ghana began emergency food relief campaigns and initiated the Ghana Rural Water Project, which dug boreholes across the country.[60] On the heels of these large-scale initiatives, they then elaborated a more regularized program of child sponsorship and community development in the North.[61] Professionals who wanted to work in the region found in NGOs like World Vision a path to employment in the face of a shrinking civil service. Mahama Tampuri had been sent to the colonial primary school in Gambaga as a young man and had risen through the ranks of the education service so that, by the 1970s, he was stationed in the regional administration in Tamale. While his cohort had been politicized in the nationalist era—joining the NPP or CPP in roughly equal proportions—by the 1970s a number of paths to success were possible in and out of politics. Some, like prominent politician Mumuni Bawumia, were successful at riding out the political vicissitudes of the 1970s, but others, like Tampuri, assiduously avoided making potentially damaging political connections, in his case by finding a path through commitment to the civil service and through his long-standing connection to the Anglican Church.

In 1983, Tampuri had recently moved from a secure position in the central regional administration to a more junior role in the district capital of Walewale, in order to settle family affairs after the death of his wife's father. World Vision's food relief efforts seem to have appealed not just to his sense of Christian charity but to his desire to find transparency, intellectual rigor, and local commitment in the work that he did.[62] To ascertain food relief needs in the Northern Region, he and his colleagues conducted an informal survey of farmers throughout the region, to "see how the farmers were" and "find out really where the shortages were," instead of "imposing [food relief] on the area without asking." After working in these crisis-relief efforts, Tampuri was invited to stay on with the organization as it set up community development projects in the Northern Region. As a project leader, and then after his promotion to project manager for the Northern Region, he participated in and oversaw the selection of locations and partners for community development work.[63]

When Tampuri and other World Vision agents arrived in Kpasenkpe in 1987, an obvious starting point was the Assemblies of God church.

Established in the early years of Sebiyam's chieftaincy by missionaries from Walewale, the Assemblies of God had remained the center of Christian religious life in Kpasenkpe. The Assemblies of God church was an institution associated with but not dominated by the chiefly family in Kpasenkpe. The church had also maintained a hand in village development work, beginning with the Mass Education literacy and building projects of the 1950s. Pastor Daniel Barijesira Azundow, the Wulugunaba's brother and the church's first pastor in the 1940s, returned to Kpasenkpe in the 1980s to become the church's pastor again. At the time, he was in his early sixties and had pursued a varied career in the northern city of Bolgatanga, where he worked in public health initiatives, ran a photography studio, launched his children into professional careers, and remained active at the regional headquarters of the Assemblies of God.[64] To Pastor Azundow and others, the World Vision project was an extension of the church's previous activities in town, part of their evangelism efforts in the wider area.[65] Sebiyam was, by all reports, a strong supporter of World Vision's work, but he did not run it.[66] Similarly, many PNDC activists in town were church members, but none was in a position of authority in World Vision's work.[67]

Pastor Azundow described the church's relationship with World Vision as that of host, or landlord, rather than client of an outside agency. The church, he argued, was "like their [World Vision's] landlords, so they came to stay in our [the church's] house. So all of the things [they brought], they would come and put them in this place [the church]." As Kpasenkpe residents recount it, local initiative is what brought World Vision to town. Pastor Azundow recalls that his relationship with World Vision came out of connections he had made in his career and not his relationship with the Wulugunaba. He remembers hearing about World Vision from two sources: his brother B. B. Wahaga, a teacher and friend of Tampuri; and from his colleagues at the Assemblies of God church in the nearby town of Wulugu.[68] One of Pastor Azundow's nephews remembers seeing World Vision's work in Wulugu, where he was working as a teacher, and encouraging his uncle and other relations to agitate for World Vision to come to Kpasenkpe.

It is worth dwelling, for a moment, on how different this narrative is from the language of participation and partnership offered by World Vision, in which local "partners" were taught to "own" local development only through participatory processes led by the NGO itself.[69] Instead, as landlords, the church listened to what World Vision agents like Tampuri were offering as well as what they required, and they made a plan. The church first created a local World Vision organizing body, the Central Committee, which consisted solely of members of the Assemblies of God and had Pastor Azundow as its chairman. For distribution of relief items, Pastor Azundow explained how Tampuri and other regional staff would "just bring them to my yard here . . . [and] the people would come and we would disburse them." Pastor Azundow remembered that this structure reaffirmed the church's centrality and insulated World Vision's work from the official structures of PNDC government. Locally, because the cadre members were not church elders, he argued that they could be involved but not "up to where we [the Central Committee] are." Furthermore, because World Vision brought food aid "straight to the spot [Kpasenkpe]" rather than relying on the district government, it avoided what Pastor Azundow saw as the inevitable kickbacks that district officials might extract.[70]

The role of host when distributing aid was rather straightforward, but when it came to community development projects the work could often be more complex. Tampuri described the process by which he negotiated the extent and focus of World Vision activity in a community as "lead[ing] them to arrive at what they want, and what is possible." In a series of meetings, first with chiefs, elders, and other local hosts, then with larger groups of constituents, World Vision staff would create a list of community desires and then describe the list of activities that World Vision would be able to help them undertake—primarily drilling wells, building schools and other buildings, and small-scale agricultural projects. Tampuri would tell residents that World Vision would give them support for eight years, so they should think of projects that could be completed within that time. For example, he might have to dissuade projects—"such as a Post Office"— that were outside of the realm of the possible.[71] Thus, as World Vision's hosts in Kpasenkpe, the Central Committee helped identify projects that fit the organization's portfolio, much as district officials worked to identify projects that fit particular donor criteria.

After projects were defined, hosts like Kpasenkpe's Central Committee had to then deliver on the organization's primary demand of village labor. Pastor Azundow recalled the Central Committee's work raising labor as part of a local process of innovation, in which they drew on existing scripts and mechanisms of organization pioneered in earlier decades of development practice. Pastor Azundow and other committee members needed to mobilize "participation" by church members and nonmembers alike. To do this, they looked to reinvigorate the practice of self-help labor in Kpasenkpe. Structurally, their organization of labor recalled the Wulu-gunaba's previous efforts to systematically require labor from households for both *nayiri kpaariba* and village development. Creating a second organizational structure, dubbed a "Council of Elders," the Central Committee identified leaders, both Christians and non-Christians, from each of six "sections" in town, which they created by subdividing each of the three existing sections or quarters (*fɔŋŋu*).[72] The leaders of these sections were charged with raising a contribution of one labor day per week from each farm household in the section for the duration of any World Vision project (usually several weeks). Six sections meant that Kpasenkpe residents were called out in six one-day shifts per week, followed by a worship service on Sundays. The Council of Elders avoided fully aligning development labor collections with recognition of chiefly authority or of the PNDC cadres, but they often partnered with both. Sometimes they would ask the Wulugunaba to call laborers, while at other times the PNDC cadres would "mobilize" workers to participate.[73] At still other times, World Vision would call for labor by relying on the skills of individual members of the Council of Elders.[74]

As in previous decades, however, the meanings that Kpasenkpe residents attached to labor were as diverse as the official concepts of self-help to which they responded. Like in the hospital project of the 1970s, residents recall that section leaders relied on a variety of labor mobilization strategies. Men and women would be requested for different tasks—women frequently remember carrying water. For the most part, residents do not describe contributions being particularly onerous, and many discuss the project with a sense of pride in local initiative. When describing why they contributed labor to World Vision development projects, Kpasenkpe residents often used the terminology of "help" (*suŋŋi*). As in the 1950s and 1960s, and with the hospital project of the 1970s, residents argued that World Vision had come to *suŋŋi ti* ("help us"), and so it was necessary to *suŋŋi ba* ("help them").[75]

Organizers were able to enforce labor extraction without the frequent explicit use of force or punishment. One World Vision organizer mentioned that the Central Committee retained the right to fine anyone who refused to contribute labor, but, at least in retrospect, it was difficult to find anyone who remembered fines being used with any regularity.[76] If we are attentive to the structure of World Vision's work, however, it becomes easier to see how coercion need not have been exercised at the level of individuals. Structurally, collective demands for labor were backed by the collective threat that World Vision could always take its resources elsewhere. Across the region, Tampuri recalls pairing labor demands with explicit warnings that he could always "close the project" if there were any "problems."[77]

The institution of unpaid development labor was a way for World Vision to cut costs and become "sustainable," but it was also their key measure of local support. When I asked how the organization chose village projects to fund, Tampuri described a process of identifying several towns and setting up introductory goal-setting meetings. Over the course of a few visits, Tampuri argued, you "can tell if the people are united." Asking for examples, I tried to gauge to what extent this perception of "unity" hinged on the power of specific authority figures—chiefs or church leaders. Instead, I was surprised to hear Tampuri describe towns in which World Vision had found "unity" despite long-standing local disputes or a lack of strong local Christian institutions. Instead of appealing to a sense of cohesion under leaders, he defined "unity" almost exclusively in relation to the ease and economy with which residents of a town could meet World Vision's demands for labor.[78]

As Kelsall and Mercer argue based on their research on World Vision Tanzania in the 1990s, the organization's emphasis on participation and empowerment often "equivocate[d] on the question" of whether it was interested in individual or community transformation. Reading individual labor contributions as evidence of community empowerment regardless of how they were mobilized, the organization effectively downplayed local hierarchies and assumed community homogeneity.[79] More broadly, organizations like World Vision insisted on reading local labor as a representation of support for development that was neatly circumscribed in a local arena, rather than creating new mechanisms for Kpasenkpe residents to make claims in political and economic orders. In World Vision's view, Kpasenkpe residents were expected to contribute development labor because of "unity" and a desire to "lead themselves." But the organization's idea of where this work would lead was limited by its vision of "what was possible" in development—small-scale, "sustainable" projects that Kpasenkpe residents would have to work to retain.

"IT WILL BY ALL MEANS COME TO THIS HOUSE": FAMILY CONNECTIONS, EXPERTISE, AND HARDSHIP IN THE NEOLIBERAL ERA

Looking at World Vision's tenure in Kpasenkpe illustrates how neoliberal village projects relied on local innovation and improvisation, even as they drew on long-standing patterns of labor extraction and limited the explicit connections that residents could make to wider political and social orders. A look at the chiefly family helps demonstrate how decades of accumulated experience and networks with the state allowed certain Kpasenkpe residents to weather the vicissitudes of the 1980s by making village work part of careers that had taken them away from Kpasenkpe in the past.

The economic instabilities of the 1980s played out for different Sebiyam family members in ways that reflected the relationships with the state that had been cultivated in previous decades. A period of decline and contraction on Sebiyam's farms came, as it did for many Kpasenkpe farmers, with the reductions in state agricultural support during the structural adjustment era. Sebiyam's commercial rice farm in Katigri appears to have continued production into the mid-1980s, helped in part by his acquisition of a combine harvester in 1979–81. While Katigri is less than twenty kilometers away from Kpasenkpe, the rainy season made roads difficult to travel, and full-time management of the farm meant that family members would be away from Kpasenkpe for weeks at a time. Pastor Azundow returned to Kpasenkpe in part to help run the Katigri farm, along with one of Sebiyam's sons who had just started his teaching career. For at least a few years, this enterprise seemed like a sustainable career path, and the son recalls with pride that the second year he drove the combine harvester they harvested over twelve hundred bags of rice.[80]

As state agricultural funding declined over the course of the 1980s, however, even Sebiyam's expansions in farming began to erode. These contractions hit especially hard on Sebiyam's wives and the brothers whose livelihoods were most bound up in the farming enterprise. When speaking about the eventual decline of Sebiyam's farming enterprise, family members told stories that referenced the decline of government support for agriculture and its concurrence with Sebiyam's own aging.[81] The collapse of government marketing mechanisms seems to have been particularly devastating. While Sebiyam remained able to access improved inputs on a private basis, family members recall the 1980s as a time in which "the Agric people stopped coming in a timely way" to buy tobacco, cotton, and, eventually, rice as well. The decline of Sebiyam's commercial rice farm closed the possibility that Sebiyam's educated sons would take up farming as a career path and, instead, other relatives were left to preside over an increasingly precarious enterprise of feeding members of the family who remained in town.

In the face of these hardships, the fortunes of Sebiyam's junior and senior wives began to diverge in relation to their children's success in professional life. Wives who had married Sebiyam in the 1940s and 1950s began to reach old age and "retire" from domestic work, and many of their oldest children's success in civil service professions seems to have softened the effects of the family's hardships. However, for younger wives, particularly those married as young girls in the 1960s, the 1980s brought rapid changes in fortune. Women with younger children shouldered the consequences of farming's decline, particularly with regard to feeding their children. While more senior wives remember that Sebiyam "would not allow" them to have their own plots, wives that Sebiyam married in the 1960s and 1970s recall that in his old age it was necessary to begin farming on their own.[82] Like other Kpasenkpe residents, these women struggled with farming in the 1980s, and their farming stories reflect increasing desperation. Unlike Sebiyam's brothers who established their own farms in the 1960s and 1970s, by the time that wives began farming for themselves in the 1980s they could not rely on Sebiyam for access to fertilizer or tractor services. Instead, they relied on their own resources, using money from trading to hire labor and tractors or bullocks.[83]

Meanwhile, even for educated family members, the future seemed less certain in the early 1980s.[84] Budgetary shortfalls and austerity policies caused the availability and desirability of civil service jobs to drop sharply.[85] At the same time, the ascension to national prominence of the Wulugunaba's senior son, Dr. Nabila, was followed by an abrupt fall when Rawlings' second coup in 1981 dissolved the government of Hilla Limann, in which he was serving as a senior minister. After the coup, Dr. Nabila spent three years in political detention. For some educated Sebiyam siblings and children, the Rawlings coup and Dr. Nabila's imprisonment refocused their interest in staying out of politics and shoring up their positions in civil service by gaining experience and mobilizing connections among the growing network of educated family members. Pawura rose through the ranks to become an assistant community development officer in the 1980s and eventually a district community development officer, continuing to host nieces and nephews while they completed secondary and technical schooling and launched their careers. Sebiyam's senior daughters continued to host family members in Bawku, and a junior sister who had schooled in Bawku was then posted to Yendi, where a number of junior family members came to stay.

Contractions in the civil service and the growing salience of new political and nongovernmental networks encouraged others of Sebiyam's children to think of forging careers in which village work in Kpasenkpe would take a prominent role. Within months of the coup against Limann, several of Dr. Nabila's younger brothers took up positions in the local arms of the PNDC government (which had ousted their brother and about which many had real rancor). One of Dr. Nabila's junior brothers became the first "zonal coordinator" for Rawlings's revolutionary cadres. Soon after his appointment, several other junior brothers in the Sebiyam family assumed positions in the PNDC government, with another brother ultimately becoming zonal coordinator from 1988 to 1991. Rather than explaining this as a source of family division (though there was some of that), these folks thought of the PNDC as a new form of the work that civil servants and even the chief had done in the past. Meanwhile, by the second half of the 1980s, state austerity measures and the rise of neoliberal development practice meant that NGOs, especially World Vision, became a way for family members to continue the Wulugunaba's work and find an outlet for their training.

In addition to being led by the Wulugunaba's brother, a son-in-law played a prominent role in World Vision's Central Committee, and many other family members were active in the Assemblies of God. Once established in Kpasenkpe, the operation of World Vision projects then also relied heavily on the Sebiyam family network, both formally through employment but also informally through the networks necessary to deliver and organize supplies. A number of Sebiyam's children recall the informal or sporadic roles they played in World Vision's activities, mostly because of their ability to fill "skilled" roles that the organization required. In keeping with its efforts to reduce costs, World Vision would often hire trucks locally or ask communities to provide sand for mixing cement. Two brothers who lived in different northern towns remember organizing deliveries of sand and gravel for building projects. When I asked each of these brothers why they had been involved, even though they had no formal connection to World Vision, they explained that they were nearby and that Pastor Azundow and others had asked them to help. When I commented that World Vision was, in some ways, "a family business," one of them laughed in agreement with me.

As NGO work came to compete more broadly with the civil service as a source of employment for professionals from the North, it is perhaps unsurprising that one of Sebiyam's daughters soon came to work for World

Vision at the regional level, first on secondment from her civil service job as a public health nurse and, ultimately, leaving government employ to work for World Vision full time in Tamale. Thus, in the last years of the ten-year community development project in Kpasenkpe, she was in charge of monitoring work in the Kpasenkpe site run by her uncle, brother-in-law, and a number of siblings. I would not argue that these relationships represent anything nefarious but instead observe merely that at the dawn of the neoliberal era, when government and NGO initiatives began to emphasize decentralization and "local ownership," these projects were built upon decades of regional and national connections. As government development projects and NGOs came to town, educated Sebiyam family members nearly always acted as "opinion leaders," group coordinators, and local secretaries.

When discussing this reality, family members emphasized long-term processes, naming two dynamics that highlight the difficulty of understanding the present without understanding the past. First, family members described the importance of personal connections among educated relatives in allowing them to use the family network to accumulate political and professional status. Comments that attributed success to the fact that the family "never put its eggs in one basket" emphasized the importance of diversity in the network (among political affiliations as well as among different locations, civil service agencies, and between government and NGO work) for helping individuals manage the contingencies of working in the Ghanaian state over the course of the twentieth century. However, family members emphasized the clear point that personal connections among family members were inseparable from a second dynamic, in which the schooling and training that family members made possible for each other in turn made family members extremely qualified for government work. In the early years of the Kpasenkpe School when, as one son noted, it was basically the "the Sebiyam family school," Sebiyam's children began to do small tasks for outsiders. "Any governmental worker that is coming there," he explained, "or any [project] that is coming there, they will see that 'oh this boy, he's capable of doing it!' and they are picking somebody from my house." By the 1990s, family members were involved in so many different political, civil service, and NGO positions that one son discussed a new version of this dynamic, insightfully arguing that because of their schooling and experience, whenever an agency wanted to undertake a development project in Kpasenkpe, it would "by all means come to this house."

The robustness of the family networks as a whole did not mitigate any individual's vulnerability to the uncertainties of the neoliberal era. Sebiyam's youngest children went to school and began careers in the late 1980s and 1990s, becoming nurses, teachers, and NGO workers. The youngest cohort recalls the difficulties of managing the dual uncertainties of the neoliberal era and of marshaling resources during their father's old age and after his death. These youngest children relied on their mothers and their siblings particularly heavily, as they scrambled to pursue schooling and civil service careers without assistance from their father (who died in 1992). Many continued to stay with and learn from older siblings who worked in the fields they had chosen. However, when interviewed in the 2010s, while still in the midst of building their careers, they often spoke about the unpredictability of government work—where you might work for several years without salary or, alternately, you might fight or luck your way into an opportunity for advancement. One of Sebiyam's junior sons, for example, received a Ford Foundation Fellowship to study development in the United States. A daughter, in contrast, spoke of avoiding civil service work to instead trade used clothing and send steady money to her sisters in the North.

When Sebiyam died in 1992, Dr. Nabila, who had returned to civilian life as a professor at the University of Ghana, stood for Kpasenkpe's chieftaincy. After he was appointed, he continued to live and work primarily in Accra, which put him in a good position to advocate for development in and around Kpasenkpe and to build a new national career around chiefly affairs (when I started my research in 2008, for example, he was president of the National House of Chiefs).[86] By the 1990s, it was clear why Kpasenkpe's chief would be someone like Dr. Nabila, who had forged his career elsewhere and could bring his connections to bear on local development. It was also clear why, for people like Dr. Nabila, village work in Kpasenkpe could play an important role in a career that was anything but "local" in scope. Some of Sebiyam's children and siblings thus built on the model of progressive chieftaincy that Sebiyam had forged in the 1950s. By the 1990s, these performances of local expertise and leadership were robust, flexible, and time tested. They no longer relied on the institution of chieftaincy or on particular state-centered networks. Instead, family members who had schooled and worked in towns and cities across the North found Kpasenkpe to be alternately a refuge and a promising site for networking with national and international agencies, demonstrating expertise, and continuing careers in the face of an unpredictable future.

Meanwhile, many in the family network, like many in the region as a whole, found their avenues to prosperity and their ability to engage the state limited by the contractions and uncertainties of the neoliberal era.

⇜

The 1980s saw the expansion and diversification of village work as a form of statecraft in northern Ghana. As the state dismantled blanket programs of agricultural subsidies and ambitions to "reach every farmer," village development projects became the primary mode of statecraft in the region. The PNDC and organizations like World Vision offered visions of citizen engagement, including "people's power" and "transformation" that were radically different than the valorization of markets and individuals represented by structural adjustment. Despite their ambitions, new initiatives continued patterns of hinterland statecraft and reaffirmed ideas that villages were all the same. For the PNDC, fiscal stringency meant relying on bilateral and nongovernmental organizations to fund and implement small-scale development in the northern hinterland. Organizations like World Vision, in turn, adopted old strategies of treating northern villages as substitutable, selecting project sites based on demonstrations of labor and leadership.

The tensions and hypocrisies of village development were not new, but as residents took up old scripts of progressive leadership and self-help, the pace and urgency of these performances increased. New funders demanded labor as a way to cut costs, but they were also keenly interested in the appearance of community support. In some ways, new funders were not so much extracting labor as they were extracting "success," and thus they wanted labor to be a performance of local community that could simultaneously justify development work and downplay the politics of its content. As one of countless NGOs and international organizations that implemented village development projects in northern Ghana, World Vision's focus on competitive, small-scale, "sustainable" interventions reinforced what structural adjustment had wrought: a gradual limitation of the possibilities of development and an increasingly distant ability to attach local action to demands beyond the village. Meanwhile, residents of Ghana's North continued to improvise and innovate. District officials managed the gutting of their budgets by courting and managing a diverse set of outside funders, often using demands for local labor as a flexible all-purpose glue that bound otherwise contradictory agendas together. Local leaders convinced groups of people to contribute time and money so that they could argue for a project to come to their particular village, and then they acted as hosts to manage the demands of funders when they came. For a small set of people, like some members of Kpasenkpe's chiefly family, the proliferation of village development projects both demanded and allowed the cultivation of a rich web of connections to national and international networks.

In 1992, after more than a decade as a military leader, Jerry John Rawlings prepared to run for president. The revolutionary Provisional National Defense Council (PNDC) became the National Democratic Congress (NDC) and made way for the reformation of opposition parties and resurgence of partisan contests. Ghana's return to multiparty democratic rule was bound up in the politics and promises of development at all levels of government. In the late 1980s and 1990s the Rawlings regime managed to remain a World Bank "star pupil" by pairing its economic reforms with a series of policy changes—including decentralization, an emphasis on participatory development, and, ultimately, a transition to party political competition—that responded to domestic political pressures and the World Bank's increasing interest in what it called "good governance."[87] The PNDC began with local government, focusing on decentralization in a bid to avoid a more wholesale overhaul of military rule. In 1988–89, the regime held nonpartisan elections for new local government units called District Assemblies, which were charged with planning and decision making over local development (though in practice, they were given few resources to do so and continued to rely on donors and NGOs).[88] When this failed to quell both local and international discontent, the PNDC negotiated its way toward drawing up a constitution and holding national elections, meanwhile courting elites and investing heavily in national road and electrification projects widely perceived as a bid for political support.[89]

As presidential hopefuls, MPs, and District Assembly candidates began to campaign on local and national development promises, analysts debated the promises and dangers of a new era. By the late 1990s, social scientists began to analyze election returns and development spending to judge whether electoral competition at the local and national levels made government more efficient, accountable, or participatory.[90] This chapter suggests, however, that by the 1990s the expansion of village work as government had already deeply shaped what residents of northern Ghana could demand of the state. Politicians who continued to treat Ghana's northern regions as an economic and electoral hinterland easily perpetuated the politics of neoliberal stringency, learning that competition for projects could be a very effective way of both rewarding political networks and quelling local critique. At the local level, continued reliance on donors and NGOs meant that rural people were faced with even more powerful incentives to avoid open dissent and to invest in specific performances of community participation and village leadership. More broadly, the terms of debate over how villages like Kpasenkpe and the northern hinterland as a whole could be integrated into Ghanaian national development plans had been narrowed to the set of small-scale projects that have dominated politics in the decades since.

Epilogue

On a Sunday afternoon in January 2012, world-famous economist Jeffrey Sachs, U2 lead singer and activist Bono, and journalist and *Observer* editor John Mulholland arrived in Kpasenkpe.[1] They noticed the bumpy road and stopped to visit the Kpasenkpe clinic, which was now significantly less well staffed and stocked than when it was commissioned in the 1970s. They made their way past the market site, several World Vision boreholes, and the path to the primary and middle schools before arriving at an outdoor pavilion where community gatherings are often held. From the pavilion, they could see the palace compounds of both the former chief, Wulugu-naba Sebiyam, and the current chief, his son, Wulugunaba Professor John Sebiyam Nabila. They stood in the shadow of the old colonial courthouse, which had, among other things, served as Kpasenkpe's first classroom while local residents built the primary school. Like decades of developers before them, however, the trio saw little of the history that was all around them and focused instead on the future that they hoped to bring about. They had traveled to Kpasenkpe to announce that it had been identified as one of several settlements that, together, would make up the latest site for the Millennium Villages Project—a well-funded, high-profile effort that identified sites in ten African countries for a range of interventions and intended to "prove that by fighting poverty at the village level . . . rural Africa [could] . . . escape from the poverty trap."[2] A few months later, another prominent British journalist, Ian Birrell, traveled to Kpasenkpe as part of a critique of the Millennium Villages Project, dubbing it the "village where every family gets £7,000 from the British taxpayer."[3]

Over the five years of its operation, the Ghanaian press associated the project not with Sachs or Bono but with its Ghanaian sponsor, the Savannah Accelerated Development Authority (SADA), an agency that was established under President John Evans Atta-Mills and the National Democratic Congress in 2010. The SADA–Millennium Village Project was the object of both praise and critique by Ghanaians, who used it as a forum to discuss the government's effectiveness more generally, particularly in light of corruption and wastage scandals plaguing the SADA organization.[4] In 2018, after the release of an evaluation of the project by the UK's Department for International Development, Ian Birrell returned to Kpasenkpe and its surroundings to document what he saw as its wastefulness and encouragement of a "dependency culture."[5] Ghanaians, however, had already moved on to another development controversy, this time about the now-ruling National Patriotic Party president Nana Akufo-Addo's "One-Village-One-Dam" (1V1D) project, which had begun to announce sites and garner praise and critique.[6] Kpasenkpe was not among the sites chosen for the 1V1D project. Kpasenkpe's clinic did have new visitors, however, when contractors working for the China Aid project began to dig a borehole, one of a thousand that the Chinese government had committed to building in villages across the country.[7]

In the nearly three decades that have elapsed since Ghana's return to multiparty democracy in 1992, party political networks and bilateral and nongovernmental organizations have continued to use small-scale projects and an imaginary of interchangeable rural villages to legitimize the little work they do to address the developmental demands of people from Ghana's North. Photo opportunities and press releases on individual village development projects are immediately legible as a way for developers to tell stories about larger agendas in an attempt to garner funding or votes. Meanwhile, others use exposés of the wastage, fraud, or patronage involved in particular projects to tell stories that decry party leaders, donors, or the development enterprise itself. Despite the ubiquity of these narratives, neither Sachs and Bono, Atta-Mills and Akufo-Addo, nor the Department for International Development and China Aid are the main characters in the story of village development work in Northern Ghana. Rather, the twenty-first-century apparatuses of party politics, celebrity aid, and international assistance that currently bring village projects to northern Ghana are built on the twentieth-century dynamics of hinterland statecraft—dynamics that were forged, over decades, by local government agents, progressive chiefs, NGO workers, and a wide range of residents.

Through decades of small-scale projects, developmentalism was knit into the fabric of rural government in areas, like northern Ghana, that states saw as peripheral. This position has not made the region distant from something we might call "the state," but it has instead made the region a center of a certain kind of governance. The concept of hinterland statecraft, employed here, describes how states used simplified mechanisms of rule that both allowed local innovation and circumscribed people's ability to translate their actions into legible claims. In hinterlands, officials working with limited resources relied on useable fictions like the idea of interchangeable rural villages and on cheap and flexible systems of labor extraction. The colonial imaginary of the North as a hinterland of the cocoa- and gold-producing South led to policies that both forced and encouraged labor migration from the region and led to its underdevelopment. Its position as an economic hinterland also made it a bureaucratic hinterland, in which the colonial government expended very few resources and relied on the sporadic imposition of force. In the day-to-day practice of interwar colonialism, a simplified imaginary of rural villages became an essential tool of government, one that ordered DCs' agendas as much as official ideologies of tribal governance and ethnic boundaries. In the second half of the twentieth century, the North's historic underdevelopment made it an attractive target for a new agenda of development that was taken up by late colonial, nationalist, and postnationalist governments. While states espoused their commitment to rural communities, development projects in rural northern villages continued a pattern of limited investment, for reasons ranging from the Nkrumah government's low prioritization of rural development to the exclusion of small-scale infrastructure from myriad 1970s agricultural schemes and the neoliberal obsession with efficiency and stringency.

From the interwar period through "Nkrumah's time," across the upheavals of the 1970s and into the neoliberal era, officials, leaders, and constituents pieced together surprising continuities through periods of dramatic change. Official imaginaries of the generic northern village endured because they became, again and again, useful tools of administration. Developers have never been that interested in pinning down exactly what a "village" is in rural Ghana. The term has been used to apply to dispersed and clustered settlements, to tiny hamlets and small towns, and to places near and far from regional capitals and major roads. Since funding was never sufficient enough that all villages would be sites for schools, clinics, and dams, officials set about looking for particularly attractive villages for projects. These scattered village projects, when cast as emblematic of a rural development agenda, could then be used as evidence that the state was developing the region as a whole.

In the twentieth century, the central way that rural people engaged with village imaginaries was through their labor. States and, later, NGOs have extracted local labor as a condition of development funding, a way of differentiating "progressive" or "successful" villages from the rest. From the late colonial period to the present, small-scale development projects have incorporated demands that residents mold blocks, clear roads, and carry water. Whether or not labor was voluntarily given for development, structures of development have been extractive of labor, and rural people have experienced, navigated, and made meaning of extractive systems. The imaginary of villages, self-help, and development has not simply been imposed from above. A multitude of people have used demonstrations of self-help in a variety of political projects—supporting and opposing chiefs, supporting and opposing governments or parties, or supporting and opposing particular development projects themselves. Moreover, at the local level, state agents were often only dimly aware of how they should make decisions about where to site projects and how to organize work. They were often learning from local hosts who had, over time, honed a range of strategies and tools for organizing development.

Successive states' abilities to command labor were contingent on rural leaders' performances of leadership and expertise. Such is the story of Kpasenkpe's chief, Wulugunaba Sebiyam, who served from 1942 until his death in 1992. Early on, Sebiyam styled himself as a progressive chief, building on the models pioneered by northern chiefs such as Builsa's Sandemnaab Azantilow in the early decades of the century. Performances of progressive chieftaincy allowed the Wulugunaba to navigate the era of decolonization and nationalist rule by harnessing the promise of modernization to gain the support of local people as well as a changing cast of state agents. In the middle decades of the century, however, chieftaincy became just one of the paths for people in rural northern Ghana to connect with developmentalist states. The Wulugunaba's siblings and children attended schools, took up jobs in government and nongovernmental agencies, and formed a network that connected Kpasenkpe to regional, national, and international centers of education and employment. Just as some villages accumulated experience as "project villages," some people used schooling and familial connections to become agents of the developmentalist state. Because family networks were not bounded by location or institution, members used them to creatively blur boundaries between "local" knowledge and "outside" expertise and to create connections across agencies and among politicians, chiefs, civil servants, and NGOs.

Village work, in important ways, delineated both the possibilities and the limitations of citizenship. Over time, people from the North used labor and leadership to pursue diverse forms of engagement with states and to fashion continuities in the face of instability. But rural Ghanaians connected to larger state structures principally through their ability to reinforce an imagination of local community, making government a very slippery entity. The village imaginary obscured an uneven landscape in which some rural spaces and certain people were particularly tied to regional, national, and international networks of developmentalist statecraft. Moreover, while rural people might have imbued their labor and leadership with political meanings that were both local and national in scope, developers could easily subsume those meanings into a more simplified model of rural support or opposition to an abstracted idea of development.

Hinterland statecraft and the village imaginary have also continued to depoliticize the paucity of investment in the region overall. In recent decades, praise and critique of particular projects have reinforced the obvious reality that development is a political enterprise—revealing the contours of party competition and the unequal relationships among development funders and recipient regions. But controversies framed in terms of success and failure, of party patronage or "dependency culture," tend to ignore the underlying scarcity of resources on which the apparatus of village development is premised. More importantly, perhaps, this focus has continued to limit the ability of rural citizens to demand more fundamental changes—changes that might not only seek to address ongoing regional inequality but would also recognize the knowledge, expertise, and critical analysis of government that rural people have honed over decades of village work.

Notes

INTRODUCTION

1 The civil court system and employment with the civil service are the other daily manifestations of government.

2 Ben Jones, *Beyond the State in Rural Uganda* (Edinburgh: Edinburgh University Press, 2009), xiv.

3 Standing at the bridge and thinking about the map of northern Ghana (see maps I.1 and I.2), it is easy to see how this area could figure into the unrealized dreams of regional transformation. For a 130-km stretch starting just north of the regional capital of Tamale and reaching to the boundary of Upper East region at Pwalugu, Ghana's main North/South highway stands 30–40 km from the White Volta River. The central Volta River Basin's sparsely populated valleys have periodically captured the imaginations of developers since the early 1930s, and riverside towns have often seemed like potential gateways to an area of untapped resources.

4 Mampruli orthography follows Tony Naden, ed., *GILLBT Mampruli Dictionary* (Tamale, N/R, Ghana: GILLBT, 2016). Carola Lentz gives a wonderfully detailed history of these dynamics in Dagara and Sisala villages in northwest Ghana and southwest Burkina Faso. See Carola Lentz, *Land, Mobility, and Belonging in West Africa: Natives and Strangers* (Bloomington: Indiana University Press, 2013).

5 Paulla A. Ebron, *Performing Africa* (Princeton, NJ: Princeton University Press, 2002), 5.

6 I want to thank one of the manuscript's anonymous reviewers for making this connection explicit.

7 Frederick Cooper, *Africa since 1940: The Past of the Present* (Cambridge: Cambridge University Press, 2002), 85.

8 Gregory Mann, *From Empires to NGOs in the West African Sahel: The Road to Nongovernmentality* (Cambridge: Cambridge University Press, 2015), 172.

9 The quotation is from Frederick Cooper and Randall M. Packard, "Introduction," in *International Development and the Social Sciences: Essays on*

the History and Politics of Knowledge, ed. Frederick Cooper and Randall M. Packard (Berkeley: University of California Press, 1997), 4.

10 Frederick Cooper, "Writing the History of Development," *Journal of Modern European History* 8 (2010): 5–23; Cooper and Packard, *International Development and the Social Sciences*; M. P. Cowen and R. W. Shenton, *Doctrines of Development*, Taylor and Francis e-Library ed. (London: Routledge, 2005); Joseph Morgan Hodge, *Triumph of the Expert: Agrarian Doctrines of Development and the Legacies of British Colonialism* (Athens: Ohio University Press, 2007); Gilbert Rist, *The History of Development: From Western Origins to Global Faith*, 5th ed. (London: Zed Books, 2019).

11 Leslie Hadfield and John Aerni-Flessner, "Introduction: Localizing the History of Development in Africa," *International Journal of African Historical Studies* 50, no. 1 (January 2017): 1–9.

12 Allen F. Isaacman and Barbara S. Isaacman, *Dams, Displacement and the Delusion of Development: Cahora Bassa and Its Legacies in Mozambique, 1965–2007* (Athens: Ohio University Press, 2013); Stephan Miescher, "Building the City of the Future: Visions and Experiences of Modernity in Ghana's Akosombo Township," *Journal of African History* 53, no. 3 (2012): 367–90; Jamie Monson, *Africa's Freedom Railway: How a Chinese Development Project Changed Lives and Livelihoods in Tanzania* (Bloomington: Indiana University Press, 2011); Dzodzi Tsikata, *Living in the Shadow of the Large Dams: Long Term Responses of Downstream and Lakeside Communities of Ghana's Volta River Project* (Leiden: Brill, 2006).

13 Peter J. Bloom, Stephan Miescher, and Takyiwaa Manuh, eds., *Modernization as Spectacle in Africa* (Bloomington: Indiana University Press, 2014).

14 Priya Lal, *African Socialism in Postcolonial Tanzania: Between the Village and the World* (Cambridge: Cambridge University Press, 2015); Leander Schneider, *Government of Development: Peasants and Politicians in Postcolonial Tanzania* (Bloomington: Indiana University Press, 2014); Michael Jennings, *Surrogates of the State: NGOs, Development, and Ujamaa in Tanzania* (Bloomfield, CT: Kumarian Press, 2008); James C. Scott, *Seeing Like a State: How Certain Schemes to Improve the Human Condition Have Failed* (New Haven, CT: Yale University Press, 1998).

15 Hadfield and Aerni-Flessner, "Introduction," 3.

16 Several excellent studies of particular small-scale development initiatives by anthropologists and geographers include Richard Schroeder, *Shady Practices: Agroforestry and Gender Politics in the Gambia* (Berkeley: University of California Press, 1999); Erica Bornstein, *The Spirit of Development: Protestant NGOs, Morality, and Economics in Zimbabwe* (Stanford, CA: Stanford University Press, 2005); China Scherz, *Having People, Having Heart: Charity, Sustainable Development, and Problems of Dependence in Central Uganda* (Chicago: University of Chicago Press, 2014); Pauline E. Peters, ed., *Development Encounters: Sites of Participation and*

Knowledge (Cambridge, MA: Harvard University Press, 2000). Recent examples of historical works that consider the local politics of development include John Aerni-Flessner, *Dreams for Lesotho: Independence, Foreign Assistance, and Development* (Notre Dame, IN: University of Notre Dame Press, 2018); Priya Lal, *African Socialism*; Kara Moskowitz, *Seeing Like a Citizen: Decolonization, Development, and the Making of Kenya, 1945–1980* (Athens: Ohio University Press, 2019).

17 A prominent exception is Dorothy Louise Hodgson's excellent study from nearly two decades ago, *Once Intrepid Warriors: Gender, Ethnicity, and the Cultural Politics of Maasai Development* (Bloomington: Indiana University Press, 2001), which has unfortunately not been followed by similarly long-term histories of development practice in particular places.

18 James Ferguson, *The Anti-politics Machine: "Development," Depoliticization, and Bureaucratic Power in Lesotho* (Cambridge: Cambridge University Press, 1990), 87. For other foundational texts in this vein, see Arturo Escobar, *Encountering Development: The Making and Unmaking of the Third World* (Princeton, NJ: Princeton University Press, 1995); Timothy Mitchell, *Rule of Experts: Egypt, Techno-Politics, Modernity* (Berkeley: University of California Press, 2002). For an analysis of this dynamic in northern Ghana, see Karl Botchway, "Are Development Planners Afraid of History and Contextualization? Notes on Reading a Development Report on Northern Ghana," *Canadian Journal of African Studies / Revue Canadienne Des Études Africaines* 35, no. 1 (2001): 32–66.

19 Sabelo J. Ndlovu-Gatsheni, *Empire, Global Coloniality and African Subjectivity* (New York: Berghahn Books, 2013); Sabelo J. Ndlovu-Gatsheni, *Coloniality of Power in Postcolonial Africa* (CODESRIA, 2013). For a larger discussion of decolonial political economy and its relevance to development discourse in recent decades, see T. D. Harper-Shipman, *Rethinking Ownership of Development in Africa* (Milton: Routledge, 2019), 17–20.

20 Tania Murray Li, *The Will to Improve: Governmentality, Development, and the Practice of Politics* (Durham, NC: Duke University Press, 2007), introduction. The quotations are from pages 28 and 12. In Indonesia, Li shows how attempts by international NGOs and the World Bank to "render technical" the issues of forest conservation and village development became entangled with rural political action that built on decades of experience with governmental agents who purported to act as "trustees" of their interests.

21 Nicole Sackley, "The Village as Cold War Site: Experts, Development, and the History of Rural Reconstruction," *Journal of Global History* 6, no. 3 (2011): 484.

22 Daniel Immerwahr, *Thinking Small: The United States and the Lure of Community Development* (Cambridge, MA: Harvard University Press, 2018); Sackley, "The Village as Cold War Site."

23 Andrea Cornwall, "Introductory Overview–Buzzwords and Fuzzwords: Deconstructing Development Discourse," in *Deconstructing Development Discourse: Buzzwords and Fuzzwords*, ed. Andrea Cornwall and Deborah Eade (Warwickshire, UK: Practical Action Publishing, 2010), 5.

24 In recent decades, extensive work has been done by academics to explode the idea of village homogeneity and isolation in Africa and elsewhere, building in particular on Charles Piot, *Remotely Global: Village Modernity in West Africa* (Chicago: University of Chicago Press, 1999), and Anna Lowenhaupt Tsing, *In the Realm of the Diamond Queen: Marginality in an Out-of-the-Way Place* (Princeton, NJ: Princeton University Press, 1993). Conversely, Stacy Leigh Pigg's work on Nepal helps to illuminate how developmentalist ideas of village homogeneity, isolation, and stasis can become part of the social imaginary in places where they have become common. Stacy Leigh Pigg, "Inventing Social Categories through Place: Social Representations and Development in Nepal," *Comparative Studies in Society and History* 34, no. 3 (July 1992): 491–513. For recent challenges to developmentalist views of villages, see Ben Jones, *Beyond the State in Rural Uganda* (Edinburgh: Edinburgh University Press, 2009); Judith Scheele, *Village Matters: Knowledge, Politics and Community in Kabylia, Algeria* (Woodbridge, Suffolk: James Currey, 2009); and Lillian Trager, *Yoruba Hometowns: Community, Identity, and Development in Nigeria* (Boulder, CO: Lynne Rienner Publishers, 2001). This literature is closely related to a rich body of work in development studies that challenges and complicates developmentalist imaginaries of "community." See, for example, Giles Mohan and Kristian Stokke, "Participatory Development and Empowerment: The Dangers of Localism," *Third World Quarterly* 21, no. 2 (2000): 247–68, as well as the multiple critiques in Bill Cooke and Uma Kothari, eds., *Participation: The New Tyranny?* (London: Zed Books, 2001). See also the critical approach and summary of literature in Nana Akua Anyidoho, "'Communities of Practice': Prospects for Theory and Action in Participatory Development," *Development in Practice* 20, no. 3 (May 1, 2010): 318–28.

25 Nana Akua Anyidoho, "Theorising the Intersection of Public Policy and Personal Lives through the Lens of 'Participation,'" *Africa Development* 35, no. 3 (2010): 1–11. In the context of policy makers, see Thomas Yarrow, "Life/History: Personal Narratives of Development amongst NGO Workers and Activists in Ghana," *Africa* 78, no. 3 (2008): 334–58.

26 For a good overview of planned "territorialization" of village space in Africa, see Achim von Oppen, "The Village as Territory: Enclosing Locality in Northwest Zambia, 1950s to 1990s," *Journal of African History* 47, no. 1 (2006): 57–75. Limited schemes of planned resettlement accompanied large-scale development projects in Ghana, including the Gonja Development Project, the building of Tema Harbor, and the Volta River Project. See Jeffrey Grischow, *Shaping Tradition: Civil Society, Community*

and Development in Colonial Northern Ghana, 1899–1957 (Leiden: Brill, 2006), chapter 8; and Stephan Miescher, "Building the City of the Future: Visions and Experiences of Modernity in Ghana's Akosombo Township," *Journal of African History* 53, no. 3 (2012): 367–90.

27 Kwesi Kwaa Prah, "Culture, the Missing Link in Development Planning in Africa," *Présence Africaine* 163/164 (2001): 91.

28 The World Bank's influential 1989 report *Sub-Saharan Africa: From Crisis to Sustainable Growth* (Washington, DC: World Bank, 1989) is frequently cited as a distillation of the World Bank's revised thinking and messaging.

29 Mkandawire argues that the new governance agenda initially drew on the input of a number of African scholars who sought to alter the World Bank's neglect of structural and political forces, but that the ensuing institutional and intellectual journey of "good governance" turned it into "one more instrument for ensuring the implementation of adjustment programmes." Thandika Mkandawire, "'Good Governance': The Itinerary of an Idea," in Cornwall and Eade, *Deconstructing Development Discourse*, 265–68. In other work, he shows that development institutions instead drew heavily on schools of thought, including those that emphasized neopatrimonialism and those that emphasized public choice that tended to posit (rather than analyze) a generic African state responsible for economic failure. In the case of the neopatrimonial school, he points out that authors envisioned government either floating above a distant and untouched society or, alternately, posited that it had been helplessly "captured" by African hierarchies and cultures. Much of the most influential writing on African politics, then, both relied on and reinforced the pernicious idea that Africans were at some level either ungoverned or ungovernable. Thandika Mkandawire, "Neopatrimonialism and the Political Economy of Economic Performance in Africa: Critical Reflections," *World Politics* 67, no. 3 (2015): 563–612. For more on the continued relevance of pejorative ideas of African states despite a recent turn to national "ownership" of development, see Harper-Shipman, *Rethinking Ownership of Development in Africa*, introduction and chapter 1.

30 The phrase "the local turn" is from Carol Warren and Leontine Visser, "The Local Turn: An Introductory Essay Revisiting Leadership, Elite Capture and Good Governance in Indonesian Conservation and Development Programs," *Human Ecology* 44, no. 3 (June 1, 2016): 277–86. For an excellent analysis of the lack of historical consciousness in contemporary discussions of community development, see the epilogue in Daniel Immerwahr's *Thinking Small*, 164–86.

31 Concerns about local accountability and "elite capture," for example, have long been prominent in development studies and development economics. For foundational examples, see Arun Agrawal and Jesse Ribot, "Accountability in Decentralization: A Framework with South Asian and West African Cases," *Journal of Developing Areas* 33, no. 4 (1999): 473–502;

Pranab K. Bardhan and Dilip Mookherjee, "Capture and Governance at Local and National Levels," *American Economic Review* 90, no. 2 (2000): 135–39. By 2013, even the World Bank recognized that the outpouring of small-scale projects "proceeded, in large part, with little systematic effort to understand the particular challenges entailed in inducing participation or to learn from the failures. . . . The process is, arguably, still driven more by ideology and optimism than by systematic analysis, either theoretical or empirical." Ghazala Mansuri and Vijayendra Rao, *Localizing Development: Does Participation Work?* (Washington, DC: World Bank, 2013), 3.

32 Okia's two books on communal labor in Kenya are convincing on this front. Opolot Okia, *Communal Labor in Colonial Kenya: The Legitimization of Coercion, 1912–1930* (New York: Palgrave Macmillan, 2012); Opolot Okia, *Labor in Colonial Kenya after the Forced Labor Convention, 1930–1963* (New York: Palgrave Macmillan, 2019). Benedetta Rossi illuminates this connection well in her 2015 monograph as well as in her introduction to a special issue of *International Labor and Working-Class History.* Benedetta Rossi, *From Slavery to Aid: Politics, Labour, and Ecology in the Nigerien Sahel, 1800–2000* (Cambridge: Cambridge University Press, 2015); Benedetta Rossi, "What 'Development' Does to Work," *International Labor and Working-Class History* 92 (Fall 2017): 7–23. See also the collection of articles in Benedetta Rossi, ed., "Developmentalism, Labor, and the Slow Death of Slavery in Twentieth Century Africa," special issue, *International Labor and Working-Class History* 92 (2017); Alexander Keese, "Slow Abolition within the Colonial Mind: British and French Debates about 'Vagrancy,' 'African Laziness,' and Forced Labour in West Central and South Central Africa, 1945–1965," *International Review of Social History* 59, no. 3 (2014): 377–407.

33 Pablo Alejandro Leal, "Participation," in Cornwall and Eade, *Deconstructing Development Discourse,* 89–100; Andrea Cornwall and Karen Brock, "What Do Buzzwords Do for Development Policy? A Critical Look at 'Participation,' 'Empowerment' and 'Poverty Reduction,'" *Third World Quarterly* 26, no. 7 (2005): 1043–60. For a multifaceted examination of participation in Tanzanian development practice in the 1990s and 2000s, see Maia Green, *The Development State: Aid, Culture and Civil Society in Tanzania* (Woodbridge, Suffolk: James Currey, 2014).

34 Emma Hunter, "Voluntarism, Virtuous Citizenship, and Nation-Building in Late Colonial and Early Postcolonial Tanzania," *African Studies Review* 58, no. 2 (2015): 43–61; Lal, *African Socialism*; Moskowitz, *Seeing Like a Citizen,* chapters 6 and 7. For more on continuities between late colonial and Nkrumah-era community development initiatives, see the series of articles by Kate Skinner that traces mass education initiatives throughout Ghana. Kate Skinner, "'It Brought Some Kind of Neatness to Mankind': Literacy, Development and Democracy in 1950s Asante,"

Africa 79, no. 4 (2009); "From Pentecostalism to Politics: Mass Literacy and Community Development in Late Colonial Northern Ghana," *Paedagogica Historica* 46, no. 3 (2010): 307–23; "Who Knew the Minds of the People? Specialist Knowledge and Developmentalist Authoritarianism in Post-colonial Ghana," *Journal of Imperial and Commonwealth History* 39, no. 2 (2011).

35 Two notable exceptions focus on long-term labor exploitation of populations identified as the descendants of enslaved people. See Rossi, *From Slavery to Aid*, and Elisabeth McMahon, "Developing Workers: Coerced and 'Voluntary' Labor in Zanzibar, 1909–1970," *International Labor and Working-Class History* 92 (Fall 2017): 114–33.

36 Naaborko Sackeyfio-Lenoch, *The Politics of Chieftaincy: Authority and Property in Colonial Ghana, 1920–1950* (Rochester, NY: University of Rochester Press, 2014); Carola Lentz, *Land, Mobility, and Belonging*; Christian Lund, *Local Politics and the Dynamics of Property in Africa* (Cambridge: Cambridge University Press, 2008); Grischow, *Shaping Tradition*; Catherine Boone, *Political Topographies of the African State: Territorial Authority and Institutional Choice* (Cambridge: Cambridge University Press, 2003); Sara Berry, *Chiefs Know Their Boundaries: Essays on Property, Power, and the Past in Asante, 1896–1996* (Portsmouth, NH: Heinemann, 2001); Kwame Arhin, *Transformations in Traditional Rule in Ghana (1951–1996)* (Accra: Sedco, 2001); Richard Rathbone, *Nkrumah and the Chiefs: The Politics of Chieftaincy in Ghana, 1951–60* (Athens: Ohio University Press, 2000); Jean Marie Allman, *The Quills of the Porcupine: Asante Nationalism in an Emergent Ghana* (Madison: University of Wisconsin Press, 1993). For Anglophone West Africa more broadly, see Olufemi Vaughan, *Nigerian Chiefs: Traditional Power in Modern Politics, 1890s–1990s* (Rochester, NY: University of Rochester Press, 2000); Peter Geschiere, "Chiefs and Colonial Rule in Cameroon: Inventing Chieftaincy, French and British Style," *Africa: Journal of the International African Institute* 63, no. 2 (1993): 151–75; J. D. Y. Peel, *Ijeshas and Nigerians: The Incorporation of a Yoruba Kingdom, 1890s–1970s* (Cambridge: Cambridge University Press, 1983).

37 Erik Green, "Indirect Rule and Colonial Intervention: Chiefs and Agrarian Change in Nyasaland, ca. 1933 to the Early 1950s," *International Journal of African Historical Studies* 44, no. 2 (2011): 249–74; Myles Osborne, "The Kamba and Mau Mau: Ethnicity, Development, and Chiefship, 1952–1960," *International Journal of African Historical Studies* 43, no. 1 (2010): 63–87; Hodgson, *Once Intrepid Warriors*; Monica M. van Beusekom, *Negotiating Development: African Farmers and Colonial Experts at the Office Du Niger, 1920–1960* (Portsmouth, NH: Heinemann, 2002); William A. Munro, *The Moral Economy of the State: Conservation, Community Development, and State Making in Zimbabwe* (Athens: Ohio University Press, 1998).

38 For detailed examinations of the "politics of custom" in the late twentieth and early twenty-first centuries, see the introduction and essays in John L. Comaroff and Jean Comaroff, *The Politics of Custom: Chiefship, Capital, and the State in Contemporary Africa* (Chicago: University of Chicago Press, 2018). For earlier analyses of these dynamics in West Africa, see T. Bierschenk, J. P. Chauveau, and Jean-Pierre Olivier de Sardan, *Courtiers En Développement: Les Villages Africains En Quête de Projets* (Paris: Karthala, 2000); J. C. Ribot, "Decentralisation, Participation, and Accountability in Sahelian Forestry," *Africa* 69, no. 1 (1999).

39 David Carson Davis, "Continuity and Change in Mampurugu" (PhD diss., Northwestern University, 1984), chapter 5.

40 A. A. Iliasu, "The Establishment of British Administration in Mamprugu, 1898–1937," *Transactions of the Historical Society of Ghana* 16, no. 1 (1975): 1–28; Davis, "Continuity and Change in Mampurugu," chapter 7; and David Carson Davis, "'Then the White Man Came with His Whitish Ideas . . .': The British and the Evolution of Traditional Government in Mampurugu," *International Journal of African Historical Studies* 20, no. 4 (1987): 627–46.

41 On the deep history of host-guest dynamics in northern Ghana, see Lentz, *Land, Mobility, and Belonging*, especially chapter 4. While less comprehensive analysis has been done in Mamprusi areas, several works discuss the variety of interactions that are understood to be governed by relationships among hosts (or "landlords") and guests. See Steve Tonah, "Diviners, Malams, God, and the Contest for Paramount Chiefship in Mamprugu (Northern Ghana)," *Anthropos* 101, no. 1 (2006): 21–35; Steve Tonah, "Migration and Farmer-Herder Conflicts in Ghana's Volta Basin," *Canadian Journal of African Studies / Revue Canadienne Des Études Africaines* 40, no. 1 (2006): 152–78; Michael Schlottner, "'We Stay, Others Come and Go': Identity among the Mamprusi in Northern Ghana," in *Ethnicity in Ghana: The Limits of Invention*, ed. Carola Lentz and Paul Nugent (London: Macmillan, 2000), 49–67.

42 My jumping off point is Christine Oppong's classic study *Marriage among a Matrilineal Elite*, and, more recently, Behrends and Lentz's work on "Education, Careers, and Home Ties," both of which focus on the importance of civil service work in shaping family relationships. Christine Oppong, *Marriage among a Matrilineal Elite: A Family Study of Ghanaian Senior Civil Servants* (Cambridge: Cambridge University Press, 1974); Andrea Behrends and Carola Lentz, "Education, Careers, and Home Ties: The Ethnography of an Emerging Middle Class from Northern Ghana," *Zeitschrift Für Ethnologie* 137, no. 2 (2012): 139–64.

43 Joseph R. A. Ayee, "The Measurement of Decentralization: The Ghanaian Experience, 1988–92," *African Affairs* 95 (1996): 31–50; Melissa T. Labonte, "From Patronage to Peacebuilding? Elite Capture and Governance from Below in Sierra Leone," *African Affairs* 111, no. 442 (2012):

90–115; William Muhumuza, "Pitfalls of Decentralization Reforms in Transitional Societies: The Case of Uganda," *Africa Development / Afrique et Développement* 33, no. 4 (2008): 59–81. My research is principally concerned with how village projects have shaped Ghanaians' interactions with developmentalist states and vice versa. It is less well suited to a discussion of the differential effects of developmentalism on economic and social life more broadly (on, for example, food security, education, or the burdens of farm labor). Throughout the manuscript, I attempt to direct readers to the wealth of historical and social scientific literature on these topics.

44 Cooper argues that colonial state building rendered all sorts of networks, including family networks, essential to how Africans navigate colonial and postcolonial "gatekeeper states." See Frederick Cooper, *Africa Since 1940*.

45 For Ghana, for example, see Gracia Clark's extensive work with women traders, in particular her analysis of "family survival" in the neoliberal era, and Kojo Amanor's work on how states have shaped familial struggles over land and labor. Gracia Clark, "Negotiating Asante Family Survival in Kumasi, Ghana," *Africa: Journal of the International African Institute* 69, no. 1 (1999): 66–86; Kojo Sebastian Amanor, "Family Values, Land Sales and Agricultural Commodification in South-Eastern Ghana," *Africa: Journal of the International African Institute* 80, no. 1 (2010): 104–25; Kojo Sebastian Amanor, *Land, Labour and the Family in Southern Ghana: A Critique of Land Policy under Neo-liberalisation* (Uppsala: Nordic Africa Institute, 2001). On contemporary networks, see Ming-Chang Tsai and Dan-Bright S. Dzorgbo, "Familial Reciprocity and Subjective Well-Being in Ghana," *Journal of Marriage and Family* 74, no. 1 (2012): 215–28; Valentina Mazzucato and Djamila Schans, "Transnational Families and the Well-Being of Children: Conceptual and Methodological Challenges," *Journal of Marriage and Family* 73, no. 4 (2011): 704–12; Kim Caarls and Valentina Mazzucato, "Transnational Relationships and Reunification: Ghanaian Couples between Ghana and Europe," *Demographic Research* 34 (2016): 587–614. I am very excited about a new project started by Lentz, Meda, and Lobnibe to write a monograph based on extensive interviews and their own engagement as members of an extended family network in northwestern Ghana and southwestern Burkina Faso. The project is detailed in Carola Lentz, Isidore Lobnibe, and Stanislas Meda, "Family History as Family Enterprise? A Wissenschaftskolleg Focus Group's Views of a West African Family," *TRAFO—Blog for Transregional Research*, August 2, 2018, https://trafo.hypotheses.org/11214.

46 This idea has come in different forms from different scholars, but I have been particularly influenced by Emily Lynn Osborn's work, which traces both the colonial imposition of separate spheres ideology and the enduring entanglement of "household-making and state-making" in the Milo

River Valley from the seventeenth to the early twentieth centuries. See Emily Lynn Osborn, *Our New Husbands Are Here: Households, Gender, and Politics in a West African State from the Slave Trade to Colonial Rule* (Athens: Ohio University Press, 2011). I give a longer discussion of recent scholarship on families and states in chapter 3.

47 Moses Mosonsieyiri Kansanga et al., "A Feminist Political Ecology of Agricultural Mechanization and Evolving Gendered On-Farm Labor Dynamics in Northern Ghana," *Gender, Technology and Development* 23, no. 3 (2019): 210; Jacqueline Alyce Ignatova, "Seeds of Contestation: Genetically Modified Crops and the Politics of Agricultural Modernization in Ghana" (PhD diss., University of Maryland, 2015), 143n29.

48 For examples of analyses that use individual biographies and career trajectories to examine change over time, see Akosoa K. Darkwah, "Education: Pathway to Empowerment for Ghanaian Women?," in *Feminisms, Empowerment, and Development: Changing Women's Lives*, ed. Andrea Cornwall and Jenny Edwards (London: Zed Books, 2014), 87–103; Behrends and Lentz, "Education, Careers, and Home Ties."

49 Christine Okali, "Gender Analysis: Engaging with Rural Development and Agricultural Policy Processes" (working paper, FAC, Future Agricultures Consortium, Brighton, UK, 2012), 2.

50 In fact, I am sure I remembered this corner after seeing the strikingly similar image in Piot's book *Nostalgia for the Future: West Africa after the Cold War* (Chicago: University of Chicago Press, 2010), 133–34. While Piot's work shows in great depth and variety that these were certainly "signs of the times," I also want to point out that the practices of neoliberal government drew on experiences of previous eras.

51 If this was not obvious at first, it was certainly clear by the second or third year of visits that continued to yield more conversations and no projects.

52 Government of Ghana, *1960 Population Census of Ghana* (Accra: Census Office, 1962); Government of Ghana, *1970 Population Census of Ghana* (Accra: Census Office, 1973); Government of Ghana, *1984 Population Census of Ghana* (Accra: Statistical Service, 1989).

53 Schlottner, "'We Stay, Others Come and Go'"; Susan Drucker-Brown, *Ritual Aspects of the Mamprusi Kingship* (Leiden: Afrika-studiecentrum, 1975).

54 Ebron, *Performing Africa*, chapter 5.

55 In 2019, I returned to Kpasenkpe for several days to check quotations, share and confirm with interviewees how I was using and interpreting their stories, and ask how they would like their names to appear in the book. In this work I was generously aided by Emmanuel Sebiyam.

CHAPTER 1: LABOR, CHIEFTAINCY, AND COLONIAL STATECRAFT

1 Public Records and Archives Administration, Tamale, Ghana (hereafter cited as PRAAD-Tamale) NRG3.22.1 Labour—Northern Territories,

Memo no. 634/30/5/50, "Maintenance of Roads Under the Forced Labour Convention," from Acting Colonial Secretary G. C. du Boulay, July 20, 1933. Some archival material from PRAAD-Tamale has been digitized and made available through the British Library's Endangered Archives Programme (hereafter cited as EAP) at http://eap.bl.uk. For this material, where possible, I have included the original record number from PRAAD-Tamale followed by the reference from EAP in parentheses. Where an EAP reference is not given, files were accessed in person at PRAAD-Tamale.

2 PRAAD-Tamale NRG8.10.14, letter from chief commissioner of the Northern Territories to Colonial Secretary, March 9, 1936.

3 The phrase "in the direct interest for the community" is from ILO, "Forced Labour Convention," Convention CO29, June 28, 1930, articles 2, 9, and 10. http://www.ilo.org/dyn/normlex/en/f?p=1000:12100:0::NO:: P12100_ILO_CODE:C029.

4 Opolot Okia, *Labor in Colonial Kenya after the Forced Labor Convention, 1930–1963* (New York: Palgrave Macmillan, 2019), chapters 5 and 6.

5 Elisabeth McMahon, "Developing Workers: Coerced and 'Voluntary' Labor in Zanzibar, 1909–1970," *International Labor and Working-Class History* 92 (Fall 2017).

6 Roger G. Thomas, "Military Recruitment in the Gold Coast during the First World War (Recrutement Militaire En Gold Coast Pendant La Première Guerre Mondiale)," *Cahiers d'Études Africaines* 15, no. 57 (1975): 57–83; Roger G. Thomas, "Forced Labour in British West Africa: The Case of the Northern Territories of the Gold Coast 1906–1927," *Journal of African History* 14, no. 1 (1973): 79–103; Cassandra Mark-Thiesen, *Mediators, Contract Men, and Colonial Capital: Mechanized Gold Mining in the Gold Coast Colony, 1879–1909* (Rochester, NY: University of Rochester Press, 2018); Kwabena Opare Akurang-Parry, "Colonial Forced Labor Policies for Road-Building in Southern Ghana and International Anti-forced Labor Pressures, 1900–1940," *African Economic History* 28 (January 2000): 1–25.

7 Allman and Parker argue, "Outside of moments of direct coercion, the British presence [in the region] only made a difference in people's daily lives when it was allotted a role in local narratives, that is, when it intersected with local configurations of power." Jean Allman and John Parker, *Tongnaab: The History of a West African God* (Bloomington: Indiana University Press 2005), 91.

8 Scholars of colonial forced labor have often treated chiefs as simple instruments of colonial extraction, which, while identifying how ongoing coercion and brutality belied the rhetoric of "indirect rule," also limits historians' ability to see the way that chiefs crafted rule and, crucially, how they forged practices that would last.

9 Benedict G. Der, *The Slave Trade in Northern Ghana* (Accra: Woeli Publishing Services, 1998); Akosua Adoma Perbi, *A History of Indigenous*

Slavery in Ghana from the 15th to the 19th Centuries (Accra: Sub-Saharan Publishers, 2004); Natalie Swanepoel, "Every Periphery Is Its Own Center: Sociopolitical and Economic Interactions in Nineteenth-Century Northwestern Ghana," *International Journal of African Historical Studies* 42, no. 3 (2009): 411–32.

10 A number of excellent studies have considered the dynamics of precolonial statecraft in northern Ghana, notably Ivor Wilks, *Wa and the Wala: Islam and Polity in Northwestern Ghana* (Cambridge: Cambridge University Press, 1989); Allman and Parker, *Tongnaab*; Carola Lentz, *Land, Mobility, and Belonging in West Africa: Natives and Strangers* (Bloomington: Indiana University Press, 2013).

11 Bayo Holsey, *Routes of Remembrance: Refashioning the Slave Trade in Ghana* (Chicago: University of Chicago Press, 2008); Allman and Parker, *Tongnaab*, chapter 1.

12 Martin Staniland, *The Lions of Dagbon: Political Change in Northern Ghana* (Cambridge: Cambridge University Press, 1975), 39; Jeffrey Grischow, *Shaping Tradition: Civil Society, Community and Development in Colonial Northern Ghana, 1899–1957* (Leiden: Brill, 2006), 23. The terminology of "Gold Coast hinterland" comes from George Ekem Ferguson's influential reports of expeditions to the region in the 1890s, and the terminology of "Ashanti hinterland" comes from R. S. Rattray's 1932 colonial ethnography. See George Ekem Ferguson, *The Papers of George Ekem Ferguson: A Fanti Official of the Government of the Gold Coast, 1890–1897*, ed. Kwame Arhin, vol. 7 (Leiden: Afrika-Studiecentrum, 1974); Robert Sutherland Rattray, *The Tribes of the Ashanti Hinterland*, 2 vols. (Oxford: Clarendon Press, 1932). As scholars have shown, it is important not to naturalize the idea of the "hinterland," and it is often equally productive to think of Ghana's southern regions as "hinterlands" of processes centered in the North. See Lentz, *Land, Mobility, and Belonging*; Allman and Parker, *Tongnaab*. My intent here is to point out that the region's classification as a hinterland by the colonial government had important and enduring consequences for forms and dynamics of statecraft.

13 Jacob Songsore, *Regional Development in Ghana: The Theory and the Reality* (Accra: Woeli Publishing Services, 2003); R. B. Bening, "Colonial Development Policy in Northern Ghana 1898–1950," *Bulletin of the Ghana Geographical Association* 17 (January 1975): 65–79; Iliasu, "The Establishment of British Administration in Mamprugu, 1898–1937," *Transactions of the Historical Society of Ghana* 16, no. 1 (1975); Nii K. Plange, "Underdevelopment in Northern Ghana: Natural Causes or Colonial Capitalism?," *Review of African Political Economy* 15/16 (May–December 1979): 4–14; Inez Sutton, "Colonial Agricultural Policy: The Non-development of the Northern Territories of the Gold Coast," *International Journal of African Historical Studies* 22, no. 4 (1989): 637–69.

Brukum points out that even Guggisberg's explicit statements rejecting previous neglect did not change the fundamental treatment of the region as a labor reserve. N. J. K. Brukum, "Sir Gordon Guggisberg and Socio-economic Development of Northern Ghana, 1919–1927," *Transactions of the Historical Society of Ghana*, New Series 9 (2005), 6.

14 Thomas, "Military Recruitment"; Thomas, "Forced Labour"; Mark-Thiesen, *Mediators, Contract Men, and Colonial Capital*; Akurang-Parry, "Colonial Forced Labor Policies."

15 Carola Lentz, *Ethnicity and the Making of History in Northern Ghana* (Edinburgh: Edinburgh University Press, 2006), chapter 5; Samuel Ntewusu, "Settling In and Holding On: A Socio-economic History of Northern Traders and Transporters in Accra's Tudu: 1908–2008" (PhD diss., University of Leiden, 2011), chapter 2.

16 Lentz, *Ethnicity*, chapter 5.

17 Grischow, *Shaping Tradition*, 2–3. Grischow echoes Cowen and Shenton's foundational argument that British "doctrines of development" in the nineteenth and twentieth centuries incorporated the idea of colonial trusteeship to make development the object of state policy and to reconcile ideas of progress and of community. M. P. Cowen and R. W. Shenton, *Doctrines of Development*, Taylor and Francis e-Library ed. (London: Routledge, 2005), chapter 1, especially 53–55.

18 This vision led officials to turn a blind eye to domestic slavery in a broad sense and to further classify various forms of labor exploitation by chiefs as forms of taxation. Grischow, *Shaping Tradition*, 31–32. For example, in January of 1919, DC Michael Dasent in Tumu reported that while supervising "improvement" in Tumu town, "The Chief of Tumu has at last realized that it is one of the privileges of a chief to be able to obtain labour for the improvement of his house, which he is now doing." PRAAD-Tamale NRG8.4.5 (EAP541/1/4/5), Tumu Informal Diary January 1919. While domestic enslavement existed in the Northern Territories, indications are that forced labor recruited by chiefs relied on a variety of relationships of dependence and would have fallen on a variety of constituents. It is unclear from the records exactly how different chiefs raised labor, but there is little indication that enslaved people were a particular target.

19 Sara Berry, "Hegemony on a Shoestring: Indirect Rule and Access to Agricultural Land," *Africa* 62, no. 3 (1992): 327–55.

20 The comparable figures in Ashanti and the Colony were 17,425 people/1,006 square miles and 27,253 people/593 square miles. Staniland, *The Lions of Dagbon*, 46–47.

21 Staniland, 44.

22 David Kimble, *A Political History of Ghana: The Rise of Gold Coast Nationalism, 1850–1928* (Oxford: Clarendon Press, 1963), 534; Grischow, *Shaping Tradition*, 47. Staniland quotes an earlier statement from Governor

Hodgson in 1899 that not "a single penny more than was absolutely necessary" would be expended on the area. Staniland, *The Lions of Dagbon*, 43.

23 With few exceptions, studies of forced labor in Ghana and elsewhere have focused on mass mobilization, often involving long-distance migration, for large-scale infrastructure and for private enterprises. Akurang-Parry, "Colonial Forced Labor Policies"; Iliasu, "The Establishment of British Administration in Mamprugu"; Thomas, "Forced Labour in British West Africa"; Alexander Keese, "Slow Abolition within the Colonial Mind: British and French Debates about 'Vagrancy,' 'African Laziness,' and Forced Labour in West Central and South Central Africa, 1945–1965," *International Review of Social History* 59, no. 3 (2014): 377–407; Marie Rodet, "Forced Labor, Resistance, and Masculinities in Kayes, French Sudan, 1919–1946," *International Labor and Working-Class History* 86 (Fall 2014): 107–23; Monica M. van Beusekom, *Negotiating Development: African Farmers and Colonial Experts at the Office Du Niger, 1920–1960* (Portsmouth, NH: Heinemann, 2002). Two prominent recent exceptions are Sarah Kunkel, "Forced Labour, Roads, and Chiefs: The Implementation of the ILO Forced Labour Convention in the Gold Coast," *International Review of Social History* 63, no. 3 (2018): 449–76, and Romain Tiquet, "Challenging Colonial Forced Labor? Resistance, Resilience, and Power in Senegal (1920s–1940s)," *International Labor and Working-Class History* 93 (2018): 135–50. Libbie Freed's dissertation on road building in French Central Africa also does excellent work to explore ideologies and practices of forced labor. See Libbie Freed, "Conduits of Culture and Control: Roads in Colonial French Central Africa, 1890–1960" (PhD diss., University of Wisconsin, 2006).

24 For more on forced labor and trekking, see Staniland, *The Lions of Dagbon*, 45–48.

25 Staniland notes that 1,344 carriers were recruited in Western Dagomba district in 1920, representing what the DC estimated as "ten-thousand man-days" of lost agricultural labor. Staniland, *The Lions of Dagbon*, 46.

26 As Allman and Parker argue, "British administration . . . was experienced as brutal, illegitimate, and unpredictable, but it was also encountered unevenly, episodically, and in ways that were often marginal to the rituals and work of daily life." Allman and Parker, *Tongnaab*, 90.

27 Particularly compelling accounts of the extension of colonial rule in noncentralized political systems of northern Ghana include Allman and Parker, *Tongnaab*; Lentz, *Ethnicity*; and Benjamin Talton, *Politics of Social Change in Ghana: The Konkomba Struggle for Political Equality* (New York: Palgrave Macmillan, 2010).

28 Grischow, *Shaping Tradition*, 39. See also Lentz, *Ethnicity*, chapter 2; Allman and Parker, *Tongnaab*, chapter 2.

29 Contemporary spellings varied among Navarro/Navaro/Navoro and Zuaragu/Zuarugu. Cardinall began his time in the Gold Coast Civil Service

as a twenty-seven-year-old in 1914 and was first posted to the North in 1916. Staniland offers details of the educational and military background of a number of northern administrators as well as their dates of service in the colony and in the North; see Staniland, *The Lions of Dagbon*, 48–49.

30 The book was published in 1920. See A. W. Cardinall, *The Natives of the Northern Territories of the Gold Coast: Their Customs, Religion and Folklore* (London: Routledge, 1920). Cardinall's district diaries are sporadic and vague in reporting labor recruitment and works construction. In early 1919, he wrote of progress on roads and station buildings, but he also discussed the need to limit labor demands because of the district's heavy losses from the influenza epidemic, which he estimated had killed ten thousand residents by January. In November of 1919, he reported that he preferred that labor be recruited "voluntarily by private individuals" rather than by DCs. PRAAD-Tamale NRG8.4.3 (EAP541/1/4/3), Navrongo-Zuarungu Informal Diary, January–November 1919.

31 PRAAD-Tamale NRG8.4.3 (EAP541/1/4/3) Navrongo-Zuarungu Informal Diary, March and October 1919.

32 PRAAD-Tamale NRG8.4.3 (EAP541/1/4/3) Navrongo-Zuarungu Informal Diary, August and September 1919.

33 PRAAD-Tamale NRG8.4.3 (EAP541/1/4/3) Navrongo-Zuarungu Informal Diary, July 1919.

34 Staniland, *The Lions of Dagbon*, 49. Allman and Parker confirm the months of dry-season labor demands. Allman and Parker, *Tongnaab*, 60.

35 See Allman and Parker, *Tongnaab*, 86–87. By the time my research began in Kpasenkpe in 2010, I was unable to find any residents who personally remembered this era.

36 PRAAD-Tamale NRG8.4.10 (EAP541/1/4/10) Navrongo-Zuarungu Informal Diary, March and July 1920.

37 PRAAD-Tamale NRG8.4.6 (EAP541/1/4/6) Gambaga Informal Diary, September, October, and December 1919. In 1907, the Northeastern Province was split into two districts, Gambaga and Navrongo (sometimes Navrongo-Zuarungu, after a district office was opened in Zuarungu in 1910). See Grischow, *Shaping Tradition*, 34–36. By 1919, another district, Bawku (or Kusasi), had been carved out of the Gambaga District. See Roger G. Thomas, "The 1916 Bongo 'Riots' and Their Background: Aspects of Colonial Administration and African Response in Eastern Upper Ghana," *Journal of African History* 24, no. 1 (1983): 58. By 1926, Gambaga District was referred to as Southern Mamprusi (and Navrongo, Zuarungu, and Bawku/Kusasi as "Northern Mamprusi"). In 1932, Southern Mamprusi was amalgamated with Kusasi, Navrongo, and Zuarungu into the Mamprusi District. See Grischow, *Shaping Tradition*, 95.

38 PRAAD-Tamale NRG8.4.9 (EAP541/1/4/9) Tumu Informal Diary, June 1920. Jeffisi is often "Jeffies" in colonial diaries.

39 PRAAD-Tamale NRG8.4.9 (EAP541/1/4/9) Tumu Informal Diary, July 1920.

40 PRAAD-Tamale NRG8.4.9 (EAP541/1/4/9) Tumu Informal Diary, July 1920.

41 PRAAD-Tamale NRG8.4.9 (EAP541/1/4/9) Tumu Informal Diary, August 1920, remarking on work at Bellu. Shields was transferred to Wa District in August.

42 Scholars have also chronicled the use of fines, imprisonment, and other forms of coercion as well as the prevalence of desertion and avoidance in response to recruitment for colonial road building in southern Ghana: Akurang-Parry, "Colonial Forced Labor Policies"; Iliasu, "The Establishment of British Administration in Mamprugu"; Thomas, "Forced Labour."

43 PRAAD-Tamale NRG8.4.10 (EAP541/1/4/10) Navrongo-Zuarungu Informal Diary, July 1920.

44 PRAAD-Tamale NRG8.4.15 (EAP541/1/4/15) Lawra Informal Diary, October 1920.

45 PRAAD-Tamale NRG8.4.15 (EAP541/1/4/15) Lawra Informal Diary, August 1920. The poem is from E. C. Adams, *Lyra Nigeriæ* (London: T. F. Unwin, 1911), http://archive.org/details/lyranigeriaeooadamiala.

46 PRAAD-Tamale NRG8.4.11 (EAP 541/1/4/11) Gambaga Informal Diaries, February and March 1920. For more on the scheme, see Lentz, *Ethnicity*, 142–43, and Thomas, "Forced Labour," 91–94.

47 PRAAD-Tamale NRG8.4.6 (EAP 541/1/4/6) Gambaga Informal Diaries, November and December 1919. Thomas gives several accounts of both the methods (from threats to bribery) and the "logic-chopping" that administrators engaged in when they attempted to convince their superiors as well as the chiefs on whom demands fell that the quota system was only to recruit "voluntary" laborers. Thomas, "Forced Labour," 97–98.

48 PRAAD-Tamale NRG8.4.11 (EAP 541/1/4/11) Gambaga Informal Diaries, March 1920.

49 Between the 25th and 26th of August, Navrongo-Zuarungu DC Freeman said that more than three hundred recruits reported to his office, and he had "to stop now on account of literally having no more money to subsist any more people." PRAAD-Tamale NRG8.4.10 (EAP541/1/4/10) Navrongo-Zuarungu Informal Diary, August 1920. A month later, however, Freeman began to report on the widespread return of recruited laborers. In September, after complaining of the "nuisance" of "dealing with deserters from Railway labor," Freeman relayed the news from two such "deserters" that two men had drowned while trying to cross a flooded road. PRAAD-Tamale NRG8.4.10 (EAP541/1/4/10) Navrongo-Zuarungu Informal Diary, September 1920. In October, a headman from Bare reported, "The clerk they were handed to said they would have to go underground," which led his entire gang to refuse the work. PRAAD-Tamale NRG8.4.10 (EAP541/1/4/10) Navrongo-Zuarungu Informal Diary, October 1920. Thomas argues that northern migrants to southern gold mines

were often tasked with "the dangerous and unpleasant underground work"; see Thomas, "Forced Labour," 80. The official terminology of "desertion" and the existence of punishments further confirm that there was little that was "voluntary" about labor recruitment.

50 He reported, for example, that he "collected 46 deserted labourers, paid them extra subsistence and sent them back." PRAAD-Tamale NRG8.4.10 (EAP541/1/4/10) Navrongo-Zuarungu Informal Diary, October 1920. Similar instances are evident in PRAAD-Tamale NRG8.4.11 (EAP 541/1/4/11) Gambaga Informal Diaries, July 1920.

51 On a larger scale, the Northern Territories also became a destination for refugees from Upper Volta and Côte d'Ivoire who, as A. I. Asiwaju argues, migrated in protest of the repression and dispossession that accompanied French colonial rule. A. I. Asiwaju, "Migrations as Revolt: The Example of the Ivory Coast and the Upper Volta before 1945," *Journal of African History* 17, no. 4 (1976): 577–94.

52 PRAAD-Tamale NRG8.4.5 (EAP541/1/4/5) Tumu Informal Diary, January 1919.

53 PRAAD-Accra ADM56.1.278, letter from E. O. Rake, DC of Tumu, to commissioner of the Northwestern Province, February 19, 1919.

54 PRAAD-Accra ADM56.1.278, letter from H. M. Berkeley, commissioner of the Northwestern Province, to the acting commissioner of the Northeastern Province, April 30, 1919.

55 PRAAD-Accra ADM56.1.278, letter from S. D. Nash, commissioner of the Northeastern Province, to the acting district commissioner of Navarro-Zuaragu, June 4, 1919. For more on Nash and Cardinall as unusually perceptive administrators, see Allman and Parker, *Tongnaab*, chapters 1 and 2.

56 PRAAD-Accra ADM56.1.278, letter from DC A. W. Cardinall to the acting commissioner of Northern Province, June 14, 1919.

57 In his reply, he pointed out the hypocrisy of restricting these migrants at a time when the government was promoting and enforcing long-distance labor: "I would further ask you, if the natives in question had migrated to Gambaga, Tamale, or Coomassie, would you have asked for their return?" PRAAD-Accra ADM56.1.278, letter from S. D. Nash, commissioner of the Northeastern Province, to the commissioner of the Northwestern Province, June 28, 1919.

58 PRAAD-Accra ADM56.1.278, letter from H. M. Berkeley, commissioner of the Northwestern Province, to H. W. Leigh, acting chief commissioner of the Northern Territories, October 27, 1919.

59 Leigh, presumably concerned with sparking conflict among his few DCs, left the issue unresolved, instructing in vague terms that "a personal investigation by the District Commissioner affected" should determine government action, without specifying how to resolve an issue on which two "affected" DCs disagreed so fundamentally. PRAAD-Accra ADM56.1.278,

letter from H. W. Leigh, acting chief commissioner of the Northern Territories, to the commissioner of the Northwestern Province, November 5, 1919.

60 Continued correspondence in 1920 and 1921 between Nash and Duncan-Johnstone, the DC of Lawra-Tumu, can be found in PRAAD-Accra ADM56.1.278. When Michael Dasent returned three and a half years after his initial interaction with the Santejan case to find that the terms of debate had escalated, he argued that Cardinall's "fulsome journalese" was merely a cover for biased rulings and administrative inadequacy, pointing out that "under the administration of (Mr. A.W. CARDINALL) little or no Labour for outside has been recruited." PRAAD-Accra ADM56.1.278, letter from Michael Dasent, DC of Lawra-Tumu, to the commissioner of the Northern Province, June 17, 1922.

61 Grischow, *Shaping Tradition*, 60.

62 Grischow, *Shaping Tradition*, 60–61, citing R. E. Wraith, *Guggisberg* (London: Oxford University Press, 1967), 100. At first glance, one might assume that the appearance of private lorry transport would have brought new opportunities to northern farmers and traders. Recent studies by Ntewusu and Soeters suggest that while in the 1920s traders began to rely on lorry transport in addition to older methods of transport (by canoe, head porters, carts, and bicycles), the vast majority of trade north of Tamale continued to be carried by head-load. See Ntewusu, "Settling In and Holding On," chapter 6, and Sebastiaan Soeters, "Tamale 1907–1957: Between Colonial Trade and Colonial Chieftainship" (PhD diss., University of Leiden, 2012), chapters 2 and 3. Even a few lorries could take a heavy toll on unpaved roads, however, meaning that one of the first widespread effects of motor transport was not increased mobility but, rather, an increase in the frequency with which residents of the Northern Territories were called to repair the roads. Hart points out that "early commercial motor lorries were a poor fit for early twentieth-century road conditions in the Gold Coast. At a time when few roads were metalled [paved] the heavy weight of imported European lorries caused dirt and gravel roads to deteriorate quickly." Jennifer Hart, *Ghana on the Go: African Mobility in the Age of Motor Transportation* (Bloomington: Indiana University Press, 2016), 45. For complaints about the impact of lorries on roads, see excerpts from Lawra-Tumu Diary, December 1926, in PRAAD-Tamale NRG8.4.18 (EAP541/1/4/18); Informal Diaries Northern Province; and from Mamprusi Diary, January 1933, PRAAD-Tamale NRG8.4.69 (EAP541/1/4/67). Extracts from Informal Diaries of the commissioner of the Southern Province.

63 For more on the contradictions between ambition and funding in Guggisberg's road-building plans, see Hart, *Ghana on the Go*, chapter 1. Nominal payments for road gangs, pegged at the low rate of 6 pence per day, do not seem to have served as an incentive for road work, as officials continued

to struggle to enforce labor demands. For comparison, Thomas argues that in 1920 men from the North who were forced into labor gangs for southern railways were paid three times this amount (1 shilling 6 pence), that those forced into mine work were (at least theoretically) paid four times as much (2 shillings), and that wages for both "government" and mine work in the South paled in comparison to what migrants earned on southern cocoa farms. Thomas, "Forced Labour," 93–94. Furthermore, it is relatively certain that the payments themselves were sporadic, as officials were adamant in the 1930s that they could not afford to pay all the labor regularly requisitioned by the government, even at these low rates. It is also worth mentioning that fines for refusing to perform local labor—often 10 to 20 shillings—massively outweighed the payments laborers received.

64 Making roads accessible to motor vehicles without spending much money also spurred additional schemes. By 1930, Whittall estimated that "5 or 6 hundred pounds" would be necessary to pay the labor used annually to repair the drifts on the road between Tamale and Navrongo—a laughably large expense for around one hundred miles of road. This estimate of the tradeoffs between labor and materials hit at the heart of the financial rationale for road labor. An all-weather road, which would drastically reduce annual labor costs, was, the governor noted, simply out of the question. PRAAD-Tamale NRG8.4.33 (EAP 541/1/4/32), Informal Diary Chief Commissioner Northern Territories, January 1930. In June to July of 1926, Northern Provincial Commissioner P. F. Whittall began to experiment with local manufacture of road-making materials. Ordering the laborers at his station in Navrongo to make a kiln out of an old government bungalow, he then had them pack it with clay-and-earth bricks to use on local culverts and bridges. While Whittall's staff at his station appear to have been permanent employees, the brick-making scheme relied on forced labor, recruited and enforced by colonial staff. The underlying threat of violence should not be underestimated. In June, Whittall reported that a constable who was supervising carriers delivering clay from the town of Tili (over forty miles away) had become "annoyed" at one carrier's sickness and had "made them strip and lie down on the stony road and roll along as punishment." PRAAD-Tamale (EAP541/1/4/30), Northern Provincial Commissioner Diary, June 1926.

65 PRAAD-Tamale NRG8.4.18 (EAP 541/1/4/18), Informal Diaries Northern Province, October 1926. New technical staff could add to the demands on local labor even when commissioners were not aware of it, as evidenced by periodic investigations into African colonial staff's use of carriers and "free labour" "in [the DC's] name." Whittall noted that "Yesterday I got hold of a Sawyer who last year succeeded in getting a lot of free labour out of the Chief of BELUNGU in my name, whereas he has never cut for me." PRAAD-Tamale (EAP 541/1/4/30), Northern Provincial

Commissioner Diary, April 1926. See also Whittall's notes on Veterinary Assistant Engman, PRAAD-Tamale NRG8.4.18 (EAP541/1/4/18), Informal Diaries Northern Province, December 1926.

66 PRAAD-Tamale (EAP541/1/4/30) Excerpts from Wa Monthly Informal Diaries, June 1926 and September–October 1928.

67 In May, Whittall noted that "in March . . . they all had their choice to follow Sandema or go." PRAAD-Tamale (EAP541/1/4/30), Provincial Commissioner's Diary, May 1926. In July, in response to reports from the Sandemnaab that "certain Mamprusis are trying to come into Kanjarga country," Whittall instructed the DC of Southern Mamprusi "to warn his people that this country has already got more people than it can carry and no more can be admitted. We want to encourage migration South not North." PRAAD-Tamale (EAP541/1/4/30), Provincial Commissioner's Diary, July 1926.

68 PRAAD-Tamale NRG8.4.18 (EAP 541/1/4/18), Informal Diaries Northern Province, Northern Provincial Commissioner's Diary, October 1926; Informal Diaries Northern Province, Southern Mamprusi Diary, November 1926.

69 PRAAD-Tamale NRG8.4.18 (EAP 541/1/4/18), Informal Diaries Northern Province, Provincial Commissioner's Diary, November 1926; PRAAD-Tamale (EAP541/1/4/30), Southern Mamprusi Diary, December 1926. The term "boundary jump" is from PRAAD-Tamale NRG8.4.18 (EAP 541/1/4/18), Informal Diaries Northern Province, Lawra-Tumu Diary, November 1926.

70 PRAAD-Tamale (EAP541/1/4/30), Provincial Commissioner's Diary, April 1928. The full quotation reads, "There is something wrong in that corner and we must try and find out what it is. People are constantly moving over to the GAMBAGA side from there."

71 PRAAD-Tamale NRG8.4.15 (EAP541/1/4/15), Lawra Informal Diary, September and October 1920. On September 3, Duncan Johnstone noted that the chief of Lambussie was observing roads in Lawra to make his own. On September 11, he wrote that the chief of Nandaw was widening his road, and in October he argued that road widening signaled that "all the Chiefs seem keen on making a name for themselves." He also noted in September that the newly installed Magajias (women's leader) in Lawra had organized five hundred women to do road labor around town.

72 There do appear to have been limits to what Whittall would praise, for in November of 1926 he asked the Sandemnaab not to "have his road beaten 'on his own'" in order to "keep the labour for more urgently required work." PRAAD-Tamale NRG8.4.18 (EAP541/1/4/18), Informal Diaries Northern Province, Provincial Commissioner's Diary, November 1926.

73 PRAAD-Tamale NRG8.4.18 (EAP541/1/4/18), Informal Diaries Northern Province, Extracts from Lawra-Tumu Diary, December 1926.

74 Lentz, *Ethnicity*, 287n106.

75 PRAAD-Tamale NRG8.4.18 (EAP541/1/4/18), Informal Diaries Northern Province, Extracts from Lawra-Tumu Diaries, December 1926.

76 PRAAD-Tamale (EAP541/1/4/30), Extracts from Lawra-Tumu Diaries, January and February 1927; PRAAD-Tamale NRG 8.4.22 (EAP541/1/4/22), Informal Diaries Northern Province, 1927, Extracts from Lawra-Tumu Diaries, May and June 1927; PRAAD-Tamale NRG8.4.30 (EAP541/1/4/29), Informal Diaries, 1927, Extract from Lawra-Tumu Diary, September 1927.

77 PRAAD-Tamale (EAP541/1/4/30), Extracts from Lawra-Tumu Diary, January 1927.

78 See also Sean Hawkins, *Writing and Colonialism in Northern Ghana: The Encounter between the LoDagaa and "The World on Paper", 1892–1991* (Toronto: University of Toronto Press, 2002), 111–13, 176.

79 Duncan Johnstone's discussions of Tugu roads and Kayani's relationships with constituents appear in the diaries for June, July, August, and September of 1920. The quotations are from October 8 and September 19, 1920. PRAAD-Tamale NRG8.4.15 (EAP541/1/4/15), Lawra Informal Diary.

80 PRAAD-Tamale NRG8.4.18 (EAP541/1/4/18), Informal Diaries Northern Province, Extracts from Lawra-Tumu Diary, December 1926.

81 PRAAD-Tamale NRG8.4.30 (EAP 541/1/4/29), Informal Diaries, Lawra District documents for August and September 1927. The quotation is from a letter from the district commissioner of Lawra-Tumu to the commissioner of the Northern Province on August 23, 1927. The "Slavery Convention" passed by the League of Nations in 1926 highlighted new European debates about when colonial forced labor constituted "conditions analogous to slavery." See Frederick Cooper, "Conditions Analogous to Slavery: Imperialism and Free Labour Ideology in Africa," in *Beyond Slavery: Explorations of Race, Labor, and Citizenship in Postemancipation Societies*, ed. Frederick Cooper, Thomas C. Holt, and Rebecca J. Scott (Chapel Hill: University of North Carolina Press, 2000), 107–50. Over the course of 1927 and 1928, Northern Province officials acted on a growing concern about chiefs' demands for farm labor, reminding chiefs (as if the two could be separated) that they should call farm labor under "their own authority and not the D.C.'s authority" and that demands would be limited to five days per year. The quotation is from PRAAD-Tamale NRG8.4.22 (EAP541/1/4/22), Informal Diaries Northern Province, Extracts from Lawra-Tumu Diary, December 1927. By 1928, officials began articulating a limit of five days per year that chiefs would be permitted to demand constituent labor on their farms. See PRAAD-Tamale NRG8.4.22 (EAP541/1/4/22), Informal Diaries Northern Province, Extracts from Lawra-Tumu Diary, March 1928; PRAAD-Tamale (EAP541/1/4/30), Southern Mamprusi Diary, June 1928, and Kusasi Diary, July 1928.

82 PRAAD-Tamale NRG8.4.30 (EAP 541/1/4/29), Informal Diaries, letter from the district commissioner of Lawra-Tumu to the commissioner of the Northern Province on August 23, 1927.

83 He was allowed to return to "live quietly" in Tugu in February of 1928. PRAAD-Tamale NRG8.2.14 (EAP 541/1/2/10), Tugu Affairs, correspondence September 1927 to February 1928.

84 PRAAD-Tamale NRG8.2.14 (EAP 541/1/2/10), Tugu Affairs, letter from the acting DC of Lawra-Tumu to the commissioner of the Northern Province, April 15, 1930, letters from the commissioner of Northern Province to the acting DC of Lawra-Tumu, May 8, 1930, and June 5, 1930.

85 See Richard Roberts, "Coerced Labor in Twentieth-Century Africa," in *The Cambridge World History of Slavery*, ed. David Eltis et al., vol. 4, *AD 1804–AD 2016* (Cambridge: Cambridge University Press, 2017), 583–609; Marlous van Waijenburg, "Financing the African Colonial State: The Revenue Imperative and Forced Labor," *Journal of Economic History* 78, no. 1 (March 2018): 40–80.

86 For more on activism against forced labor as well as legislative changes in colonial Africa in the 1930s, see Frederick Cooper, "Conditions Analogous to Slavery"; Opolot Okia, *Labor in Colonial Kenya after the Forced Labor Convention*; Romain Tiquet, "Challenging Colonial Forced Labor?"; Babacar Fall, "Le Trevail Force en Afrique Occidentale Française (1900–1946)," *Civilisations* 41, no. 1/2 (1993): 329–36.

87 The law was to come into effect in the Northern Territories in 1932. PRAAD-Tamale NRG3.22.1, Labour—Northern Territories, confidential letter from the acting chief commissioner of the Northern Territories to the DC Mamprusi Gambaga, November 10, 1932.

88 Kunkel, "Forced Labour, Roads, and Chiefs."

89 Frederick D. Lugard, *The Dual Mandate in British Tropical Africa* (London: William Blackwood & Sons, 1922), https://hdl.handle.net/2027/mdp.39015020087949. Architects of indirect rule hoped that local taxes would make each Native Authority revenue neutral while also demonstrating "the value of local government" through public works. This vision came up against the practical impossibility of raising significant funds through direct taxation in large areas of the North.

90 Kunkel, "Forced Labour, Roads, and Chiefs."

91 Kunkel.

92 British and international advocacy on the subject of forced labor relied on drawing distinctions between forced labor for private enterprise, which was condemned, and for public works, which would simply need to be regulated. Furthermore, and particularly important in light of their reliance on chiefs, the British successfully advocated for the retention of labor demanded by "native custom" and in "personal service" to chiefs who were otherwise not compensated for their administrative work. Suzanne Miers, *Slavery in the Twentieth Century: The Evolution of a Global Problem* (Walnut Creek, CA: Altamira, 2003), chapter 10. Cooper suggests that this distinction in fact legitimized many forms of forced labor: "Whatever was not declared coerced was therefore not analogous to

slavery and would acquire the distinction of having been exonerated in terms of the only moral criteria the League and the ILO were applying to colonial labor." Cooper, "Conditions Analogous to Slavery," 132. For more on how "communal labor" allowed labor extraction to continue in colonial Kenya, see Okia, *Communal Labor in Colonial Kenya*, and Okia, *Labor in Colonial Kenya after the Forced Labor Convention.*

93 ILO, "Forced Labour Convention," Convention CO29, June 28, 1930, http://www.ilo.org/dyn/normlex/en/f?p=1000:12100:0::NO::P12100_ILO_CODE: C029. Article 10 of the ILO Forced Labour Convention is also quoted in PRAAD-Tamale NRG3.22.1, Labour—Northern Territories, Memo no. 634/30/5/50, "Maintenance of Roads Under the Forced Labour Convention," from Acting Colonial Secretary G. C. du Boulay, July 20, 1933.

94 PRAAD-Tamale NRG3.22.1, Labour—Northern Territories, letter from W. J. A Jones, chief commissioner of the Northern Territories, to the colonial secretary, Accra, June 5, 1935.

95 PRAAD-Tamale NRG3.22.1, Labour—Northern Territories, letter from the colonial secretary to the chief commissioner of the Northern Territories, May 18, 1936.

96 As Berry argues, policies of indirect rule "wove instability—in the form of changing relations of authority and conflicting interpretations of rules—into the fabric of colonial administration." Berry, "Hegemony on a Shoestring," 336.

97 See, for example, Lentz, *Ethnicity*; Christian Lund, *Local Politics and the Dynamics of Property in Africa* (Cambridge: Cambridge University Press, 2008); Talton, *Politics of Social Change.*

98 Lentz, *Ethnicity*, 126. By the 1940s, Cardinall's 1920 formulation of a "benevolent despot" had apparently been replaced by what Lentz notes as DC Amherst's praise for the Lawra Na as a "benevolent progressive despot."

99 PRAAD-Tamale NRG8.10.14, letter from George E. London, acting governor of the Gold Coast, to Malcolm MacDonald, secretary of state for the colonies, July 10, 1935.

100 Franz Kröger, "Colonial Officers and Bulsa Chiefs," *Buluk* 7 (2013), https://buluk.de/new/. In the 1920s, as colonial officials used the instruments of colonial force as well as chiefs' "own initiative" to construct roads and rest houses, they also embarked on parallel efforts to understand, catalog, and, in many cases, reshape local structures of authority in the interest of designating "head chiefs" who could act as counterparts to colonial district commissioners. Most complex and controversial were debates surrounding the position of *tindanas* ("earthpriests"); see Allman and Parker, *Tongnaab*; Lentz, *Ethnicity*; Lund, *Local Politics.*

101 In the First World War, the Builsa area also became known to colonial officials as a key site for military recruitment, for which Azantilow's brother, Afoko, was presented a medallion. Franz Kröger, "Extracts from Bulsa

History: Sandema Chiefs before Azantilow," *Buluk* 6 (2012), https://buluk .de/new/.

102 Kröger, "Extracts from Bulsa History"; Franz Kröger, "Kunkwa, Kategra and Jadema: The Sandemnaab's Lawsuit," *Buluk* 6 (2012), https://buluk .de/new/.

103 "Funeral Service for the Late Nab Dr. Ayieta Azantilow, 1900–2006," 2006, original copy from the personal files of Namiyelana E. D. Sebiyam. Text also available in *Buluk* 6, https://buluk.de/new/.

104 PRAAD-Tamale NRG8.10.14, letter from W. A. Jones to colonial secretary, March 9, 1936.

105 Grischow, *Shaping Tradition*, 138–42.

106 In 1925, Governor Guggisberg solicited a "secret report" to ascertain the "principal chiefs of the Gold Coast . . . the amount of influence they exert and their loyalty to the Government or otherwise." In a June 1927 reply, the district commissioner of Southern Mamprusi reported Barijesira as "VERY LOYAL," (other chiefs in the area were described as "modern," "old style," or "lazy"), noting that he was "most intelligent" and "makes great efforts to understand what is required and carry it out. Has a small division but excellent influence over his people." PRAAD-Tamale NRG 3.3.1. However, by the late 1930s the Kpasenkpe area was mentioned only in connection with refusals of labor, disputes over jurisdiction, and official neglect. See PRAAD-Tamale NRG8.4.70 (EAP541/1/4/68), Informal Diary Gambaga, November 1933 and April 1934; PRAAD-Tamale NRG8.4.72 (EAP541/1/4/70), Informal Diary Gambaga, January and July 1935; PRAAD-Tamale NRG8.4.90 (EAP541/1/4/87), Informal Diary Gambaga, May 1938.

107 PRAAD-Tamale NRG8.10.14, letter from chief commissioner of the Northern Territories to colonial secretary, January 21, 1939.

108 District officer notes, December 3, 1939, cited by Kröger in his notes on Sandema records at PRAAD Accra, available at http:// www.kroeger1937.homepage.t-online.de/Materialien/. Officials also noted that Azantilow used the school to learn English; see Roger Thomas, "Education in Northern Ghana, 1906–1940: A Study in Colonial Paradox," *International Journal of African Historical Studies* 7, no. 3 (1974): 459.

109 PRAAD-Tamale NRG8.10.14, letter from W. A. Jones to colonial secretary, December 11, 1939.

110 Mixed farming programs envisioned that chiefs would "demonstrate" crops and techniques advocated by the recently established northern agricultural service. District officials used chiefs' farming to measure the success of agricultural programs and the competency of particular chiefs. PRAAD-Tamale NRG8.4.98, Informal Diaries Navrongo, July 1943 and January 1944.

111 Since the Sandemnaab, like Wulugunaba Sebiyam, was deceased at the time of research, oral evidence comes from constituents and family

members whose recollections are invariably influenced by his long involvement with development, making it particularly difficult to isolate this initial period.

112 PRAAD-Tamale NRG8.4.98, Informal Diaries Navrongo, April 1940.

113 For more on northern migrants' ideas about knowledge and development, see Gariba B. Abdul-Korah, "'Ka Bie Ba Yor': Labor Migration among the Dagaaba of the Upper West Region of Ghana, 1936–1957," *Nordic Journal of African Studies* 17, no. 1 (2008): 1–19.

114 PRAAD-Tamale NRG8.4.98, Informal Diaries Navrongo, February and March 1940.

115 PRAAD-Tamale NRG8.4.98, Informal Diaries Navrongo, February 1940.

116 PRAAD-Tamale NRG8.4.98, Informal Diaries Navrongo, March 1940.

117 Former students recall mixed reactions to the Sandemnaab's efforts to recruit students and teachers in the 1940s and 1950s; see Ghanatta Ayaric, ed., "Eric Akanpaanab Ayaric Recalls His School Days in the 1930s and 1940s (taken from an audio-recorded account by Akanpaanab in 2000)," *Buluk* 7 (2013), https://buluk.de/new/; Franz Kröger, "Going to a Bulsa School: Enrolment, Motivation and Resistance," *Buluk* 3 (2001), https://buluk.de/new/. For more on colonial schooling in Northern Ghana, see Lacy S. Ferrell, "'We Were Mixed with All Types': Educational Migration in the Northern Territories of Colonial Ghana," in *Children on the Move in Africa: Past and Present Experiences of Migration*, ed. Elodie Razy and Marie Rodet (Woodbridge, Suffolk: James Currey, 2016), 141–58. Notes on the cattle kraal and opening of the middle school are in "Funeral Service for the Late Nab Dr. Ayieta Azantilow, 1900–2006."

118 Franz Kröger, "Mr. Abu Gariba, One of the First to Combine Traditional and Modern Bulsa Values," *Buluk* 8 (2014), https://buluk.de/new/.

119 In other parts of British colonial Africa, the Second World War offered an opportunity for officials to justify forced labor as an emergency measure. Keese, "Slow Abolition within the Colonial Mind." In northern Ghana, however, mechanisms of coercion remained piecemeal and there is even some evidence that colonial subjects were able to bargain for increases in the low daily rate for road labor. In 1942, the colonial government constructed a military airfield (or aerodrome) that, while never used for military maneuvers, briefly employed over a thousand laborers. In June of 1942, when a colony-wide decision to offer a "cost of living" bonus was implemented unevenly between workers employed by the Native Authorities and the aerodrome project, district officials indicated difficulties hiring road labor until the pay difference was eliminated. As the harvest began in September, the aerodrome competed with agricultural labor, which occasioned an increase in daily wages from 8 to 9 pence per day. Similarly, in July of 1943, DC Davies argued that wages for building a forest ranger's bungalow needed to be increased to attract labor during the planting season. PRAAD-Tamale NRG8.4.98, Informal Diaries Navrongo,

June–August 1942, September–October 1942, and July 1943. For a similar phenomenon in Lawra-Tumu District, see Lentz, *Ethnicity*, 69.

120 Grischow, *Shaping Tradition*, chapter 6.

121 PRAAD-Tamale NRG8.4.98, Informal Diaries Navrongo, April 1942. This comment likely reflects growing official concern about native courts in southern Ghana; see Sara Berry, *Chiefs Know Their Boundaries: Essays on Property, Power, and the Past in Asante, 1896–1996* (Portsmouth, NH: Heinemann, 2001), 38–43.

122 PRAAD-Tamale NRG8.4.98, Informal Diaries Navrongo, April 1943.

123 PRAAD-Tamale NRG8.4.98, Informal Diaries Navrongo, February 1943.

124 PRAAD-Tamale NRG8.4.98, Informal Diaries Navrongo, 1940–47. Early on, officials remarked that the chief of nearby Chiana was "of the Sandem-nab standard," and the two chiefs dominated colonial officials' accounts of area development projects in the 1940s. PRAAD-Tamale NRG8.4.98, Informal Diaries Navrongo, May 1940.

125 PRAAD-Tamale NRG8.4.98, Informal Diaries Navrongo, January 1944. Underlining is from the chief commissioner, who noted "Good" in the margin.

CHAPTER 2: STATECRAFT AND VILLAGE DEVELOPMENT IN "NKRUMAH'S TIME"

1 PRAAD-Tamale NRG3.13.33, Meetings of the Regional Commissioner and District Commissioners 1962–66, "Minutes of Meeting of the Regional Commissioner and District Commissioners Held at the Regional Office on the 11th October, 1962."

2 Throughout Ghana, chiefs were active in forging new rhetorical and practical connections between chieftaincy and changing political and governmental structures. See Jean Marie Allman, *The Quills of the Porcupine: Asante Nationalism in an Emergent Ghana* (Madison: University of Wisconsin Press, 1993); Naaborko Sackeyfio-Lenoch, *The Politics of Chieftaincy: Authority and Property in Colonial Ghana, 1920–1950* (Rochester, NY: University of Rochester Press, 2014).

3 PRAAD-Tamale NRG8.5.18, Conference of Chiefs 1942–48, "Address by His Excellency the Governor to the Northern Territories Chiefs at the Durbar Held at Tamale on 27th January 1945."

4 For insight into these dual imperial goals, see Fredrick Cooper, "Modernizing Bureaucrats, Backward Africans, and the Development Concept," in *International Development and the Social Sciences: Essays on the History and Politics of Knowledge*, ed. Frederick Cooper and Randall Packard (Berkeley: University of California Press, 1997), 64–92; Joseph Morgan Hodge, *Triumph of the Expert: Agrarian Doctrines of Development and the Legacies of British Colonialism* (Athens: Ohio University Press, 2007), chapter 7.

5 Frederick Cooper, "Writing the History of Development," *Journal of Modern European History* 8, no. 1 (2010): 5–23. As Cooper points out,

former colonial powers similarly took the opportunity to delegitimize the claims of new nations vis-à-vis their colonizers.

6 Jeffrey S. Ahlman, *Living with Nkrumahism: Nation, State, and Pan-Africanism in Ghana* (Athens: Ohio University Press, 2017), 50–51.

7 Carola Lentz, *Ethnicity and the Making of History in Northern Ghana* (Edinburgh: Edinburgh University Press, 2006), 145–46.

8 Jeffrey Ahlman's *Living with Nkrumahism* gives a nuanced account of the intellectual and ideological development of Nkrumahism as well as the ways that Ghanaians shaped and navigated its tensions. See also several chapters on Nkrumah's Ghana in Peter J. Bloom, Stephan Miescher, and Takyiwaa Manuh, eds., *Modernization as Spectacle in Africa* (Bloomington: Indiana University Press, 2014).

9 For more on the regional disparities of postcolonial development planning, see Jacob Songsore, *Regional Development in Ghana: The Theory and the Reality* (Accra: Woeli Publishing Services, 2003).

10 Paul André Ladouceur, *Chiefs and Politicians: The Politics of Regionalism in Northern Ghana*, Legon History Series (London: Longman, 1979), 202–5.

11 For a discussion of Konkomba mobilization and political imagination in this era, see Talton, *Politics of Social Change in Ghana: The Konkomba Struggle for Political Equality* (New York: Palgrave Macmillan, 2010), chapter 4. See also the discussion of decolonization and local political mobilization in Lentz, *Ethnicity*, chapters 7 and 8.

12 For recent discussions of the CPP's differential treatment of chieftaincy in the North, see Boone, *Political Topographies of the African State: Territorial Authority and Institutional Choice* (Cambridge: Cambridge University Press, 2003), 174–77, and Lentz, *Ethnicity*, 180–82. The clearest example of Nkrumah-era politics of northern difference comes from the antinudity campaigns that I discuss in chapter 3. See Jean Allman, "'Let Your Fashion Be in Line with Our Ghanaian Costume': Nation, Gender and the Politics of Clothing in Nkrumah's Ghana," in Jean Allman, *Fashioning Africa: Power and the Politics of Dress* (Bloomington: Indiana University Press, 2004), 144–66. A deeper examination of the role that imaginaries of northern difference have played in coastal political imagination comes from Bayo Holsey, *Routes of Remembrance: Refashioning the Slave Trade in Ghana* (Chicago: University of Chicago Press, 2008), chapter 3.

13 Frederick Cooper, "Possibility and Constraint: African Independence in Historical Perspective," *Journal of African History* 49, no. 2 (2008): 167–96.

14 Frederick Cooper, *Africa Since 1940: The Past of the Present* (Cambridge: Cambridge University Press, 2002), 85; Stephan Miescher, Peter J. Bloom, and Takyiwaa Manuh, "Introduction," in Bloom, Miescher, and Manuh, *Modernization as Spectacle*, 1.

15 John Aerni-Flessner, *Dreams for Lesotho: Independence, Foreign Assistance, and Development* (Notre Dame, IN: University of Notre Dame

Press, 2018); Ahlman, *Living with Nkrumahism*; Priya Lal, *African Socialism in Postcolonial Tanzania: Between the Village and the World* (Cambridge: Cambridge University Press, 2015); Kara Moskowitz, *Seeing Like a Citizen: Decolonization, Development, and the Making of Kenya, 1945–1980* (Athens: Ohio University Press, 2019).

16 For more on the "multiple Nkrumahisms" that existed even among Ghanaians who were more entwined with the structures of the Nkrumah state, see Ahlman, *Living with Nkrumahism*, 21.

17 The common use of "Nkrumah's time" is noted in ethnographies (and is also used commonly in the press and in academic publications). For example, see Gracia Clark, "Negotiating Asante Family Survival in Kumasi, Ghana," *Africa: Journal of the International African Institute* 69, no. 1 (1999): 74; Thomas Yarrow, "Remains of the Future: Rethinking the Space and Time of Ruination through the Volta Resettlement Project, Ghana," *Cultural Anthropology* 32, no. 4 (2017): 566–91. Like Yarrow, I want to point out the way that this periodization allows Ghanaians to make arguments about the past. He argues that, for people who live in what remains of the Volta Resettlement Project, the idea of "Nkrumah's time" represents a "nostalgia for modernization" that is associated with not only the aims of that project but for the hopes for the future that Nkrumah's modernizing agenda represented. In Kpasenkpe, in contrast, I am interested in how the framing of "Nkrumah's time" collapses late colonial and nationalist development efforts, pointing out continuities where scholars might otherwise see disjuncture.

18 As elsewhere in Ghana, this hierarchy is more of a framework for argumentation than it is a settled structure. Both historically and in the present, claims to the chieftaincy in a Mamprusi settlement were made by mobilizing historical and genealogical claims that locate both the settlement and the claimant.

19 David Carson Davis, "Continuity and Change in Mampurugu" (PhD diss., Northwestern University, 1984), 14–16. In both northern and southern Ghana, chieftaincies are referred to metonymically as either "stools" (southern Ghana) or "skins" (northern Ghana). Thus a northern Ghanaian chief is "enskinned" (like a southern Ghanaian chief is "enstooled," or like a British queen or king is "enthroned").

20 Shortly after the end of World War II, Agricultural Extension Officer Charles Lynn accepted a post as the DC of Mamprusi, on the condition that he would continue his agricultural extension work. Charles Lynn, Marjorie Lynn, and Sylvia Lynn, *The Long Garden Master in the Gold Coast: The Life and Times of a Colonial Agricultural Officer in the Gold Coast, 1929–1947* (Bedfordshire, UK: Authors OnLine, 2012), chapter 9. Memories of bullock training and *nigi puu* are from an interview with Sakparana Sandow Batisima, Kpasenkpe, June 28, 2010, and interviews with Pastor Daniel Barijesira Azundow, Kpasenkpe, September and October 2010.

21 PRAAD-Tamale NRG3.16.3, letter from chief commissioner of the Northern Territories to DC Gambaga, September 10, 1947; PRAAD-Tamale, NRG3.16.3, letter from N. O. Dobbs to chief commissioner of the Northern Territories, October 22, 1948.

22 Data preserved in district records is partial. Unlike national or colony-wide aggregates, however, it appears amidst practical discussions of how funds were allocated. It is thus much more likely to reflect the actual disbursements at the district level. Figures are compiled from PRAAD-Tamale NRG8.10.27, Direct Taxation 1945–54; NRG8.10.32, Community and Local Development Committees (Grants-in-Aid) 1948–51; NRG8.10.36, Grants-in-Aid 1950–51; NRG8.10.38, Government Grants-in-Aid to Native Authority (Local Authorities) 1951–57; NRG8.10.58, Regional Development and Funds 1956–57; and NRG8.3.224, Report Development Aid Local Authorities 1957–59.

23 Jeffrey Grischow, Shaping Tradition: Civil Society, Community and Development in Colonial Northern Ghana, 1899–1957 (Leiden: Brill, 2006), 169.

24 Grischow, Shaping Tradition, chapter 7; Kate Skinner, "'It Brought Some Kind of Neatness to Mankind': Literacy, Development and Democracy in 1950s Asante," Africa 79, no. 4 (2009).

25 Lentz, Ethnicity, 188, citing Peter du Sautoy, Community Development in Ghana (Oxford: Oxford University Press, 1958). The most fully articulated program for small-scale northern development was the Mass Education program, which aimed to combine mass literacy campaigns with community development work. Drawing on missionary networks and administered through the newly formed Department of Social Welfare and Community Development, Mass Education initiatives hoped to use literacy to both control African political initiative and meet new demands for education in the "interstices of political nationalism." Kate Skinner, "From Pentecostalism to Politics: Mass Literacy and Community Development in Late Colonial Northern Ghana," Paedagogica Historica 46, no. 3 (2010): 308.

26 Benedetta Rossi, "What 'Development' Does to Work," International Labor and Working-Class History 92 (Fall 2017): 7–23.

27 Nicole Sackley, "The Village as Cold War Site: Experts, Development, and the History of Rural Reconstruction," Journal of Global History 6, no. 3 (2011): 481–504.

28 Daniel Immerwahr, Thinking Small: The United States and the Lure of Community Development (Cambridge, MA: Harvard University Press, 2018), 67–69.

29 Intellectual and social histories of the Etawah project and the Indian community development program are in Nicole Sackley, "Village Models: Etawah, India, and the Making and Remaking of Development in the Early Cold War," Diplomatic History 37, no. 4 (2013): 749–78; Immerwahr, Thinking Small, chapter 3.

30 Joanna Lewis, *Empire State-Building: War and Welfare in Kenya, 1925–52* (Oxford: James Currey, 2000), chapter 6.

31 D. A. Low and J. M. Lonsdale, "Introduction," in *History of East Africa*, ed. D. A. Low and A. Smith, *vol.* 3 (Oxford: Clarendon Press, 1976), 12–16. For a recent examination of these dynamics in Nigeria, see Bekeh Utietiang Ukelina, *The Second Colonial Occupation: Development Planning, Agriculture, and the Legacies of British Rule in Nigeria* (Lanham, MD: Lexington Books, 2017).

32 Hodge, *Triumph of the Expert*, chapter 7. Nicole Sackley persuasively argues that the postwar era was marked by the "'scientization' of rural reform" that treated village projects as "laboratories" for social scientific knowledge production. Sackley, "The Village as Cold War Site," 482.

33 Skinner, "From Pentecostalism to Politics."

34 The title of "district commissioner" was changed to "district administrative officer" in the mid-1950s, but they remained "DCs" in local parlance.

35 PRAAD-Tamale NRG3.25.32, Development—Northern Territories 1948–51, memo from chief commissioner of the Northern Territories to all DCs and assistant DCs, October 12, 1948.

36 PRAAD-Tamale NRG3.25.32, Development—Northern Territories 1948–51, memo from DC Bawku, October 29, 1948.

37 Officials debated the best way to allocate grants among districts, working with formulas that included considerations of taxes collected by the new local government bodies, the population of districts, and previous grant allocations. See PRAAD-Tamale NRG8.10.38, Government Grants-in-Aid to Native Authority (Local Authorities), 1951–57. In contrast, questions of how to allocate projects within districts remained at the discretion of individual administrators.

38 PRAAD-Tamale NRG3.25.32, Development—Northern Territories 1948–51, letter from ADC Gambaga to chief commissioner of the Northern Territories, December 22, 1948.

39 PRAAD-Tamale, NRG8.10.32, Community and Local Development Committees (Grants in Aid), "Community Development and Local Development Committees," memo from the Ministry of Social Welfare and Community Development to chief commissioner of the Northern Territories, September 19, 1949.

40 PRAAD-Tamale NRG 8.10.32, Community and Local Development Committees (Grants in Aid). Problems with implementation are evident in subsequent notes from DCs following the memo on September 19, 1949.

41 Grischow, *Shaping Tradition*, chapter 6.

42 PRAAD-Tamale NRG8.20.12, Personal File N. O. Dobbs. See letter from chief commissioner of the Northern Territories to N. O. Dobbs, September 26, 1950, and copy of Colonial Service Personal Record for Neil Osborne Dobbs. Davis notes that Dobbs was instrumental in instituting a

system of elections for the Mamprusi kingship in 1948, a system that was reversed in 1964. See Davis, "Continuity and Change in Mampurugu."

43 PRAAD-Tamale NRG 3.4.8, Informal Diary (Gambaga) 1951–54, and NRG 3.4.7, Diaries and Newsletters (Gambaga) 1954–55.

44 Davis, "Continuity and Change in Mampurugu"; Susan Drucker-Brown, *Ritual Aspects of the Mamprusi Kingship* (Leiden: Afrika-Studiecentrum, 1975); A. A. Iliasu, "The Establishment of British Administration in Mamprugu, 1898–1937," *Transactions of the Historical Society of Ghana* 16, no. 1 (1975): 1–28. Scholars of the area differentiate between the Mamprusi heartland areas, where there has been little historic contestation of the Mamprusi king's authority, and peripheral areas that were incorporated under colonial rule and have since been disputed. While challenges to Mamprusi authority outside the heartland have been framed in ethnic terms, ethnic solidarity has not been central to the kingdom's power at the center. As Michael Schlottner argues, Mamprusi identity is based not on "common origins or 'ethnogenesis'" but instead on "loyalty to a specific [system of] political authority." Michael Schlottner, "'We Stay, Others Come and Go': Identity among the Mamprusi in Northern Ghana," in *Ethnicity in Ghana: The Limits of Invention*, ed. Carola Lentz and Paul Nugent (London: Macmillan, 2000), 49–67. Drucker-Brown made a similar observation in a survey of linguistic groups in South Mamprusi in 1965. See Drucker-Brown, *Ritual Aspects*, 22.

45 David Carson Davis's careful reconstruction of Mamprusi political history from the seventeenth century to end of colonial rule highlights the historical resilience of *naam* to political changes over the nineteenth and twentieth centuries, a resilience that Schlottner credits to the Mamprusi leaders' strategies of integrating a changing set of constituents. Davis, "Continuity and Change in Mampurugu"; Schlottner, "'We Stay, Others Come and Go,'" 57.

46 For an excellent account of the motivations, experiences, and changing self-perceptions of migrants from Lawra District as well as their relationships with government officials and chiefs, see Lentz, *Ethnicity*, chapter 5.

47 Interviews in Kpasenkpe with Balihira Seiya, October 2, 2010; Kambonaba Ziblim Takora, June 28, 2010; Samanaba Sumani Takora, July 12, 2010; Sandowbila Nantomah, May 1, 2011; Suurana Yakubu Pusu, July 2, 2010; Tindanpoa Awa Saari, June 30, 2010; Wudana Daboo Saaka, October 3, 2010; Zanloorana Tia Cheera, July 29, 2010; Abiba Pugumba Baŋmarigu, October 4, 2010; Alhassan Sulemana and Seidu Sulemana, June 15, 2013.

48 Interview with Sakparana Sandow Batisima in Kpasenkpe, June 28, 2010. Solomon Dawuni Sebiyam provided the direct translation.

49 Seiya Hammi later became the chairman of Kpasenkpe's Local Council when it became a district in 1962. PRAAD-Tamale NRG8.5.226, Kpasenkpe Local Council Minutes, 1962–66, and interview with Balihira Seiya, Kpasenkpe, October 2, 2010.

50 For more on the cultural history of *akpeteshie* and its particularly potent political resonances in 1950s and 1960s Ghana, see Emmanuel Kwaku Akyeampong, *Drink, Power, and Cultural Change: A Social History of Alcohol in Ghana, c. 1800 to Recent Times* (Portsmouth, NH: Heinemann, 1996), chapters 5 and 6.

51 Interview with Balihira Seiya, Kpasenkpe, October 2, 2010.

52 For recent discussions of *anibue*, see Gracia Clark, *African Market Women: Seven Life Stories from Ghana* (Bloomington: Indiana University Press, 2010), 230–31; Jennifer Hart, *Ghana on the Go: African Mobility in the Age of Motor Transportation* (Bloomington: Indiana University Press, 2016), chapter 3; and Skinner, "'It Brought Some Kind of Neatness to Mankind.'" For discussions of *olaju*, see J. D. Y. Peel, "Olaju: A Yorba Concept of Development," *Journal of Development Studies* 14, no. 2 (1978): 139–65; Lisa A. Lindsay, *Working with Gender* (Portsmouth, NH: Heinemann, 2003), introduction. Abdul-Korah's discussion of migrants' recollections in the Upper West region similarly emphasizes the importance, particularly during this era, of "knowing the world." Gariba B. Abdul-Korah, "'Ka Bie Ba Yor': Labor Migration among the Dagaaba of the Upper West Region of Ghana, 1936–1957," *Nordic Journal of African Studies* 17, no. 1 (2008): 1–19.

53 Interview with Bugurana Ibrahim Manmara, Kpasenkpe, October 5, 2010.

54 Interviews with Pastor Daniel Barijesira Azundow, Kpasenkpe, September 1 and October 2, 2010. The Wulugunaba's relationships with both colonial administrators and Assemblies of God missionaries also helped attract the Mass Education Programme, which relied heavily on chiefs and the recommendation of DCs. PRAAD-Tamale NRG8.1.26, Mass Education Policy, 1949–55.

55 Interview with Alhassan Pusu, Kpasenkpe, July 6, 2010. Solomon Dawuni Sebiyam provided the direct translation.

56 The number of primary schools in the Northern Territories, while extremely low compared to Gold Coast Colony and Ashanti, jumped from 10 in 1935 to 83 in 1950 and to 219 in 1957. See Lacy S. Ferrell, "'We Were Mixed with All Types': Educational Migration in the Northern Territories of Colonial Ghana," in *Children on the Move in Africa: Past and Present Experiences of Migration*, ed. Elodie Razy and Marie Rodet (Woodbridge, Suffolk: James Currey, 2016), 141–58.

57 Bawumia recalled that, at the time, "no employee of the Native Authority wanted a posting to Kpasenkpe" because it lacked an all-season road. Arriving in Kpasenkpe in 1947, Bawumia's first task was to supervise the construction of the school building itself, which had not been completed. Mumuni Bawumia, *A Life in the Political History of Ghana* (Accra: Ghana Universities Press, 2004), 13–14.

58 Ferrell, "'We Were Mixed with All Types.'" The description of who was sent to the Kpasenkpe school comes from an interview with Hajia Mariama (Bani) Bawumia, Walewale, September 21, 2010.

59 Interviews in Kpasenkpe with Pastor Daniel Barijesira Azundow, September 1 and October 2, 2010; Bugurana Ibrahim Manmara, October 5, 2010; Alhassan Sulemana and Seidu Sulemana, June 15, 2013.

60 Interview with Alhassan Sulemana and Seidu Sulemana, June 15, 2013.

61 Interview in Kpasenkpe with Tindana Issah Tongo, Samanaba Sumani Takora, and Faara Tongo, June 7, 2013.

62 Interview with Kakpanaba Somka Nluki, Kpasenkpe, July 2, 2019.

63 Interview in Kpasenkpe with Wurugurunaba Nsoanyanni Sandow, June 29, 2010. Solomon Dawuni Sebiyam provided the direct translation.

64 Interview in Kpasenkpe with Adam Abdullai Seiya, July 5, 2010.

65 Interview in Kpasenkpe with Adisa Tampulima, April 30, 2011.

66 Interview with Bugurana Ibrahim Manmara, July 2, 2019.

67 Attempts by northern chiefs to relocate markets have frequently been the subject of constituent protest, but Sebiyam effectively overcame any local objections, not least because he appeared to have influence with the newly interventionist administration. Interviews with Bugurana Ibrahim Manmara, Kpasenkpe, October 5, 2010, and Wudana Daboo Saaka, Kpasenkpe, October 3, 2010. Examples of nearby disputes over market relocation include Chiana 1953–55 (PRAAD-Tamale NRG8.4.111, Navrongo Monthly Diary, March 1955), Kunkwa 1971 (PRAAD-Tamale NRG 3.3.37, Complaints and Petitions, 1968–70), and Walewale 1970 (PRAAD-Tamale NRG8.5.369, Management Committee Walewale-Kpasenkpe Local Council, 1970–71).

68 PRAAD-Tamale NRG3.4.7, Diaries and Newsletters (Gambaga), 1954–55.

69 PRAAD-Tamale NRG3.4.7, Diaries and Newsletters (Gambaga), March 1955. Dobbs went on to note that they "found this was such hot work that we had to retire to Madame Bonsu's bar."

70 Interviews in Kpasenkpe with Pastor Daniel Barijesira Azundow, October 1, 2010, and Bugurana Ibrahim Manmara, Kpasenkpe, October 5, 2010; corroborated in PRAAD-Tamale NRG3.4.7, Diaries and Newsletters (Gambaga), 1954–55.

71 Kate Skinner shows that, in the context of Mass Education initiatives, location and historical context deeply shaped how calls for labor were viewed. In Kwaso, a small town near Kumasi, Skinner provides a detailed study of how residents recall participants' ideas of *anibue*, "environmental cleanliness," and good character as well as a variety of practices in which farmers worked together to clear individuals' plots. In contrast, she provides some suggestive evidence from Northern Ghana that histories of forced labor influenced responses to Mass Education. See Skinner, "'It Brought Some Kind of Neatness to Mankind'"; Skinner, "From Pentecostalism to Politics."

72 Interviews in Kpasenkpe with Warana Nkrumah Baba, September 30, 2010, and May 1, 2011; Jacob Pitigi Tampulima, October 1, 2010; and Zanloorana Tia Cheera, April 30, 2011; interview with Namiyelana E. D. Sebiyam, Bolgatanga, May 5, 2011. In the 1950s, *nayiri kpaariba*

extended the general institution of farm labor sharing, called *kpaariba* (*nayiri* means chief).

73 As Lund has argued with regard to land rights, evidence from Kpasenkpe suggests that the chiefly "right" to raise communal labor was both a product and a generator of the Wulugunaba's authority vis-à-vis Kpasenkpe constituents as well as regional and national officials; see Christian Lund, "Negotiating Property Institutions: On the Symbiosis of Property and Authority in Africa," in *Negotiating Property in Africa*, ed. K. Juul and C. Lund (Portsmouth, NH: Heinemann, 2002), 14.

74 Interview with Bugurana Ibrahim Manmara, Kpasenkpe, October 5, 2010. Solomon Dawuni Sebiyam provided the direct translation.

75 Interview with Pastor Daniel Barijesira Azundow, Kpasenkpe, October 3, 2010.

76 Interviews in Kpasenkpe with Sakparana Sandow Batisima, June 28, 2010, and Bugurana Ibrahim Manmara, October 5, 2010.

77 Interview with Sakparana Sandow Batisima, Kpasenkpe, June 28, 2010. Thank you to Abigail Sulemana for assisting with the direct translation of this quotation.

78 The example he gave of such punishments was from a slightly earlier time, when he was young in the 1940s and Sebiyam had raised labor to build the colonial courthouse. After one compound failed to send a laborer to quarry stones for the building, Sebiyam stopped the work until that house's people came to clear the road to the quarry so that laborers could pass more easily. While laborers were often fed by the chief, those undertaking this additional assignment were not. Interview in Kpasenkpe with Bugurana Ibrahim Manmara, July 2, 2019.

79 Skinner, "From Pentecostalism to Politics," 318. Interviews in Kpasenkpe with Wudana Daboo Saaka, October 3, 2010; Kambonaba Ziblim Takora, June 28, 2010.

80 Interview with Memubla Boonba, Kpasenkpe, June 7, 2013. Seiya Namyoaya Enoch provided the direct translation.

81 Interview with Pastor Daniel Barijesira Azundow, Kpasenkpe, October 2, 2010.

82 Interviews in Kpasenkpe with Wudana Daboo Saaka, October 3, 2010; Musah Yidana, October 2, 2010.

83 PRAAD-Tamale NRG3.4.7, Diaries and Newsletters (Gambaga), February 1955.

84 As Carola Lentz has noted, people in the North often downplay formal independence in 1957 in favor of glossing all of the 1950s as the "time when politics came," a term that suggests ambivalence, casting "politics" as an outside force that tied party political distinctions to local conflicts. Lentz, *Ethnicity*, 199.

85 Paul André Ladouceur, *Chiefs and Politicians*, 81.

86 Unable to secure concessions on these points with the CPP, the NPP entered into an uneasy alliance with the CPP's main source of opposition, the Asante-based National Liberation Movement, which was also formed

in 1954. NPP leaders acknowledged that federalism would disadvantage the region. Throughout 1954–56, NPP politicians attempted to maintain a distinct call for regional autonomy as opposed to federalism, as they negotiated this "second best" alternative; see Ladouceur, *Chiefs and Politicians*, 133, quoting Mumuni Bawumia. The other explicit demand of the NPP was the preservation of chieftaincy in the North. However, the distinction between chief and politician in the North was much less apparent than elsewhere in colonial Ghana, and, as is evident in Kpasenkpe, both the CPP and NPP became embroiled in the intricate politics of northern chieftaincy. Colonial policies that restricted northern education to the sons of chiefs in the interwar era meant that the educated elites who dominated northern party politics in the 1950s overwhelmingly belonged to chiefly families; see Ladouceur, *Chiefs and Politicians*, 84–86. While the CPP launched frequent rhetorical attacks on the institution of chieftaincy, in practice the party tried to use chiefly struggles to its advantage. See Richard Rathbone, *Nkrumah and the Chiefs: The Politics of Chieftaincy in Ghana 1951–60* (Athens: Ohio University Press, 2000). Note that after 1957, the NPP became part of the joint opposition party, the United Party (UP).

87 Nkrumah's Regional Development Fund, established in 1955, began to funnel additional funds to districts. In 1955, as the CPP prepared to contest the decisive 1956 elections, this was joined by an abrupt £700,000 grant for capital works at the regional level, including a nonnegotiable "bonus" of £80,000 to the Ashanti region over the population-apportioned estimates for the rest of the colony. PRAAD-Tamale NRG8.10.38, Government Grants-in-Aid to Native Authority (Local Authorities) 1951–57, internal notes April 1955.

88 Bawumia, *A Life in the Political History of Ghana*, 70.

89 In the excerpts of Legislative Assembly debates from 1953 and 1954 that are reproduced in his memoirs, Bawumia shows himself advocating for a hospital and pipe-borne water to "convince the Nayiri . . . that progress in this country is really what we preach," and berating the government for not beginning promised construction on the Nasia-Pwalugu bridge and another bridge across the Volta at Adomi, in addition to water supply projects for Bawku. See Bawumia, *A Life in the Political History of Ghana*, 97–98, 103–5.

90 PRAAD-Tamale NRG3.5.3 and NRG3.5.4, General Elections South Mamprusi West, 1954 and 1956.

91 Lentz, *Ethnicity*, 181–82.

92 See, for example, Paul Stacey, "'The Chiefs, Elders, and People Have for Many Years Suffered Untold Hardships': Protests by Coalitions of the Excluded in British Northern Togoland, UN Trusteeship Territory, 1950–7," *Journal of African History* 55, no. 3 (November 2014): 423–44; Talton, *Politics of Social Change*; Lentz, *Ethnicity*, chapter 8.

93 PRAAD-Tamale NRG8.2.133 (EAP 541/1/2/120), Petitions and Resolutions 1957–58, Kpembewura, "Welcome Address to the Regional Commissioner Mr. L.R. Abavana," Kpembe, 1957.

94 PRAAD-Tamale NRG8.2.133 (EAP 541/1/2/120), Petitions and Resolutions 1957–58, Navropio A. Adda, "Welcome Address to the Regional Commissioner," Navrongo, March 18, 1958.

95 PRAAD-Tamale NRG8.2.133 (EAP 541/1/2/120), Petitions and Resolutions 1957–58, Ya Na Abudulai III, "Address by the Ya Na of Dagbon on the First Independence Anniversary Celebration," Yendi, March 1958.

96 PRAAD-Tamale NRG8.2.133 (EAP 541/1/2/120), Petitions and Resolutions 1957–58, petition to the regional commissioner from W. H. Wahab, April 9, 1958.

97 PRAAD-Tamale NRG8.2.133 (EAP 541/1/2/120), Petitions and Resolutions 1957–58, letter from E. C. E. Asiama, Government Agent Salaga, to the regional commissioner, May 28, 1958.

98 PRAAD-Tamale NRG8.2.133 (EAP 541/1/2/120), Petitions and Resolutions 1957–58, petition from Sabuli Naa Gariba, Kariba Naa Bayor, Gbari Naa Nyunaa, and Tugu Naa Tanbaa to the regional commissioner, August 1, 1958; petition from A. P. Severo-Termaghre to regional secretary UGFC, September 23, 1958; petition from C. K. Saame to the minister of interior, n.d.

99 PRAAD Tamale NRG8.2.150, Mamprusi Traditional Council 1960–67, letter from the district commisioner Gambaga to the regional commissioner, September 22, 1960. After independence in March of 1957, opposition remained alive in the north until the Local Council elections of May–June 1958 confirmed that even residents of the North (including those in Kpasenkpe) overwhelmingly supported the CPP. Ladouceur, *Chiefs and Politicians*, 170.

100 Both sides made claims that they were simply upholding tradition, while their opponents were playing politics with chieftaincy by either unseating or advancing claimants on the basis of political affiliation.

101 PRAAD-Tamale NRG 8.2.150, Mamprusi Traditional Council 1960–67, letter from Naamtabilba Mamprusi to President Kwame Nkrumah, January 30, 1961.

102 For more detail on the politics of Bawumia's decision to "cross the carpet," see Ladouceur, *Chiefs and Politicians*, 168–71. For Bawumia's own account, see Bawumia, *A Life in the Political History of Ghana*, 131–34.

103 Bawumia, *A Life in the Political History of Ghana*, 140–43.

104 PRAAD-Tamale NRG8.5.223, South Mamprusi West Area Committee 1961, petition from Kunkwanaba Anabila to President Kwame Nkrumah, June 6, 1961.

105 PRAAD-Tamale NRG8.2.150, Mamprusi Traditional Council 1960–67, letter from the district commissioner Gambaga to the regional commissioner, September 22, 1960, and letter from the district commissioner Gambaga to Kunkwanaba August 5, 1961.

106 Interview with Pastor Daniel Barijesira Azundow, Kpasenkpe, October 1, 2010.
107 Osuanyi Quaicoo Essel and Emmanual R. K. Amissah, "Smock Fashion Culture in Ghana's Dress Identity-Making," *Historical Research Letter* 18 (2015): 32–38. The smock meant many different things to different people. For many in the South who associated northern garb with manual labor, it was a symbol of working-class populism. As Essel and Amissah point out, this is the interpretation offered by Ama Biney in *The Political and Social Thought of Kwame Nkrumah* (New York: Palgrave Macmillan, 2011), 77. See also Richard Rathbone, "Casting 'the Kingdome into Another Mold': Ghana's Troubled Transition to Independence," *Round Table* 97, no. 398 (2008): 716. For others, the handspun cloth might have signaled the visible rejection of colonial markers of respectability as well as the embrace of local manufacturing. For people from the North, however, the symbol was layered with the contradictions and ambiguities that characterized the region's relationship with the nationalist project of modernization itself. Northern members of Nkrumah's Convention People's Party who had hoped that independence would end colonial reliance on chiefs may have wondered at the president's choice of a garment most closely associated with northern chieftaincy. Those who had been students would have recalled their recent protests over a colonial policy that forced them to wear smocks, marking their difference and preventing them from presenting themselves in the trousers and shirts that Ghanaians associated with modern students; see Ferrell, "'We Were Mixed with All Types,'" 151–52.
108 Ahlman, *Living with Nkrumahism*, chapter 2.
109 Ahlman, *Living with Nkrumahism*, 27, chapter 3.
110 These works explore the intellectual roots and practical politics of both programs, along with exploring how citizens encountered and used them. Lal shows how, in Tanzania, the ongoing tension between a rhetoric of self-sufficiency and the reality of central government funding in the Mtwara region created space for competing interpretations of "self-reliance" by actors on local, regional, and national stages. In contrast, Moskowitz shows how self-help in the first decades of independence became a way for Kenyan citizens to make claims on the state at the same time that it became entwined with the politics of patronage. Lal, *African Socialism*; Moskowitz, *Seeing Like a Citizen*, chapters 6 and 7.
111 John Aerni-Flessner, "Self-Help Development Projects and Conceptions of Independence in Lesotho, 1950s–1970s," *International Journal of African Historical Studies* 50, no. 1 (January 2017): 11–33.
112 Lal discusses Chinese support for Tanzania, while Leander Schneider's work also emphasizes the early support of the World Bank and highlights the diversity of models and experiences that the Tanzanian state drew on in its pursuit of villagization. Moskowitz discusses support from the USAID and the Rockefeller Foundations, and Aerni-Flessner discusses

support from the United States, Britain, and a variety of nongovernmental organizations. Lal, *African Socialism*, chapter 1; Leander Schneider, *Government of Development: Peasants and Politicians in Postcolonial Tanzania* (Bloomington: Indiana University Press, 2014); Moskowitz, *Seeing Like a Citizen*, chapter 6; Aerni-Flessner, "Self-Help Development Projects."

113 Kwame Nkrumah, *Guide to Party Action: Address by Osagyefo Dr. Kwame Nkrumah at the First Seminar at the Winneba Ideological School on 3rd February, 1962* (Accra: Central Committee of Convention People's Party, 1962). Quoted in Skinner, "Who Knew the Minds of the People?," 306.

114 For more on the relationship of the Nkrumah government to chieftaincy in the North, see Boone, *Political Topographies of the African State*, chapter 4; Lentz, *Ethnicity*, 180–83.

115 Talton shows how Konkomba activists organized self-help labor to demonstrate unity and contest political exclusion. Benjamin Talton, *Politics of Social Change*, chapter 4.

116 Skinner, "Who Knew the Minds of the People?," 302.

117 After 1957, it becomes much harder to chart the amount of national funds devoted to small-scale development projects in northern Ghana, as frequent changes in accounting and reporting practices make data consistency an issue. Joseph Ayee, citing a 1968 government report, charts the national decline in funding for local government units in Ghana as a whole, from over ¢4 million (¢ is the symbol for cedi, the basic monetary unit in Ghana) in 1960–61 to under ¢2 million in 1963–64 and under ¢1.5 million in 1966. See Joseph R. A. Ayee, *An Anatomy of Public Policy Implementation: The Case of Decentralization Policies in Ghana* (Brookfield, VT: Ashgate, 1994), 62. With the continuously falling world price of cocoa, national revenues as a whole became unstable and were quickly outpaced by expenditures. National statistics confirm that the Nkrumah government emphasized large-scale development projects over funding for local government. Ministry of Finance, *Ghana Economic Surveys 1957, 1958, 1959* (Accra: Ministry of Finance, 1957–60); Ghana Central Bureau of Statistics, *Ghana Economic Surveys 1960, 1961, 1962, 1963, 1964, 1965, 1966* (Accra: Ghana Central Bureau of Statistics, 1960–66).

118 In other parts of the country, wealthy individuals or strategic political concerns might allow calls for self-help to generate revenue from individuals and politicians who wished to demonstrate their concern for local communities, and local councils that had struggled to establish independent bases of revenue might use self-help as a call for increased local taxation. See examples in Skinner, "Who Knew the Minds of the People?," 307–8. When the National Liberation Council attempted to take over the Town/Village Development Committees in the months following the coup that overthrew Nkrumah, however, letters from regional officers in other regions suggest that while the committees were quite active in raising

funds and labor in other areas of the country, they were not in the North. PRAAD-Tamale NRG8.5.274, Local Government Council Development Committee General 1962–71, memo from the NLC secretariat to regional administrative officers, July 20, 1966, and replies July–September 1966.

119 For the text of Nkrumah's announcement of the Programme of Work and Happiness, see Kwame Nkrumah, *Revolutionary Path* (London: Panaf Books, 1973), 185. Ladouceur argues that in the late Nkrumah era the Regional Administration became the mechanism by which people in the North were "permitted by and large to run their own affairs, within a context of limited resources." See Ladouceur, *Chiefs and Politicians*, 187.

120 PRAAD-Tamale NRG3.13.33, Meetings of the Regional Commissioner and District Commissioners 1962–66, "Minutes of Meeting of the Regional Commissioner and District Commissioners Held at the Regional Office on the 29th June 1962."

121 PRAAD-Tamale NRG3.13.33, Meetings of the Regional Commissioner and District Commissioners 1962–66, minutes of meetings between the regional commissioner and district commissioners, Tamale, for June 29, 1962, October 11, 1962, February 28, 1963, and May 30, 1963.

122 The number of local authorities dropped from 282 to 70; see Joe K. Ansere, *The Role of Local Government in Nation Building* (Accra: Institute of Adult Education, University of Ghana, 1973), 4.

123 Ayee argues that, especially in areas where the district commissioner and the Local Council were all seated in the same town, development spending had a heavy headquarters bias. Ayee, *An Anatomy of Public Policy Implementation*, 58.

124 From 70 to 183. Ansere, *The Role of Local Government in Nation Building*, 5.

125 Initially sited at the far western town of Yagaba, it quickly moved to Kpasenkpe. While the stated reason was Yagaba's "inaccessibility," the move was popularly credited also to the close connections among Damma Wuni, Mumuni Bawumia, and Wulugunaba Sebiyam. PRAAD Tamale NRG3.13.33, minutes of meetings between regional commissioner and district commissioners, May and June 1962. With the movement of the capital, the Kpasenkpe District became a clearly political creation, with boundaries that corresponded to neither the colonial Local Council divisions, the traditional chiefly jurisdictions, nor the major geographic division at the White Volta River.

126 Interview with Duunaba Bennett Baani, Walewale, June 17, 2010.

127 Informal conversations with Kpatuanaba Jude Sugri Sebiyam, Kpasenkpe, June–July 2010; interview with Duunaba Bennett Baani, Walewale, June 17, 2010.

128 Interview in Kpasenkpe with Tindana Issah Tongo, May 1, 2011.

129 Bawumia noted that grants fell from £53,000 in 1961–62 to £19,900 in 1963. PRAAD-Tamale, NRG3.13.33, Meetings of the Regional Commissioner

and District Commissioners 1962–66, "Minutes of Meeting of the Regional Commissioner and District Commissioners, Chairmen and Clerks of Local Councils and Secretaries of Town Councils Held at the Regional Office on the 29th August 1963." A 1962 grant for "town roads" in the region was apportioned specifically to tar between one-half and three miles of road in each district capital. Similarly, regional development funds and road improvement grants were divvied up among districts. Town roads are discussed in the minutes for October 11, 1962, regional development funds on May 20, 1963, and road improvement funds on August 5, 1965.

130 Former staff of the Kpasenkpe District confirm that funding relied on decisions by the regional government, and that meager local tax revenues were barely enough to cover the costs of hiring local casual laborers. Interview with Duunaba Bennett Baani, Walewale, June 17, 2010.

131 PRAAD-Tamale NRG3.13.33, Meetings of the Regional Commissioner and District Commissioners 1962–66, "Minutes of a Meeting of the Regional Commissioner and District Commissioners Held at the Regional Office on the 20th May 1963."

132 PRAAD-Tamale NRG3.3.35, National Development Plan Progress Report 1965–66. In 1965, when creating a map of the old South Mamprusi District, Drucker-Brown includes this spur road as the only major road in Western Mamprugu. Drucker-Brown, *Ritual Aspects*, 4.

133 PRAAD-Tamale NRG3.13.33, Meetings of the Regional Commissioner and District Commissioners 1962–66, "Minutes of Meeting of the Regional Commissioner and District Commissioners Held at the Regional Office on the 26th July 1963," confirmed in interview with Kpatuanaba Jude Sugri Sebiyam, Kpasenkpe, October 1, 2010.

134 Interviews in Kpasenkpe with Duundana Yakubu Kolugu, June 28, 2010; Sakparana Sandowbila, July 1, 2010. Duunaba Bennett Baani, who served as the treasurer for the Kpasenkpe District from 1962 to 1966, recalled that funds were meager but that the small amount of local taxation from market, cattle, and bicycle rates went to paying district laborers. Interview with Duunaba Bennett Baani, Walewale, June 17, 2010.

135 Interview in Kpasenkpe with Jacob Pitigi Tampulima, July 1, 2010

136 Interviews in Kpasenkpe with Duundana Yakubu Kolugu, June 28, 2010; Kambontia Yaado Piyisiba, June 28, 2010; Wurugurunaba Nsoanyanni Sandow, June 29, 2010; and Sakparana Sandow Batisima, June 28, 2010.

137 PRAAD-Tamale NRG3.13.33, Meetings of the Regional Commissioner and District Commissioners 1962–66, "Minutes of Meeting of the Regional Commissioner and District Commissioners Held at the Regional Office on the 11th October, 1962."

CHAPTER 3: LABOR AND STATECRAFT IN A CHIEFLY FAMILY

1 Bawumia recalls that there were eighteen students, Pawura recalled thirteen. Mumuni Bawumia, *A Life in the Political History of Ghana* (Accra:

Ghana Universities Press, 2004), 13; interview with Poanaba Pawura Paulina Barijesira, Kpasenkpe, August 31, 2010.

2 Bawumia recounts the story of his parents' decision to send him to school. Bawumia, A *Life in the Political History of Ghana*, 3.

3 Northern politicians, almost all from chiefly families themselves, often relied on such families as a starting point for their visions of change, though their ambitions reached much further. For the relationships of politicians to chiefly families, see table 8 in Paul André Ladouceur, *Chiefs and Politicians: The Politics of Regionalism in Northern Ghana*, Legon History Series (London: Longman, 1979), 86.

4 When Sebiyam became chief in 1942, he had one wife and a young son.

5 Behrends and Lentz point out that particularly because only some members of families in northern Ghana went to school, "class divisions therefore exist not only between, but also within extended families." Andrea Behrends and Carola Lentz, "Education, Careers, and Home Ties: The Ethnography of an Emerging Middle Class from Northern Ghana," *Zeitschrift Für Ethnologie* 137, no. 2 (2012): 140.

6 Emily Lynn Osborn, *Our New Husbands Are Here: Households, Gender, and Politics in a West African State from the Slave Trade to Colonial Rule* (Athens: Ohio University Press, 2011), 11–12.

7 Colonial intermediaries, for example, "did not necessarily . . . separate their domestic lives from their public lives." Osborn, *Our New Husbands Are Here*, 174. Conversely, as Kenda Mutongi illustrates, families could provide moral vocabularies by which colonial subjects engaged the state. Kenda Mutongi, *Worries of the Heart: Widows, Family, and Community in Kenya* (Chicago: University of Chicago Press, 2007). A number of recent works have illuminated how multiracial families, interracial sex, and conjugal ties served as key sites in which colonial subjects both navigated and unsettled the changing hierarchies and ideologies of race, gender, and class that underpinned colonial rule. Carina E. Ray, *Crossing the Color Line: Race, Sex, and the Contested Politics of Colonialism in Ghana* (Athens: Ohio University Press, 2015); Rachel Jean-Baptiste, *Conjugal Rights: Marriage, Sexuality, and Urban Life in Colonial Libreville, Gabon* (Athens: Ohio University Press, 2014); Christopher J. Lee, *Unreasonable Histories: Nativism, Multiracial Lives, and the Genealogical Imagination in British Africa* (Durham, NC: Duke University Press, 2014); Hilary Jones, *The Métis of Senegal: Urban Life and Politics in French West Africa* (Bloomington: Indiana University Press, 2013). For a wonderful recent examination of the historiography on kinship as well as a critique of African historians' frequent discomfort with kinship as an arena of analysis, see Giblin's summary of kinship in African history. James L. Giblin, "Kinship in African History," in *A Companion to African History*, ed. William H. Worger, Charles H. Ambler, and Nwando Achebe (Hoboken, NJ: Wiley Blackwell, 2019), 163–77.

8 Sean Hawkins, *Writing and Colonialism in Northern Ghana: The Encounter between the LoDagaa and "The World on Paper," 1892–1991* (Toronto: University of Toronto Press, 2002). See also N. J. K. Brukum, "Sir Gordon Guggisberg and Socio-economic Development of Northern Ghana, 1919–1927," *Transactions of the Historical Society of Ghana,* New Series 9 (2005): 1–15; Lacy S. Ferrell, "'We Were Mixed with All Types': Educational Migration in the Northern Territories of Colonial Ghana," in *Children on the Move in Africa: Past and Present Experiences of Migration,* ed. Elodie Razy and Marie Rodet (Woodbridge, Suffolk: James Currey, 2016), 145; Jeffrey Grischow, *Shaping Tradition: Civil Society, Community and Development in Colonial Northern Ghana, 1899–1957* (Leiden: Brill, 2006).

9 The first colonial document I could find that referred to Barijesira was in 1927. After Governor Guggisberg solicited a "secret report" to ascertain the "principal chiefs of the Gold Coast . . . the amount of influence they exert and their loyalty to the Government or otherwise," a June 1927 reply from the DC of Gambaga reported Barijesira (spelled "Barajesira") as "VERY LOYAL," noting that he was "most intelligent" and "makes great efforts to understand what is required and carry it out. Has a small division but excellent influence over his people." For comparison, other chiefs in the area were noted as "modern," "old style," or "lazy." PRAAD Tamale NRG 3.3.1, Reports of Chiefs 1925–51.

10 For members of the first generation of people from the North to attend government schools, going to school meant traveling long distances, often on foot, and staying away from family for long stretches. Interview with Bunaba Chimsi, Burugu, August 29, 2010; interview with Tia Adjei, Walewale, July 11, 2010; interview with Robert Tia Abudulai, Walewale, July 11, 2010. See also Ferrell, "'We Were Mixed with All Types.'"

11 Charles Lynn, Marjorie Lynn, and Sylvia Lynn, *The Long Garden Master in the Gold Coast: The Life and Times of a Colonial Agricultural Officer in the Gold Coast, 1929–1947* (Bedfordshire, UK: Authors OnLine, 2012), locations 1832, 1936.

12 Susan Drucker-Brown, *Ritual Aspects of the Mamprusi Kingship* (Leiden: Afrika-Studiecentrum, 1975), 17, 19–20. While often couched in language of timelessness, Drucker-Brown's scholarship is largely based on fieldwork done in the mid-1960s and captures a snapshot of this particular moment in the area.

13 Jean Allman and John Parker, *Tongnaab: The History of a West African God* (Bloomington: Indiana University Press, 2005). See especially the discussion in chapter 5 of colonial reactions to accumulation by Golibdaana Tengol, whose entrepreneurship weaves throughout the book.

14 Grischow, *Shaping Tradition,* 137–38. See also Carola Lentz, *Ethnicity and the Making of History in Northern Ghana* (Edinburgh: Edinburgh University Press, 2006), 63–64.

15 Grischow, *Shaping Tradition*, 160–67.
16 Grischow gives the example of the family of Chief Gandah of Birifu. In addition to Gandah, Lentz points out that the educated Lawra Naa J. A. Karbo eventually had sixty-five wives. Grischow, *Shaping Tradition*, 150–51; Lentz, *Ethnicity*, 64.
17 Grischow, *Shaping Tradition*, 134–35. Grischow gives a comprehensive history of the ideology and practice of agricultural development in colonial northern Ghana, showing how related colonial concerns about food security, overpopulation, and political stability shaped successive waves of small-scale agricultural intervention in the 1930s, 1940s, and 1950s, culminating in the large-scale mechanized farming scheme of the Gonja Development Company in 1948–57.
18 The church was established in 1951.
19 Marrying this many women was not particularly unusual for chiefs, and certain successful chiefs in the 1930s were noted to have upwards of fifty wives. See, for example, Lentz, *Ethnicity*, 63–64; Allman and Parker, *Tongnaab*, 273n98.
20 Sometimes the period was described simply as "those days," "that time," "colonial days," or, most frequently, "Nkrumah's time." Given the age of the interviewees and surrounding context, I would usually be able to date these descriptions to the broad postwar era, from 1942 to the first coup in 1966.
21 See James Leonard Giblin, *A History of the Excluded: Making Family a Refuge from State in Twentieth-Century Tanzania* (Woodbridge, Suffolk: James Currey, 2005); Barbara Cooper, *Marriage in Maradi: Culture and Gender in a Hausa Society in Niger, 1900–1983* (Portsmouth, NH: Heinemann, 1997). In the 1950s and 1960s, brothers farmed together rather than individually, but the identities and provenance of these brothers changed rapidly over the period. Similarly, Sebiyam's growing household continued to eat from "one pot," but the size of the pot, the number of consumers, and the number of women involved in food preparation all changed.
22 Interview with Na Gunga Barijesira, Kpasenkpe, October 1, 2010; interview with Zanloorana Tia Cheera, Kpasenkpe, September 1, 2010; interview with Pastor Daniel Barijesira Azundow, Kpasenkpe, September 1, 2010.
23 After Barijesira's death in 1942, Sebiyam not only became Wulugunaba but also the head of his father's small cluster of farms, called Chibiri, Ti Libsi, and Na Chiga, on which he and several of his brothers were already farming. Barijesira was not remembered, either locally or in colonial documents, as a particularly enthusiastic farmer.
24 Interview with Jacob Pitigi Tampulima, Kpasenkpe, July 1, 2010. While an exact timeline is difficult to reconstruct, it appears that the heyday of Barangaŋi lasted at least until the early 1960s.

25 The expansion at Baranganj also relied heavily on the expansion of *nayiri kpaariba* labor, supplied by Sebiyam's constituents, as detailed in chapter 2. Hailu confirms that bullock farming in northern Ghana probably changed the timing but not the quantity of labor required for an acre of production. Zegeye Hailu, "The Adoption of Modern Farm Practices in African Agriculture: Empirical Evidence about the Impacts of Household Characteristics and Input Supply Systems in the Northern Region of Ghana," Nyankpala Agricultural Research Report (Nyankpala, Ghana, and Eschborn, West Germany: Nyankpala Agricultural Experiment Station and GTZ, 1990).

26 Sebiyam's expanded use of *nayiri kpaariba* labor allowed him to address peak labor demands for clearing, weeding, and harvest, but expanded farms also required a steady supply of family labor for management and for more daily tasks like keeping away pests.

27 Not like "today," when, interviewees argued, individuals farm for their wives, children, and other dependents.

28 Cooper, *Marriage in Maradi*, 43–45.

29 Family members' descriptions echo the familial norms Fortes and Jack Goody observed in nearby areas of northern Ghana in the 1940s and 1950s. Writing on the idea of "development cycle of domestic groups," they and contemporary anthropologists emphasized the ways that dynamics of family "systems" changed over time. A particular family unit, in this model, would go through periods of "expansion," "fission," and "replacement" depending on the ages of its members and would change because of marriages, births, and deaths. Members of the Sebiyam family, like these scholars, emphasized continuity and the primacy of familial events in explaining changes in farming and residence patterns. Jack Goody, ed., *The Developmental Cycle in Domestic Groups* (Cambridge: Cambridge University Press, 1958).

30 Material for this paragraph comes from interviews in Kpasenkpe with Aarana Daboo Kayuri, October 4, 2010; Dakurugu Yampuhigiya, May 2, 2011; Jacob Pitigi Tampulima, July 1, 2010; Musah Yidana (Tailor), October 2, 2010; Zanloorana Tia Cheera, June 29, 2010. My arrangement with these interviewees specified that I would not disaggregate responses in the published book.

31 Agnes Atia Apusigah, "The Gendered Politics of Farm Household Production and the Shaping of Women's Livelihoods in Northern Ghana," *Feminist Africa* 12, no. 2 (2009): 51–68. In her research in the 1960s, Susan Drucker-Brown noted that men commonly cited a norm that "women 'do not farm.'" *Ritual Aspects*, 14. In a broad comparative sense, demands on female farm labor have been more limited in Mamprugu than in what are now Upper West and Upper East Regions, where Apusigah points out that women are normatively constructed as "farm hands" and are involved in most aspects of farm production. As Apusigah argues, both of

these normative arrangements position women in subordinate roles even as they are consistently relied upon for their labor as producers.

32 "Harvest," for women, included all processing associated with bringing grain from the field to the silo (shucking, drying, etc.).

33 Susan Drucker-Brown, "House and Hierarchy: Politics and Domestic Space in Northern Ghana," *Journal of the Royal Anthropological Institute* 7, no. 4 (2001): 669–85. Drucker-Brown points out that compound design has been relatively stable since her early fieldwork in the 1960s.

34 Group interview with Turenaba Sebiyam, Mariama Sebiyam, Nabila Sebiyam, Garalima Sebiyam, and Aishatu Sebiyam, Kpasenkpe, July 2, 2019.

35 In addition to Sebiyam's own wives, in the period when "brothers farmed together," the wives of two of Sebiyam's brothers also lived in the compound. Most of the brothers who worked on Sebiyam's farms were unmarried in the 1942–66 period, but two had wives that remained in the compound and participated in cooking rotation along with Sebiyam's wives. Because it was difficult to gather information on the wives of brothers who had died or who did not currently live in the compound, I am likely leaving out several sets of wives and children. For the purpose of this section, then, "wives" refers to Sebiyam's wives plus the wives of the brothers about whom I have information.

36 Material for this paragraph comes from interviews in Kpasenkpe with Wudan Duu Sebiyam, July 14, 2010; Mariama Sebiyam, July 14, 2010; Fatacheeba Sebiyam, July 12, 2010, and May 3, 2011; Wuriche Zangu Sebiyam, July 13, 2010; Napoa Sebiyam, July 12, 2010; Assana Sebiyam, July 14, 2010; Turenaba Sebiyam, July 5, 2010; and Nabila Sebiyam, July 12, 2010. My arrangement with these interviewees specified that I would not disaggregate responses in the published book.

37 Note that in the Wulugunaba's compound, as in Mamprugu more broadly, cooking responsibilities were separate from the issue of sharing Sebiyam's room, which wives recounted as following a somewhat less regular schedule and was associated with fetching water rather than food preparation.

38 Being familiar with other accounts of household feeding in Ghana, I was surprised to find that wives recalled having no responsibility for procuring household food, even relish ingredients, at this time. When I asked about daytime meals and soup (relish) ingredients, the wives insisted that these were provided by Sebiyam as well, either from food grown on the farm (okra, groundnuts) or from his cash stock. This appears to be in sharp contrast to my observations of current norms, in which the responsibility of food provision for daytime meals and of soup ingredients are not expected to fall upon the husband. While I cannot demonstrate change over time in any rigorous way, this observation accords with more widely observed trends in conjugal responsibilities in twentieth-century Ghana, in which women's responsibilities for household feeding have tended to

grow over time. Jean Allman and Victoria Tashjian, "*I Will Not Eat Stone*": *Women's History in Colonial Asante* (Portsmouth, NH: Heinemann, 2000); Gracia Clark, "Negotiating Asante Family Survival in Kumasi, Ghana," *Africa: Journal of the International African Institute* 69, no. 1 (1999): 66–86.

39 Group interview with Sebiyam's wives, Kpasenkpe, April 29, 2011; group interview with Turenaba Sebiyam, Mariama Sebiyam, Nabila Sebiyam, Garalima Sebiyam, and Aishatu Sebiyam, Kpasenkpe, July 2, 2019. Drucker-Brown observed small-scale trading as commonplace among women in South Mamprusi in the early 1960s. Drucker-Brown, *Ritual Aspects*, 17.

40 Ladouceur points out, for example, that unlike their southern counterparts, teachers made up the bulk of northern politicians in the 1950s. Ladouceur, *Chiefs and Politicians*, 87.

41 R. Bagulo Bening, *A History of Education in Northern Ghana, 1907–1976*, 2nd ed. (Accra: Gavoss Education PLC, 2015), chapter 14.

42 In fact, his uncle Wahaga, who had been educated in the decade before him, began his advanced training in the same period. Interview with Wulugunaba Professor John Sebiyam Nabila, Accra, July 12, 2015.

43 R. Bagulo Bening, *A History of Education in Northern Ghana, 1907–1976* (Accra: Ghana Universities Press, 1990), 208.

44 Interview with Wulugunaba Professor John Sebiyam Nabila, Accra, July 12, 2015. For more on the history of northern attendance at universities, see Bening, *A History of Education*, 233.

45 Bening, *A History of Education*, 2nd ed., 291–94.

46 For a discussion of the ambiguities and erasures that characterized the CPP's ideas of a gender revolution, see Jeffrey S. Ahlman, *Living with Nkrumahism: Nation, State, and Pan-Africanism in Ghana* (Athens: Ohio University Press, 2017), chapter 5. Behrends and Lentz point out that it was not simply employment that became uncertain, but many other aspects of life: "This first generation of women with a school education not only had to find ways of making use of their education, but had to create a new role model that radically departed from existing images of how women should comport themselves. Instead of quietly working for the family, they assumed a public role, making decisions and openly expressing their opinions." Behrends and Lentz, "Education, Careers, and Home Ties," 149.

47 Mary Opare and Judy E. Mill, "The Evolution of Nursing Education in a Postindependence Context—Ghana from 1957 to 1970," *Western Journal of Nursing Research* 22, no. 8 (2000): 936–44; Bening, *A History of Education*, 92–96.

48 Kate Skinner, "Who Knew the Minds of the People? Specialist Knowledge and Developmentalist Authoritarianism in Post-colonial Ghana," *Journal of Imperial and Commonwealth History* 39, no. 2 (2011).

49 Pawura did not specify which title she had when she began her work, but from the descriptions of her activities and training this appears to have been her position. Interview with Poanaba Pawura Paulina Barijesira, Kpasenkpe, August 31, 2010.

50 Interview with Poanaba Pawura Paulina Barijesira, Kpasenkpe, August 31, 2010.

51 Skinner, "Who Knew the Minds of the People?," 313.

52 For more on the intersection of nation building, women's advocacy, and regional and ethnic bigotry that characterized Nkrumah-era antinudity campaigns, see Jean Allman, "'Let Your Fashion Be in Line with Our Ghanaian Costume': Nation, Gender and the Politics of Clothing in Nkrumah's Ghana," in *Fashioning Africa: Power and the Politics of Dress* (Bloomington: Indiana University Press, 2004), 144–66. See also Jessica Cammaert, *Undesirable Practices: Women, Children, and the Politics of the Body in Northern Ghana, 1930–1972* (Lincoln: University of Nebraska Press, 2016).

53 Allman, "'Let Your Fashion Be in Line.'"

54 Interview with Poanaba Pawura Paulina Barijesira, Kpasenkpe, August 31, 2010.

55 Allman points out that the southern women who were architects and activists in the campaign prized these regional and familial connections, quoting secretary general of the Federation of Ghana Women E. Amarteifio as telling an audience of northern women to "visit your homes in the farther north and advise naked women to put on clothes." Allman, "'Let Your Fashion Be in Line,'" 149. As Skinner indicates, members of the Nkrumah-era Department of Social Welfare and Community Development more broadly took up an idea of "specialized knowledge" that valued familiarity and ability to work in specific regional and national settings. Skinner, "'Who Knew the Minds of the People?'"

56 Interview with Poanaba Pawura Paulina Barijesira, Kpasenkpe, August 31, 2010.

57 Allman interviewed Margaret Azantilow about her work in 2001. Allman, "'Let Your Fashion Be in Line.'"

58 Interview with Poanaba Pawura Paulina Barijesira, Kpasenkpe, August 31, 2010.

59 While educational opportunities for Ghanaians from the North increased dramatically in the 1950s, from secondary literature and my own interviews, it seems that the number of children Sebiyam sent to school, as well as his emphasis on both sons and daughters attending, appears quite unusual. See Bening, *A History of Education*, 142; Ladouceur, *Chiefs and Politicians*, 22.

60 Interview with Namiyelana E. D. Sebiyam, Bolgatanga, May 5, 2011; Interview with Ruth Lamisi Sebiyam, Accra, July 5, 2013. Note that a small but significant contingent of the family is now in New York City, with positions in the Department of Health and in private practice.

61 Ahlman, *Living with Nkrumahism,* "Conclusion."

62 Interview with Wulugunaba Professor John Sebiyam Nabila, Accra, July 12, 2015.

CHAPTER 4: IMPROVISING GOVERNMENT IN THE
GRANARY OF GHANA, 1966–81

1 PRAAD-Tamale NRG8.7.84, Pilot Project Aided Self Help Scheme, 1971–72, letter from Saaka Dahamani and seven others to the Management Committee, Walewale/Kpasenkpe Local Council, October 16, 1971.

2 Piet Konings, *The State and Rural Class Formation in Ghana: A Comparative Analysis* (Leiden: African Studies Centre, 1986), 175.

3 PRAAD-Tamale NRG3.2.12, Traditional Council and other, 1974–75, "Reply to Welcome Address at Welcoming Ceremony by the Head of State," Office of the National Redemption Council news release. The seven governments were the National Liberation Council (1966–69), Busia (1969–72), Acheampong (1972–78), Akuffo (1978–79), Rawlings (1979), Limann (1979–81), Rawlings (1981–92).

4 For a comprehensive summary, see Bjorn Beckman, "The Agrarian Basis of the Post-colonial State," in *Rural Development in Tropical Africa,* ed. Judith Heyer, Pepe Roberts, and Gavin Williams (London: Macmillan, 1981), 143–68. Konings also gives a good summary of national policy in Konings, *The State and Rural Class Formation,* 34–35, 167–75. Between 1966 and 1969, the military coalition that overthrew Kwame Nkrumah began to dismantle state farms under its "Stabilisation and Consolidation" plan, designed to attract the support of the IMF, and its 1968 Development Plan stated its interest in supporting "key farmers." After a transition to civilian rule in 1969, Dr. K. A. Busia's Progress Party continued liberalization policies and also embarked on an ambitious plan for rural development that aimed to pair agricultural programs with improvements in rural infrastructure and services. After the 1972 coup that overthrew Busia, General I. K. Acheampong's National Redemption Council (1972–75) and Supreme Military Council (1975–78) repudiated IMF support and liberalization policies, enacting reforms that aimed to make Ghana "self-reliant" in agricultural production. While Acheampong's "Operation Feed Yourself" initiative was supported by a series of price controls, it was clearly capitalist in its vision of agricultural production and continued the basic tenets of earlier programs.

5 Derek Byerlee and Carl K. Eicher, eds., *Africa's Emerging Maize Revolution* (Boulder, CO: Lynne Rienner Publishers, 1997); John M. Cohen, "Effects of Green Revolution Strategies on Tenants and Small-Scale Landowners in the Chilalo Region of Ethiopia," *Journal of Developing Areas* 9, no. 3 (1975): 335–58; Jeremiah I. Dibua, "Agricultural Modernization, the Environment and Sustainable Production in Nigeria, 1970–1985," *African Economic History* 30 (2002): 107–37; Carl K. Eicher,

"Zimbabwe's Maize-Based Green Revolution: Preconditions for Replication," *World Development* 23, no. 5 (1995): 805–18; Abe Goldman and Joyotee Smith, "Agricultural Transformations in India and Northern Nigeria: Exploring the Nature of Green Revolutions," *World Development* 23, no. 2 (1995): 243–63; Stein T. Holden, "Peasant Household Modelling: Farming Systems Evolution and Sustainability in Northern Zambia," *Agricultural Economics* 9, no. 3 (September 1993): 241–67. These experiments in broad-based support for green revolution technologies were limited in scope, but they served as test cases on which the prospects for agricultural growth in sub-Saharan Africa would be measured. Peter Lawrence, "The Political Economy of the 'Green Revolution' in Africa," *Review of African Political Economy* 15, no. 42 (1988).

6 PRAAD-Tamale NRG3.8.8, Roads Gambaga, letter from E. Ansah-Aboagye, DAO Gambaga, to the regional agricultural mechanisation officer, Ministry of Agriculture, Tamale, titled "Request for Tractors to Work on the Walewale-Wungu-Yama Road," February 8, 1968; PRAAD-Tamale NRG8.7.84, Pilot Project Aided Self Help Scheme, 1971–72, letter from Saaka Dahamani and seven others to the Management Committee, Walewale/Kpasenkpe Local Council, October 16, 1971.

7 The notable exception here is Julius Nyerere's project of *ujamaa* in Tanzania, though, as Priya Lal points out, studies of *ujamaa* as a development project have tended to divorce it from its continental and global context, often to the point where it is seen as a paradigmatic instance of developmentalism or of postcolonial African statecraft. Priya Lal, *African Socialism in Postcolonial Tanzania: Between the Village and the World* (Cambridge: Cambridge University Press, 2015), 10–12.

8 Cooper, for example, dates the end of the "development era" to 1973, which is useful for periodizing economic fortunes but tends to reaffirm the idea that development receded as focus of statecraft in this period. Frederick Cooper, *Africa since 1940: The Past of the Present*, New Approaches to African History (Cambridge: Cambridge University Press, 2002), 85.

9 Chazan, characterizing the period from 1969 to 1982; Chazan and Pellow characterizing the period from 1966 to 1981; Killick on the period from 1972 to 1983. Naomi Chazan, *An Anatomy of Ghanaian Politics: Managing Political Recession, 1969–1982* (Boulder, CO: Westview Press, 1983); Deborah Pellow and Naomi Chazan, *Ghana: Coping with Uncertainty* (Boulder, CO: Westview Press, 1986), 47; Tony Killick, *Development Economics in Action: A Study of Economic Policies in Ghana* (Portsmouth, NH: Heinemann, 1978). Most of the work done on particular regimes or policies of the era was produced by social scientists in the 1980s, and, for northern Ghana, a distinct set of scholarship emerged that critiqued a series of large-scale rice estate projects most closely associated with Acheampong's Operation Feed Yourself. Konings, *The State and Rural*

Class Formation; Jack Goody, "Rice-Burning and the Green Revolution in Northern Ghana," *Journal of Development Studies* 16, no. 2 (1980): 136–55; Nicholas Van Hear, "Northern Labour and the Development of Capitalist Agriculture in Ghana" (PhD diss., University of Birmingham, 1982); Andrew Shepherd, "Agrarian Change in Northern Ghana: Public Investment, Capitalist Farming and Famine," in Heyer, Roberts, and Williams, *Rural Development in Tropical Africa.*

10 In the regional and national archives, there is a clear and extreme drop in available records over the course of the 1960s and 1970s. For documentary evidence, in this chapter I rely on the select district and regional records that have been preserved, as well as uncatalogued files I could find in local government offices and unpublished policy documents and reports that are kept in the libraries of ministries and research institutions.

11 When compared to the scholarship on the Nkrumah and Rawlings eras, the scholarship on the 1970s in Ghana is sparse. In recent historical examinations of northern Ghana, the period between 1966 and 1979 has been more or less absent. The Nkrumah-Rawlings interregnum plays little role in, for example, Carola Lentz, *Ethnicity and the Making of History in Northern Ghana* (Edinburgh: Edinburgh University Press, 2006), or Christian Lund, *Local Politics and the Dynamics of Property in Africa* (Cambridge: Cambridge University Press, 2008). A notable exception is Benjamin Talton's *Politics of Social Change in Ghana: The Konkomba Struggle for Political Equality* (New York: Palgrave Macmillan, 2010), which shows the 1970s to be a crucial period for postcolonial Konkomba politics.

12 Jennifer Hart, *Ghana on the Go: African Mobility in the Age of Motor Transportation* (Bloomington: Indiana University Press, 2016), chapter 4; Bianca Murillo, *Market Encounters: Consumer Cultures in Twentieth-Century Ghana* (Athens: Ohio University Press, 2017), 140 and chapter 5.

13 In my research for this chapter, I used interviews to find and interpret documentary evidence. For example, I began to seek documents on the Ministry of Agriculture because interviews in Kpasenkpe focused on agricultural projects whose records were not in the government archives. From there, I began to interview former staff of the Ministry of Agriculture, who helped me understand what I was looking for, directed me to collections of reports and studies that were produced in the period, and helped me to understand how the documentary record reflected both the vitality and limitations of government work in the period.

14 Subsidized government loans were extended to individual farmers—often urban businessmen who had the capital to clear hundreds of acres—who also took advantage of newly subsidized fertilizer. Between 1968 and 1974, approximately twenty-six thousand hectares were cleared for rice cultivation, and rice production more than quintupled, culminating in the declaration of the country's "self-sufficiency" in rice production in 1975.

World Bank, "Ghana Agricultural Sector Review" (Washington, DC: World Bank, 1978), appendix table 8.

15 My explicit interest in farming directed me to more men than women in this subset of interviews (thirty-five men and twenty women), though I also spoke to several women who had built reputations as particularly good farmers (usually meaning that they cultivated their own plots of staple grains, though not in all cases). I use the term "small-scale" here to distinguish farmers, like those in Kpasenkpe, whose farms were not the large-scale commercial estate farms of the period. This distinction, while broad, is based on the categorizations used by policy makers and recognized by farmers. As I hope the chapter shows, I do not intend to imply a lack of variation in the size, success, and market relationships of farms in Kpasenkpe.

16 The Ghanaian Agricultural Development Bank began to focus increasingly on small-scale borrowers, turning to them almost exclusively by the late 1970s. Konings, *The State and Rural Class Formation*, 176. The GGADP also began to refocus its efforts to reach smaller-scale farmers in 1974, focusing on research and extension that would support development and dissemination of seeds and other inputs to small-scale farmers. A grant from Germany resurrected a colonial experiment station, establishing the Nyankpala Crops Research Project and Nyankpala Agricultural Extension Station to support German and Ghanaian research into new crop varieties for small-scale famers and northern Ghanaian ecosystems. GTZ, "Evaluation Report, Agricultural Experiment Station Nyankpala" (Eschborn, West Germany: GTZ, 1982), 15. In March of 1977, the project attempted to limit fertilizer distribution to small-scale farmers by establishing collection points at bullock training stations and agricultural extension points. Ministry of Agriculture and Ghana-German Agricultural Development Project, "10 Years of Ghanaian-German Technical Cooperation in the Field of Agriculture, Northern Ghana" (Tamale, Ghana: Ministry of Agriculture, 1980).

17 Chazan, *An Anatomy of Ghanaian Politics*.

18 Even when Acheampong repudiated IMF support in the mid-1970s, he intensified parallel efforts to attract support from, for example, the German government, on the basis of a similar recipe for agricultural production as his predecessors.

19 Interviews with current and former Ministry of Agriculture staff: former regional director for extension, Walewale and Tamale, informal conversations, 2010–11; former tractor operator, Walewale, August 28, 2010; former information officer Mr. Frank Adongo, Tamale, October 30, 2010; northern regional director of agriculture, Tamale, September 27, 2010; former information officer Mr. Frank Adongo and the former regional director for extension, Tamale, June 24, 2013; Information Officer Iddrisu Baba Mohammed, Tamale, June 27, 2013.

20 Ministry of Agriculture and GGADP, "10 Years of Ghanaian-German Technical Cooperation," 7–8.

21 Increases in funding were accompanied by the pervasive presence of German experts and volunteer extension agents ("A LOT of Germans" recalled the current information officer, who worked in the Information Support Unit in the 1980s). Interview with Information Officer Iddrisu Baba Mohammed, Tamale, June 27, 2013.

22 Interview with former information officer Mr. Frank Adongo, Tamale, June 24, 2013.

23 This assumption is on display, for example, in the summary of work produced by the GGADP at the end of the decade. Ministry of Agriculture and GGADP, "10 Years of Ghanaian-German Technical Cooperation."

24 For a succinct summary of the literature on the construction of "farmer" as male in African agricultural policy, see Moses Mosonsieyiri Kansanga et al., "A Feminist Political Ecology of Agricultural Mechanization and Evolving Gendered On-Farm Labor Dynamics in Northern Ghana," *Gender, Technology and Development* 23, no. 3 (2019): 210.

25 Interview with former information officer Frank Adongo and the former regional director for extension, Tamale, June 24, 2013. Nkrumah-era group farming efforts, which in Kpasenkpe had been modest, envisioned collective production and reinvestment. In contrast, new group farming schemes explicitly aimed for group members to "act as models for other farmers to emulate via the posited trickle-down effect." Kwame Amezah and Johann Hesse, "Reforms in the Ghanaian Extension System" (case study prepared for the workshop Extension and Rural Development: A Convergence of Views on International Approaches?, World Bank and USAID, Washington, DC, November 12–15, 2002), 3.

26 Interview with Suurana Yakubu Pusu, Kpasenkpe, July 2, 2010. Solomon Dawuni Sebiyam provided the direct translation. Several additional factors may have come into play when deciding who would join the groups. For example, an elder explained his membership, saying "the Wulugu-naba could not leave the elders, so he let them join." Interview with Wudana Daboo Saka, Kpasenkpe, October 3, 2010.

27 Interview with Kakpanaba Somka Nluki, Kpasenkpe, June 30, 2010.

28 Interview with Suurana Yakubu Pusu, Kpasenkpe, July 2, 2010.

29 Interviews in Kpasenkpe with Suurana Yakubu Pusu, July 2, 2010, and with Kakpanaba Somka Nluki, September 3, 2010; interview with Nelson Ndimah (Bayela), Kpasenkpe, October 2, 2010.

30 Interview with Kakpanaba Somka Nluki, Kpasenkpe, June 30, 2010.

31 Interviews in Kpasenkpe with Kakpanaba Somka Nluki, June 30, 2010, July 12, 2010, October 1, 2010, and July 2, 2019.

32 The Busia regime had issued the Aliens Compliance Order in 1969, which had abruptly expelled non-Ghanaians in the country and prevented new immigration without residence papers. Naaichi Maka did not

mention the order, but it is likely no coincidence that he arrived shortly after the coup that unseated Busia. Interview with Naaichi Maka, Kpasenkpe, July 9, 2010.

33 Interview with Naaichi Maka, Kpasenkpe, July 9, 2010.

34 Interview with Sandola Tampuri, Kpasenkpe, June 8, 2013. It is possible that what appeared to those who were not civil servants as "take and [not] pay" was a scheme in which loan repayments were deducted from civil servants' pay. I am less concerned with what was happening with repayment than I am with the way it came to capture what was perceived by some farmers as the ability of well-connected residents to negotiate beneficial arrangements with the government.

35 Interview with Sandola Tampuri, Kpasenkpe, June 8, 2013. This explanation contrasts with but is not in contradiction to the explanation from others that the group rice scheme ended when droughts and poor harvests prevented the group from paying back its loan.

36 Analyses in the late 1970s and early 1980s focused on land, labor, and capital on and around large-scale mechanized rice estates, highlighting the benefits of agricultural spending for a narrow class of large-scale estate farmers, largely businessmen and traders from urban centers. The Gonja rice projects were chronicled Jack Goody in 1980; the Dagomba rice estates were studied by Van Hear and Shepherd; the Fumbisi Valley rice estates were explored by Piet Konings. Goody, "Rice-Burning and the Green Revolution"; Nicholas Van Hear, "Northern Labour and the Development of Capitalist Agriculture in Ghana" (PhD diss., University of Birmingham, 1982); Shepherd, "Agrarian Change in Northern Ghana," 168–92; Konings, *The State and Rural Class Formation*. More recently, scholars have started to expand the frame of analysis with which estate farming is studied in order to "examine the effects of agricultural modernization on agricultural development and the responses of local farming practice to these interventions." Kojo Amanor and Opoku Pabi, "Space, Time, Rhetoric and Agricultural Change in the Transition Zone in Ghana," *Human Ecology* 35, no. 1 (2007): 51–67. Amanor and Pabi show, for example, that smallholder farmers in the immediate vicinity of the maize and rice estates of northern Brong-Ahafo Region hired plowing services from large-scale farmers and used subsidized fertilizer.

37 Scholars have pointed out that chiefs were able to turn their statutory and political influence into broader opportunities for personal accumulation. See, for example, Shepherd, "Agrarian Change in Northern Ghana," 147. Goody provides the most nuanced description of the range of people who became involved in estate farming, rejecting "a straightforward division between capitalist ('stranger' or 'absentee') farmers and local 'peasants.'" Goody, "Rice-Burning and the Green Revolution," 151.

38 "Bolga farmers" appeared to prefer living in Kpasenkpe town, with its centralized town structure and relative proximity to a main road, to staying

in the more isolated and dispersed settlements immediately surrounding their estates. Interview with Bugurana Ibrahim Manmara, Kpasenkpe, October 5, 2010. It is also possible that increasing tensions with local laborers, like those described by Goody and Konings, encouraged estate owners to keep their distance. See Goody, "Rice-Burning and the Green Revolution"; Konings, *The State and Rural Class Formation*.

39 There is little reason to believe that they were uniquely advantaged in this respect. Farmers recall that fertilizer and agricultural loans were only available thirty kilometers away in Walewale or at the agricultural station several additional kilometers away. In the Northern Region, small-scale farmers often had ready access to land but were constrained by access to labor, inputs, roads, and markets. There are good reasons to believe that the experiences of this era of policy are highly region-specific. For example, the evidence for Upper East Region, where a few studies of long-term agricultural change have been done, is influenced by the fact that population pressure has been a major force behind agricultural change. Evidence from these areas does not contradict the idea that 1970s interventions were widely used and influenced farmers' choices. See David A. Cleveland, "Migration in West Africa: A Savanna Village Perspective," *Africa: Journal of the International African Institute* 61, no. 2 (January 1, 1991): 222–46; Paul Webber, "Agrarian Change in Kusasi, North-East Ghana," *Africa: Journal of the International African Institute* 66, no. 3 (January 1, 1996): 437–57.

40 Interview with Kofi Nabila, Kpasenkpe, April 30, 2011. Solomon Dawuni Sebiyam provided the direct translation.

41 Interview with Kofi Nabila, Kpasenkpe, June 15, 2013.

42 Interviews in Kpasenkpe with Danladi Dabdu, July 6, 2010, and Tindana Issah Tongo, May 1, 2011. Farmers recall fertilizer being purchased directly from extension agents or through traders.

43 Interview with Sandow Kundunkurigu, Kpasenkpe, May 1, 2011.

44 Interviews in Kpasenkpe with Musah Ladi (Hajia), July 8, 2010, and Adam Abdullai Seiya, July 5, 2010. Many farmers' memories of the period are intimately connected to government policy, even if these effects were not always at the point of direct contact with an extension worker or a government buyer. For example, after telling me about his refusal to participate in what he thought of as an inequitable group loan scheme for rice, Sandola Tampuri then went on to point out that he did not need to rely on the farmers group. He had plenty to do on his own farms, because "at that time the fertilizer was not much [did not cost much]," and he could just buy it in the market. Interview with Sandola Tampuri, June 8, 2013.

45 Interviews in Kpasenkpe that discussed Agric and Damongo maize included Tindana Issah Tongo, June 30, 2010; Tindana Issah Tongo, Samanaba Sumani Takora, and Faara Tongo, June 7, 2013; Fati Zebagane, June 17, 2013; Alhassan Pusu, June 17, 2013; Adisa Tampulima, June 15, 2013;

Balihira Seiya, June 15, 2013; Naaichi Maka, June 17, 2013; Nelson Danladi, June 17, 2013; Kofi Nabila, June 15, 2013; and Sandow Bugri, June 17, 2013.

46 Some farmers in Kpasenkpe were able to purchase or receive loans for bullock plows as individuals, working directly with the Ministry of Agriculture department centers in Walewale and surrounding towns, and a 1970 survey of the Kpasenkpe area noted that "Bullock Plowing which is fast gaining adherents should also be encouraged," and that "Farmers in this area have also been clamouring for Tractors." PRAAD Tamale NRG3.13.37, Northern Territories Planning Commission 1968–78, "Western South Mamprusi—On the Spot Survey Report of the Regional Planning Committee Subcommittee," report sent from N. S. Belo-Giwa, regional planning secretary, to District Administrative Office Gambaga, June 26, 1970.

47 Men frequently argued that "women did not farm" in the past (interview with Kambontia Yaado Piyisiba, Kpasenkpe, June 28, 2010, for example), but it was clear that a small number of women cultivated their own plots in the late colonial and nationalist periods. However, in interviews, women confirmed that this was rare before the 1980s, and only very recently has it become more common. Interviews in Kpasenkpe with Adisa Tampulima, October 3, 2010, Musah Ladi (Hajia), July 8, 2010, and Balihira Seiya, October 2, 2010.

48 When I mentioned that many men had told me that women did not have their own farms "in the old days," she said emphatically, "It's a LIE!" Interview with Balihira Seiya, Kpasenkpe, October 2, 2010.

49 The bullock itself was not a very important source of income—she, like many of the bullock owners I interviewed, usually lent it to family members.

50 None of the Kpasenkpe residents I interviewed recalled engaging in labor on the rice estates of the Fumbisi Valley. Instead, several residents remembered competing with estate owners to attract laborers from the Kunkwa area to work on their farms. Interviews in Kpasenkpe with Sandow Kundunkurigu, May 1, 2011; Balihira Seiya, October 2, 2010; and Kakpanaba Somka Nluki, June 30, 2010.

51 The 1970 survey of the Kpasenkpe area took note of the arrangement, arguing that cooperatives should be an extension of "the rudimentary group farming that is presently in vogue." See PRAAD-Tamale NRG3.13.37, Northern Territories Planning Commission 1968–78, "Western South Mamprusi—On the Spot Survey." See also Van Hear's description of the rise of the parallel Dagomba institution of *daa kpariba* groups and their interaction with estate farming. Nicholas Van Hear, "'By Day' Boys and Dariga Men: Casual Labor versus Agrarian Capital in Northern Ghana," *Review of African Political Economy* 11, no. 31 (1984): 50.

52 Interviews in Kpasenkpe with Fulanaba Bukari Amadu, July 7, 2010, and May 1, 2011; and Comfort Mensah Dzii and Juwano Mensah Dzii, May 2, 2011.

53 Interview with Alhassan Pusu, Kpasenkpe, April 30, 2011.

54 Interview with Zamma Voonaba, Kpasenkpe, June 7, 2013.

55 Interviews in Kpasenkpe with Adisa Tampulima, June 15, 2013; and Fula-naba Bukari Amadu, July 7, 2010.

56 These recollections reflect the diversity of livelihood strategies that inter-sected with government initiatives. Fati Zebagane recalled the common practice of reharvesting rice from the large-scale plots across the river, keeping the grain that mechanical harvesters had left behind. Interview with Fati Zebagane, Kpasenkpe, June 17, 2013. Others recalled the avail-ability of American surplus wheat, supplied as relief grain by the Ache-ampong government, but this was associated not with years of hardship but instead with the general abundance of food in the period. Interviews in Kpasenkpe with Fatacheeba Sebiyam, July 12, 2010; Fulanaba Bukari Amadu, July 7, 2010; and Sandow Bugri, July 7, 2010.

57 Interview with Fati Zebagane, Kpasenkpe, June 17, 2013.

58 Interviews in Kpasenkpe with Adisa Tampulima, June 15, 2013; and Nel-son Danladi, June 17, 2013.

59 Interview with Naaichi Maka, Kpasenkpe, June 17, 2013.

60 Kansanga et al., "A Feminist Political Ecology"; Hanson Nyantakyi-Frimpong and Rachel Bezner Kerr, "A Political Ecology of High-Input Agriculture in Northern Ghana," *African Geographical Review* 34, no. 1 (2015): 13–35. One important focus of these studies is on the relationship between input-intensive agriculture and gendered labor demands, a topic that I was unable to study in depth beyond the Sebiyam family network. For an excellent examination of changing livelihood strategies in several families and its relationship to a larger economic, policy, and ecological change, see Ann Whitehead, "Tracking Livelihood Change: Theoretical, Methodological and Empirical Perspectives from North-East Ghana," *Journal of Southern African Studies* 28, no. 3 (2002): 575–98.

61 Interviews with Balihira Seiya, October 2, 2010, and June 15, 2013.

62 Dennis Austin, *Ghana Observed: Essays on the Politics of a West African Republic* (Manchester, UK: Manchester University Press, 1976), 102.

63 PRAAD-Tamale NRG3.13.35, minutes of a meeting between the district administrative officer and local heads of departments, Gambaga, Octo-ber 7, 1967.

64 PRAAD-Tamale NRG8.21.19, Handing Over Reports LA Staff, 1961–72.

65 PRAAD-Tamale NRG3.4.9, Diary (Gambaga) 1968–71; PRAAD-Tamale NRG8.7.64, Local Councils Regional Development Projects, 1972–74; PRAAD-Tamale NRG8.3.288 (EAP 541/1/3/260), Monthly Reports, Dis-trict Council, 1975–76.

66 PRAAD-Tamale NRG3.8.8, Roads Gambaga 1967–71, letter from J. A. Mahama, clerk of council Walewale/Kpasenkpe Local Council to the DAO Gambaga, February 17, 1969; letter from the DAO Gambaga to the clerk of council Walewale/Kpasenkpe Local Council, March 17, 1969.

67 PRAAD-Tamale NRG3.8.8, Roads Gambaga 1967–71, letter from DAO Gambaga C. K. Amanfu to the Bunkpurugu-Naba, August 31, 1970.

68 PRAAD-Tamale NRG8.5.274, Local Government Councils Development Committees General, 1962–71, memo from the NLC Secretariat to regional administrative officers, July 20, 1966, and replies July–September 1966. The determination that Northern committees were "inactive" appears in a handwritten note by Northern Regional Office staff on October 24, 1966. This summation followed the reports from numerous districts that village development committees were, to use Gambaga District Administrative Officer J. E. Nsaful's phrasing, "existing in name [only] and cannot be said to have contributed anything toward the development of their villages." PRAAD-Tamale NRG8.5.274, Local Government Councils Development Committees General, 1962–71, memo from J. E. Nsaful, DAO Gambaga, to Ag. regional administrative officer, Tamale, September 21, 1966.

69 PRAAD-Tamale NRG3.13.35, Monthly Meetings DAO and Departments 1966–71, minutes of a meeting of the Gambaga Town Development Committee, February 9, 1968.

70 Naah also highlighted the role of each village chief (as chairman of the committee), arguing that they should transcend conflict within communities by choosing members from "all sections" and irrespective of "political differences" by looking for those with "public spiritedness, honesty, devotion and sense of responsibility." PRAAD-Tamale NRG8.5.274, Local Government Councils Development Committees General, 1962–71, letter, with speech attached, from DAO A. B. Naah to RAO Tamale, May 27, 1970.

71 PRAAD-Tamale NRG3.2.12, Traditional Council Enskinnment of Chiefs and Other Matters, 1974–75, letter from M. D. Bonirima, senior assistant community development officer, Department of Social Welfare and Community Development Gambaga, to all head chiefs and subjects in South Mamprusi, January 25, 1974.

72 PRAAD-Tamale NRG3.13.37, Northern Territories Planning Commission 1968–78, "Western South Mamprusi—On the Spot Survey Report of the Regional Planning Committee Subcommittee," report sent from N. S. Belo-Giwa, regional planning secretary, to District Administrative Office Gambaga, June 26, 1970. The team, aiming to focus their survey on the "Overseas" area, never made it across the river because they went in the rainy season and there was no bridge.

73 PRAAD-Tamale NRG3.13.37, Northern Territories Planning Commission 1968–78, "Western South Mamprusi—On the Spot Survey Report of the Regional Planning Committee Subcommittee," report sent from N. S. Belo-Giwa, regional planning secretary, to District Administrative Office Gambaga, June 26, 1970.

74 PRAAD-Tamale NRG8.3.284 (EAP541/1/3/256), Districts Monthly Reports 1972–74. Quotations are from Salaga District, July 1972, and Gambaga, January 1973.

75 PRAAD-Tamale NRG3.13.35, Monthly Meetings DAO and Departments 1966–71, meeting between the DAO and local heads of departments, Walewale/Kpasenkpe Local Council Hall, Walewale, January 22, 1969.

76 PRAAD-Tamale NRG8.7.84, Pilot Project Aided Self Help Scheme 1971–72, internal notes to RAO, May 10, 1970.

77 From my archival research at PRAAD Tamale and (for later periods) the registry offices of the West Mamprusi and East Mamprusi District Assemblies, I made a database of 232 petitions that were sent between 1957 and 1991. For the period under consideration in this chapter, there are 130 petitions, most from between 1968 and 1974. Out of these, 65 mention local development projects (the others focus on local government boundaries or other administrative matters). I also considered as a "petition" anything that reported on a verbal petition received by officials. Petitions about development projects reflect the range of actors and geographies in the database as a whole. Those that do not mention local contributions of labor and funds either (a) make a general case for need; (b) make a more specific case that a particular project or area can generate revenue; (c) argue that particular areas have been neglected by existing local councils; or (d) complain about delays by local government or particular contractors. Petitions on development for this time period appeared in the following PRAAD Tamale files: NRG3.3.37, Complaints and Petitions (Gambaga), 1968–70; NRG3.8.8, Roads (Gambaga), 1967–71; NRG8.28.126, Local Government (Northern Region), 1969; NRG8.28.127, Establishment of District and Local Councils (Northern Region), 1967–72; NRG8.7.64, Local Council Regional Development Projects (Northern Region), 1972–79; NRG8.7.84, Pilot Project Aided Self Help Scheme, 1971–72.

78 PRAAD-Tamale NRG3.3.37, Complaints and Petitions (Gambaga), 1968–70, petition from Communal Labor Group to drivers, Bunkpurugu, September 5, 1968.

79 PRAAD-Tamale NRG3.3.37, Complaints and Petitions (Gambaga), 1968–70, petition from school leavers to DAO Gambaga, August 19, 1969.

80 PRAAD-Tamale NRG3.3.37, Complaints and Petitions (Gambaga), 1968–70, petitions from Kunkwa residents to the Walewale Local Council, December 10, 1971.

81 PRAAD-Tamale NRG8.28.126, Local Government (Northern Region), 1969, petition from Kanakulaiwura and subchiefs to the electoral commissioner and minister of internal affairs, Accra, November 23, 1971. For more on the East Gonja dispute, see Paul Stacey, "'The Chiefs, Elders, and People Have for Many Years Suffered Untold Hardships': Protests by Coalitions of the Excluded in British Northern Togoland, UN Trusteeship Territory, 1950–7," *Journal of African History* 55, no. 3 (2014): 423–44.

82 PRAAD-Tamale NRG3.8.8, Roads Gambaga, letter from E. Ansah-Aboagye, DAO Gambaga, to the regional agricultural mechanisation

officer, Ministry of Agriculture, Tamale, titled "Request for Tractors to Work on the Walewale-Wungu-Yama Road," February 8, 1968.

83 PRAAD-Tamale NRG8.7.84, Pilot Project Aided Self Help Scheme 1971–72, letter from Saaka Dahamani and seven others to the Management Committee, Walewale/Kpasenkpe Local Council, October 16, 1971.

84 PRAAD Tamale NRG 8.7.84, Pilot Project Aided Self-Help Scheme, petition from Chief Lungbun to regional social welfare officer, November 4, 1971; PRAAD Tamale NRG3.8.8, Roads Gambaga, 1967–71, E. Ansah-Aboagye, DAO Gambaga, to regional agricultural mechanisation officer, February 8, 1968; PRAAD Tamale NRG 8.7.64, Local Council Regional Development Projects, 1972–79, N. Parimag, clerk of council Damongo LC to Department of Social Welfare and Community Development, Tamale, November 23, 1973; PRAAD Tamale NRG 8.7.64, Local Council Regional Development Projects 1972–79, C. S. Ayamkah asst. district administrative officer Damongo to regional administrative officer, May 17, 1973; PRAAD Tamale NRG 8.7.64, Local Council Regional Development Projects, 1972–79, H. Dason secretary of Takoro-Bolega Development Committee to the chairman of the Tolon Local Council Development Committee, January 27, 1974.

85 PRAAD Tamale NRG 8.7.64, Local Council Regional Development Projects, 1972–79, petition from members of the Kpachiyilli Town Development Committee to the Department of Social Welfare and Community Development, February 25, 1974; PRAAD Tamale NRG 8.7.64, Local Council Regional Development Projects, 1972–79, petition from Yakubu Abudulai to clerk of council Savelugu LC, December 24, 1973; PRAAD Tamale NRG 8.7.64, Local Council Regional Development Projects 1972–79, letter from Yapeiwura Bakar to district administrative officer Damongo, January 28, 1974.

86 PRAAD Tamale NRG 8.7.84, Pilot Project Aided Self-Help Scheme, petition from Chief Lungbun to regional social welfare officer, November 4, 1971.

87 PRAAD Tamale NRG 8.7.64, Local Council Regional Development Projects, 1972–79, petition from John Fusheini Alhassan, copied to Regional Office, Tamale, December 26, 1973.

88 PRAAD Tamale NRG 8.7.64, Local Council Regional Development Projects, 1972–79, Zabzugu Youth Association to regional social welfare officer, October 1, 1973.

89 PRAAD Tamale NRG 8.7.64, Local Council Regional Development Projects, 1972–79, petition from John Fusheini Alhassan, copied to Regional Office, Tamale, December 26, 1973.

90 After receiving public funding in 1968 under a national project allocating 64,000 cedis for fifty-four health posts around the country (roughly £22,000), the Kpasenkpe health post received periodic mention in surviving development documents, including repairs and a materials list. See

PRAAD-Tamale NRG3.13.37, Northern Territories Planning Commission 1968–78, "Progress Report Summary for the Quarter Ending 31st Dec 1972," Regional Resource Planning Division, development planning secretary to district administrative officers, March 2, 1972; PRAAD-Tamale NRG8.7.61, Projects Undertaken by Regional Organization Under Direct Labour, 1971–76, materials list for Kpasenkpe Health Post, March 23, 1973; PRAAD-Tamale NRG8.7.64, Local Council Regional Development Projects, 1972–79, letter from Regional Administrative Office to ag. regional engineer entitled "Kpasenkpe Health Post," May 19, 1976.

91 PRAAD-Tamale NRG3.13.37, Northern Territories Planning Commission 1968–78. The quotation from the Wulugunaba is in "Western South Mamprusi—On the Spot Survey," and the allocations and commencement date for Kpasenkpe, along with fifty-four other health posts across the country, is from "Progress Report Summary for the Quarter Ending 31st December 1972," from P. S. Mensah, ag. prin. reg. planning officer to DAO Gambaga, March 2, 1973.

92 While this system structurally mimicked parts of the *nayiri kpaariba* system, self-help labor in this period became divorced from chiefly calls for farm labor.

93 Interviews in Kpasenkpe with Balihira Seiya, October 2, 2010; Lamisi Taanaba, Tipoa Baŋmarigu, and Azimi, June 6, 2013; Chimsi Wubgu, June 8, 2013; Jacob Pitigi Tampulima, October 1, 2010; Kambontia Yaado Piyisiba, June 28, 2010; Samanaba Sumani Takora, July 12, 2010; Wurugurunaba Nsoanyanni Sandow, June 29, 2010; Wuriche Dabdu, October 5, 2010.

94 Interviews with Jacob Pitigi Tampulima, Kpasenkpe, July 1, 2010, and October 1, 2011.

95 Interview with Wurugurunaba Nsoanyanni Sandow, Kpasenkpe, June 29, 2010.

96 During the 1980s and 1990s, Amasachina would become involved in channeling donor money from USAID, UNICEF, the World Bank, and others toward projects in the Northern Region. In the late 1960s and 1970s, however, it appears to have grown through decentralized local efforts that sometimes matched government and external funding to local projects. For example, reports from Western Dagomba District in July and August of 1976 detail the district chief executive inaugurating and funding Amasachina self-help activities in Tirakpaa and Nanton. See PRAAD-Tamale NRG8.3.288 (EAP 541/1/3/260), Monthly Reports for Western Dagomba, July and August 1976. For more on the group, see Eboe Hutchful, *Ghana's Adjustment Experience: The Paradox of Reform* (Geneva: UNRISD, 2002), 184; Lynne Brydon and Karen Legge, *Adjusting Society: The World Bank, the IMF and Ghana* (London: Tauris Academic Studies, 1996), 38; Ian Gary, "Confrontation, Co-operation, or Co-optation: NGOs and the Ghanaian State during Structural Adjustment," *Review of African Political Economy* 23, no. 68 (1996): 159.

97 Interviews in Kpasenkpe with Baba Baŋmarigu and Magazia Dibooriyoma, October 2, 2010; Adisa Tampulima, October 3, 2010; Mensah Dzii (Carpenter), October 3, 2010; and Musah Yidana (Tailor), October 2, 2010.

98 Interview with Adisa Tampulima, Kpasenkpe, October 3, 2010.

99 PRAAD Tamale NGR8.2.218, Mamprusi Traditional Council 1974–88, monthly report for February 1975, Mamprusi Traditional Council.

100 PRAAD Tamale NRG3.2.12, Traditional Council Enskinment of Chiefs and Other Matters, "Address by Lt.-Col. Festus Addae, Regional Commissioner Northern Region to the Members of the Northern Regional House of Chiefs during the Inaugural Meeting of the House," May 23, 1975. John Sebiyam Nabila recalls formally commissioning the hospital during the Limann years with Limann's minister of health. Interview with Wulugunaba Professor John Sebiyam Nabila, Accra, August 17, 2010.

101 It is difficult to get an exact date for the move to Kpawaŋa — it appears that Sebiyam began farming there before he owned a tractor but that gradually, over the decade, the food-farming activities of the family moved to this farm.

102 Sebiyam's first tractor, a Ferguson purchased when Sebiyam bought out the tractor loan from the Kpasenkpe farmers group in the 1970s, was a key way that Sebiyam retained access to services and money from a variety of constituents. One resident recalls paying Sebiyam for tractor services. Another recalls Sebiyam providing the tractor for him in "barter trade" for care of Sebiyam's cattle. Interview with Tindana Issah Tongo, Kpasenkpe, May 1, 2011; interview with Fulanaba Bukari Amadu, Kpasenkpe, May 1, 2011. The closeness of Sebiyam's new farms to town and to constituents' farms likely facilitated these exchanges, as a variety of constituents could contribute labor nearer to their own farms.

103 It has long been clear that commercial agriculture, hired labor, and industrial inputs have not in themselves reduced the importance of family networks in agricultural production. See Sara Berry, *No Condition Is Permanent: The Social Dynamics of Agrarian Change in Sub-Saharan Africa* (Madison: University of Wisconsin Press, 1993).

104 Another two died in the same period. Of the brothers who left full-time work on the family farm in the late 1960s, five were still alive to interview during my research.

105 Brothers who separated came from all of the groups that had worked on Sebiyam's farms in the 1940s and 1950s. Thus, it does not appear that the decision to "separate" depended on descent.

106 At the same time, inputs could be used to secure the necessary occasional labor of family members who now had their own farms — even if Sebiyam did not explicitly trade inputs for labor as with constituents, expectations loomed.

107 Material for this paragraph comes from interviews in Kpasenkpe with Aarana Daboo Kayuri, October 4, 2010; Dakurugu Yampuhigiya, May 2,

2011; Musah Yidana (Tailor), October 2, 2010; Na Gunga Barijesira, October 1, 2010; Sandowbila Nantomah, May 1, 2011; Warana Nkrumah Baba, September 30, 2010; and Zanloorana Tia Cheera, September 1, 2010. My arrangement with these interviewees specified that I would not disaggregate responses in the published book.

108 Material for the next two paragraphs comes from interviews in Kpasenkpe with Aishatu Sebiyam, July 12, 2010; Assana Sebiyam, July 14, 2010; Fatacheeba Sebiyam, May 3, 2011; Nabila Sebiyam, July 12, 2010; Poakoma Sebiyam, July 13, 2010; Turenaba Sebiyam, July 5, 2010; Wuriche Zangu Sebiyam, July 13, 2010; group interview with Sebiyam's wives, April 29, 2011; group interview with Turenaba Sebiyam, Mariama Sebiyam, Nabila Sebiyam, Garalima Sebiyam, and Aishatu Sebiyam, Kpasenkpe, July 2, 2019. My arrangement with these interviewees specified that I would not disaggregate responses in the published book.

109 After learning about Sebiyam's first twenty years as a chief, I was surprised to find that he married only a handful of additional wives between 1966 and his death in 1992, even as his success as a farmer made continued marriages an obvious option.

110 A fermented preparation of maize that, unlike other common preparations of staple grains, is often purchased by households from sellers who prepare it in bulk.

111 This was of course intriguing, but I was never able to get any more information on the context for Sebiyam preventing *akpeteshie* sales.

112 After his first coup of June 4, 1979, Rawlings immediately instituted civilian elections, which took place just two weeks later and brought into power the newly constructed People's National Party (PNP) and its presidential candidate Hilla Limann, a northern academic notable primarily for his uncontroversial career. While the PNP garnered regionally and ethnically heterogeneous support, it catapulted a number of young educated people from the North into national office. Chazan, *An Anatomy of Ghanaian Politics*, 286, 295–96; 306–25.

113 Interview with Kpatuanaba Jude Sugri Sebiyam, Kpasenkpe, June 6, 2013. For more on changes in the middle school curriculum in the post-Nkrumah years, see R. Bagulo Bening, *A History of Education in Northern Ghana, 1907–1976* (Accra: Ghana Universities Press, 1990), 228–30. Interview with Sandow Sebiyam, Walewale, July 2, 2015.

114 Interview with Namiyelana E. D. Sebiyam, Bolgatanga, May 5, 2011.

115 Chazan, *An Anatomy of Ghanaian Politics*, chapter 1.

CHAPTER 5: PROJECT VILLAGE

1 West Mamprusi District Assembly Registry Files (hereafter, WMDA) WMD/ADM/46/v.1, Development Projects 1982–91, speech made by the West Mamprusi District administrative officer at the inauguration of a World Vision Community Development Project at Duu, January 25, 1989.

2 This phrase was a common refrain from international newspaper headlines in the mid-1980s, spiking during coverage of the Live Aid concert in 1985.

3 In a piece on World Vision's successful television fundraising, Ken Waters cites a former World Vision official who argued that after World Vision telethons and documentaries took off in the 1970s and 1980s, "funds flowed into World Vision so quickly that a new division was created to find and fund worthy projects in Africa." Ken Waters, "How World Vision Rose from Obscurity to Prominence: Television Fundraising, 1972–1982," *American Journalism* (Fall 1998): 92. Famine relief began in northern Ghana in 1983–84, and by 1986 child sponsorship and community development had begun.

4 An explanation of the use of "Two-Thirds World," a phrase that gained popularity in evangelical circles in this period, appears in the first issue of World Vision's publication *Together*, which was aimed at practitioners. "The Two-Thirds World," *Together*, no. 1 (October–December 1983): 5. For the growing use of the idea of "transformational development" in the 1980s and 1990s, see David P. King, *God's Internationalists: World Vision and the Age of Evangelical Humanitarianism* (Philadelphia: University of Pennsylvania Press, 2019), 175, 221–23. King points out that World Vision staff were well aware of the disconnect between their visions of community development and sponsors' interest in individual children; see King, *God's Internationalists*, 310n61.

5 When it was launched in October of 1983 (it ran until 2000), the editors of World Vision's journal *Together* aimed to respond to the organization's need to "share [its] findings and to expose them to criticism" and to be a "forum for honestly held views from the worldwide community of faith" among "strategists as well as practitioners" as it grew and branched into a network of field and support offices around the world. "Where we come from and where we are going." World Vision International, *Together*, no. 1 (October–December 1983): 4–5. While the publication occasionally reproduced official policy statements from the organization, the vast majority of its pages were dedicated to editorials, book reviews, and accounts of research and experience from academics and practitioners in World Vision's orbit. *Together* did, in many ways, fulfill its mission to present complex and dissonant views—with articles debating strategies for combatting famine and desertification, discussing the impact of liberation theology on its work, or debating whether its vision of "community" should be limited to professed Christians. World Vision International, *Together*, no. 5 (October–December 1984); no. 7 (April–June 1985); no. 12 (July–September 1986).

6 The term "pacesetter" is from Chalfin, *Neoliberal Frontiers: An Ethnography of Sovereignty in West Africa (Chicago: University of Chicago Press, 2010)*, 6. See the introduction to *Neoliberal Frontiers* for a longer discussion of the application of the term "neoliberal" to policy reforms in Ghana.

7 Charles Piot, *Nostalgia for the Future: West Africa after the Cold War* (Chicago: Chicago University Press, 2010), chapter 5.

8 Richard Schroeder, *Shady Practices: Agroforestry and Gender Politics in the Gambia* (Berkeley: University of California Press, 1999).

9 Dorothy Louise Hodgson, *Once Intrepid Warriors: Gender, Ethnicity, and the Cultural Politics of Maasai Development* (Bloomington: Indiana University Press, 2001).

10 For recent books that reframe the history of twentieth-century government and tackle this problem more broadly, see Gregory Mann, *From Empires to NGOs in the West African Sahel: The Road to Nongovernmentality* (Cambridge: Cambridge University Press, 2015); Kara Moskowitz, *Seeing Like a Citizen: Decolonization, Development, and the Making of Kenya, 1945–1980* (Athens: Ohio University Press, 2019). By offering stories of African political life that begin in the postwar period, span independence, and continue to the 1980s, both books show that key features of neoliberal statecraft are part of overlapping and decades-long experiments in and negotiations over the content of sovereignty and citizenship.

11 Paul Nugent, *Africa since Independence* (New York: Palgrave Macmillan, 2004), 335.

12 Jonathan Derrick, "West Africa's Worst Year of Famine," *African Affairs* 83, no. 332 (1984): 281; E. Gyimah-Boadi, ed., *Ghana under PNDC Rule* (Dakar: Codesria, 1993), 104.

13 In general, the tensions between the politics of revolution and adjustment have been analyzed at the level of official policy, with respect to Rawlings's urban supporters, or in detailed studies of particular institutions or sets of actors. From the macroeconomic and macropolitical perspective, this literature demonstrates a range of views from Herbst's early lauding of Ghana's "success" at achieving adjustment to Aryeetey et al.'s and Hutchful's more critical characterizations of, respectively, "the miracle and the mirage" and "the paradox of reform." Jeffrey Herbst, *The Politics of Reform in Ghana, 1982–1991* (Berkeley: University of California Press, 1993), 4; Ernest Aryeetey, Jane Harrigan, and Machiko Nissanke, eds., *Economic Reforms in Ghana: The Miracle and the Mirage* (Woodbridge, Suffolk: James Currey, 2000); Eboe Hutchful, *Ghana's Adjustment Experience: The Paradox of Reform* (Geneva: UNRISD, 2002). A number of works offer more detailed political analysis of Rawlings and his top advisors. See, *inter alia*, Kevin Shillington, *Ghana and the Rawlings Factor* (London: Macmillan, 1992); Kwame A. Ninsin, "The PNDC and the Problem of Legitimacy," in *Ghana: The Political Economy of Recovery*, ed. Donald Rothchild (Boulder, CO: Lynne Rienner Publishers, 1991), 49–67; Emmanuel Hansen, *Ghana under Rawlings: The Early Years* (Lagos: Malthouse Press, 1991). Paul Nugent's 1994 book, *Big Men, Small Boys, and Politics in Ghana: Power, Ideology, and the Burden of History, 1982–1994* (New York: Pinter, 1995), gives the richest political economic picture to

date of these years, carefully anatomizing the PNDC government. While Nugent makes a series of claims about how revolutionary organs interacted with local political economies, he admits that the particulars of local political engagement outside of the Volta Region were beyond the scope of his analysis. His call for more research on the local politics of PNDC rule has remained largely unanswered over the twenty-five years since the book's publication. A few scholars have focused specifically on the dynamics of local government and center-local relations. See Richard Crook and James Manor, *Democracy and Decentralisation in South Asia and West Africa: Participation, Accountability, and Performance* (Cambridge: Cambridge University Press, 1998); Joseph R. A. Ayee, *An Anatomy of Public Policy Implementation: The Case of Decentralization Policies in Ghana* (Brookfield, VT: Ashgate, 1994).

14 Deborah Wetzel, "The Promises and Pitfalls in Public Expenditure," in Aryeetey, Harrigan, and Nissanke, *Economic Reforms in Ghana*, 115–31; Ernest Aryeetey and Markus Goldstein, "The Evolution of Social Policy," in Aryeetey, Harrigan, and Nissanke, *Economic Reforms in Ghana*, 284–303. In agriculture, as Moseley, Schnurr, and Bezner Kerr put it for the continent as a whole, "The era of food self-sufficiency in African food policy circles came to a crashing halt in the early 1980s with the rise of neoliberalism." William Moseley, Matthew Schnurr, and Rachel Bezner Kerr, "Interrogating the Technocratic (Neoliberal) Agenda for Agricultural Development and Hunger Alleviation in Africa," *African Geographical Review* 34, no. 1 (2015): 1–7. In Ghana, the ERPs sought to revive agricultural productivity in cocoa, most notably by increasing producer prices of cocoa in relation to other crops. At the same time, the government began to eliminate subsidies on agricultural inputs and privatize agricultural marketing. V. K. Nyanteng and W. Seini, "Agricultural Policy and the Impact on Growth and Productivity, 1970–1995," in Aryeetey, Harrigan, and Nissanke, *Economic Reforms in Ghana*, 270.

15 Nugent, *Big Men, Small Boys*, chapter 2.

16 In its revolutionary rhetoric, the PNDC included rural producers, particularly those outside of chiefly families, in its definition of "the people." However, as Nugent elaborates, it is much harder to establish that Rawlings ever gained systematic support from rural producers, either in the cocoa regions or elsewhere. Nugent, *Big Men, Small Boys*, 72–78.

17 Nugent, *Big Men, Small Boys*, 134–36, 157; Ninsin, "The PNDC and the Problem of Legitimacy," 54–57. Hutchful draws attention to the "paradox" of increased governmental control being necessary to push through unpopular neoliberal policies ostensibly designed to decrease government control. Hutchful, *Ghana's Adjustment Experience*, 198.

18 Kwadwo Konadu-Agyemang, "The Best of Times and the Worst of Times: Structural Adjustment Programs and Uneven Development," *Professional Geographer* 52, no. 3 (August 2000): 469. Scholars of the structural

adjustment period are generally tentative in their conclusions about how devaluation and other structural adjustment reforms affected agriculture outside of the cocoa sector, largely because of very incomplete data. See, for example, Nyanteng and Seini, "Agricultural Policy and the Impact on Growth and Productivity"; Kwabena Donkor, *Structural Adjustment and Mass Poverty in Ghana* (Brookfield, VT: Ashgate, 1997), 162–71; Herbst, *The Politics of Reform in Ghana*, 82–83. However, there is general consensus that the ERP's emphasis on cocoa may have had negative effects on food farmers. Ernest Aryeetey and Jane Harrigan, "Macroeconomic and Sectoral Developments since 1970," in Aryeetey, Harrigan, and Nissanke, *Economic Reforms in Ghana*, 26.

19 Hailu describes in detail how the end of subsidies in fertilizer, seeds, and chemicals, along with the end of subsidized loans for implements, made green revolution technologies less available to northern farmers. Zegeye Hailu, "The Adoption of Modern Farm Practices in African Agriculture: Empirical Evidence about the Impacts of Household Characteristics and Input Supply Systems in the Northern Region of Ghana," Nyankpala Agricultural Research Report (Nyankpala, Ghana, and Eschborn, West Germany: Nyankpala Agricultural Experiment Station and GTZ, 1990). An excellent array of recent studies has detailed how and why Ghanaians remained dependent on high-input agricultural strategies, despite the increasing difficulty of accessing inputs. These authors show how farmers creatively used inputs to meet a variety of goals that often contradicted the ideas of planners. See Kojo Sebastian Amanor, "From Farmer Participation to Pro-poor Seed Markets: The Political Economy of Commercial Cereal Seed Networks in Ghana," *IDS Bulletin* 42, no. 4 (2011): 48–58; Nazaire Houssou et al., "Changes in Ghanaian Farming Systems: Stagnation or a Quiet Transformation?," *Agriculture and Human Values* 35, no. 1 (2018): 41–66; Hanson Nyantakyi-Frimpong and Rachel Bezner Kerr, "A Political Ecology of High-Input Agriculture in Northern Ghana," *African Geographical Review* 34, no. 1 (2015): 13–35; Jacqueline Alyce Ignatova, "Seeds of Contestation: Genetically Modified Crops and the Politics of Agricultural Modernization in Ghana" (PhD diss., University of Maryland, 2015).

20 In addition to the dismantling of agricultural subsidies under the ERPs, the mid-1980s brought to an end some of the most important aspects of the Ghana-German Agricultural Development Project, including extension services, reducing both capital and staff available for northern agricultural projects. Interview with Frank Adongo, Tamale, October 30, 2010; interview with Christian Kofi Letsu, Walewale, August 28, 2010; informal conversations with Andrew Kuyipwa, Walewale, 2010–11.

21 For quotation, see Nugent, *Big Men, Small Boys*, 72. The Kpasenkpe evidence affirms Nugent's contention that the Rawlings revolution "went off with more of a whimper" in rural areas than in cities. Nugent, *Big Men*,

Small Boys, 40–105. However, many of the men I spoke to who had been in their twenties in 1979 and 1981 remembered the first PNDC mobilization with fondness, regardless of their positions in later partisan divides. Interviews in Kpasenkpe with Bugurana Ibrahim Manmara, October 5, 2010; Solomon Dawuni Sebiyam, July 12, 2010; Nelson Ndimah (Bayela), June 22, 2010; and informal conversations with Sulemana Sebiyam, 2010 and 2011.

22 The cadres' only (limited) influence on economic life in town came in the early PNDC years, when they conducted sporadic price-setting activities in Kpasenkpe. Some residents emphasized the coercive nature of the state in these years. The PDCs, argued one NDC member, were "just the policemen," and one elder said that while Rawlings was not the first military leader in Ghana, the PNDC was the first "soldier government" in Kpasenkpe. Interview with Mensah Dzii (Carpenter), Kpasenkpe, July 1, 2010; interview with Samanaba Sumani Takora, Kpasenkpe, July 12, 2010. However, many people remembered the cadres only having influence over "government things" like soap and sugar. As trader Hajia Musah Ladi told me, the PNDC had no interest in the price of the groundnuts she was selling, and as for the "government items," well, "only rich people were [ever] buying those." Interview in Kpasenkpe, July 8, 2010. Traders who sold these products in Kpasenkpe remember the time as one in which they were under constant surveillance, though not subject to the kinds of harassment and violence characterizing trader-state relations elsewhere. They also seem to have relatively easily turned to sale of local products to supplement sale of imported goods. Interviews in Kpasenkpe with Aishatu Musah (Zangu Poa) (Hajia), June 29, 2010; and Sanatu Seidu, July 7, 2010.

23 Interview with Achiri Kwaku, Kpasenkpe, July 12, 2010; interview with Sandow Bugri, Kpasenkpe, April 30, 2011.

24 Interview with Samanaba Sumani Takora, Kpasenkpe, July 12, 2010.

25 Nugent, *Africa since Independence*, 347–52.

26 For the statistics until 1991 see Kojo Amanor, Aloysius Denkabe, and Kate Wellard, "Ghana," in *Non-governmental Organizations and the State in Africa*, ed. Kate Wellard and James G. Copestake (London: Routledge, 1993), 187. See also Ian Gary, "Confrontation, Co-operation, or Co-optation: NGOs and the Ghanaian State during Structural Adjustment," *Review of African Political Economy* 23, no. 68 (1996): 149–68. The more recent "hyper-proliferation" of NGOs in Ghana is detailed by Gershon Osei, "Self-Help without the Self: Critique of Non-governmental Organizational Approaches to Rural Development in Ghana," *International Social Work* 60, no. 2 (2017): 497. In the article as a whole, Osei argues persuasively that, in recent decades, perceived homogeneity among villages acts as an engine of underdevelopment and a barrier to meaningful rural engagement with the state. See also

Julie Hearn, "African NGOs: The New Compradors?," *Development & Change* 38, no. 6 (2007): 1095–110.

27 Lynne Brydon and Karen Legge, *Adjusting Society: The World Bank, the IMF and Ghana* (London: Tauris Academic Studies, 1996), 37–38. Amanor et al. point out, for example, that in 1986, 72 percent of implement distribution was channeled through church projects, versus 19 percent through the Ministry of Agriculture. Amanor, Denkabe, and Wellard, "Ghana," 193.

28 Background on PAMSCAD in the context of changing World Bank policy is given in Hutchful, *Ghana's Adjustment Experience*, chapter 7.

29 Government of Ghana, "Programme of Actions to Mitigate the Social Costs of Adjustment (PAMSCAD)," (Accra, July 1987), quoted in Hutchful, *Ghana's Adjustment Experience*, 116.

30 Ernest Aryeetey and Markus Goldstein, "The Evolution of Social Policy," 291–92. Ato Quayson describes the "pamscadization" of Ghana, referring to the obvious disparity between rhetoric and effect that was, he implies, not just an erosion of social services but also a popular recognition of official bad faith — the "laugh-to-keep-yourself-from-crying motif that was one of the marked Ghanaian responses to the vicissitudes of the 1980s." See Ato Quayson, "Signs of the Times: Discourse Ecologies and Street Life on Oxford St., Accra," *City and Society* 22, no. 1 (2010): 90.

31 For a review of some of the literature, see Mathieu Hilgers, "The Historicity of the Neoliberal State," *Social Anthropology* 20, no. 1 (2012): 80–94. The phrase "neoliberal turn" is from Chalfin, *Neoliberal Frontiers*, 2. In rural areas across the continent, scholars have shown that even though policies were often framed in terms of individual citizens and corporate entities, both states and local leaders used neoliberal frameworks of non-governmentalization and market reform to double down on the imaginary of villages or communities as the essential unit of rural policy. A series of insightful and wide-ranging explorations of these dynamics appears in John L. Comaroff and Jean Comaroff, *The Politics of Custom: Chiefship, Capital, and the State in Contemporary Africa* (Chicago: University of Chicago Press, 2018).

32 WMDA, WMD/42/v.1, Self Help Projects, 1989–92, "General List of Self-Help Projects Completed and On Going 1986–1989, West Mamprusi District," sent to West Mamprusi DAO by Works Foreman Richard Abagoami, April 10, 1989. The remaining projects either do not specify funders or were assisted by churches, particularly the Seventh Day Adventist Church (six projects). It is unclear if ADRA was associated with the SDA projects.

33 Interview with Musah Mohammed, Walewale, September 1, 2010. Mohammed listed the primary organizations that worked in West Mamprusi as Christian World Service, Natfund, ADRA, UNICEF, and World Vision.

34 WMDA, WMD/ADM/102/v.1, Mobilization Documents, 1983–2001.

35 WMDA, WMD/ADM/46/v.1, Development Projects 1982–91, "National Mobilisation Program, Walewale District Working Plan for 1985, Development, Self-Help, and Programmes." Over twenty-four projects, the only government funding listed is for a dam at Nayorku, funded by Water and Sewage. Eight projects are listed as receiving NORRIP funding and one, a school project in Wulugu, as receiving World Vision funding.

36 Interview with Musah Mohammed, Walewale, September 1, 2010.

37 The World Bank and other international development organizations later took up a radically depoliticized idea of "participation" over the course of the 1990s and 2000s. See Andrea Cornwall and Karen Brock, "What Do Buzzwords Do for Development Policy? A Critical Look at 'Participation,' 'Empowerment' and 'Poverty Reduction,'" *Third World Quarterly* 26, no. 7 (2005): 1043–60.

38 An insightful table on the varied historical permutations of participation in twentieth-century development thinking, along with a short and pithy historical discussion, are in Samuel Hickey and Giles Mohan, "Towards Participation as Transformation: Critical Themes and Challenges," in *Participation, from Tyranny to Transformation? Exploring New Approaches to Participation in Development*, ed. Samuel Hickey and Giles Mohan (London: Zed Books, 2004), 5–11.

39 Succinct historical summaries are in Pablo Alejandro Leal, "Participation," in *Deconstructing Development Discourse: Buzzwords and Fuzzwords*, ed. Andrea Cornwall and Deborah Eade (Warwickshire, UK: Practical Action Publishing, 2010), 89–100; Hickey and Mohan, "Towards Participation."

40 Hickey and Mohan, "Towards Participation," 11. In the volume as a whole, authors draw on, summarize, and challenge a wealth of critical scholarship on participation that emerged in the 1990s.

41 Karl Botchway, *Understanding "Development" Intervention in Northern Ghana: The Need to Consider Political and Social Forces Necessary for Transformation* (New York: Edwin Mellen Press, 2004), 119–23, and Karl Botchway, "Are Development Planners Afraid of History and Contextualization? Notes on Reading a Development Report on Northern Ghana," *Canadian Journal of African Studies / Revue Canadienne Des Études Africaines* 35, no. 1 (2001): 32–66. Botchway also traces how the organization's rhetoric reproduced an image of Northern Ghana as an undifferentiated mass of isolated, primordial villages and how it systematically ignored the historical development of extractive structures of underdevelopment.

42 Botchway, *Understanding "Development" Intervention*, 157, 161.

43 WMDA, WMD/ADM/37/v1 (Box3b/File1), Department of Social Welfare and Community Development, 1979–99, wireless message from the Ministry of Local Government, Accra, to all regional secretaries, March 16, 1989.

44 WMDA, WMD/ADM/37/v1 (Box3b/File1), Department of Social Welfare and Community Development, 1979–99, Ag RAO E. K. Musah from the PAMSCAD Secretariat to PNDC district secretaries, March 31, 1989, "Guidelines and Criteria for Selection of PAMSCAD CIPs."

45 WMDA, WMD/ADM/37/v1 (Box3b/File1), Department of Social Welfare and Community Development, 1979–99. On June 9, the PNDC District Secretary Assistant Director R. S. Kuutegu submitted a list of the eight projects to the regional administrative officer. The list was then resubmitted by District Administrative Officer J. S. Wuni Gambu Naba, when it became clear that it had not been forwarded to the PAMSCAD secretariat earlier. The criteria for inclusion and exclusion are unclear, as all but one of the selected projects had been initiated before March 1989 and all of the rejected projects had been initiated in March, thus potentially falling afoul of PAMSCAD's desire to fund projects that were already underway, one of the only criteria that subsequent discussion seems to suggest that the secretariat enforced. Subsequent memos from the PAMSCAD Secretariat indicate that, once the Regional Office had compiled such a list, no additional inquiries would be made as to how and why the projects were selected.

46 WMDA, WMD/ADM/37/v1 (Box3b/File1), Department of Social Welfare and Community Development, 1979–99, letters January 11, April 28, and June 12, 1989.

47 WMDA, WMD/42/Vol.1, Self Help Projects, letter from D. D. Zibah, secretary of the Wungu Town Development Committee to Ghana Highways Authority, Walewale, August 22, 1985; WMDA, WMD/ADM/46/v.1, Development Projects 1981–92, letter from Wuni Yidana, chairman of Diani Town Development Committee, to Department of Community Development, Tamale, December 4, 1985.

48 WMDA, WMD/ADM/46/v.1, Development Projects 1981–92, letter from Emmanuel Yakubu, CDRS secretary, and Adam Abdulai, TDC chairman, Shelinova, to World Vision International, Accra, through the coordinator of World Vision International, Mamprusi District, February 1, 1988; letter from Gilbert Sagri, secretary, and Albert Sandow, CDRS chairman, Wungu Town Development Committee, to World Vision International, Accra, through the coordinator of World Vision International, Mamprusi District, February 2, 1988. The strong similarities between these letters suggest that someone, perhaps the Mamprusi District coordinator for World Vision, helped craft them.

49 WMDA, WMD/ADM/37/v1 (Box3b/File1), Department of Social Welfare and Community Development 1979–99, letter from Amidu Iddrisu, secretary Walewale Town Development Committee, to the PNDC district secretary, March 21, 1989; letter from R. T. Abudulai, chairman Wungu Town Development Committee, to the PNDC district secretary, March 25, 1989, West Mamprusi District Assembly Registry Files.

50 WMDA, WMD/ADM/46/v.1, Development Projects, 1981–92, "National Mobilisation Program, Walewale District Working Plan for 1985, Development, Self-Help, and Programmes."

51 Residents remembered Amasachina as continuing into the Rawlings years. Occasional references to farming and fishing groups appear in district files, including WMDA, WMD/ADM/37/v1 (Box3b/File1), Department of Social Welfare and Community Development, 1979–99, and WMD/ADM/20/v1, Department of Cooperatives.

52 WMDA, WMD/ADM/46/v.1, Development Projects 1981–92, "National Mobilisation Program, Walewale District Working Plan for 1985, Development, Self-Help, and Programmes."

53 A number of social scientists have done excellent analyses of World Vision activities in Africa in the 2000s, probing the tensions and possibilities generated by World Vision's concept of "transformational" Christian development in particular locations. Erica Bornstein, *The Spirit of Development: Protestant NGOs, Morality, and Economics in Zimbabwe* (Stanford, CA: Stanford University Press, 2005); Susan Mary McDonic, "Witnessing, Work and Worship: World Vision and the Negotiation of Faith, Development and Culture" (PhD diss., Duke University, 2004); Tim Kelsall and Claire Mercer, "Empowering People? World Vision and 'Transformatory Development' in Tanzania," *Review of African Political Economy* 30, no. 96 (2003): 293–304. Historical examinations of World Vision projects have been extremely limited, with the recent exception of David King's monograph on the organization as a whole, and in particular World Vision US. King, *God's Internationalists*.

54 In the 1950s, World Vision's child sponsorship scheme began by giving funding for particular orphanages. By the 1980s, funds for a particular community were pooled to support individual children and to fund wider community development projects. King, *God's Internationalists*, 73–74, 178.

55 King points out that this reality was the subject of internal debate at World Vision as well as beyond. King, *God's Internationalists*, 180–81. For wider critiques of the "starving child" imagery and of child sponsorship more generally that circulated in the early 1980s, see Jorgen Lissner, "Merchants of Misery," *New Internationalist* (June 1981), https://newint.org /features/1981/06/01/merchants-of-misery; Peter Stalker, "Please Do Not Sponsor This Child," *New Internationalist* (May 1982), https://newint.org /features/1982/05/01/keynote.

56 Whaites argues that "The internationalisation process was one of decentralisation and federalization." In 1989, the organization articulated a core mission that all forty country organizations could sign on to. Alan Whaites, "Pursuing Partnership: World Vision and the Ideology of Development—a Case Study," *Development in Practice* 9, no. 4 (1999): 410–23.

57 King, *God's Internationalists*, 178.
58 King, *God's Internationalists*, 221–23. Bornstein's research in Zimbabwe, which took place in the late 1990s after Participatory Rural Appraisal (PRA) had been fully institutionalized in the organization, has an excellent extended discussion of participatory approaches. See Bornstein, *The Spirit of Development*, chapter 2. Much of the wider critique of participation has focused on Chambers and PRA; see Bill Cooke and Uma Kothari, eds., *Participation: The New Tyranny?* (London: Zed Books, 2001).
59 In a four-part series that ran in the first four issues of *Together*, editor John A. Kenyon and Associate Director of Project Evaluation Bill Warnock outlined an "ideal process of community development" in which a "community . . . participates fully" in evaluation and planning of development activities and thus is able to "truly own the process of its development." The articles clearly reflect the influence of participatory development theory. John A. Kenyon, "When a Community Describes Itself," *Together*, no. 1 (October–December 1983): 21–23; John A. Kenyon and Bill Warnock, "When a Community Defines Its Situation," *Together*, no. 2 (January–March 1984): 22–27; John A. Kenyon and Bill Warnock, "When a Community Analyzes Its Problems," *Together*, no. 3 (April–June 1984): 34–37.
60 The organization began work in Ghana as a whole in the late 1970s: https://www.wvi.org/ghana, accessed April 2019. References to the history of the Ghana Rural Water Project's beginnings can be found in Nana Ama Serwah Poku Sam, "Gender Mainstreaming and Integration of Women in Decision-Making: The Case of Water Management in Samari-Nkwanta, Ghana," *Wagadu: A Journal of Transnational Women's and Gender Studies* 3 (Spring 2006): 27.
61 Interview with Mahama Tampuri, Walewale, July 10, 2010.
62 Interview with Mahama Tampuri, Walewale, July 10, 2010.
63 Interview with Mahama Tampuri, Walewale, July 10, 2010.
64 Interviews in Kpasenkpe with Pastor Daniel Barijesira Azundow, September 1, 2010, October 1–3, 2010, and May 2, 2011. See also "A Celebration of Life: Rev. Daniel Barijesira Azundow, 1925–2011," a booklet produced for the funeral, kindly lent by the late Philip Azundow in July 2017.
65 Informal conversations in Kpasenkpe with Nelson Ndimah (Bayela) and Pastor Daniel Barijesira Azundow, 2010–11.
66 One of the Wulugunaba's senior sons recalled World Vision as a joint intervention of "the church along with NGOs," rather than a direct imposition of the chief. A junior son who also served as PNDC zonal coordinator recollects that World Vision "came through the church" and not the chief or the PNDC. Interview with Wulugunaba Professor John Sebiyam Nabila, Accra, August 17, 2010; interview with Sulemana Sebiyam, Kpasenkpe, September 1, 2010.
67 Interview with Pastor Daniel Barijesira Azundow, Kpasenkpe, September 1, 2010.

68 Interview with Pastor Daniel Barijesira Azundow, Kpasenkpe, September 1, 2010.
69 In this idealized process, the editors argue that community members' contributions of time and labor in meetings and workshops would not only produce a plan but would produce a new affective relationship to planning itself, summed up in the idea of "ownership." John A. Kenyon, "When a Community Describes Itself"; John A. Kenyon and Bill Warnock, "When a Community Defines Its Situation"; John A. Kenyon and Bill Warnock, "When a Community Analyzes Its Problems."
70 Interview with Pastor Daniel Barijesira Azundow, Kpasenkpe, September 1, 2010.
71 Interview with Mahama Tampuri, Walewale, July 10, 2010.
72 Not to be confused with the group of traditional officeholders in Kpasenkpe, known as "elders"—though the two groups do appear to have had some overlap.
73 Interview with Achiri Kwaku, Kpasenkpe, July 12, 2010.
74 Interview with Pastor Daniel Barijesira Azundow, Kpasenkpe, September 1, 2010; interview with Sulemana Sebiyam, Kpasenkpe, July 6, 2010.
75 Interview with Sandow Bugri, July 7, 2010.
76 Interview with Nelson Ndimah (Bayela), Kpasenkpe, June 27, 2010.
77 Tampuri told a story of threatening to pull projects out of a village where there were disputes about the actions of the local World Vision committee. While he organized an election of new committee members, he also "schooled the troublemakers" who had made complaints for "refusing to do their part." Interview with Mahama Tampuri, Walewale, July 10, 2010.
78 Interview with Mahama Tampuri, Walewale, July 10, 2010.
79 Kelsall and Mercer, "Empowering People?," 294.
80 Interview with Sulemana Sebiyam, Kpasenkpe, July 6, 2010. A former Ministry of Agriculture tractor driver recalls coming to Kpasenkpe in the early 1980s to plow for group farms and to hire out subsidized services for individual farmers. When I asked who he remembered in Kpasenkpe, he said "the chief alone." Interview with Christian Kofi Letsu, Walewale, August 28, 2010.
81 Interview with Sulemana Sebiyam and Nelson Ndimah (Bayela), Kpasenkpe, July 6, 2010. Associated reductions in the subsidies on fertilizer and other inputs likely made this unpredictability even more damaging to the long-term prospects for commercial farming. The instability of markets may have also made commercial farming more susceptible to variations in weather, as several family members cite particular years of drought or flooding as reasons for the dramatic reduction in cash-crop production during the mid-1980s.
82 Some of these farming activities began as separate cash ventures, but by the 1980s several wives recall that farming became a necessity. There appear to have been two senior wives who began farming before the 1970s.

One recalls farming groundnuts through a government program for women's farming (the only time I heard one of Sebiyam's wives mention such programs), and one of Sebiyam's brother's wives began farming on her own shortly before her own husband died. Junior wives often recounted opening plots in the 1980s or "after [Sebiyam's] tractor had spoiled," often on land they "begged" from Sebiyam, elders, or relatives.

83 Material for this paragraph comes from interviews in Kpasenkpe with Aishatu Sebiyam, July 12, 2010; Assana Sebiyam, July 14, 2010; Boasina Wudana Aguriba, September 2, 2010; Fatacheeba Sebiyam, July 12, 2010, and May 3, 2011; Nabila Sebiyam, July 12, 2010; Wudan Duu Sebiyam, July 14, 2010; and group interview with Turenaba Sebiyam, Mariama Sebiyam, Nabila Sebiyam, Garalima Sebiyam, and Aishatu Sebiyam, Kpasenkpe, July 2, 2019. My arrangement with these interviewees specified that I would not disaggregate responses in the published book. It is likely that the reintroduction of school fees under the Economic Recovery Programme of 1983 further taxed wives' budgets, as some wives remember supplementing Sebiyam's payments with their own. Older siblings also recall helping younger siblings with school fees. For more on school fees and structural adjustment, see Jon Kraus, "The Struggle over Structural Adjustment in Ghana," *Africa Today* 38, no. 4 (1991): 19–37.

84 Material for this section comes from interviews with Adjei Sebiyam, Walewale, July 5, 2019; Agnes Soori Sebiyam, Kpasenkpe, June 15, 2013; Ali Sebiyam, Walewale, June 29, 2015; Azumah Sebiyam, Kpasenkpe, September 2, 2010, and June 17, 2013; Ben Bawa Sebiyam, Walewale, June 28, 2015; Emmanuel Sebiyam, Kpasenkpe, July 3, 2019; Eric D. Sebiyam, Tamale, July 6, 2015; Gbeena Owusu, Accra, July 14, 2015; Georgina Sebiyam, Walewale, June 28, 2015; Ibrahim Sebiyam, Tamale, July 6, 2015; Joel Dawuni Sebiyam, Tamale, July 7, 2015; Johnson Sebiyam, Tamale, July 7, 2015; Joseph Sebiyam, Kpasenkpe, July 7, 2010; Kpatuanaba Jude Sugri Sebiyam, Kpasenkpe, June 6, 2013; Mampaya Sebiyam, Accra, July 12, 2015; Namiyelana E. D. Sebiyam, Bolgatanga, May 5, 2011; Ruth Lamisi Sebiyam, Accra, July 5, 2013; Sandow Sebiyam, Walewale, July 2, 2015; Solomon Dawuni Sebiyam, Kpasenkpe, July 12, 2010, and September 3, 2010; Sulemana Sebiyam, Kpasenkpe, July 6, 2010, and September 1, 2010; Teni Sebiyam, July 5, 2015; Wulugunaba Professor John Sebiyam Nabila, Accra, July 12, 2015; Yakubu Sebiyam, Walewale, June 30, 2015; and Zaratu Sebiyam, Tamale, July 6, 2015. My arrangement with these interviewees specified that I would not disaggregate responses in the published book.

85 In the late 1970s, as the Acheampong government faced budgetary shortfalls and increasing political opposition, Chazan argues that its "military-bureaucratic" coalition disintegrated, challenging many of the established institutional paths for educated professionals to advance, sparking protest from students and professional organizations in the mid-1970s. After General F. W. Akuffo's 1978 coup, austerity measures sparked further protests

by students and professional organizations. Naomi Chazan, *An Anatomy of Ghanaian Politics: Managing Political Recession, 1969–1982* (Boulder, CO: Westview Press, 1983), 240, 246.

86 By the early 2010s, when the first "queen mothers" were installed in northern Ghana, Pawura became Poanaba for the Kpasenkpe traditional area, bringing her years of community development expertise to bear on new village projects for women in development. Ghana News Agency, "Northern Traditional Councils—Role of Queen Mothers," *Modern Ghana*, August 5, 2011, https://www.modernghana.com/blogs/343874/northern -traditional-councils-role-of-queen-mothers.html.

87 Hutchful, *Ghana's Adjustment Experience*, part 4; Eboe Hutchful, "Why Regimes Adjust: The World Bank Ponders Its 'Star Pupil,'" *Canadian Journal of African Studies / Revue Canadienne Des Études Africaines* 29, no. 2 (1995): 303–17. The World Bank's 1989 *Sub-Saharan Africa: From Crisis to Sustainable Growth* argued that "Private sector initiative and market mechanisms are important, but they must go hand in hand with good governance—a public service that is efficient, a judicial system that is reliable, and an administration that is accountable to its public." World Bank, *Sub-Saharan Africa: From Crisis to Sustainable Growth* (Washington, DC: World Bank, 1989), xii. The World Bank's emphasis on decentralization and participatory development was again laid out in World Bank, *Governance and Development* (Washington, DC: World Bank, 1992). For a summary of changing thinking at the World Bank, see John Pender, "From 'Structural Adjustment' to 'Comprehensive Development Framework': Conditionality Transformed?," *Third World Quarterly* 22, no. 3 (2001): 397–411. By the late 1990s, this new form of conditionality had been formalized into the "Comprehensive Development Framework." For a recent critique, see T. D. Harper-Shipman, "How Comprehensive Is Comprehensive? Using Wangari Maathai as a Critique of the World Bank's Contemporary Development Model," *Third World Quarterly* 40, no. 4 (April 2019): 633–50.

88 Joseph R. A. Ayee, "The Adjustment of Central Bodies to Decentralization: The Case of the Ghanaian Bureaucracy," *African Studies Review* 40, no. 2 (1997): 37–57.

89 Nugent, *Big Men, Small Boys*, 202–20.

90 Crook and Manor, *Democracy and Decentralisation*; Ayee, "The Adjustment of Central Bodies to Decentralization"; Gordon Crawford, "'Making Democracy a Reality'? The Politics of Decentralisation and the Limits to Local Democracy in Ghana," *Journal of Contemporary African Studies* 27, no. 1 (2009): 57–83.

EPILOGUE

1 For an account of their visit, see John Mulholland, "'In 10 Years' Time, Ghana May Not Require Any Aid at All,'" *The Guardian*, January 15, 2012, http://www.guardian.co.uk/world/2012/jan/15/ghana-aid-10-years.

2 "Millennium Villages—The Earth Institute—Columbia University," accessed August 7, 2019, https://www.earth.columbia.edu/articles/view/1799.

3 Ian Birrell, "How Your Money Is Being Squandered: African Village Where Every Family Gets £7,000 from the British Taxpayer," Mail Online (Daily Mail), June 25, 2012, http://www.dailymail.co.uk/news/article -2166697/African-village-family-gets-7-000-British-taxpayer.html.

4 Albert Sore, "Improving Lives through SADA: SADA MVP Hands Over Projects at Mamprugu Moaduri—MyJoyOnline.Com," Joy News, August 2, 2016, https://www.myjoyonline.com/news/2016/August -2nd/improving-lives-through-sada-sada-mvp-hands-over-projects-at -mamprugu-moaduri.php; Nathan Gadugah, "Bawumia Is Unfair; SADA Projects Are Not Ad-Hoc-SADA Boss," myjoyonline.com, August 29, 2012, http://edition.myjoyonline.com/pages/news/201208/93015.php.

5 Ian Birrell, "£11 million Foreign Aid Scheme Backed by Bono Failed to Reduce Hunger," Mail Online (Daily Mail), October 14, 2018, https:// www.dailymail.co.uk/news/article-6273693/Proof-foreign-aid-DOESNT -work-Scathing-report-reveals-11million-scheme-backed-Bono-failed .html. Kpasenkpe was just part of the larger rural area encompassed by the MVP, but because it was the place where Mulholland wrote about Sachs and Bono's visit, in the British press it was identified as "the village" where the project would take place.

6 "'One Village, One Dam' Will Boost Agric Sector—Lecturer," Citi 97.3 FM (blog), February 22, 2018, http://citifmonline.com/2018/02/one-village -one-dam-will-boost-agric-sector-lecturer/; "I Have Built 'More Dams' than Akufo-Addo—A. B. A Fuseini," GhanaWeb, January 26, 2018, https:// www.ghanaweb.com/GhanaHomePage/NewsArchive/I-have-built-more -dams-than-Akufo-Addo-A-B-A-Fuseini-621150.

7 Edmund Smith-Asante, "Chinese Govt Funds 1,000 Boreholes in Ghana—Graphic Online," Graphic Online, June 7, 2018, https://www .graphic.com.gh/news/general-news/chinese-govt-funds-1-000-boreholes -in-ghana.html; Daily Graphic, "Chinese Govt Provides 1,029 Boreholes in Remote Communities," Graphic Online, February 6, 2019, https://www .graphic.com.gh/news/general-news/ghana-news-chinese-govt-provides-1 -029-boreholes-in-remote-communities.html.

Bibliography

ARCHIVES

East Mamprusi District Assembly, Registry, Gambaga, Ghana
Public Records and Archives Administration (PRAAD), Accra, Ghana
Public Records and Archives Administration (PRAAD), Tamale, Ghana
West Mamprusi District Assembly, Registry, Walewale, Ghana

INTERVIEWS

Aarana Daboo Kayuri. Kpasenkpe. July 29, 2010 and October 4, 2010.
Abiba Pugumba Baŋmarigu. Kpasenkpe. October 4, 2010.
Abudu Fio. Walewale. June 17, 2010.
Achina Musah Sugri. Kpasenkpe. July 5, 2010.
Achiri Kwaku. Kpasenkpe. July 12, 2010.
Adam Abdullai Seiya. Kpasenkpe. July 5, 2010.
Adam Seiya Gumbenaba. Kpasenkpe. June 18, 2013.
Adisa Tampulima. Kpasenkpe. October 3, 2010, April 30, 2011, and June 15, 2013.
Adjei Sebiyam. Walewale. July 5, 2019.
Agnes Soori Sebiyam. Kpasenkpe. June 15, 2013.
Aishatu Musah (Zangu Poa) (Hajia). Kpasenkpe. June 29, 2010.
Aishatu Sebiyam. Kpasenkpe. July 12, 2010, June 17, 2013, and July 2, 2019.
Akara Kundunkurigu Kumbunaba. Kpasenkpe. June 29, 2010.
Alhassan Pusu. Kpasenkpe. July 6, 2010, April 30, 2011, and June 17, 2013.
Alhassan Sulemana and Seidu Sulemana. Kpasenkpe. June 15, 2013.
Ali Sebiyam. Walewale. June 29, 2015.
Andrew Kuyipwa. Walewale and Tamale. Informal conversations, 2010–11 and
    June 24, 2013.
Assana Sebiyam. Kpasenkpe. July 14, 2010.
Azara Zetabu. Kpasenkpe. June 6, 2013.
Azimi. Kpasenkpe. June 6, 2013, and June 8, 2013.
Azumah Pitigi. Kpasenkpe. June 6, 2013.
Azumah Sebiyam. Kpasenkpe. September 2, 2010, and June 17, 2013.
Baba Baŋmarigu. Kpasenkpe. July 6, 2010.
Balihira Seiya. Kpasenkpe. October 2, 2010, and June 15, 2013.

Ben Achiri. Kpasenkpe. Informal conversations, 2010.
Ben Bawa Sebiyam. Walewale. June 28, 2015.
Boasina Wudana Aguriba. Kpasenkpe. September 2, 2010.
Bugurana Ibrahim Manmara. Kpasenkpe. October 5, 2010, June 17, 2013, and
    July 2, 2019.
Bunaba Chimsi. Burugu. August 29, 2010.
Chimsi Wubgu. Kpasenkpe. June 8, 2013.
Christian Kofi Letsu. Walewale. August 28, 2010.
Comfort Mensah Dzii and Juwano Mensah Dzii. Kpasenkpe. May 2, 2011.
Dakurugu Yampuhigiya. Kpasenkpe. May 2, 2011.
Damini Bukari. Kpasenkpe. June 7, 2013.
Danladi Dabdu. Kpasenkpe. July 6, 2010.
Dirana Tampuri. Kpasenkpe. June 28, 2010.
Duunaba Bennett Baani. Walewale. June 17, 2010.
Duundana Yakubu Kolugu. Kpasenkpe. June 28, 2010.
Edward Kudow. Kpasenkpe. October 4, 2010.
Emmanuel Karimani Issa Dambanaba. Kpasenkpe. October 1, 2010.
Emmanuel Sebiyam. Kpasenkpe. July 3, 2019.
Eric D. Sebiyam. Tamale. July 6, 2015.
Faara Tongo. Kpasenkpe. June 7, 2013.
Fatacheeba Sebiyam. Kpasenkpe. July 12, 2010, and May 3, 2011.
Fati Zebagane. Kpasenkpe. June 17, 2013.
Frank Adongo. Tamale. October 30, 2010, and June 24, 2013.
Fulanaba Bukari Amadu. Kpasenkpe. July 7, 2010, and May 1, 2011.
Garalima Sebiyam. Kpasenkpe. September 2, 2010, and July 2, 2019.
Gbeena Owusu. Accra. July 14, 2015.
Georgina Sebiyam. Walewale. June 28, 2015.
Ibrahim Sebiyam. Tamale. July 6, 2015.
Iddrisu Baba Mohammed. Tamale. June 27, 2013.
Inusah Zafara. Kpasenkpe. June 29, 2010.
Jacob Pitigi Tampulima. Kpasenkpe. July 1, 2010, and October 1, 2010.
Joel Dawuni Sebiyam. Tamale. July 7, 2015.
John Gumah. Kpasenkpe. June 29, 2010.
Johnson Sebiyam. Tamale. July 7, 2015.
Joseph Dadoo Maleo. Yagaba. January 25, 2010.
Joseph Faalong. Tamale. September 27, 2010.
Joseph Sebiyam. Kpasenkpe. July 7, 2010.
Kakpanaba Somka Nluki. Kpasenkpe. June 30, 2010, July 12, 2010, Septem-
    ber 3, 2010, October 1, 2010, and July 2, 2019.
Kambonaba Ziblim Takora. Kpasenkpe. June 28, 2010.
Kambontia Yaado Piyisiba. Kpasenkpe. June 28, 2010.
Kasua Zanloorana. Kpasenkpe. June 6, 2013.
Kofi Malitenga (Langlangri). Kpasenkpe. June 15, 2013.
Kofi Nabila. Kpasenkpe. July 13, 2010, April 30, 2011, and June 15, 2013.

Kpatuanaba Jude Sugri Sebiyam. Kpasenkpe. Informal conversations, 2010–11 and June 6, 2013.
Kumasileya Azumah. Kpasenkpe. October 4, 2010.
Kunjerigi Saataba. Kpasenkpe. July 8, 2010, and June 15, 2013.
Lamisi Taanaba. Kpasenkpe. June 6, 2013.
Laraba Danladi. Kpasenkpe. June 8, 2013.
Limam Musah Abdullai (Alhaji). Kpasenkpe. July 1, 2010, and April 30, 2011.
Magazia Dibooriyoma. Kpasenkpe. October 2, 2010.
Magazia Fati Yakubu. Kpasenkpe. July 6, 2010.
Mahama Awusi. Kpasenkpe. June 8, 2013.
Mahama Tampuri. Walewale. July 10, 2010.
Malam Imoro Maanuga. Kpasenkpe. July 8, 2010.
Mampaya Sebiyam. Accra. July 12, 2015.
Mariama (Bani) Bawumia (Hajia). Walewale. September 21, 2010.
Mariama Sebiyam. Kpasenkpe. July 14, 2010, June 17, 2013, and July 2, 2019.
Mary Aboyer Azundow. Kpasenkpe. July 1, 2010.
Masu Salifu Sandema. Kpasenkpe. June 18, 2013.
Masu Wuni Sandema. Kpasenkpe. July 2, 2010.
Memubla Boonba. Kpasenkpe. June 7, 2013.
Mensah Dzii (Carpenter). Kpasenkpe. July 1, 2010, and October 3, 2010.
Musah Ladi (Hajia). Kpasenkpe. July 8, 2010.
Musah Mohammed. Walewale. September 1, 2010.
Musah Yidana (Tailor). Kpasenkpe. October 2, 2010.
Na Gunga Barijesira. Kpasenkpe. October 1, 2010.
Naaichi Maka Kpasenkpe. July 9, 2010, and June 17, 2013.
Nabila Sebiyam. Kpasenkpe. July 12, 2010, June 17, 2013, and July 2, 2019.
Namiyelana E. D. Sebiyam. Bolgatanga. May 5, 2011.
Napoa Sebiyam. Kpasenkpe. July 12, 2010, and June 17, 2013.
Nelson Danladi. Kpasenkpe. June 17, 2013.
Nelson Ndimah (Bayela). Kpasenkpe. Informal conversations, 2010–2011 and June 1, 2013.
Pastor Daniel Barijesira Azundow. Kpasenkpe. September 1, 2010, October 1–3, 2010, and May 2, 2011.
Philip Azundow. Accra. July 13, 2015.
Poakoma Sebiyam. Kpasenkpe. July 13, 2010, and June 17, 2013.
Poanaba Pawura Paulina Barijesira. Kpasenkpe. August 31, 2010.
Robert Tia Abudulai. Walewale. July 11, 2010.
Ruth Lamisi Sebiyam. Accra. July 5, 2013.
Safiya Issa. Kpasenkpe. June 6, 2013.
Sakparana Sandow Batisima. Kpasenkpe. June 28, 2010.
Sakparana Sandowbila. Kpasenkpe. July 1, 2010.
Samanaba Sumani Takora. Kpasenkpe. July 12, 2010, and June 07, 2013.
Sampoa Tindana Nluki. Kpasenkpe. June 17, 2013.
Sanatu Seidu. Kpasenkpe. July 7, 2010.

Sandola Tampuri. Kpasenkpe. June 8, 2013.
Sandow Bugri. Kpasenkpe. June 17, 2013, July 7, 2010, and April 30, 2011.
Sandow Kundunkurigu. Kpasenkpe. May 1, 2011.
Sandow Sebiyam. Walewale. July 2, 2015.
Sandowbila Nantomah. Kpasenkpe. May 1, 2011.
Shetu Damini. Kpasenkpe. June 7, 2013.
Solomon Dawuni Sebiyam. Kpasenkpe. July 12, 2010, and September 3, 2010.
Sulemana Sebiyam. Kpasenkpe. July 6, 2010 and September 1, 2010. Informal
    conversations, 2010–11.
Sumbo David. Bolgatanga. June 12, 2013.
Suurana Yakubu Pusu. Kpasenkpe. July 2, 2010, and September 3, 2010.
Teni Sebiyam. Tamale. July 5, 2015.
Thomas Kpenguburgiya Aboagye. Kpasenkpe. June 8, 2013.
Tia Adjei. Walewale. July 11, 2010.
Tindana Issah Tongo. Kpasenkpe. June 30, 2010, May 1, 2011, and June 7, 2013.
Tindanpoa Awa Saari. Kpasenkpe. June 30, 2010.
Tipoa Baŋmarigu. Kpasenkpe. June 6, 2013.
Tipoa Bugri. Kpasenkpe. June 15, 2013.
Turenaba Sebiyam. Kpasenkpe. July 5, 2010, June 17, 2013, and July 2, 2019.
Warana Nkrumah Baba. Kpasenkpe. September 30, 2010, and May 1, 2011.
Wudan Duu Sebiyam. Kpasenkpe. July 14, 2010.
Wudana Daboo Saaka. Kpasenkpe. October 3, 2010.
Wudana Sugri Saaka. Kpasenkpe. July 7, 2010.
Wulugunaba Professor John Sebiyam Nabila. Kpasenkpe and Accra. June 24–
    25, 2010, August 17, 2010, and July 12, 2015.
Wuriche Dabdu. Kpasenkpe. October 5, 2010.
Wuriche Zangu Sebiyam. Kpasenkpe. July 5, 2010, and July 13, 2010.
Wurugurunaba Nsoanyanni Sandow. Kpasenkpe. June 29, 2010, and June 6, 2013.
Yahaya Bamaŋa. Kpasenkpe. June 6, 2013.
Yakubu Sebiyam. Walewale. June 30, 2015.
Yidana (Kunkwa). Walewale. August 30, 2010.
Zamma Voonaba. Kpasenkpe. June 7, 2013.
Zanloorana Tia Cheera. Kpasenkpe. July 29, 2010. Informal conversations,
    2010–11.
Zaratu Sebiyam. Tamale. July 6, 2015.
Zariginaba Kunbahiyori Issaka. Kpasenkpe.
Zenaba Fusheini. Kpasenkpe. June 6, 2013.

PUBLISHED SOURCES

Abdul-Korah, Gariba B. "'Ka Bie Ba Yor': Labor Migration among the
    Dagaaba of the Upper West Region of Ghana, 1936–1957." *Nordic Journal
    of African Studies* 17, no. 1 (2008): 1–19.
Abu, Katie. "GGAEP Target Group Survey, Dagbon Area in Northern
    Ghana." Tamale, Ghana: GGAEP, March 1992.

Achebe, Nwando. *Female King of Colonial Nigeria: Ahebi Ugbabe*. Blooming-ton: Indiana University Press, 2011.

Adams, E. C. *Lyra Nigeriæ*. London: T. F. Unwin, 1911.

Aerni-Flessner, John. *Dreams for Lesotho: Independence, Foreign Assistance, and Development*. Notre Dame, IN: University of Notre Dame Press, 2018.

———. "Self-Help Development Projects and Conceptions of Independence in Lesotho, 1950s–1970s." *International Journal of African Historical Studies* 50, no. 1 (January 2017): 11–33.

Agrawal, Arun, and Jesse Ribot. "Accountability in Decentralization: A Frame-work with South Asian and West African Cases." *Journal of Developing Areas* 33, no. 4 (1999): 473–502.

Ahlman, Jeffrey S. *Living with Nkrumahism: Nation, State, and Pan-Africanism in Ghana*. Athens: Ohio University Press, 2017.

Akurang-Parry, Kwabena Opare. "Colonial Forced Labor Policies for Road-Building in Southern Ghana and International Anti-forced Labor Pres-sures, 1900–1940." *African Economic History* 28 (January 2000): 1–25.

Akyeampong, Emmanuel. *Drink, Power, and Cultural Change: A Social History of Alcohol in Ghana, c. 1800 to Recent Times*. Portsmouth, NH: Heinemann, 1996.

Allman, Jean. "'Let Your Fashion Be in Line with Our Ghanaian Costume': Nation, Gender and the Politics of Clothing in Nkrumah's Ghana." In *Fashioning Africa: Power and the Politics of Dress*, 144–66. Bloomington: Indiana University Press, 2004.

———. *The Quills of the Porcupine: Asante Nationalism in an Emergent Ghana*. Madison: University of Wisconsin Press, 1993.

Allman, Jean, and John Parker. *Tongnaab: The History of a West African God*. Bloomington: Indiana University Press, 2005.

Allman, Jean, and Victoria Tashjian. *"I Will Not Eat Stone": A Women's History of Colonial Asante*. Portsmouth, NH: Heinemann, 2000.

Amanor, Kojo Sebastian. "Family Values, Land Sales and Agricultural Com-modification in South-Eastern Ghana." *Africa: Journal of the International African Institute* 80, no. 1 (2010): 104–25.

———. "From Farmer Participation to Pro-poor Seed Markets: The Political Economy of Commercial Cereal Seed Networks in Ghana." *IDS Bulletin* 42, no. 4 (2011): 48–58.

———. *Land, Labour and the Family in Southern Ghana: A Critique of Land Policy under Neo-liberalisation*. Uppsala: Nordic Africa Institute, 2001.

Amanor, Kojo, Aloysius Denkabe, and Kate Wellard. "Ghana." In *Non-governmental Organizations and the State in Africa*, edited by Kate Wellard and James G. Copestake, 183–94. London: Routledge, 1993.

Amanor, Kojo, and Opoku Pabi. "Space, Time, Rhetoric and Agricultural Change in the Transition Zone in Ghana." *Human Ecology* 35, no. 1 (2007): 51–67.

Amezah, Kwame, and Johann Hesse. "Reforms in the Ghanaian Extension System." Case study prepared for the workshop Extension and Rural Development: A Convergence of Views on International Approaches?, World Bank and USAID, Washington, DC, November 12–15, 2002.

Ansere, Joe K. *The Role of Local Government in Nation Building.* Accra: Institute of Adult Education, University of Ghana, 1973.

Anyidoho, Nana Akua. "'Communities of Practice': Prospects for Theory and Action in Participatory Development." *Development in Practice* 20, no. 3 (2010): 318–28.

———. "On Whose Terms? Negotiating Participatory Development in a Fluid Policy Landscape." In *Reclaiming the Human Sciences and Humanities through African Perspectives,* edited by Helen Lauer and Kofi Anyidoho, vol. 1, 401–12. Accra: Sub-Saharan Publishers, 2012.

———. "Theorising the Intersection of Public Policy and Personal Lives through the Lens of 'Participation.'" *Africa Development* 35, no. 3 (2010): 1–11.

Apusigah, Agnes Atia. "The Gendered Politics of Farm Household Production and the Shaping of Women's Livelihoods in Northern Ghana." *Feminist Africa* 12 (2009): 51–68.

———. "Ghanaian Development: Technical versus Street Evidence." In *Reclaiming the Human Sciences and Humanities through African Perspectives,* edited by Helen Lauer and Kofi Anyidoho, vol. 1, 388–400. Accra: Sub-Saharan Publishers, 2012.

Arhin, Kwame. *Transformations in Traditional Rule in Ghana (1951–1996).* Accra: Sedco, 2001.

Aryeetey, Ernest, and Markus Goldstein. "The Evolution of Social Policy." In *Economic Reforms in Ghana: The Miracle and the Mirage,* edited by Ernest Aryeetey, Jane Harrigan, and Machiko Nissanke, 284–303. Woodbridge, Suffolk: James Currey, 2000.

Aryeetey, Ernest, and Jane Harrigan. "Macroeconomic and Sectoral Developments since 1970." In *Economic Reforms in Ghana: The Miracle and the Mirage,* edited by Ernest Aryeetey, Jane Harrigan, and Machiko Nissanke, 5–31. Woodbridge, Suffolk: James Currey, 2000.

Aryeetey, Ernest, Jane Harrigan, and Machiko Nissanke, eds. *Economic Reforms in Ghana: The Miracle and the Mirage.* Woodbridge, Suffolk: James Currey, 2000.

Asiwaju, A. I. "Migrations as Revolt: The Example of the Ivory Coast and the Upper Volta before 1945." *Journal of African History* 17, no. 4 (1976): 577–94.

Austin, Dennis. *Ghana Observed: Essays on the Politics of a West African Republic.* Manchester: Manchester University Press, 1976.

Austin, Gareth. *Labour, Land, and Capital in Ghana: From Slavery to Free Labour in Asante, 1807–1956.* Rochester, NY: University of Rochester Press, 2005.

Ayaric, Ghanatta, ed. "Eric Akanpaanab Ayaric Recalls His School Days in the 1930s and 1940s (Taken from an Audio-Recorded Account by Akanpaanab in 2000)." *Buluk* 7 (2013). https://buluk.de/new.

Ayee, Joseph R. A. "The Adjustment of Central Bodies to Decentralization: The Case of the Ghanaian Bureaucracy," *African Studies Review* 40, no. 2 (1997): 37–57.

———. *An Anatomy of Public Policy Implementation: The Case of Decentralization Policies in Ghana*. Brookfield, VT: Ashgate, 1994.

———. "The Measurement of Decentralization: The Ghanaian Experience, 1988–92." *African Affairs* 95, no. 378 (1996): 31–50.

Bardhan, Pranab K., and Dilip Mookherjee. "Capture and Governance at Local and National Levels." *American Economic Review* 90, no. 2 (2000): 135–39.

Bassett, Thomas J. *The Peasant Cotton Revolution in West Africa, Côte d'Ivoire, 1880–1995*. Cambridge: Cambridge University Press, 2001.

Bawumia, Mumuni. *A Life in the Political History of Ghana*. Accra: Ghana Universities Press, 2004.

Becker, Felicitas. *The Politics of Poverty: Policy-Making and Development in Rural Tanzania*. Cambridge: Cambridge University Press, 2019.

Beckman, Bjorn. "The Agrarian Basis of the Post-colonial State." In *Rural Development in Tropical Africa*, edited by Judith Heyer, Pepe Roberts, and Gavin Williams, 143–68. London: Macmillan, 1981.

Behrends, Andrea, and Carola Lentz. "Education, Careers, and Home Ties: The Ethnography of an Emerging Middle Class from Northern Ghana." *Zeitschrift Für Ethnologie* 137, no. 2 (2012): 139–64.

Bening, R. Bagulo. "Colonial Development Policy in Northern Ghana 1898–1950." *Bulletin of the Ghana Geographical Association* 17 (January 1975): 65–79.

———. *Ghana: Regional Boundaries and National Integration*. Accra: Ghana Universities Press, 1999.

———. *A History of Education in Northern Ghana, 1907–1976*. Accra: Ghana Universities Press, 1990.

———. *A History of Education in Northern Ghana, 1907–1976*. 2nd ed. Accra: Gavoss Education PLC, 2015.

Berry, Sara. *Chiefs Know Their Boundaries: Essays on Property, Power, and the Past in Asante, 1896–1996*. Portsmouth, NH: Heinemann, 2001.

———. "Chieftaincy, Land, and the State in Ghana and South Africa." In *The Politics of Custom: Chiefship, Capital, and the State in Contemporary Africa*, edited by John L. Comoroff and Jean Comoroff, 79–109. Chicago: University of Chicago Press, 2018.

———. "Hegemony on a Shoestring: Indirect Rule and Access to Agricultural Land." *Africa* 62, no. 3 (1992): 327–55.

———. *No Condition Is Permanent: The Social Dynamics of Agrarian Change in Sub-Saharan Africa*. Madison: University of Wisconsin Press, 1993.

———. "Questions of Ownership: Proprietorship and Control in a Changing Rural Terrain—A Case Study from Ghana." *Africa: Journal of the International African Institute* 83, no. 1 (2013): 36–56.

Bierschenk, Thomas, J. P. Chauveau, and Jean-Pierre Olivier de Sardan. *Courtiers En Développement: Les Villages Africains En Quête de Projets.* Paris: Karthala, 2000.

Bierschenk, Thomas, and Jean-Pierre Olivier de Sardan. "Powers in the Village: Rural Benin between Democratisation and Decentralisation." *Africa: Journal of the International African Institute* 73, no. 2 (2003): 145–73.

———. *States at Work: Dynamics of African Bureaucracies.* Leiden: Brill, 2014.

Biney, Ama. *The Political and Social Thought of Kwame Nkrumah.* New York: Palgrave Macmillan, 2011.

Bloom, Peter J., Stephan Miescher, and Takyiwaa Manuh, eds. *Modernization as Spectacle in Africa.* Bloomington: Indiana University Press, 2014.

Boone, Catherine. *Political Topographies of the African State: Territorial Authority and Institutional Choice.* Cambridge: Cambridge University Press, 2003.

Bornstein, Erica. *The Spirit of Development: Protestant NGOs, Morality, and Economics in Zimbabwe.* Stanford, CA: Stanford University Press, 2005.

Botchway, Karl. "Are Development Planners Afraid of History and Contextualization? Notes on Reading a Development Report on Northern Ghana." *Canadian Journal of African Studies / Revue Canadienne Des Études Africaines* 35, no. 1 (2001): 32–66.

———. *Understanding "Development" Intervention in Northern Ghana: The Need to Consider Political and Social Forces Necessary for Transformation.* New York: Edwin Mellen Press, 2004.

Britwum, Akua O., and Angela D. Akorso. "Qualitative Gender Evaluation of Agricultural Intensification Practices in Northern Ghana." Technical Report, Africa RISING. Ibadan, Nigeria: International Institute of Tropical Agriculture, December 2016.

Brukum, N. J. K. "Sir Gordon Guggisberg and Socio-economic Development of Northern Ghana, 1919–1927." *Transactions of the Historical Society of Ghana.* New Series 9 (2005): 1–15.

Brydon, Lynne, and Karen Legge. *Adjusting Society: The World Bank, the IMF and Ghana.* London: Tauris Academic Studies, 1996.

Byerlee, Derek, and Carl K. Eicher, eds. *Africa's Emerging Maize Revolution.* Boulder, CO: Lynne Rienner Publishers, 1997.

Caarls, Kim, and Valentina Mazzucato. "Transnational Relationships and Reunification: Ghanaian Couples between Ghana and Europe." *Demographic Research* 34, no. 21 (2016): 587–614.

Cammaert, Jessica. *Undesirable Practices: Women, Children, and the Politics of the Body in Northern Ghana, 1930–1972.* Lincoln: University of Nebraska Press, 2016.

Cardinall, A. W. *The Natives of the Northern Territories of the Gold Coast: Their Customs, Religion and Folklore.* London: Routledge, 1920.

Chalfin, Brenda. *Neoliberal Frontiers: An Ethnography of Sovereignty in West Africa.* Chicago: University of Chicago Press, 2010.

———. *Shea Butter Republic: State Power, Global Markets, and the Making of an Indigenous Commodity.* New York: Routledge, 2004.

Chazan, Naomi. *An Anatomy of Ghanaian Politics: Managing Political Recession, 1969–1982.* Boulder, CO: Westview Press, 1983.

Clark, Gracia. *African Market Women: Seven Life Stories from Ghana.* Bloomington: Indiana University Press, 2010.

———. "Negotiating Asante Family Survival in Kumasi, Ghana." *Africa: Journal of the International African Institute* 69, no. 1 (1999): 66–86.

Cleveland, David A. "Migration in West Africa: A Savanna Village Perspective." *Africa: Journal of the International African Institute* 61, no. 2 (1991): 222–46.

Cohen, John M. "Effects of Green Revolution Strategies on Tenants and Small-Scale Landowners in the Chilalo Region of Ethiopia." *Journal of Developing Areas* 9, no. 3 (1975): 335–58.

Comaroff, John L., and Jean Comaroff, eds. *The Politics of Custom: Chiefship, Capital, and the State in Contemporary Africa.* Chicago: University of Chicago Press, 2018.

Cooke, Bill, and Uma Kothari, eds. *Participation: The New Tyranny?* London: Zed Books, 2001.

Cooper, Barbara. *Marriage in Maradi: Culture and Gender in a Hausa Society in Niger, 1900–1983.* Portsmouth, NH: Heinemann, 1997.

Cooper, Frederick. *Africa since 1940: The Past of the Present.* New Approaches to African History. Cambridge: Cambridge University Press, 2002.

———. *Citizenship between Empire and Nation: Remaking France and French Africa, 1945–1960.* Princeton, NJ: Princeton University Press, 2014.

———. "Conditions Analogous to Slavery: Imperialism and Free Labour Ideology in Africa." In *Beyond Slavery: Explorations of Race, Labor, and Citizenship in Postemancipation Societies,* edited by Frederick Cooper, Thomas C. Holt, and Rebecca J. Scott, 107–50. Chapel Hill: University of North Carolina Press, 2000.

———. *Decolonization and African Society: The Labor Question in French and British Africa.* Cambridge: Cambridge University Press, 1996.

———. "Modernizing Bureaucrats, Backward Africans, and the Development Concept." In *International Development and the Social Sciences: Essays on the History and Politics of Knowledge,* edited by Frederick Cooper and Randall Packard, 64–92. Berkeley: University of California Press, 1997.

———. "Possibility and Constraint: African Independence in Historical Perspective." *Journal of African History* 49, no. 2 (2008): 167–96.

———. "Writing the History of Development." *Journal of Modern European History* 8, no. 1 (2010): 5–23.

Cooper, Frederick, and Randall M. Packard, eds. *International Development and the Social Sciences: Essays on the History and Politics of Knowledge.* Berkeley: University of California Press, 1997.

Cornwall, Andrea, and Karen Brock. "What Do Buzzwords Do for Development Policy? A Critical Look at 'Participation', 'Empowerment' and 'Poverty Reduction.'" *Third World Quarterly* 26, no. 7 (2005): 1043–60.

Cornwall, Andrea, and Deborah Eade, eds. *Deconstructing Development Discourse: Buzzwords and Fuzzwords.* Warwickshire, UK: Practical Action Publishing, 2010.

Cowen, M. P., and R. W. Shenton. *Doctrines of Development.* Taylor and Francis e-Library ed. London: Routledge, 2005.

Crawford, Gordon. "'Making Democracy a Reality'? The Politics of Decentralisation and the Limits to Local Democracy in Ghana." *Journal of Contemporary African Studies* 27, no. 1 (2009): 57–83.

Crook, Richard, and James Manor. *Democracy and Decentralisation in South Asia and West Africa: Participation, Accountability, and Performance.* Cambridge: Cambridge University Press, 1998.

Darkwah, Akosoa K. "Education: Pathway to Empowerment for Ghanaian Women?" In *Feminisms, Empowerment, and Development: Changing Women's Lives,* edited by Andrea Cornwall and Jenny Edwards, 87–103. London: Zed Books, 2014.

Davis, David Carson. "Continuity and Change in Mampurugu." PhD diss., Northwestern University, 1984.

———. "'Then the White Man Came with His Whitish Ideas . . .': The British and the Evolution of Traditional Government in Mampurugu." *International Journal of African Historical Studies* 20, no. 4 (1987): 627–46.

Der, Benedict G. *The Slave Trade in Northern Ghana.* Accra: Woeli Publishing Services, 1998.

Derrick, Jonathan. "West Africa's Worst Year of Famine." *African Affairs* 83, no. 332 (1984): 281–99.

Dibua, Jeremiah I. "Agricultural Modernization, the Environment and Sustainable Production in Nigeria, 1970–1985." *African Economic History* 30 (2002): 107–37.

Donkor, Kwabena. *Structural Adjustment and Mass Poverty in Ghana.* Brookfield, VT: Ashgate, 1997.

Doss, Cheryl R. "Men's Crops? Women's Crops? The Gender Patterns of Cropping in Ghana." *World Development* 30, no. 11 (2002): 1987–2000.

Doss, Cheryl R., and Michael L. Morris. "How Does Gender Affect the Adoption of Agricultural Innovations?" *Agricultural Economics* 25, no. 1 (2000): 27–39.

Drucker-Brown, Susan. "House and Hierarchy: Politics and Domestic Space in Northern Ghana." *Journal of the Royal Anthropological Institute* 7, no. 4 (2001): 669–85.

———. *Ritual Aspects of the Mamprusi Kingship.* Leiden: Afrika-Studiecentrum, 1975.

Dunn, John, and A. F. Robertson. *Dependence and Opportunity: Politics in Ahafo*. Cambridge: Cambridge University Press, 1973.

du Sautoy, Peter. *Community Development in Ghana*. Oxford: Oxford University Press, 1958.

Dzorgbo, Dan-Bright. *Ghana in Search of Development*. Brookfield, VT: Ashgate, 2001.

Ebron, Paulla A. *Performing Africa*. Princeton, NJ: Princeton University Press, 2002.

Eicher, Carl K. "Zimbabwe's Maize-Based Green Revolution: Preconditions for Replication." *World Development* 23, no. 5 (1995): 805–18.

Escobar, Arturo. *Encountering Development: The Making and Unmaking of the Third World*. Princeton, NJ: Princeton University Press, 1995.

Essel, Osuanyi Quaicoo, and Emmanual R. K. Amissah. "Smock Fashion Culture in Ghana's Dress Identity-Making." *Historical Research Letter* 18, no. 2225-096 (2015): 32–38.

Fall, Babacar. "Le Travail Forcé en Afrique Occidentale Française (1900–1946)." *Civilisations* 41, no. 1/2 (1993): 329–36.

Ferguson, George Ekem. Vol. 7, *The Papers of George Ekem Ferguson: A Fanti Official of the Government of the Gold Coast, 1890–1897*, edited by Kwame Arhin. Leiden: Afrika-Studiecentrum, 1974.

Ferguson, James. *The Anti-politics Machine: "Development," Depoliticization, and Bureaucratic Power in Lesotho*. Cambridge: Cambridge University Press, 1990.

———. *Expectations of Modernity Myths and Meanings of Urban Life on the Zambian Copperbelt*. Berkeley: University of California Press, 1999.

———. *Global Shadows: Africa in the Neoliberal World Order*. Durham, NC: Duke University Press, 2006.

Ferguson, James, and Akhil Gupta. "Spatializing States: Toward an Ethnography of Neoliberal Governmentality." *American Ethnologist* 29, no. 4 (2002): 981–1002.

Ferrell, Lacy S. "'We Were Mixed with All Types': Educational Migration in the Northern Territories of Colonial Ghana." In *Children on the Move in Africa: Past and Present Experiences of Migration*, edited by Elodie Razy and Marie Rodet, 141–58. Woodbridge, Suffolk: James Currey, 2016.

Freed, Libbie. "Conduits of Culture and Control: Roads in Colonial French Central Africa, 1890–1960." PhD diss., University of Wisconsin, 2006.

"Funeral Service for the Late Nab Dr. Ayieta Azantilow, 1900–2006." 2006. Original copy from the personal files of Namiyelana E. D. Sebiyam. Text also available in *Buluk*, vol 6. https://buluk.de/new/.

Gariba, Sulley. "The Peasantry and the State in Ghana: The Political Economy of Agrarian Stagnation and Rural Development in Northern Ghana." PhD diss., Carleton University, 1989.

Gary, Ian. "Confrontation, Co-operation, or Co-optation: NGOs and the Ghanaian State during Structural Adjustment." *Review of African Political Economy* 23, no. 68 (1996): 149–68.

Geschiere, Peter. "Chiefs and Colonial Rule in Cameroon: Inventing Chieftaincy, French and British Style." *Africa: Journal of the International African Institute* 63, no. 2 (1993): 151–75.

Ghana Central Bureau of Statistics. "Ghana Economic Surveys 1960, 61, 62, 63, 64, 65, 66." Accra: Ghana Central Bureau of Statistics, 1960–66.

Giblin, James Leonard. *A History of the Excluded: Making Family a Refuge from State in Twentieth-Century Tanzania.* Woodbridge, Suffolk: James Currey, 2005.

———. "Kinship in African History." In *A Companion to African History*, edited by William H. Worger, Charles H. Ambler, and Nwando Achebe, 163–77. Hoboken, NJ: Wiley Blackwell, 2019.

Goldman, Abe, and Joyotee Smith. "Agricultural Transformations in India and Northern Nigeria: Exploring the Nature of Green Revolutions." *World Development* 23, no. 2 (1995): 243–63.

Goody, Jack. *The Developmental Cycle in Domestic Groups.* Cambridge: Cambridge University Press, 1958.

Goody, Jack, ed. "Rice-Burning and the Green Revolution in Northern Ghana." *Journal of Development Studies* 16, no. 2 (1980): 136–55.

Government of Ghana. *1960 Population Census of Ghana.* Accra: Census Office, 1962.

———. *1970 Population Census of Ghana.* Accra: Census Office, 1973.

———. *1984 Population Census of Ghana.* Accra: Statistical Service, 1989.

Green, Erik. "Indirect Rule and Colonial Intervention: Chiefs and Agrarian Change in Nyasaland, ca. 1933 to the Early 1950s." *International Journal of African Historical Studies* 44, no. 2 (2011): 249–74.

Green, Maia. *The Development State: Aid, Culture and Civil Society in Tanzania.* Woodbridge, Suffolk: James Currey, 2014.

Grischow, Jeffrey. *Shaping Tradition: Civil Society, Community and Development in Colonial Northern Ghana, 1899–1957.* Leiden: Brill, 2006.

GTZ. "Evaluation Report, Agricultural Experiment Station Nyankpala." Eschborn: GTZ, 1982.

Guyer, Jane I. "Household and Community in African Studies." *African Studies Review* 24, no. 2/3 (1981): 87–137.

———. "Representation without Taxation: An Essay on Democracy in Rural Nigeria, 1952–1990." *African Studies Review* 35, no. 1 (1992): 41–79.

Gyimah-Boadi, E., ed. *Ghana under PNDC Rule.* Dakar: Codesria, 1993.

Hadfield, Leslie, and John Aerni-Flessner. "Introduction: Localizing the History of Development in Africa." *International Journal of African Historical Studies* 50, no. 1 (January 2017): 1–9.

Hailu, Zegeye. "The Adoption of Modern Farm Practices in African Agriculture: Empirical Evidence about the Impacts of Household Characteristics and Input Supply Systems in the Northern Region of Ghana." Nyankpala Agricultural Research Report. Nyankpala, Ghana, and Eschborn, West Germany: Nyankpala Agricultural Experiment Station and GTZ, 1990.

Hansen, Emmanuel. *Ghana under Rawlings: The Early Years.* Lagos: Malt-house Press, 1991.

Hansen, Emmanuel, and K. A. Ninsin. *The State, Development, and Politics in Ghana.* Dakar: Codesria Book Series, 1989.

Harper-Shipman, T. D. "How Comprehensive Is Comprehensive? Using Wangari Maathai as a Critique of the World Bank's Contemporary Development Model." *Third World Quarterly* 40, no. 4 (April 2019): 633–50.

———. *Rethinking Ownership of Development in Africa.* Milton: Routledge, 2019.

Hart, Jennifer. *Ghana on the Go: African Mobility in the Age of Motor Transportation.* Bloomington: Indiana University Press, 2016.

Hawkins, Sean. *Writing and Colonialism in Northern Ghana: The Encounter between the LoDagaa and "The World on Paper," 1892–1991.* Toronto: University of Toronto Press, 2002.

Hearn, Julie. "African NGOs: The New Compradors?" *Development & Change* 38, no. 6 (2007): 1095–110.

Herbst, Jeffrey. *The Politics of Reform in Ghana, 1982–1991.* Berkeley: University of California Press, 1993.

Hickey, Samuel, and Giles Mohan, eds. *Participation, from Tyranny to Transformation? Exploring New Approaches to Participation in Development.* London: Zed Books, 2004.

———. "Towards Participation as Transformation: Critical Themes and Challenges." In *Participation, from Tyranny to Transformation? Exploring New Approaches to Participation in Development,* edited by Samuel Hickey and Giles Mohan, 3–24. London: Zed Books, 2004.

Hilgers, Mathieu. "The Historicity of the Neoliberal State." *Social Anthropology* 20, no. 1 (2012): 80–94.

Hodge, Joseph Morgan. *Triumph of the Expert: Agrarian Doctrines of Development and the Legacies of British Colonialism.* Athens: Ohio University Press, 2007.

Hodgson, Dorothy Louise. *Once Intrepid Warriors: Gender, Ethnicity, and the Cultural Politics of Maasai Development.* Bloomington: Indiana University Press, 2001.

Holden, Stein T. "Peasant Household Modelling: Farming Systems Evolution and Sustainability in Northern Zambia." *Agricultural Economics* 9, no. 3 (1993): 241–67.

Holsey, Bayo. *Routes of Remembrance: Refashioning the Slave Trade in Ghana.* Chicago: University of Chicago Press, 2008.

Houssou, Nazaire, Michael Johnson, Shashidhara Kolavalli, and Collins Asante-Addo. "Changes in Ghanaian Farming Systems: Stagnation or a Quiet Transformation?" *Agriculture and Human Values* 35, no. 1 (2018): 41–66.

Hunter, Emma. "Voluntarism, Virtuous Citizenship, and Nation-Building in Late Colonial and Early Postcolonial Tanzania." *African Studies Review* 58, no. 2 (2015): 43–61.

Hutchful, Eboe. *Ghana's Adjustment Experience: The Paradox of Reform*. Geneva: UNRISD, 2002.

Ignatova, Jacqueline Alyce. "Seeds of Contestation: Genetically Modified Drops and the Politics of Agricultural Modernization in Ghana." PhD diss., University of Maryland, 2015.

Iliasu, A. A. "The Establishment of British Administration in Mamprugu, 1898–1937." *Transactions of the Historical Society of Ghana* 16, no. 1 (1975): 1–28.

Immerwahr, Daniel. *Thinking Small: The United States and the Lure of Community Development*. Cambridge, MA: Harvard University Press, 2018.

International Labour Organization. Forced Labour Convention, Convention CO29 § (1930). https://www.ilo.org/dyn/normlex/en/f?p=NORMLEXPUB: 12100:0::NO::P12100_ILO_CODE:C029.

Isaacman, Allen F., and Barbara S. Isaacman. *Dams, Displacement and the Delusion of Development: Cahora Bassa and Its Legacies in Mozambique, 1965–2007*. Athens: Ohio University Press, 2013.

Jean-Baptiste, Rachel. *Conjugal Rights: Marriage, Sexuality, and Urban Life in Colonial Libreville, Gabon*. Athens: Ohio University Press, 2014.

Jennings, Michael. *Surrogates of the State: NGOs, Development, and Ujamaa in Tanzania*. Bloomfield, CT: Kumarian Press, 2008.

Jones, Ben. *Beyond the State in Rural Uganda*. Edinburgh: Edinburgh University Press, 2009.

Jones, Hilary. *The Métis of Senegal: Urban Life and Politics in French West Africa*. Bloomington: Indiana University Press, 2013.

Kansanga, Moses Mosonsieyiri, Roger Antabe, Yujiro Sano, Sarah Mason-Renton, and Isaac Luginaah. "A Feminist Political Ecology of Agricultural Mechanization and Evolving Gendered On-Farm Labor Dynamics in Northern Ghana." *Gender, Technology and Development* 23, no. 3 (2019): 207–33.

Keese, Alexander. "Slow Abolition within the Colonial Mind: British and French Debates about 'Vagrancy,' 'African Laziness,' and Forced Labour in West Central and South Central Africa, 1945–1965." *International Review of Social History* 59, no. 3 (2014): 377–407.

Kelly, Bob, and R. B. Bening. "Ideology, Regionalism, Self-Interest and Tradition: An Investigation into Contemporary Politics in Northern Ghana." *Africa* 77, no. 2 (2007): 180–206.

Kelsall, Tim, and Claire Mercer. "Empowering People? World Vision and 'Transformatory Development' in Tanzania." *Review of African Political Economy* 30, no. 96 (2003): 293–304.

Killick, Tony. *Development Economics in Action: A Study of Economic Policies in Ghana*. Portsmouth, NH: Heinemann, 1978.

Kimble, David. *A Political History of Ghana: The Rise of Gold Coast Nationalism, 1850–1928*. Oxford: Clarendon Press, 1963.

King, David P. *God's Internationalists: World Vision and the Age of Evangelical Humanitarianism*. Philadelphia: University of Pennsylvania Press, 2019.

Konadu-Agyemang, Kwadwo. "The Best of Times and the Worst of Times: Structural Adjustment Programs and Uneven Development." *Professional Geographer* 52, no. 3 (August 2000): 469–83.

Konings, Piet. *The State and Rural Class Formation in Ghana: A Comparative Analysis.* Leiden: African Studies Centre, 1986.

Kraus, Jon. "The Struggle over Structural Adjustment in Ghana." *Africa Today* 38, no. 4 (1991): 19–37.

Kröger, Franz. "Colonial Officers and Bulsa Chiefs." *Buluk* 7 (2013). https://buluk.de/new/.

———. "Extracts from Bulsa History: Sandema Chiefs before Azantilow." *Buluk* 6 (2012). https://buluk.de/new/.

———. "Going to a Bulsa School: Enrolment, Motivation and Resistance." *Buluk* 3 (2001). https://buluk.de/new/.

———. "Kunkwa, Kategra and Jadema: The Sandemnaab's Lawsuit." *Buluk* 6 (2012). https://buluk.de/new/.

———. "Mr. Abu Gariba, One of the First to Combine Traditional and Modern Bulsa Values." *Buluk* 8 (2014). https://buluk.de/new/.

Kröger, Franz, and Barbara Meier. *Ghana's North: Research on Culture, Religion, and Politics of Societies in Transition.* Frankfurt: Peter Lang Publishing, 2003.

Kunkel, Sarah. "Forced Labour, Roads, and Chiefs: The Implementation of the ILO Forced Labour Convention in the Gold Coast." *International Review of Social History* 63, no. 3 (2018): 449–76.

Labonte, Melissa T. "From Patronage to Peacebuilding? Elite Capture and Governance from Below in Sierra Leone." *African Affairs* 111, no. 442 (2012): 90–115.

Ladouceur, Paul André. *Chiefs and Politicians: The Politics of Regionalism in Northern Ghana.* Legon History Series. London: Longman, 1979.

Lal, Priya. *African Socialism in Postcolonial Tanzania: Between the Village and the World.* Cambridge: Cambridge University Press, 2015.

———. "Militants, Mothers, and the National Family: Ujamaa, Gender and Rural Development in Postcolonial Tanzania." *Journal of African History* 51, no. 1 (2010): 1–20.

Lawrance, Benjamin N., Emily Lynn Osborn, and Richard L. Roberts. *Intermediaries, Interpreters, and Clerks: African Employees in the Making of Colonial Africa.* Madison: University of Wisconsin Press, 2006.

Lawrence, Peter. "The Political Economy of the 'Green Revolution' in Africa." *Review of African Political Economy* 15, no. 42 (1988): 59–75.

Leal, Pablo Alejandro. "Participation." In *Deconstructing Development Discourse: Buzzwords and Fuzzwords,* edited by Andrea Cornwall and Deborah Eade, 89–100. Warwickshire, UK: Practical Action Publishing, 2010.

Lee, Christopher J. *Unreasonable Histories: Nativism, Multiracial Lives, and the Genealogical Imagination in British Africa.* Durham, NC: Duke University Press, 2014.

Lentz, Carola. "The Chief, the Mine Captain and the Politician: Legitimating Power in Northern Ghana." *Africa: Journal of the International African Institute* 68, no. 1 (1998): 46–67.

———. *Ethnicity and the Making of History in Northern Ghana.* Edinburgh: Edinburgh University Press, 2006.

———. *Land, Mobility, and Belonging in West Africa: Natives and Strangers.* Bloomington: Indiana University Press, 2013.

Lentz, Carola, Isidore Lobnibe, and Stanislas Meda. "Family History as Family Enterprise? A Wissenschaftskolleg Focus Group's Views of a West African Family." *TRAFO—Blog for Transregional Research,* August 2, 2018. https://trafo.hypotheses.org/11214.

Lewis, Joanna. *Empire State-Building: War and Welfare in Kenya, 1925–52.* Oxford: James Currey, 2000.

Li, Tania Murray. *The Will to Improve: Governmentality, Development, and the Practice of Politics.* Durham, NC: Duke University Press, 2007.

Lindsay, Lisa A. *Working with Gender.* Portsmouth, NH: Heinemann, 2003.

Lissner, Jorgen. "Merchants of Misery." *New Internationalist* 100 (June 1981). https://newint.org/features/1981/06/01/merchants-of-misery.

Low, D. A., and J. M. Lonsdale. "Introduction." In *History of East Africa,* edited by D. A. Low and A. Smith, *vol.* 3, 12–16. Oxford: Clarendon Press, 1976.

Lugard, Frederick D. *The Dual Mandate in British Tropical Africa.* London: William Blackwood & Sons, 1922.

Lund, Christian. *Local Politics and the Dynamics of Property in Africa.* Cambridge: Cambridge University Press, 2008.

———. "Negotiating Property Institutions: On the Symbiosis of Property and Authority in Africa." In *Negotiating Property in Africa,* edited by Kristine Juul and Christian Lund, 11–44. Portsmouth, NH: Heinemann, 2002.

Lynn, Charles, Marjorie Lynn, and Sylvia Lynn. *The Long Garden Master in the Gold Coast: The Life and Times of a Colonial Agricultural Officer in the Gold Coast, 1929–1947.* Bedfordshire, UK: Authors OnLine, 2012.

Mamdani, Mahmood. *Citizen and Subject: Contemporary Africa and the Legacy of Late Colonialism.* Princeton, NJ: Princeton University Press, 1996.

Mann, Gregory. *From Empires to NGOs in the West African Sahel: The Road to Nongovernmentality.* Cambridge: Cambridge University Press, 2015.

Mansuri, Ghazala, and Vijayendra Rao. *Localizing Development: Does Participation Work?* Washington, DC: World Bank, 2013.

Mark-Thiesen, Cassandra. *Mediators, Contract Men, and Colonial Capital: Mechanized Gold Mining in the Gold Coast Colony, 1879–1909.* Rochester, NY: University of Rochester Press, 2018.

Mazzucato, Valentina, and Djamila Schans. "Transnational Families and the Well-Being of Children: Conceptual and Methodological Challenges." *Journal of Marriage and Family* 73, no. 4 (2011): 704–12.

McCaskie, T. C. *Asante Identities: History and Modernity in an African Village, 1850–1950*. Bloomington: Indiana University Press, 2000.

McDonic, Susan Mary. "Witnessing, Work and Worship: World Vision and the Negotiation of Faith, Development and Culture." PhD diss., Duke University, 2004.

McMahon, Elisabeth. "Developing Workers: Coerced and 'Voluntary' Labor in Zanzibar, 1909–1970." *International Labor and Working-Class History* 92 (Fall 2017): 114–33.

Miers, Suzanne. *Slavery in the Twentieth Century: The Evolution of a Global Problem*. Walnut Creek, CA: Altamira, 2003.

Miescher, Stephan. "Building the City of the Future: Visions and Experiences of Modernity in Ghana's Akosombo Township." *Journal of African History* 53, no. 3 (2012): 367–90.

Miescher, Stephan, and Dzodzi Tsikata. "Hydro-Power and the Promise of Modernity and Development in Ghana: Comparing the Akosombo and Bui Dam Projects." In "Revisiting Modernization." Special issue, *Ghana Studies* 12–13 (2009–10): 15–53.

Ministry of Agriculture and Ghana-German Agricultural Development Project. *10 Years of Ghanaian-German Technical Cooperation in the Field of Agriculture, Northern Ghana*. Tamale, Ghana: Ministry of Agriculture, 1980.

Ministry of Finance. "Ghana Economic Surveys 1957, 58, 59." Accra: Ministry of Finance, 1957–59.

Mitchell, Timothy. *Rule of Experts: Egypt, Techno-Politics, Modernity*. Berkeley: University of California Press, 2002.

Mkandawire, Thandika. "'Good Governance': The Itinerary of an Idea." In *Deconstructing Development Discourse: Buzzwords and Fuzzwords*, edited by Andrea Cornwall and Deborah Eade, 265–68. Warwickshire, UK: Practical Action Publishing, 2010.

———. "Neopatrimonialism and the Political Economy of Economic Performance in Africa: Critical Reflections." *World Politics* 67, no. 3 (2015): 563–612.

———. "Thinking about Developmental States in Africa." *Cambridge Journal of Economics* 25, no. 3 (2001): 289–313.

Mohan, Giles, and Kristian Stokke. "Participatory Development and Empowerment: The Dangers of Localism." *Third World Quarterly* 21, no. 2 (2000): 247–68.

Monson, Jamie. *Africa's Freedom Railway: How a Chinese Development Project Changed Lives and Livelihoods in Tanzania*. Bloomington: Indiana University Press, 2011.

Moseley, William, Matthew Schnurr, and Rachel Bezner Kerr. "Interrogating the Technocratic (Neoliberal) Agenda for Agricultural Development and Hunger Alleviation in Africa." *African Geographical Review* 34, no. 1 (2015): 1–7.

Moskowitz, Kara. *Seeing Like a Citizen: Decolonization, Development, and the Making of Kenya, 1945–1980.* Athens: Ohio University Press, 2019.

Mosse, David. *Cultivating Development: An Ethnography of Aid Policy and Practice.* Ann Arbor, MI: Pluto Press, 2005.

Muhumuza, William. "Pitfalls of Decentralization Reforms in Transitional Societies: The Case of Uganda." *Africa Development / Afrique et Développement* 33, no. 4 (2008): 59–81.

Munro, William A. *The Moral Economy of the State: Conservation, Community Development, and State Making in Zimbabwe.* Athens: Ohio University Press, 1998.

Murillo, Bianca. *Market Encounters: Consumer Cultures in Twentieth-Century Ghana.* Athens: Ohio University Press, 2017.

Mutongi, Kenda. *Worries of the Heart: Widows, Family, and Community in Kenya.* Chicago: University of Chicago Press, 2007.

Ndlovu-Gatsheni, Sabelo J. *Coloniality of Power in Postcolonial Africa.* Dakar: Council for the Development of Social Science Research in Africa, 2013.

———. *Empire, Global Coloniality and African Subjectivity.* New York: Berghahn Books, 2013.

Ninsin, Kwame A. "The PNDC and the Problem of Legitimacy." In *Ghana: The Political Economy of Recovery,* edited by Donald Rothchild, 49–67. Boulder, CO: Lynne Rienner Publishers, 1991.

Nkrumah, Kwame. *Revolutionary Path.* London: Panaf Books, 1973.

Ntewusu, Samuel. "Settling In and Holding On: A Socio-economic History of Northern Traders and Transporters in Accra's Tudu: 1908–2008." PhD diss., University of Leiden, 2011.

Nugent, Paul. *Africa since Independence.* New York: Palgrave MacMillan, 2004.

———. *Big Men, Small Boys, and Politics in Ghana: Power, Ideology, and the Burden of History, 1982–1994.* New York: Pinter, 1995.

Nyaaba, Ali Yakubu, and George M. Bob-Milliar. "The Economic Potentials of Northern Ghana: The Ambivalence of the Colonial and Post-colonial States to Develop the North." *African Economic History* 47, no. 2 (2019): 45–67.

Nyantakyi-Frimpong, Hanson, and Rachel Bezner Kerr. "A Political Ecology of High-Input Agriculture in Northern Ghana." *African Geographical Review* 34, no. 1 (2015): 13–35.

Nyanteng, V. K., and W. Seini. "Agricultural Policy and the Impact on Growth and Productivity, 1970–1995." In *Economic Reforms in Ghana: The Miracle and the Mirage,* edited by Ernest Aryeetey, Jane Harrigan, and Machiko Nissanke, 267–83. Woodbridge, Suffolk: James Currey, 2000.

———. "Smallholders and Structural Adjustment in Ghana." In *The African Food Crisis: Lessons from the Asian Green Revolution,* edited by Göran Djurfeldt, H. Holmén, M. Jirström, and R. Larssön, 219–38. Cambridge, MA: Centre for Agriculture and Bioscience International (CABI), 2005.

Odotei, Irene, and A. Awedoba, eds. *Chieftaincy in Ghana: Culture, Governance and Development*. Accra: Sub-Saharan Publishers, 2006.

Okali, Christine. "Gender Analysis: Engaging with Rural Development and Agricultural Policy Processes." Working paper, FAC, Future Agricultures Consortium, Brighton, UK, 2012.

Okia, Opolot. *Communal Labor in Colonial Kenya: The Legitimization of Coercion, 1912–1930*. New York: Palgrave Macmillan, 2012.

———. *Labor in Colonial Kenya after the Forced Labor Convention, 1930–1963*. New York: Palgrave Macmillan, 2019.

Opare, Mary, and Judy E. Mill. "The Evolution of Nursing Education in a Postindependence Context—Ghana from 1957 to 1970." *Western Journal of Nursing Research* 22, no. 8 (2000): 936–44.

Oppong, Christine. *Marriage among a Matrilineal Elite: A Family Study of Ghanaian Senior Civil Servants*. Cambridge: Cambridge University Press, 1974.

Osborn, Emily Lynn. "'Circle of Iron': African Colonial Employees and the Interpretation of Colonial Rule in French West Africa." *Journal of African History* 44, no. 1 (2003): 29–50.

———. *Our New Husbands Are Here: Households, Gender, and Politics in a West African State from the Slave Trade to Colonial Rule*. Athens: Ohio University Press, 2011.

Osborne, Myles. "The Kamba and Mau Mau: Ethnicity, Development, and Chiefship, 1952–1960." *International Journal of African Historical Studies* 43, no. 1 (2010): 63–87.

Osei, Gershon. "Self-Help without the Self: Critique of Non-governmental Organizational Approaches to Rural Development in Ghana." *International Social Work* 60, no. 2 (2017): 494–506.

Peel, J. D. Y. *Ijeshas and Nigerians: The Incorporation of a Yoruba Kingdom, 1890s–1970s*. Cambridge: Cambridge University Press, 1983.

———. "Olaju: A Yorba Concept of Development." *Journal of Development Studies* 14, no. 2 (1978): 139–65.

Pellow, Deborah, and Naomi Chazan. *Ghana: Coping with Uncertainty*. Boulder, CO: Westview Press, 1986.

Pender, John. "From 'Structural Adjustment' to 'Comprehensive Development Framework': Conditionality Transformed?" *Third World Quarterly* 22, no. 3 (2001): 397–411.

People's National Party (Ghana). *Twenty-Seven Months of the People's National Party Administration: 24th Sept 1979–31st Dec, 1981: PNP in Retrospect*. Accra: People's National Party, 1992.

Perbi, Akosua Adoma. *A History of Indigenous Slavery in Ghana from the 15th to the 19th Centuries*. Accra: Sub-Saharan Publishers, 2004.

Peters, Pauline E., ed. *Development Encounters: Sites of Participation and Knowledge*. Cambridge, MA: Harvard University Press, 2000.

Pigg, Stacy Leigh. "Inventing Social Categories through Place: Social Representations and Development in Nepal." *Comparative Studies in Society and History* 34, no. 3 (1992): 491–513.

Piot, Charles. *Nostalgia for the Future: West Africa after the Cold War.* Chicago: Chicago University Press, 2010.

———. *Remotely Global: Village Modernity in West Africa.* Chicago: University of Chicago Press, 1999.

Plange, Nii K. "Underdevelopment in Northern Ghana: Natural Causes or Colonial Capitalism?" *Review of African Political Economy* 15/16 (May–December 1979): 4–14.

Prah, Kwesi Kwaa. "Culture, the Missing Link in Development Planning in Africa." *Présence Africaine* 163/164 (2001): 90–102.

Quayson, Ato. "Signs of the Times: Discourse Ecologies and Street Life on Oxford St., Accra." *City and Society* 22, no. 1 (2010): 72–96.

Rathbone, Richard. "Casting 'the Kingdome into Another Mold': Ghana's Troubled Transition to Independence." *Round Table* 97, no. 398 (2008): 705–18.

———. *Nkrumah and the Chiefs: The Politics of Chieftaincy in Ghana, 1951–60.* Athens: Ohio University Press, 2000.

Rattray, Robert Sutherland. *The Tribes of the Ashanti Hinterland.* 2 vols. Oxford: Clarendon Press, 1932.

Ray, Carina E. *Crossing the Color Line: Race, Sex, and the Contested Politics of Colonialism in Ghana.* Athens: Ohio University Press, 2015.

Ribot, J. C. "Decentralisation, Participation, and Accountability in Sahelian Forestry." *Africa: Journal of the International Institute of African Languages and Cultures* 69, no. 1 (1999): 23–65.

Ribot, J. C., A. Chhatre, and T. Lankina. "Introduction: Institutional Choice and Recognition in the Formation and Consolidation of Local Democracy." *Conservation and Society* 6, no. 1 (2008): 1–11.

Rimmer, Douglas. *Staying Poor: Ghana's Political Economy 1950–1990.* Oxford: Pergammon, 1992.

Rist, Gilbert. *The History of Development: From Western Origins to Global Faith.* 5th ed. London: Zed Books, 2019.

Roberts, Richard. "Coerced Labor in Twentieth-Century Africa." In *The Cambridge World History of Slavery,* edited by David Eltis, David Richardson, Seymour Drescher, and Stanley L. Engerman, vol. 4, *AD 1804–AD 2016,* 583–609. Cambridge: Cambridge University Press, 2017.

Robertson, Claire C. *Sharing the Same Bowl: A Socioeconomic History of Women and Class in Accra, Ghana.* Bloomington: Indiana University Press, 1984.

Rodet, Marie. "Forced Labor, Resistance, and Masculinities in Kayes, French Sudan, 1919–1946." *International Labor and Working-Class History* 86 (Fall 2014): 107–23.

Rodney, Walter. *How Europe Underdeveloped Africa.* Revised ed. Washington, DC: Howard University Press, 1981.

Rossi, Benedetta. *From Slavery to Aid: Politics, Labour, and Ecology in the Nigerien Sahel, 1800–2000.* Cambridge: Cambridge University Press, 2015.

———. "What 'Development' Does to Work." *International Labor and Working-Class History* 92 (Fall 2017): 7–23.

Rossi, Benedetta, and Franco Barchiesi, eds. "Developmentalism, Labor, and the Slow Death of Slavery in Twentieth Century Africa." Special issue, *International Labor and Working-Class History* 92 (Fall 2017).

Saaka, Yakubu, ed. *Regionalism and Public Policy in Northern Ghana.* New York: Peter Lang, 2001.

Sackeyfio-Lenoch, Naaborko. *The Politics of Chieftaincy: Authority and Property in Colonial Ghana, 1920–1950.* Rochester, NY: University of Rochester Press, 2014.

Sackley, Nicole. "The Village as Cold War Site: Experts, Development, and the History of Rural Reconstruction." *Journal of Global History* 6, no. 3 (2011): 481–504.

———. "Village Models: Etawah, India, and the Making and Remaking of Development in the Early Cold War." *Diplomatic History* 37, no. 4 (2013): 749–78.

Sam, Nana Ama Serwah Poku. "Gender Mainstreaming and Integration of Women in Decision-Making: The Case of Water Management in Samari-Nkwanta, Ghana." *Wagadu: A Journal of Transnational Women's and Gender Studies* 3 (Spring 2006). http://sites.cortland.edu/wagadu/wp-content/uploads/sites/3/2014/02/ama.pdf.

Scheele, Judith. *Village Matters: Knowledge, Politics and Community in Kabylia, Algeria.* Woodbridge, Suffolk: James Currey, 2009.

Scherz, China. *Having People, Having Heart: Charity, Sustainable Development, and Problems of Dependence in Central Uganda.* Chicago: University of Chicago Press, 2014.

Schlottner, Michael. "'We Stay, Others Come and Go': Identity among the Mamprusi in Northern Ghana." In *Ethnicity in Ghana: The Limits of Invention,* edited by Carola Lentz and Paul Nugent, 49–67. London: Macmillan, 2000.

Schneider, Leander. *Government of Development: Peasants and Politicians in Postcolonial Tanzania.* Bloomington: Indiana University Press, 2014.

Schroeder, Richard. *Shady Practices: Agroforestry and Gender Politics in the Gambia.* Berkeley: University of California Press, 1999.

Scott, James C. *Seeing Like a State: How Certain Schemes to Improve the Human Condition Have Failed.* New Haven, CT: Yale University Press, 1998.

Shepherd, Andrew. "Agrarian Change in Northern Ghana: Public Investment, Capitalist Farming and Famine." In *Rural Development in Tropical Africa,* edited by Judith Heyer, Pepe Roberts, and Gavin Williams, 168–92. London: Macmillan, 1981.

Shillington, Kevin. *Ghana and the Rawlings Factor.* London: Macmillan, 1992.

Skinner, Kate. "From Pentecostalism to Politics: Mass Literacy and Community Development in Late Colonial Northern Ghana." *Paedagogica Historica* 46, no. 3 (2010): 307–23.

———. *The Fruits of Freedom in British Togoland: Literacy, Politics and Nationalism, 1914–2014.* Cambridge: Cambridge University Press, 2015.

———. "'It Brought Some Kind of Neatness to Mankind': Literacy, Development and Democracy in 1950s Asante." *Africa: Journal of the International African Institute* 79, no. 4 (2009): 479–99.

———. "Who Knew the Minds of the People? Specialist Knowledge and Developmentalist Authoritarianism in Post-colonial Ghana." *Journal of Imperial and Commonwealth History* 39, no. 2 (2011): 297–323.

Soeters, Sebastiaan. "Tamale 1907–1957: Between Colonial Trade and Colonial Chieftainship." PhD diss., University of Leiden, 2012.

Songsore, Jacob. *Regional Development in Ghana: The Theory and the Reality.* Accra: Woeli Publishing Services, 2003.

Stacey, Paul. "'The Chiefs, Elders, and People Have for Many Years Suffered Untold Hardships': Protests by Coalitions of the Excluded in British Northern Togoland, UN Trusteeship Territory, 1950–7." *Journal of African History* 55, no. 3 (2014): 423–44.

Stalker, Peter. "Please Do Not Sponsor This Child." Special issue, *New Internationalist* 111 (May 1982). https://newint.org/features/1982/05/01/keynote.

Staniland, Martin. *The Lions of Dagbon: Political Change in Northern Ghana.* Cambridge: Cambridge University Press, 1975.

Sutton, Inez. "Colonial Agricultural Policy: The Non-development of the Northern Territories of the Gold Coast." *International Journal of African Historical Studies* 22, no. 4 (1989): 637–69.

Swanepoel, Natalie. "Every Periphery Is Its Own Center: Sociopolitical and Economic Interactions in Nineteenth-Century Northwestern Ghana." *International Journal of African Historical Studies* 42, no. 3 (2009): 411–32.

Talton, Benjamin. *Politics of Social Change in Ghana: The Konkomba Struggle for Political Equality.* New York: Palgrave Macmillan, 2010.

Thomas, Roger. "Education in Northern Ghana, 1906–1940: A Study in Colonial Paradox." *International Journal of African Historical Studies* 7, no. 3 (1974): 427–67.

———. "Forced Labour in British West Africa: The Case of the Northern Territories of the Gold Coast 1906–1927." *Journal of African History* 14, no. 1 (1973): 79–103.

———. "Military Recruitment in the Gold Coast during the First World War (Recrutement Militaire En Gold Coast Pendant La Première Guerre Mondiale)." *Cahiers d'Études Africaines* 15, no. 57 (1975): 57–83.

———. "The 1916 Bongo 'Riots' and Their Background: Aspects of Colonial Administration and African Response in Eastern Upper Ghana." *Journal of African History* 24, no. 1 (1983): 57–75.

Tiquet, Romain. "Challenging Colonial Forced Labor? Resistance, Resilience, and Power in Senegal (1920s–1940s)." *International Labor and Working-Class History* 93 (2018): 135–50.

Tonah, Steve. "Diviners, Malams, God, and the Contest for Paramount Chiefship in Mamprugu (Northern Ghana)." *Anthropos* 101, no. 1 (2006): 21–35.

———. "Migration and Farmer-Herder Conflicts in Ghana's Volta Basin." *Canadian Journal of African Studies / Revue Canadienne Des Études Africaines* 40, no. 1 (2006): 152–78.

Trager, Lillian. *Yoruba Hometowns: Community, Identity, and Development in Nigeria.* Boulder, CO: Lynne Rienner Publishers, 2001.

Tsai, Ming-Chang, and Dan-Bright S. Dzorgbo. "Familial Reciprocity and Subjective Well-Being in Ghana." *Journal of Marriage and Family* 74, no. 1 (2012): 215–28.

Tsikata, Dzodzi. "Gender, Land and Labour Relations and Livelihoods in Sub-Saharan Africa in the Era of Economic Liberalisation: Towards a Research Agenda." *Feminist Africa* 12 (December 2009): 11–30.

———. *Living in the Shadow of the Large Dams: Long Term Responses of Downstream and Lakeside Communities of Ghana's Volta River Project.* Leiden: Brill, 2006.

Tsing, Anna Lowenhaupt. *In the Realm of the Diamond Queen: Marginality in an Out-of-the-Way Place.* Princeton, NJ: Princeton University Press, 1993.

Ukelina, Bekeh Utietiang. *The Second Colonial Occupation: Development Planning, Agriculture, and the Legacies of British Rule in Nigeria.* Lanham, MD: Lexington Books, 2017.

van Beusekom, Monica M. *Negotiating Development: African Farmers and Colonial Experts at the Office Du Niger, 1920–1960.* Portsmouth, NH: Heinemann, 2002.

van Beusekom, Monica M., and Dorothy L. Hodgson. "Lessons Learned? Development Experiences in the Late Colonial Period." Special issue, *Journal of African History* 41, no. 1 (2000): 29–33.

Van Hear, Nicholas. "'By Day' Boys and Dariga Men: Casual Labor versus Agrarian Capital in Northern Ghana." *Review of African Political Economy* 11, no. 31 (1984): 44–56.

———. "Northern Labour and the Development of Capitalist Agriculture in Ghana." PhD diss., University of Birmingham, 1982.

van Waijenburg, Marlous. "Financing the African Colonial State: The Revenue Imperative and Forced Labor." *Journal of Economic History* 78, no. 1 (March 2018): 40–80.

Vaughan, Olufemi. *Nigerian Chiefs: Traditional Power in Modern Politics, 1890s–1990s.* Rochester, NY: University of Rochester Press, 2000.

Vercillo, Siera, and Miriam Hird-Younger. "Farmer Resistance to Agriculture Commercialisation in Northern Ghana." *Third World Quarterly* 40, no. 4 (April 2019): 763–79.

von Oppen, Achim. "The Village as Territory: Enclosing Locality in Northwest Zambia, 1950s to 1990s." *Journal of African History* 47, no. 1 (2006): 57–75.

Warren, Carol, and Leontine Visser. "The Local Turn: An Introductory Essay Revisiting Leadership, Elite Capture and Good Governance in Indonesian Conservation and Development Programs." *Human Ecology* 44, no. 3 (June 2016): 277–86.

Waters, Ken. "How World Vision Rose from Obscurity to Prominence: Television Fundraising, 1972–1982." *American Journalism* 15, no. 4 (Fall 1998): 69–93.

Webber, Paul. "Agrarian Change in Kusasi, North-East Ghana." *Africa: Journal of the International African Institute* 66, no. 3 (1996): 437–57.

Weller, Kate, and James G. Copestake, eds. *Non-governmental Organizations and the State in Africa.* London: Routledge, 1993.

Wetzel, Deborah. "The Promises and Pitfalls in Public Expenditure." In *Economic Reforms in Ghana*, edited by Ernest Aryeetey, Jane Harrigan, and Machiko Nissanke, 115–31. Woodbridge, Suffolk: James Currey, 2000.

Whaites, Alan. "Pursuing Partnership: World Vision and the Ideology of Development—a Case Study." *Development in Practice* 9, no. 4 (1999): 410–23.

Whitehead, Ann. "Tracking Livelihood Change: Theoretical, Methodological and Empirical Perspectives from North-East Ghana." *Journal of Southern African Studies* 28, no. 3 (2002): 575–98.

Wiemers, Alice. "'It Is All He Can Do to Cope with the Roads in His Own District': Labor, Community, and Development in Northern Ghana, 1919–1936." *International Labor and Working-Class History* 92 (Fall 2017): 89–113.

———. "A 'Time of Agric': Rethinking the 'Failure' of Agricultural Programs in 1970s Ghana." *World Development* 66 (February 2015): 104–17.

———. "'When the Chief Takes an Interest': Development and the Reinvention of 'Communal' Labor in Northern Ghana, 1935–1960." *Journal of African History* 58, no. 2 (2017): 239–57.

Wilks, Ivor. *Wa and the Wala: Islam and Polity in Northwestern Ghana.* Cambridge: Cambridge University Press, 1989.

World Bank. *Accelerated Development in Sub-Saharan Africa: An Agenda for Action.* Washington, DC: World Bank, 1981.

———. *Ghana Agricultural Sector Review.* Washington, DC: World Bank, 1978.

———. *Ghana: Managing the Transition.* Washington, DC: World Bank, 1984.

———. *Ghana: Policies and Program for Adjustment.* Washington, DC: World Bank, 1983.

———. *Governance and Development.* Washington, DC: World Bank, 1992.

———. *Sub-Saharan Africa: From Crisis to Sustainable Growth.* Washington, DC: World Bank, 1989.

World Vision International. *Together.* Monrovia, CA: World Vision International, 1983.

Wraith, R. E. *Guggisberg.* London: Oxford University Press, 1967.

Yarrow, Thomas. *Development beyond Politics: Aid, Activism and NGOs in Ghana*. New York: Palgrave Macmillan, 2011.

——. "Life/History: Personal Narratives of Development amongst NGO Workers and Activists in Ghana." *Africa* 78, no. 3 (2008): 334–58.

——. "Remains of the Future: Rethinking the Space and Time of Ruination through the Volta Resettlement Project, Ghana." *Cultural Anthropology* 32, no. 4 (2017): 566–91.

Yembilah, Nicholas. "The Onchocerciasis Control Programme (OCP) and Socio-economic Development in the Fumbisi Valley, UER." MPhil thesis, University of Ghana, Legon, 2001.

Yokying, Phanwin, and Isabel Lambrecht. "Landownership and the Gender Gap in Agriculture: Disappointing Insights from Northern Ghana." IFPRI Discussion Paper. International Food Policy Research Institute, 2019.

Ziai, Aram. *Development Discourse and Global History: From Colonialism to the Sustainable Development Goals*. London: Routledge, 2015.

Index

Page numbers in italics refer to figures.

73, 98, 101, 102, 199n16, 203n46; Sebiyam's family involved in, 56, 61, 80, 83, 113–14, 192n25; training for, 176n20
Bunkpurugu, 105, 107
Busia, Kofi Abrefa, 95, 104, 105, 196nn3–4, 200n32

Canadian Fund for Local Initiative, 128
Cardinall, A. W., 35–36, 39–40, 162n29, 163n30, 166n60, 171n98
carriers, 34, 162n25, 167nn64–65
cattle kraals, 49
Chalfin, Brenda, 211n6, 216n31
Chambers, Robert, 130, 220n58
Chazan, Naomi, 197n19, 222n85
chieftaincy, 7, 16–18, 27, 28–29, 155nn36–37; in the 1970s, 96, 106; accumulation and, 49–50, 80, 112–16, 190n13, 201n37; agriculture and, 80, 98–99, 172n110; and "benevolent despots," 35, 171n98; and British removal of chiefs, 43, 46, 49, 50; colonial anxieties regarding, 80, 169n81, 172n106, 174n121, 190n13; in the colonial era, 31–53, 55–59, 78–81, 159n8, 163n35, 167n65, 171n100, 183n86, 185n107, 190n9; and colonial officials, 35, 169n81, 171n100; and communal or self-help labor, 13–16, 26–28, 30, 44–47, 50–51, 58, 61–65, 75, 96, 105–8, 110–11, 133–35; CPP and, 71, 183n86; and development, 16–21; education and, 47, 60, 78–82, 87–89, 91–92, 112, 116, 140, 147–48, 195n59; electoral politics and, 68–69, 71, 183n86, 184n100, 189n3; families of, and the colonial state, 79–81; funding procured by, 27, 45–51, 56, 58–59, 62–64, 74–75, 98–99, 106–9, 111, 120–21; indirect rule and, 44–47; labor extraction by, for chiefs' farms, 42–43, 44–45, 50, 62–64, 159n8, 161n18, 169n79, 169n81; labor refusals and, 35–40, 41–43, 64, 182n78; locals not "following," 35–36, 41–42, 50; marriages of, 191n16, 191n19; in "Nkrumah's time," 52–76, 174n2; punishment of, 36, 43, 50; in the Rawlings era, 122; relevance of, 16, 17–18; "right" of, to raise labor, 182n73; and the state,

labor decoupled from, 134. See also progressive chiefs
childcare centers, 127, 128
child sponsorship, 118, 129–30
China, funding from, 70, 145, 185n112
Christianity: and Catholic activism, 68; in Kpasenkpe, 60, 81, 131–32, 191n18; Seventh Day Adventists, 216n32; and World Vision, 118–19. See also Assemblies of God Church; churches
Christian World Service, 216n33
chronology, 26
churches: development funded by, 124, 216n27, 216n32; as distribution points, 133, 216n27; as partners or hosts of development organizations, 120–21, 131–33
citizenship, 14, 70–71, 148, 212n10
civil service, 79, 90–91, 92, 116; continuity of, in the north, 104; families' role in, 18–19, 21, 77–79, 88–92, 115–17, 137–40, 147–48, 156n42; lack of jobs in, 137, 138, 140; NGOs and, continuity between, 119, 138; retrenchment, 119–20, 122–23, 131, 137–38; World Vision as alternative to, 119
Clark, Gracia, 157n45
clothing: antinudity campaigns, 20, 90–91, 175n12, 195n52, 195n55; smocks, 70, 185n107
cocoa production, 33, 71; ERPs and, 213n14, 214n18; payment for, 167n63; price crash, 93, 96, 186n117
the Cold War, 10–11, 57
collective responsibilities vs. individualism, 82–83
colonial governments, 30–51; chiefs established or removed by, 43, 46, 49, 50; deniability of, regarding forced labor, 44–45, 62, 164n47, 170n92; development ideologies of, 161n17, 191n17; local presence of, 159n7, 162n26; violence of, 31, 35, 36, 37, 47, 50, 167n64. See also colonialism; the state
colonialism, 2, 7; chiefly families and, 79–81; chiefs and, 31–53, 55–59, 78–81, 155n36, 159n8, 163n35, 167n65, 171n100, 183n86, 185n107, 190n9; in the Cold War, 56–57; and colonial imaginaries, 11, 26, 45, 46, 74–75, 146;

colonialism (*cont.*)
  critiques of, 30–31; and families, 78–
    81, 189n7; French, 78, 165n51; in the
    hinterland, 32–43; and "Nkrumah's
    time," continuities between, 20,
    53–55, 75, 79, 146–47, 154n34, 176n17;
    resistance to, 50–51, 54–55; and trust-
    eeship, 161n17. *See also* development,
    colonial funding for; district diaries
Comaroff, Jean, 216n31
Comaroff, John L., 216n31
Committees for the Defense of the
    Revolution (CDRs), 122
commoners, 25
communal labor, 13–16, 30, 44–47,
    50–51, 56, 58, 61–65, 74–75, 104–8,
    110–11, 123, 154n32; communities
    and groups leveraging, 108–11;
    NGOs and, 128; for private vs.
    public works, 170n92; publicity cel-
    ebrating, 63. *See also* labor; labor
    extraction; participation; self-help
community development. *See* develop-
    ment
Community Initiative Projects (CIPs),
    126, 127–28
compound design, 193n33
consumer politics, 95
continuity, maintaining, 104, 176n17,
    192n29
Convention People's Party (CPP), 53–
    54; defunct development commit-
    tees of, 105, 205n68; funds funneled
    to districts by, 183n87; and gender
    equality, 88, 194n46; northern
    Ghana and, 65–69, 71–76, 175n12,
    182n86, 184n99, 185n107; smocks
    and, 70, 185n107; taxation by, 68
Cooper, Barbara, 83
Cooper, Frederick, 7, 53, 54, 157n44,
    170n92, 174n5, 197n8
Cornwall, Andrea, 11
Council of Elders, 134, 221n72
Cowen, M. P., 161n17
Crook, Richard, 213n13

daa kpariba groups, 203n51
dams, 50, 52, 53, 74, 97, 108, 111, 145,
    217n35. *See also* water sources
Danladi, Nelson, 103
Dasent, Michael, 39, 161n18, 166n60
Davies (District Commissioner), 49, 50,
    173n119
Davis, David Carson, 178n42, 179n45

decolonization and the state, 27, 54–55,
    65–66, 70, 74–75, 147
Denkabe, Aloysius, 216n27
Department of Social Welfare and Com-
    munity Development, 56, 88, 89–91,
    92, 105, 177n25, 195n55
dependents, accumulating, 80
depoliticizing state power, 5–6, 8, 10,
    16, 148
desertion, 38, 164n49, 165n50
Deutsche Gesellschaft für Technische
    Zusammenarbeit (GTZ), 97
development: ambiguity of, 8, 53–54;
    bureaucracy of, 17, 44, 70–75, 98,
    125–28; and child sponsorship, 118,
    129–30; churches funding, 124,
    216n27, 216n32; and cultivation of
    careers, 16–21; and developmen-
    talist states, 5–7, 12, 18, 75, 78, 91,
    147–48, 157n43; electoral politics
    and, 66–69, 142–43, 145; exposés
    of, 144, 145; fictions of, 10–12; local
    committees for, 58, 72, 105, 107–
    9, 124, 128–29, 186n118, 205n68,
    205n70; local hierarchies and,
    13, 19, 20, 79, 90, 125, 135, 153n31;
    localizing the history of, 9–10;
    local politics of, 10, 151nn16–17;
    local turn in, 12–13, 153nn30–31;
    nationalism and, 50–51, 53, 54–55,
    94–95; "ownership" of, 130, 139,
    221n69; pan-Africanism and, 70; as
    prevention of mass political action,
    56; and the relegitimization of
    empire, 50, 53; scale and practice
    of, 8–12, 151n20; small-scale, 9–10,
    13, 50, 73–74, 89–90, 120, 123–35,
    141–43, 145–47, 154n31, 177n25,
    186n117; "transformational," 4,
    118, 130, 211n4, 219n53. *See also*
    development, colonial funding for;
    rhetoric of development; the state;
    village projects
development, colonial funding for, 46,
    47, 48, 50, 52–53, 56; DCs respon-
    sible for, 49, 58, 59, 61–62, 178n37,
    178n40; increase in, during the
    1950s, 52–53, 58–59, 177n22
development, Ghanaian government
    funding for, 106; difficulty charting,
    186n117; district capitals receiving,
    72–73; and headquarters bias,
    187n123; lack of, in neoliberal era,
    122–25, 217n35; restrictions on,

fishing, 100, 111
ɔŋŋu (section or quarter of village/
  town), 110, 134
food as labor compensation, 110, 124
forced labor. See labor extraction
Forced Labor Convention, 44–45,
  170n87
Freed, Libbie, 162n23
Freeman (district commissioner), 42,
  164n49
French colonialism, 78, 165n51
Fumbisi Valley, rice farming in, 96,
  100–101, 201n36, 203n50
funding. See development, colonial
  funding for; development, Ghanaian government funding for;
  nongovernmental organizations
  (NGOs)

Gambaga District, 36, 37, 55, 69, 104,
  107, 163n37
Gambaga Town Development Committee, 105, 107–8, 205n68
Gambia, 120
Gandah (chief of Birifu), 191n16
gender, 18; agriculture and, 20–21, 61,
  83–85, 192n31, 193n32, 199n15,
  200n24, 203nn47–48, 204n60; and
  chiefly families, 21, 78–82; colonial
  ideologies of, 20; equality, rhetoric
  of, 88, 194n46; in interviews, 20–21,
  24; in the postcolonial order, 92;
  schooling and, 20, 21, 88, 194n46,
  195n59. See also women
Ghana, 2; in the 1970s, 94–95, 197n9;
  agricultural self-reliance of, 196n4;
  austerity measures in, 123, 126,
  137, 138, 222n85; chiefs in, 16–21;
  economy of, 3, 4, 71–72, 94–95,
  121–24, 197n9, 222n85; government
  upheavals in, 93, 95, 104, 121, 142,
  198n10, 222n85; independence of,
  53, 70; NGOs in, 21–22, 118–21,
  123–29; as "pacesetter," 119–20,
  211n6; post-Nkrumah administrations in, 93, 196n3; regional
  discrimination in, 175n12, 185n107,
  195n52; structural adjustment in,
  119–22, 123–26, 141, 212n13, 216n30;
  as World Bank "star pupil," 142.
  See also "Nkrumah's time";
  northern Ghana; the Northern
  Territories

Ghana-German Agricultural Develop-
  ment Project (GGADP), 97–98,
  104, 199n16, 200n21, 200n23, 214n20
Ghana-German Fertilizer Project
  (GGFP), 97
Ghana Rural Water Project, 131, 220n60
Giblin, James L., 189n7
Gilbert, W. E., 36
Gold Coast hinterland, 32–33, 160n12.
  See also the Northern Territories
Gold Coast Legislative Assembly, 66
Gonja Development Company, 191n17
Goody, Jack, 192n29, 201nn36–37, 202n38
Governance and Development (World
  Bank report), 223n87
Granary of Ghana, 93
the "green revolution," 4, 8, 20, 28, 93–
  117, 197n5, 201n36; female farmers
  neglected by, 20; neoliberalism's
  effect on, 214n19
Greenwood Commission for Local
  Authorities, 72, 187n122
Grischow, Jeff, 33, 56, 152n26, 161n17,
  191nn16–17
groundnuts, 100, 102
Guggisberg, Frederick Gordon, 40,
  160n13, 172n106, 190n9

Hadfield, Leslie, 9–10
Hailu, Zegeye, 192n25, 214n19
Harper-Shipman, T. D., 151n19, 153n29,
  223n87
Harrigan, Jane, 212n13
Hart, Jennifer, 95, 166n62
help, 9, 64, 65, 134. See also "self-help"
Herbst, Jeffrey, 212n13
Hickey, Samuel, 217n38, 217n40
hinterland statecraft. See northern
  Ghana; the state
hinterland statecraft, definition of, 6, 13,
  146, 160n12
Hockett, Arthur E., 108
Hodge, Joseph, 57
Hodgson, Dorothy, 120, 151n17
Hodgson, Frederick Mitchell, 161n22
Holsey, Bayo, 175n12
host-guest dynamics: in chiefly families
  generally, 80; churches and, 120–21,
  132; history of, 156n41; in Kpasenkpe, 17–19, 24, 28, 120, 132–34; and
  self-help labor, 28, 80, 133–34, 141–
  42, 147; state agents and, 147
Houssou, Nazaire, 214n19

labor (*cont.*)
    quotas, 38; terms for, 13, 64–65;
    unity demonstrated by, 83, 103,
    106, 110, 135, 186n115. *See also*
    communal labor; labor extraction;
    participation; self-help
labor extraction, 5, 7, 13–16, 147; before
    1920, 32–40; in the 1920s, 40–43;
    agriculture competing with, in the
    colonial period, 173n119; British
    deniability and, 44–45, 62, 164n47,
    170n92; for carrying colonial
    administrators, 64; for chiefs'
    farms, 42–43, 44–45, 50, 62–64,
    159n8, 161n18, 169n79, 169n81; and
    "community," 44–45, 47, 62, 63,
    104–9, 121, 135, 141, 159n3, 171n92;
    depoliticizing effect of, 16, 28;
    "desertion" and, 38, 164n49, 165n50;
    distinctions between forms of, 64,
    170n92; dry-season, 36, 110, 163n34;
    enslavement, 32, 33, 155n35, 159n19,
    161n18, 169n81, 171n92; gender
    and, 20; as "local initiative," 30–31,
    58; meanings attached to, 64–65,
    75–76, 134, 147–48; mechanisms of,
    14–15; by NGOs, 119, 124–31, 141,
    147; in "Nkrumah's time," 7, 27, 55,
    62–64, 71–76; the Northern Terri-
    tories and, 32–33; as "ownership,"
    130–31, 221n69; as "participation,"
    14, 119, 125–28, 133–35; petitions
    and, 107–9, 110, 128; private use of,
    167n65, 170n92; resistance to, 35,
    37–38, 41; for road building, 31, 34,
    36–37, 41, 42–43, 45, 104–5, 164n42,
    166nn62–63, 167n64, 168nn71–72;
    studies of, 162n23; as taxation, 15, 34,
    44, 161n18; "voluntary," 38, 45, 50,
    163n30, 164n47, 165n49; in wartime,
    173n119; for World Vision projects,
    133–34. *See also* communal labor;
    labor; participation; self-help
labor refusals: chiefs and, 35–40, 41–43,
    64, 75, 182n78; dangers leading to,
    164n49; punishing, 15–16, 36–37, 41,
    43, 50, 64, 106, 164n42, 167nn63–
    64; and the reduction in *nayiri
    kpaariba*, 69–70
labor-sharing groups, 103
Ladi, Hajia Musah, 101–2, 215n22
Ladouceur, Paul, 66, 187n119, 194n40
Lal, Priya, 70, 151n16, 185n110, 185n112,
    197n7

Land and Native Rights Ordinance, 46
language of development. *See* rhetoric of
    development
language skills, 89, 90
Lawra Confederacy, 68
Lawra-Tumu District, 37–38, 39, 40;
    labor extraction by chiefs in, 42,
    169n81; migration from, 179n46
leadership, performance of, 28
Legge, Karen, 123
Leigh, H. W., 40, 165n59
Lentz, Carola, 42–43, 45, 56, 149n4,
    156n41, 157n45, 160n10, 171n98,
    175nn11–12, 179n46, 182n84, 186n114,
    189n5, 191n16, 194n46, 198n11
Lesotho, 70
Li, Tania Murray, 10, 151n20
Limann, Hilla, 116, 137, 196n3, 209n100,
    210n112
Lobnibe, Isidore, 157n45
"localizing the history of development,"
    9–10
Lonsdale, J. M., 57
lorry transport, 48, 107, 166n62
Low, D. A., 57
Lugard, Frederick, 44
Lund, Christian, 182n73, 198n11
Lynn, Charles, 80, 176n20

maaligu (improvement), 9, 64–65, 110
maize, 97, 99, 100; "Agric," 101, 102, 103,
    202n45; "Damongo," 101, 102, 103,
    202n45; fertilizer and, 101–2, 103
Maka, Naaichi, 100, 103, 200n32
Mamprugu, 17, 32; and chieftaincy, 25,
    55, 59, 176n18, 178n42, 179nn44–
    45; and development projects, 66;
    western, "opening up," 62
Mampruli language, 149n4
Mamprusi District, 58–59
Mamprusi District Council, 66
mangasiziiya (women's leader), 89–90
Mann, Gregory, 7–8, 212n10
Manor, James, 213n13
Mansu, E. B., 80
Mansuri, Ghazala, 154n31
market relocation, 62, 181n67
marriage, 85–86, 191n16, 191n19
Mass Education Programme, 56, 60–
    61, 62, 65, 81; Assemblies of God
    Church and, 132; description of,
    177n25; forced labor and, 65, 181n71;
    Pawura's work for, 89–90; Wulugu-
    naba and, 180n54

mass political action: and decolonization, 53; development imagined as bulwark against, 56

McDonic, Susan Mary, 219n53

meals as labor compensation, 110, 124

Meda, Stanislas, 157n45

Mercer, Claire, 135, 219n53

methodology, 5–8; organization and, 26–29; sources and, 21–26

Miers, Suzanne, 170n92

Miescher, Stephan, 153n26

migration, 33, 38–39, 59–60, 146, 164n49; agricultural labor and, 40, 41–42, 59–60, 113; colonial officials mandating, 41–42; colonial officials prohibiting, 39–40, 168n67; freedom of, 40, 165n57, 165n59; from French colonial rule, 165n51; from Lawra District, 179n46

military recruitment, 48

Millennium Villages Project (MVP), 1, 144–45, 224n5

millet farming, 99, 100, 101, 114

Mineral Rights Ordinance, 46

mining, 93, 167n63

Ministry of Agriculture ("Agric"), 4, 11, 73, 95–102, 104; bullock farming funded by, 73, 98, 101, 102, 199n16, 203n46; chiefs' role in, 172n110; collapse of support from, 122, 136; DCs involved in, 176n20; defunding of, 121, 122–23, 136, 213n14, 214n19, 221n81; employment and, 91; and farmers groups, 95, 98–100, 200nn25–26, 202n44, 203n51; farmers identified by, 98, 101; funding by international and bilateral donors of, 94, 95, 97–98, 196n4, 198n18, 199n16, 200n21, 214n20; loans, nonrepayment of, 100, 201n34; Sebiyam's family and, 56, 61–62, 83, 95, 98–99, 100–101; seed distribution by, 101; strength of, post-Nkrumah, 96–103; tractors provided by, 221n80; women and, 21

Mintabah, Ali, 128

missionary networks, 177n25

Mkandawire, Thandika, 12, 153n29

Mobisquads, 122

modernization, 27; idioms of, 9; and northern Ghana, 53–54, 70; nostalgia for, 176n17; of women's dress, 90

Mohammed, Musah, 216n33

Mohan, Giles, 217n38, 217n40

Moseley, William, 213n14

Moskowitz, Kara, 70, 151n16, 185n110, 185n112, 212n10

motor vehicles, 41, 43, 48, 166n62, 167n64. See also roads

Mulholland, John, 144, 224n5

Murillo, Bianca, 95

Muslim community in Kpasenkpe, 60

Mutongi, Kenda, 189n7

Naah, A. B., 105, 205n70

naam, 59, 110, 179n45

Naba, J. S. Wuni Gambu, 218n45

Nabila, John Sebiyam (Wulugunaba), 77, 81, 87; career of, 87–88, 92, 116, 140; as chief, 140, 144; in government, 116, 137; hospital commissioned by, 209n100

Nabila, Kofi, 101

Nandom, 42, 68

nangbanyinni (labor-sharing groups), 103, 110

Nash, S. D., 39–40, 165n57

Natfund, 216n33

National Democratic Congress (NDC), 142, 145

nationalism, development and, 50–51, 53, 54–55, 94–95. See also Nkrumah, Kwame; "Nkrumah's time"

National Liberation Council (NLC), 104, 105, 186n118, 196n3

National Liberation Movement, 182n86

National Mobilization Programme (NMP), 124–25, 129

National Patriotic Party, 145

Native Authorities, 44, 45–46, 48, 49, 170n89, 180n57

"native customs," 44–45

Navrongo, 67

Navrongo-Zuarungu District, 37, 38, 39, 40, 162n29, 163n37; Azantilow and, 48; and Southern Mamprusi, migration between, 41–42, 168n70

the Nayiri, 59, 66

nayiri kpaariba (chiefly labor mobilization), 62–64, 103, 134, 181n72, 192nn25–26; Baranganji's expansion dependent on, 192n25; for hospital building, 109–10; reduction in scope of, 69–70, 114; and self-help labor, 208n92. See also chieftaincy

Ndlovu-Gatsheni, Sabelo, 10

neoliberalism, 118–43, 146–47, 148; African states vilified under, 12–13; agricultural programs dismantled under, 28, 122, 213n14, 214n19; chieftaincy and, 17, 135–41; competition for development and, 28, 120, 142–43; economy undercut by, 122, 123–24, 213n14; farming in era of, 136–37, 214n19; impact of, on Africa, 29; and "self-help," 26, 28, 121, 124, 141–42; statecraft of, 124, 212n10, 213n17, 223n87; as term, 211n6, 216n31. *See also* structural adjustment programs

neopatrimonialism, 153n29

Nigeria, Ghanaian migrants expelled from, 121

nigi puu (demonstration farm), 61, 176n20

ninneesim (enlightenment), 9, 60, 81, 180n52

Nissanke, Machiko, 212n13

Nkrumah, Kwame, 7; antinudity campaigns of, 20, 90–91, 175n12, 195n52, 195n55; bureaucracy of, 70–76; group farming efforts under, 200n25; and institutionalization of self-help, 55, 70–76, 146; large-scale development prioritized by, 70–71, 186n117; overthrow of, 92, 93, 186n118; petitions to government of, 66–69, 75; Regional Administration under, 187n119; and "regional development," 56, 183n87; rise of, 53, 55–61, 70

Nkrumahism: development of, 175n8; and "multiple Nkrumahisms," 176n16

Nkrumah-Rawlings interregnum, 198n11

"Nkrumah's time," 7, 20, 27, 52–76, 77–92; and colonialism, continuities between, 20, 53–55, 75, 79, 146–47, 154n34, 176n17; definition of, 54–55; labor extraction in, 7, 27, 55, 71, 74, 75–76; use of, 176n17, 191n20

Nluki, Somka, 99–100, 102

nongovernmental organizations (NGOs), 8, 11; civil service and, continuity between, 119, 138; conflicting goals of, 125–26; continuity of, with earlier forms of development, 119–20, 126–28; funding, district officials negotiating, 124–28; in Ghana, 21–22, 118–21, 123–29;

labor extraction by, 119, 124–31, 141, 147; labor leveraged for aid from, 128–29; "landlords" to, 132–33; local hierarchies entrenched by, 13, 19, 125, 135; and "NGO fervor," 21–22, 120, 158n50, 215n26; and the "NGO-ification" of statecraft, 123–29; and "ownership" of development, 130, 139, 221n69; Sebiyam family engagement with, 139; shifts in focus of, 120; state shortfalls replaced by, 118, 124–25

normative ideals, 82, 83, 86

Northeastern Province, 39–40, 163n37

northern Ghana: as an administrative backwater, 33–34, 53–54, 56, 77–78, 120, 142–43; CPP in, 65–69, 71–76, 175n12, 182n86, 184n99, 185n107; differential governance of, 27, 54, 56, 65, 70–75, 145, 175n9, 175n12; education in, 87–88; education in, increasing, 180n56, 195n59; as focus for development, 94; as Granary of Ghana, 93; as hinterland, 4–5, 7–8, 26–28, 30–35, 53–54, 93–94, 120, 141, 142–43, 146–47, 160n12; map of, 3, 149n3; Nkrumah government and, 70–76, 77, 175n12; precolonial statecraft in, 160n10; "savagery" attributed to, 90; structural adjustment era and, 122, 123–24, 125–28, 141, 213n18, 214nn19–20; as an unpopular posting, 104; village development committees in, 58, 72, 105, 107–9, 124, 128–29, 186n118, 205n68, 205n70. *See also* the Northern Territories

Northern Mamprusi District, 163n37

Northern People's Party (NPP), 66, 68–69, 73, 182n86

Northern Regional Rural Integrated Programme (NORRIP), 124, 125, 129, 217n35, 217n41

the Northern Territories, 27, 30, 32–34, 161n20, 161n22; as labor reserve, 32–33, 160n13; mobility of residents of, 38–40; postwar development of, 52–53, 55–56, 65–66; refugees to, 165n51. *See also* northern Ghana

Northern Territories Council, 66

Northern Territories Development Plan, 68

Northern Territories Planning Committee, 106, 205n72

Northwestern Province, 39

Nsaful, J. E., 205n68
Ntewusu, Samuel, 166n62
Nugent, Paul, 121, 122, 123, 212n13, 213n16, 214n21
Nyankpala Agricultural Extension Station, 199n16
Nyankpala Crops Research Project, 199n16
Nyantakyi-Frimpong, Hanson, 214n19
Nyerere, Julius, 70, 71, 197n7

Obeng, A. K., 127–28
Okali, Christine, 21
Okia, Opolot, 14, 154n32, 170n86, 171n92
olaju, 60
"one pot," feeding everyone from, 82, 86, 113, 191n21; labor of, 86–87
"One-Village-One-Dam" project (1V1D), 145
Operation Feed Yourself, 93, 196n4, 197n9
Oppong, Christine, 156n42
Osborn, Emily, 19–20, 78, 157n46, 189n7
Osei, Gershon, 215n26
"ownership," 130, 139, 153n29, 221n69

paanni (senior wife), 85
Pabi, Opoku, 201n36
"pacesetter," Ghana as, 119–20, 211n6
pan-Africanism, 53, 54, 70–71
Parker, John, 36, 80, 159n7, 160n10, 162n26, 163n34, 165n55, 190n13
participation, 13–14, 119, 125–28, 130, 217nn37–38, 220nn58–59; vs. "land-lord" or "host" relationship, 132–33, 220n66, 221n69; and self-help labor, 133–35; the World Bank's focus on, 14, 125, 142, 154n31, 217n37, 223n87. *See also* communal labor; labor; self-help
Participatory Rural Appraisal (PRA), 220n58
"partnership," development as, 119
payment for labor, 110, 166n63, 167n64, 173n119
Pellow, Deborah, 197n9
Pender, John, 223n87
People's Defense Committees, 121–22
People's Militia, 122
People's National Party (PNP), 210n112
Peters, Pauline, 150n16
petitions, 66–69, 75, 185n110; database of, 206n77; leveraging labor, 107–9, 110; for roads, 107–8, 111

Pigg, Stacy Leigh, 152n24
Piot, Charles, 21, 120, 152n24, 158n50
pito (millet beer), 115
plow owners. *See* bullock farming
"politics of custom," 17, 156n38
poverty, simplifying and depoliticizing, 130
Prah, Kwesi, 12
Programme of Work and Happiness, 71, 72
Program of Actions to Mitigate the Social Costs of Adjustment (PAM-SCAD), 123–24, 125–26, 127–28, 218n45; and "pamscadization," 216n30
progressive chiefs, 17–19, 27, 31–32, 45–52, 55–61, 75, 111, 140, 147, 171n98; Sebiyam among, 4, 52, 55–56, 59, 80–81, 106, 111, 147–48
"progressive farmers," 97–98
Progress Party, 105
"project villages," 3–4, 12, 106, 120–21, 147
Provisional National Defence Council (PNDC), 28, 121–23, 124, 141, 218n45; becoming the National Democratic Congress, 142; coercion of, 215n22; in Kpasenkpe, 28, 122–23, 132, 134, 138, 214n21, 215n22, 220n66; Nugent on, 213n13, 213n16, 214n21; Sebiyam family members working for, 138; World Vision and, 220n66
punishment for refusing labor, 15–16, 36–37, 41, 43, 50, 64, 106, 164n42, 167nn63–64
Pusiga Teacher Training college, 88
Pusu, Alhassan, 60, 103
Pusu, Suurana Yakubu, 98, 99

Quayson, Ato, 216n30
"queen mothers," 223n86

railroads, 40
Rake, E. O., 39
Rao, Vijayendra, 154n31
Rattray, R. S., 160n12
Rawlings, J. J., 116, 138, 196n3; Amasachina and, 219n51; J. S. Nabila's political detention by, 137; and the PNP, 210n112; and rural producers, 213n16; structural adjustment programs implemented by, 28, 121–23, 142, 212n13; supporters of, and adjustment, 212n13
Regional Administration, 187n119

resettlement, planned, 152n26
rhetoric of development, 9, 10–11, 64–
65, 89–90, 91, 110; malleability of,
53, 56–57. *See also* participation;
self-help; village imaginaries
rice farming, 93, 96–97, 99, 113; decline
of, 100, 103, 136, 201n35; industrial-
scale, 100–101, 197n9, 198n14,
201n36, 203n50; and reharvesting
rice, 204n56
roads: agricultural activity dependent
on, 94; bridge building and, 42,
48, 62, 181n69; chiefs' initiative
concerning, 42, 62, 168nn71–72;
cost of, 167n64; damage to, 166n62;
DCs demanding, 34, 36–44,
163n30; in district diaries, 36–38,
42–43, 163n30, 166n62, 167n64,
168nn71–72, 169n79, 173n119; grants
funding, 188n129; to Kpasenkpe,
73, 111, 180n57, 188n132; labor
extraction for, 31, 34, 36–37, 41,
42–43, 45, 104–5, 166n63, 167n64,
168nn71–72; lack of funding for, 62,
104, 166n63; local materials used
for, 167n64; motor vehicles and, 41,
43, 48, 166n62, 167n64; petitioning
for, 107–8, 111; rains and, 41, 105;
tractors needed for, 107–8; women
building and repairing, 111, 168n71
Rossi, Benedetta, 14, 154n32
rural reform, "scientization" of, 178n32
rural statecraft. *See* the state

saama (recent immigrants), 25
Sachs, Jeffrey, 144–45, 224n5
Sackley, Nicole, 10, 177n29, 178n32
Saka, Wudana Daboo, 64–65
Sam, Nana Ama Serwah Poku, 220n60
Sandema, 30–31, 47, 168n67
Sandow, Wurugurunaba Nsoanyanni,
61, 110
Sandowbila, Sakparana, 74
Santejan, 39, 166n60
Savannah Accelerated Development
Authority (SADA), 145
Savelugu, 63
Scherz, China, 150n16
Schlottner, Michael, 179nn44–45
Schneider, Leander, 185n112
Schnurr, Matthew, 213n14
schools and schooling, 1, 18, 128; Azan-
tilow and, 47, 49, 172n108, 173n117;

differentiation by, 82–83; fees for,
222n83; gender and, 20, 21, 88, 194n46,
195n59; increase of, in northern
Ghana, 180n56, 195n59; in Kpasenkpe, 18–19, 60–61, 73, 77–82, 87–89,
115–16, 129, 139–40, 144, 180nn57–58,
188n1; Mass Education Programme,
56, 57, 60–61, 62, 81, 177n25; in Nkrumah era, 54, 87–92; teacher demand
for, 87–88; traveling for, 190n10
Schroeder, Richard, 120, 150n16
Sebiyam (Wulugunaba), 4, 7, 16, 18,
27, 32; agricultural development
projects and, 61, 80, 81, 83, 98–101,
112–14, 136, 209n101, 209n106;
agricultural labor and, 62–63, 81,
83–85, 209n102; Bawumia and,
73, 187n125; compound of, 85,
85–86, 144, 193n35; father's farms,
191n23; finance training of, 56; and
Kpasenkpe District, 187n125; market
moved by, 62, 181n67; marriages of,
85–86, 114, 210n109; *nayiri kpaariba*
system and, 62–64, 69–70, 109–10,
192nn25–26; *ninneesim* and, 60; old
age and death of, 140; party politics
distrusted by, 92; in postwar era,
52, 55–61; as a progressive chief, 4,
52, 55–56, 59, 80–81, 106, 147–48;
relationships of, with DCs and missionaries, 59, 180n54; and self-help
labor, 62–65, 75, 106, 109–10, 134;
tractor services of, 114, 209nn101–2;
village development projects and,
61–62, 75, 106, 109–11, 134; World
Vision and, 132. *See also* Sebiyam,
brothers of; Sebiyam, wives of;
Sebiyam family
Sebiyam, brothers of, 81–83, 193n35,
209n109; in the compound, 85;
definitions of, 83–84; education
of, 80, 82; family supported by, 79,
82–83, 92; farming, 27, 56, 78, 80,
82–85, 112–14, 136, 191n21, 193n35;
interviews with, 24, 25; "separating,"
113–14, 137, 209nn104–5; World
Vision and, 132, 138. *See also* Azundow, Daniel Barijesira
Sebiyam, Emmanuel, 158n55
Sebiyam, Solomon Dawuni, 25–26
Sebiyam, wives of: cohorts of, 86–87,
114–15, 137, 210n109, 222n82; in the
compound, 85, 86; cooking, 63, 86–

87, 114, 193n38; family supported by, 27, 79, 81, 92, 114; farming, 21, 84–85, 136, 137, 221n82; including brothers' wives, 193n35; interviews with, 24, 25; labor of, 21, 82, 84–85, 86, 114–15, 136, 137, 221n82; marriages of, 85–86, 114, 210n109; normative family models, 82–83, 114; trading, 87, 112, 114, 115, 222n83

Sebiyam family, 77–92, 147–48; in the 1970s, 112–16; as agents of developmentalist statecraft, 24, 27, 28, 79, 91, 116, 139; at Barangani, 83–85; education of, 77–78, 80, 81, 82–83, 87–92, 115–16, 140, 195n59, 222n83; facing uncertainty, 112–16, 136–41; feeding, 86–87, 113, 114–15, 136, 191n21, 193nn37–38; gender in, 21, 82, 88; interviews with, 24–26; in the neoliberal era, 136–41; networks among, 91–92, 112, 115–16, 139; in "Nkrumah's time," 81–92; PNDC work of, 138; World Vision and, 132, 138–39. *See also* Sebiyam, brothers of; Sebiyam, wives of

Seiya, Adam Abdullai, 61, 102

Seiya, Balihira, 59–60, 102, 103, 203n48

self-help, 13–14, 55, 70–76, 185n110; in the 1970s, 96, 104–6; Amasachina self-help initiatives and, 21, 110–11; in colonial documents, 58; and fiscal stringency, 71–72, 75; institutionalizing, 55, 70–75, 106–9, 146; leveraging, 6, 8, 15–16, 96, 108–11, 128–29, 133–34, 141–42, 185n110, 186n115; meanings attached to, 64–65, 75–76, 134, 147–48; in the neoliberal era, 26, 28, 121, 124–28, 141–42; under Nkrumah, 70–72; and petitions for funding, 107–9, 128, 185n110; publicity celebrating, 63; raising revenue, 186n118; transnational discourses of, 70–71; unity demonstrated by, 106, 186n115; World Vision projects and, 133–34. *See also* communal labor; participation

"sense-making," 11

"separate spheres" ideology, 19–20, 157n46

sergeant major chiefs, 34

Seventh Day Adventists, 216n32

Shenton, R. W., 161n17

Shepherd, Andrew, 201n36

Shields, C. B., 36–37, 40, 164n41

Skinner, Kate, 71, 90, 154n34, 177n25, 181n71, 195n55

"Slavery Convention," 169n81

"small boys," 122

smocks, 70, 185n107

Soeters, Sebastiaan, 166n62

sources, 21–26

Southern Mamprusi District, 38, 41, 73, 163n37, 165n50, 188n132; and Navrongo-Zuarungu, migration between, 41–42, 168n70

sovereignty, 212n10

"Special Scholarship Scheme," 88

the spirits, 64

sponsoring children, 118, 129–30

"Stabilisation and Consolidation," 196n4

Staniland, Martin, 161n22, 162n25, 163n29

the state: decolonization and, 27, 54–55, 65–66, 70, 74–75, 147; developmentalist, 6, 7, 12–14, 17–18, 68–69, 75, 77–79, 147–48, 157n43, 161n17; and families, 19–20, 78–79, 80–81, 157n46; as "gatekeeper," 157n44; labor as leverage with, 7, 8, 15–16, 64, 107–9, 111, 128–29; naturalizing the power of, 10, 16; and neoliberal statecraft, 124, 211n6, 213n17, 223n87; "NGO-ification" of statecraft, 123–29; NGOs as separate from, 133; "rollback" of, 120; schooling and, 87–92; self-help and, 106–9; "triumph of the expert" and, 57; village development and, 3; village imaginaries and, 11, 26–27, 46, 74–75, 142–43, 145. *See also* colonialism; development; hinterland statecraft, definition of; northern Ghana

state farms, dismantling of, 196n4

State Farms Corporation, 70

status, technology enhancing, 48–49

structural adjustment programs, 8, 12; agriculture and, 28, 122, 213n14, 213n18, 214n19; failures of, 12–13, 14; in Ghana, 119–22, 123–26, 141, 212n13, 216n30; in northern Ghana, 122, 123–24, 125–28, 141, 213n18, 214nn19–20; "participation" and, 14, 119, 125, 126, 142, 154n31, 217n37, 223n87; Rawlings and, 28, 121–23, 142, 212n13; revolutionary politics and, 121–23; scholarship on, 120, 212n13, 213n18;

structural adjustment programs (*cont.*) school fees and, 222n83; village projects absent from early programs, 125. *See also* neoliberalism

Sub-Saharan Africa: From Crisis to Sustainable Growth (World Bank report), 153n28, 223n87

subsidies, agricultural, 97, 101, 122, 198n14, 213n14

Sulemana, Alhassan, 61

Sumner (district commissioner), 41

suŋŋi (help), 9, 64, 65, 134

Takora, Kambonaba Ziblim, 64–65

Talton, Benjamin, 71, 162n27, 175n11, 186n115, 198n11

Tamale, 23; NGOs in, 21, 22, 123, 158n50

Tamale Teacher Training College, 60, 88

Tampulima, Adisa, 61, 103, 111

Tampulima, Jacob Pitigi, 74, 110

Tampuri, Mahama, 131–32, 133, 135, 221n77

Tampuri, Sandola, 100, 202n44

Tanzania, 9, 70, 71, 120, 135, 185n110, 185n112, 197n7

tarima (commoners), 25

taxation, 72, 188n130, 188n134; Builsa chiefs and, 47, 174n121; CPP strategies of, 68; and indirect rule, 49, 170n89; labor extraction as, 15, 33–34, 44, 161n18

technology of agriculture, 48–49, 61, 94, 97–98

Tema, 53

Tengol, Golibdaana, 190n13

Thomas, Roger G., 164n47, 164n49, 167n63

Thornburn, James, 34

tindanas (earthpriests), 171n100

tinkpaŋŋa (villages), 4, 55

tiŋŋa (towns), 55

Tiquet, Romain, 162n23, 170n86

Tizza, 42–43

Together (journal), 119, 211nn4–5, 220n59

Togo, 120

Tongnaab, 80

Tongo, Tindana Issa, 73

towns, 55

tractors, 61, 73, 98, 99–100, 102; exchange of services for, 114; Ministry of Agriculture providing, 221n80; petitioning for, 107–8

traders, surveillance of, 215n22

"transformational development," 4, 118, 119, 130–31, 135, 141, 211n4, 219n53. *See also* World Vision

transportation: air travel, 89, 173n119; lorries, 48, 107, 166n62; motor vehicle, 41, 43, 48, 166n62, 167n64; roads damaged by, 166n62. *See also* roads

tsetse eradication, 47

Tsing, Anna Lowenhaupt, 152n24

Tumu District, 39, 40

"Two-Thirds World," 118, 211n4

ujamaa, 9, 71, 197n7

United Nations Children's Fund (UNICEF), 208n96, 216n33

United Party (UP), 183n86

United States Agency for International Development (USAID), 97, 185n112, 208n96

Unites States, funding from, 70

unity: family, 82–83, 103, 112, 135; labor demonstrating, 83, 103, 106, 110, 135, 186n115

university, attending, 88

University of Ghana, 88

Upper East Region, 192n31, 202n39

Upper West Region, 180n52, 192n31

Van Hear, Nicholas, 201n36, 203n51

"village development" as a "fuzzword," 11

village development committees, 58, 72, 105, 107–9, 124, 128–29, 186n118, 205n68, 205n70; chieftaincy and, 205n70; defunct, 105, 205n68

village imaginaries, 11, 19, 26–27, 46, 74–75, 142–43, 145, 146–47, 148, 152n24, 216n31

village projects: citizenship and, 14, 70–71, 148; committees, 58, 72, 105, 107–9, 124, 128–29, 186n118, 205n68, 205n70; as "laboratories," 178n32; as mode of statecraft, 6–7, 54, 65–70, 119, 141; structural adjustment programs, absence in, 125; villagers treated as resource in, 125, 134–35. *See also* development

villages, 4; ambiguities surrounding, 11–12, 34–35, 146–47, 152n24; belonging and, 4, 149n4; British use of term, 34–35; power relations in, 13, 19, 20, 79, 90, 125, 135, 153n31; "project," 3–4, 12, 106, 120–21, 147; resettlement of, 152n26; treated as interchangeable, 4–5, 13, 46, 75–76, 120,

Printed by Printforce, United Kingdom